Those Who Know Don't ~~y

Those Who Know Don't Say

*The Nation of Islam,
the Black Freedom Movement,
and the Carceral State*

Garrett Felber

The University of North Carolina Press CHAPEL HILL

The publication of this book was supported in part by a generous grant from the William R. Kenan Jr. Charitable Trust.

The University of North Carolina Press has been a member of the Green Press Initiative since 2003.

Library of Congress Cataloging-in-Publication Data
Names: Felber, Garrett, author.
Title: Those who know don't say : the Nation of Islam, the Black freedom
    movement, and the carceral state / Garrett Felber.
Other titles: Justice, power, and politics.
Description: Chapel Hill : University of North Carolina Press, [2020] | Series:
    Justice, power, and politics | Includes bibliographical references and index.
Identifiers: LCCN 2019019411| ISBN 9781469653815 (cloth : alk. paper) |
    ISBN 9781469653822 (pbk : alk. paper) | ISBN 9781469653839 (ebook)
Subjects: LCSH: Nation of Islam (Chicago, Ill.)—History. |
    Black Muslims—History. | Discrimination in criminal justice
    administration—United States. | Justice, Administration of—
    United States—History. | Black nationalism—United States.
Classification: LCC BP221 .F45 2020 | DDC 297.8/7—dc23 LC record
    available at https://lccn.loc.gov/2019019411

Cover illustration: Malcolm X with star and crescent in the background. Photo by Richard Saunders. Richard Saunders Collection, Schomburg Center for Research in Black Culture, New York Public Library.

Chapter 2 was previously published in a different form as "Shades of Mississippi: The Nation of Islam's Prison Organizing, the Carceral State, and the Black Freedom Struggle," *Journal of American History* 105, no. 1 (June 2018): 71–95.

For Dr. Manning Marable (1950–2011),
who set me on this path

Contents

Illustrations

Those Who Know Don't Say

Introduction

On the evening of April 27, 1962, patrolmen Frank Tomlinson and Stanley Kensic stopped Monroe X Jones and Fred X Jingles as they unloaded clothing out of the back of a Buick by the Nation of Islam's mosque in South Los Angeles. The ensuing altercation with police, dubbed a "blazing gunfight" and a "riot" by the *Los Angeles Times*, ended with seven unarmed Muslims injured and one dead.[1] William X Rogers was left paralyzed, and mosque secretary Ronald X Stokes was killed, shot through the heart as he walked toward officer Donald Weese with his palms raised toward the sky. Weese later told an all-white coroner's jury that Stokes "came towards me, chanting. He put his hands out. . . . I thought he was going to choke me."[2] As the other men lay on the ground, handcuffed and bleeding, they held hands and chanted *Allāhu akbar*, "God is most great." In August that same year, twelve Muslim men at Folsom Prison were holding a meeting in the prison yard when a sergeant began snapping photographs of the gathering. As the officer approached, one of the men proclaimed, "They want to take our picture, so let's give them a good one." Another suggested that they "face the east and pray to Allah." The group lined up with their hands raised waist high, palms facing up, and prayed.[3] In both instances, Muslims in the Nation of Islam (NOI) confronted with police violence and state surveillance, responded with nonviolent protest in the form of prayer.

Where do such stories fit within our narrative of the civil rights era? These episodes demonstrate that challenges to policing and prisons were central to the postwar Black Freedom movement, and the Nation of Islam was at the forefront of that struggle. They show Black Nationalism as an ideological current of Black politics, which continued to gain strength in the years between the dissolution of the United Negro Improvement Association (UNIA) in the interwar period and the rise of Black Power in the late 1960s, a period portrayed as Black Nationalist decline.[4] No group signified and catalyzed this growth more than the NOI. Popular understandings of the NOI have long characterized the group as insular, violent, apolitical, and religiously heretical. It is for these reasons, we are told, that Malcolm X left the NOI to join the civil rights struggle and practice orthodox Islam.

But far from being apolitical, Muslims were ambitious in the pursuit of political goals. They sought to build all-Black coalitions against police brutality and fought for the constitutional rights of prisoners. The circumstances surrounding Ronald Stokes's murder in Los Angeles and performative prayer under surveillance at Folsom were not anomalies, but culminations of broader, more sustained campaigns against policing and prisons. To combat the formidable challenge posed by this disciplined Black Nationalist organizing, the carceral state responded with new modes of surveillance, punishment, and ideological knowledge production. This relationship between disciplined, collective Black protest and escalating punitive state discipline—which I call the "dialectics of discipline"—laid the groundwork for the modern carceral state and the contemporary abolition movements that oppose it.[5]

These dialectics played out in prisons, courtrooms, and the streets. Prison officials tried to stamp out Muslim practice and activism through transfers, solitary confinement, and loss of good time credit, and prisoners countered with hunger strikes, sit-ins, and litigation. In cities across the country, police scrutinized and monitored the growth of Muslim mosques; hassled men selling the Nation of Islam's newspaper, *Muhammad Speaks*; and prepared officers for the inevitability of violent encounters. In addition to responding to provocations with prayer, the NOI marched on police precinct headquarters and filed lawsuits alleging police brutality, which sometimes led to successful settlements. More often as defendants rather than plaintiffs, the group used courtrooms to stage political theater and put the state on trial while building broad-based coalitions in communities of color. The dialectics of discipline describe the interplay between Muslim responses to state repression and the paradoxical acceleration of the expansion of the carceral state through new technologies of violence. *Those Who Know Don't Say* uses these dialectics as a way to demonstrate the historical process by which the Black Freedom movement and the carceral state were always in dynamic interplay.

Discipline here has a dual meaning: as a means of social control and coerciveness by the state, and as the individual and collective behavior necessary to resist and defeat it. On one hand, what has been called the "twin mechanism" of police and prisons worked to segment, manipulate, and discipline those the state identified as delinquent or dangerous.[6] Leveraged against the NOI, this discipline took the form of surveillance, infiltration, harassment, racial and religious profiling, mosque raids, solitary confinement, and even fatal police shootings. But these persecutions were met with a resistant self-discipline that was both individual and collective. It was not coincidental that the NOI catalyzed this dialectic. Personal discipline ranged from immaculate dress and healthy eating to prayer, tithing, and a refusal to smoke, drink, or curse. Public displays of collective discipline included the Fruit of Islam's (FOI) military-style drills, security at rallies, and women's demands for separate seating in courtrooms.[7] There were also methods of internal discipline within both the mosque and the prison, such as silencing, reprimand, and expulsion. Malcolm X's eventual ouster from the Nation of Islam was preceded by a commonplace procedure of three months' public silencing and removal from the community. And when prisoners at Attica in the early 1960s deliberately filled solitary confinement until no more men could be sent there, they met discipline as a means of control with disciplined resistance, thereby undermining its effectiveness as a form of punishment.

This distinction can be seen throughout the NOI's organizing work—in its political theorizing as well as in its religious practice. For example, Malcolm X distinguished between racial segregation and racial separation by emphasizing that "segregation means to regulate or control. . . . A segregated community is that forced upon inferiors by superiors. A separate community is done voluntarily by two equals."[8] As William Haywood Burns wrote, "the Muslim appears to be in complete control of himself. He moved with a quiet determination and an inner sense of personal dignity. . . . The existence of this well-disciplined self does not negate the Muslim's militancy."[9] Indeed, discipline was a form of militancy. Discipline enacted by the state was rooted in racial control, coercion, and violence. Muslim discipline was an expression of faith, racial pride, and Black self-determination.

The NOI is sometimes skeptically described as having been conscripted into political engagement. This view seems to suggest that it did not have a political program but was reluctantly drawn into these struggles through direct experiences with police brutality and incarceration. Of course, this statement could be applied to most activism. Sites of oppression are terrains of struggle. Critics of Black Nationalism more broadly point out how empire, masculinity, homophobia, and policing is reinscribed. These critiques sometimes bleed into white liberal understandings of Black Nationalism as nothing but the Janus-faced twin of white nationalism.[10] Nonetheless, Black Nationalism contains trappings and contradictions. As Keisha Blain defines it, Black Nationalism is the "political view that people of African descent constitute a separate group or nationality on the basis of their distinct culture, shared history, and experiences." It is an ideology that has often left patriarchy and capitalism uninterrogated, yet is a powerful vehicle for Black solidarity, autonomy, and peoplehood in the Diaspora. Struggling with this contradiction requires dialectical thinking. Black self-determination and self-discipline profoundly challenged state officials invested in maintaining white supremacist rule. The Nation of Islam not only challenged the carceral state but also challenged the nation-state.[11]

Just as state violence is marked by its monopoly on legitimate forms of violence, white supremacy is predicated on delegitimizing expressions of Black nationhood. To combat a disciplined organization grounded in autonomous Black sovereignty, the state criminalized, marginalized, and undercut the NOI's claims to statehood and religious legitimacy. This included charges of sedition, suspicions of communism, and accusations of violence. Beginning with the 1959 documentary *The Hate That Hate Produced*, these sprawling attempts to delegitimize the NOI coalesced around the framework of "reverse racism" or "Black hate."

Malcolm X explained how dominant media representations masked racism and state violence *against* the Nation of Islam by suggesting that Black nationalists were the true perpetrators of hatred and violence. "Every effort we make to unite among ourselves on the basis of what we are, they label it as what? Racism." Historical accounts of white supremacy were countered with accusations of fomenting hate. And then there was the trap of violence. Police profiled Muslims, invaded mosques and homes, and even shot and killed Muslims in the streets, only to try the victims in court on charges of assault and murder. Here, Malcolm explained, "they have another trap wherein they make it look criminal if any of us, who has a rope around his neck . . . do anything to stop the man from putting that rope around your neck, that's violence."[12] Just as the southern wing of the civil rights movement used nonviolent direct action to dramatize the everyday violence of Jim Crow through the spectacle of white racists attacking, hosing, and setting dogs on Black women, men, and children, the Nation of Islam exposed white liberals by building a Black nation in their midst. As Malcolm X remarked after *The Hate That Hate Produced* aired, "When the white man tries to expose 'us' they cannot help but expose themselves."[13]

Those Who Know Don't Say uses the NOI as a vehicle to explore forgotten sites and forms of Black struggle that confronted the carceral state during the mid-twentieth century. The chapters that unfold are often as much about the coalitions and opposition that formed around the Nation of Islam as the organization itself. Reconsidering the place and scope of the NOI within these histories expands the boundaries of Black liberation struggles in several significant ways. First, it reveals a more dynamic freedom movement in which objectives and strategies were always contested and debated within communities themselves. As Nikhil Singh observes, dominant narratives of the civil rights movement have failed to "recognize the historical depth and heterogeneity of Black struggles against racism, narrowing the political scope of Black agency and reinforcing a formal, legalistic view of Black equality."[14] Desegregation campaigns, voter registration drives, and nonviolent direct action were only one register of what it meant to be political. And while Muslims engaged in street protests, sit-ins, hunger strikes, and prison litigation, they also performed other politics of spatial control and everyday resistance that challenged the state. Second, it changes who we see as political theorists and agents of change. What we regard as legitimate politics informs who we recognize as legible activists. While historians of the civil rights movement have challenged male-dominated, southern-centered, and top-down narratives, incarcerated people, Black Nationalists, and Muslims rarely appear as leading figures. Lastly, it expands our spatial lens to include prison yards and courtrooms as sites of activism. Courts should not be studied solely for legal proceedings and rulings, prisons as mere warehouses to chart the rising numbers of incarcerated Black and brown people; both were arenas of struggle.[15] As C. Eric Lincoln remarked, "The Muslims appear to believe in the efficacy of the white man's law without believing in its justice."[16] Courtrooms, police precincts, solitary confinement cells, and other spaces of white rule were places to lay claims on the state and challenge its legitimacy.

That this story is dominated by men does not mean they were the sole, or even primary, theorizers of Black Nationalism. Historians of black women's political thought have refuted the long-held notion that Black Nationalism, Pan-Africanism, and Black Power were simply patriarchal visions, which women had no share in creating.[17] Keisha Blain, Asia Leeds, and Ula Taylor describe an "ongoing scholarly effort to capture the gendered contours of Pan-Africanism and to centralize Black women as key figures in shaping, refining, and redefining Pan-Africanist thought and praxis during the twentieth century."[18] Taylor demonstrates the range and complexity of relationships that women in the NOI in particular had to patriarchy, including challenging it from within while participating in a movement that "more so than any other Black nation-building movement . . . provided a space for women who had been disrespected, abused, and who had struggled to find a 'home' in racial America."[19] Farah Jasmine Griffin has described this bargain as the "promise of protection."[20] The interplay of protection and possession is evident in the discourse through which this patriarchal promise ran. A sign commonly held by men at NOI rallies read, "We must protect (our most valuable property) our women."[21]

Some of the silences surrounding women's confrontations with the carceral state reflected this price of protection. For example, in a 1957 case in Flomaton, Alabama, two Muslim women refused to leave the whites-only section of a train station when a police chief asked them to move. The two men traveling with the women asked the chief whom he was talking to. When he replied that he was speaking to the women, they shot back, "No you're not, you're talking to us."[22] The men then disarmed the chief, took his billy club, and beat him with it until they were subdued by police.[23] What began as an act of resistance by two Black women was quickly channeled into the politics of male protection.[24] Given the bodily and economic vulnerability of Black women during this period, protection was often a compromise born of women's necessity and men's presumption. By granting Black women a privilege given to their white counterparts and asserting an aspect of masculinity denied to Black men under white supremacy, Griffin argues, the "woman gets protection; the man acquires a possession."[25]

The Flomaton case exemplifies how interactions between Muslims and the state were mediated by gender. Indeed, the broader history of the Nation of Islam and the carceral state documented in this book demonstrates the deep intersections of race, gender, religion, and nationhood. Yet the Nation of Islam's historical erasure from the Black freedom movement and global Islam is in part grounded in the state's own insistence on privileging some identifications over others. As Su'ad Abdul Khabeer notes, "American multiculturalism defines communities strictly by their particular and non-overlapping racial identities. Thus the state can recognize Blacks *or* Muslims for hierarchal inclusion, but is not designed to include those who are Black *and* Muslim."[26] When the Third Circuit Court of Appeals in Philadelphia ruled in favor of plaintiffs in *Hassan v. City of New York* in 2015 regarding surveillance of Muslim communities by the New York Police Department (NYPD), the decision stated: "We have been down similar roads before," and cited "African-Americans during the civil rights movement."[27] But as Amna Akbar and Jeanne Theoharis point out, "Black, immigrant, and Muslim communities often overlap."[28] And as this book documents, Black Muslims in the NOI were particularly subject to the double jeopardy of being Black *and* Muslim during the civil rights era.[29]

The emergence and political uses of the phrase the "Black Muslims" during the 1960s (and today) to describe those in the Nation of Islam raises a third meaning of discipline: disciplinary knowledge. Michel Foucault writes that "power and knowledge directly imply one another; that there is no power relation without the correlative constitution of a field of knowledge, nor any knowledge that does not presuppose and constitute at the same time power relations." He theorizes a carceral state which swells and absorbs by deputizing an ever-expanding network of people as "judges."[30] The term "Black Muslims," which was coined by the young sociologist C. Eric Lincoln in the first book-length study of the Nation of Islam, *The Black Muslims in America*, took hold following the intense public attention paid to the NOI after *The Hate That Hate Produced*. Carceral officials read and shared Lincoln's work, grabbing hold of a phrase which signaled a dual marginality from both orthodox Islam and the secular Black politics. As Abdul Khabeer argues, "even when seeking to be inclusive, the state is blind to intersectionality." The "Black Muslims" paradigm allowed the state to pivot seamlessly between discourses of Black criminality and Muslim terrorism and otherness. All of this was inherently irreconcilable with the NOI's theology, which stated that to be Black *is to be* Muslim. But in this way, Muslims of African descent became "subject to a double burden of state violence: the war on crime and the War on Terror."[31]

This book reveals that policymaking is not solely a top-down process or the work of elites, but often emanates from the ground up from those rarely considered producers of knowledge. Police, prison officers, and wardens all gathered, compiled, interpreted, and shared information they regarded as authoritative. Their logics radiated outward to reach state capitals, governors' offices, and even the nation's capital. Thus, the dialectics of discipline describe a historical process by which the carceral state developed alongside the Black freedom movement as well as a historical method that helps us to understand their dynamic interrelationship. The origins of mass incarceration cannot be explained only by federal policy, electoral realignments, or backlash against the successes of social movements. They were also rooted in the granular interplay between prisoners and guards, and officers and those they policed.

In 1961, at the annual convention of the National Association for the Advancement of Colored People (NAACP), the country's most prominent civil rights organization issued a five-paragraph resolution denouncing the NOI as "anti-white" and "advocating racial superiority."[32] The following year, the American Correctional Association (ACA) deemed the NOI a "pseudo-religious sect . . . [which] lacks the generally recognized characteristics of religion" and urged attorneys general and corrections commissioners throughout the country to forbid Islam as practiced by the NOI in prisons.[33] Thus, a group that was engaged in an international antiracist struggle was dismissed by the NAACP as racist, and a group that launched the first major prison litigation movement for the right to practice Islam inside lacked the characteristics of a religion in the eyes of the ACA. While the NOI's political and religious commitments were sometimes in tension, they should not be seen as irreconcilable. Indeed, Edward Curtis argues that "the religion of the NOI was powerful precisely because it was simultaneously a form of political activism and religious expression."[34]

The relationship between public misrepresentations of the NOI and its actual beliefs and practices was captured in the enigmatic response given by Muslims when asked about their political engagement: "Those who say don't know, and those who know don't say."[35] The first half of this aphorism pertains to a set of journalists, scholars, and state officials who positioned themselves as experts on the Nation of Islam throughout the Cold War. Carceral officials in particular became producers of knowledge, shaping public discourse about Black Nationalism and Islam while influencing local and national policy.[36] The second half refers to Muslims in the Nation of Islam who engaged in an anticolonial, antiracist, and anticarceral religious movement despite the external labels assigned to them but often remained strategically silent regarding their political engagement. The NOI was dedicated to bringing together the Muslim world and the global Black freedom struggle and, through its commitment to Black Nationalism and disciplined actions, led a struggle against incarceration, criminalization, and policing—one that was central to the Black freedom movement and has too long been obscured.

On February 11, 1965, just days before his house was firebombed and weeks before he was assassinated, Malcolm X gave a speech at the London School of Economics in which he described the NOI as "one of the main ingredients in the civil rights struggle." He refuted framings of the Harlem uprising in 1964 as a "riot," describing it as a response to police brutality. By feeding the press racialized crime statistics and criminalizing Black protest, the police make "it possible for the power structure to set up a police-state system." As Malcolm reflected on the Bandung Conference of 1955 and the ensuing decade of African decolonization, he declared, "It is the African revolution that produced the Black Muslim movement. It was the Black Muslim movement that pushed the civil rights movement. And it was the civil rights movement that pushed the liberals out into the open, where today they are exposed as people who have no more concern for the rights of dark-skinned humanity than they do for any other form of humanity."[37] The following week, five days before his assassination, he urged the audience, "No matter what you think of the philosophy of the Black Muslim movement, when you analyze the part that it played in the struggle of Black people during the past twelve years you have to put it in its proper context and see it in its proper perspective."[38] This book is an attempt to answer that call.

THE LOST-FOUND NATION OF ISLAM, which was founded in 1930 in Detroit by a mysterious silk peddler named W. D. Fard (pronounced Far-rod), redefined what it meant to be Black in America. Like its closest precursor, the Moorish Science Temple of America (MST), the NOI rejected "Negro" identity and was engaged in what Judith Weisenfeld calls "religio-racial ways of understanding the Black self and Black history."[39] Noble Drew Ali, the founder of the MST, argued that "the name means everything." By calling members of the "Asiatic" nation "Negro, Black, colored, or Ethiopian," he wrote, "the European stripped the Moor of his power, his authority, his God, and every other worth-while possession."[40] The Nation of Islam built upon this insight, replacing "slave names" with an X. Like the unknown variable in mathematics, the X symbolized the name their ancestors lost through the transatlantic slave trade.

Yet even as the group strove to redefine what it meant to be Black, it struggled against external misrepresentations. The first academic study of the Nation of Islam—by sociologist Erdmann Beynon in 1938—relied heavily on Detroit police surveillance and labeled the group a "Voodoo Cult."[41] As Ula Taylor documents, during these early years the NOI was subjected to several instances of surveillance and targeting by police and social workers, including a raid on its first parochial school and a courtroom brawl in Chicago. Under the leadership of Elijah Muhammad in Chicago as the United States entered World War II, it was investigated by the Federal Bureau of Investigation (FBI) for its sympathies with Japan. Muslims refused to register with the military, instead claiming they were "registered with Allah." Constituting the largest group of Black men incarcerated for draft resistance, the Nation of Islam joined nearly six thousand other conscientious objectors (COs) who remade federal prisons during the war.

Chapter 1 chronicles the NOI's draft resistance and its introduction to prisons through an "Asiatic" identity which positioned Muslims as part of a global majority of color. World War II has been understood as a period of rising civil rights activism and transnational racial formation, but the prison as a site of race-making and political organizing during the war has been understudied. Conscientious objectors from historic peace movements and racial justice struggles came together to form one of the earliest prisoners' rights movements, waging hunger strikes and dining-hall sit-ins to desegregate these federal institutions. Prison officials rethought traditional notions of prison management and discipline in the face of a morally-principled movement of incarcerated activists with robust outside support. While many members of the Nation of Islam participated in this wartime milieu, the organization explicitly refused to take part in racial desegregation campaigns, instead focusing their activism on seeking religious freedoms. Most prison officials regarded Muslims as unthreatening and even "model" prisoners during World War II. By the 1960s, they were seriously concerned about incarcerated Muslims' resistance to the penal order and likened the disruption they caused to those previously posed by conscientious objectors.[42]

The Nation of Islam grew dramatically throughout the 1950s, in large part due to the efforts of an energetic young minister who was released to Detroit from Massachusetts's Charlestown State Prison in 1952: Malcolm X. At the end of World War II, membership had dipped below one thousand, and in 1945, there were just four temples—in Detroit, Chicago, Milwaukee, and Washington, D.C. By 1955, there were fifteen temples; and by 1960, there were fifty. Some accounts estimated national membership at over a quarter of a million.[43] The FBI monitored mosques in towns as remote as Henderson, Kentucky, and Racine, Wisconsin.[44] As the Nation of Islam spread across the country, a wave of independence movements in Asia and Africa confirmed the Nation of Islam's eschatology about the approaching collapse of global white supremacy.

At the height of the Cold War, the Nation of Islam solidified its relationship to anticolonial struggles and the Muslim world. It drew inspiration from a nonaligned movement that promised to challenge the polarization between the Soviet Union and the United States. The group strengthened its connection to global Islam through a small journal, *Moslem World and the U.S.A.*, and its publisher, a Pakistani immigrant named Abdul Basit Naeem. As Malcolm traveled abroad for the first time as a guest of Egyptian president Gamal Abdel Nasser, the Nation of Islam was introduced to mainstream America through the television documentary series *The Hate That Hate Produced*, which described it as shocking evidence of the rise of "Black racism."

The Nation of Islam reached out to the global Black freedom struggle and the Muslim world at the same time that it was framed by white liberals as "Black supremacy" and denounced by civil rights organizations as similar to white segregationists. Amid these debates, C. Eric Lincoln published *The Black Muslims in America*. The NOI sought to dislodge the "Black Muslims" moniker, which emphasized its perceived difference from orthodox Islam. As Malcolm X would later say, "We are Muslims. Black, brown, red, and yellow."[45] The phrase made little sense in the context of NOI theology. The group believed that 85 percent of all people are "deaf, dumb, and blind"—that is, mentally dead—and struggle against the 10 percent who exploit them. The remaining 5 percent are "poor righteous teachers" who have been spiritually and mentally awakened through Islam.[46] The term "Black Muslims" was redundant because, according to the NOI, all Black people were already Muslim. State officials argued the opposite, seeing Blackness as somehow incompatible with legitimate expressions of Islam. For example, a note from the New York State prison inspector stapled to the file of a prisoner named Demir Asam read, "This man was reported from Sing Sing as a Moslem but it must be assumed that he is of the *legitimate religion as he is white* and had a name that might be assumed to be from the Far East."[47] Islam was always racialized, albeit differently over time. My use of the term "Muslim" to refer to those in the Nation of Islam throughout the book, as opposed to the more common "Black Muslim," privileges believers' self-identification, which positioned them firmly within a global Muslim community.

As the NOI navigated the turbulent waters of growing public notoriety and government surveillance, incarcerated Muslims initiated direct-action protests and the first organized prison litigation movement, which challenged the growing suppression of Islam and Black political activism by prison officials. Chapter 2 focuses on the specific mechanisms of carceral repression that paralleled Muslim prison organizing in New York.[48] During this period, largely due to the success of Muslim prison litigation and the array of political strategies that accompanied it, prisoners won a dramatic increase in visibility and recognition of their rights. For almost a century, the 1871 ruling in *Ruffin v. Commonwealth*, which declared that incarcerated people are "slaves[s] of the State" with no constitutional rights, had guided a practice of nonintervention by the courts known as the "hands-off doctrine."[49] In 1964's *Cooper v. Pate* decision—initiated by Muslim prisoner Thomas X Cooper—the Supreme Court determined that prisoners retained their constitutional rights. Sociologist James Jacobs likened the impact of this ruling on the prisoners' rights movement to the role of *Brown v. Board* in the civil rights movement.[50]

The state's attempts to restrict and punish Muslim practice in prisons hinged on its determination that the movement was a racial hate group using religion to mask its subversive aims. Drawing from courtroom testimony and state surveillance related to the trials of *Pierce v. LaVallee* and *SaMarion v. McGinnis*, this chapter reconstructs various forms of repression by the state to bolster its claims before the courts while stemming the growth of Islam in prisons. Muslim litigants detailed these various punishments at trial, revealing their own political responses, ranging from sit-ins and hunger strikes to takeovers of solitary confinement and coordinated writ writing. Instead of focusing on the legal outcomes of these cases, I use prisoners' courtroom testimonies as oral histories that publicly documented the brutality of the state. One of the central obstacles to prison organizing was physical: the isolation of prisoners from public view. Prisoners saw the courts as a breach in the walls, which allowed them to state their political claims before the world outside. As Dan Berger writes, the "courtroom was a staging ground in which activists could continue to articulate a critique of the American state."[51] Testimony has been central to Black liberation struggles, and courtroom testimony was one way that prisoners transgressed the silencing inflicted by imprisonment.

Prison litigation forced carceral officials to justify and coordinate practices whose power rested on their arbitrary and discretionary nature. During this period, police forces across the country, which were known for their corruption, graft, and political partisanship, were undergoing a professionalization effort. But as Michael Brown has argued, "Professionalization has fostered the illusion of control over police discretion when in fact it has resulted in greater autonomy for the police."[52] Stuart Schrader points out, "Police reform is not designed to help citizens. It is designed to help police."[53] As law enforcement emphasized "expert" knowledge and proactive policing, the Nation of Islam came under further supervision, especially in two major centers of its growth: New York and Los Angeles.

When Ronald Stokes was killed by Donald Weese in the spring of 1962, civil rights groups in Los Angeles had been fighting against police violence for over a decade. Los Angeles police chief William H. Parker shielded his department from outside scrutiny by maintaining autonomy from government officials and resisting all calls for civilian oversight. The Los Angeles Police Department (LAPD) was seen nationally as the epitome of modernized policing, using community relations training programs to mask the ways in which new surveillance technologies and racial crime statistics buoyed overpolicing and violence against communities of color. As the longest tenured chief in the city's history, Parker oversaw a force that spent decades terrorizing Black and brown Angelenos while complaining that police were the actual minority under attack.[54] While the Nation of Islam was building its first major mosque on the West Coast, Parker was insulating his department from public scrutiny and political oversight while justifying overpolicing and brutality through racial crime statistics. The NOI faced repeated acts of police brutality from the late 1950s through the early 1960s, ranging from invasions of mosques and homes to beatings in the street and eventually the mass shooting of Muslims outside Mosque No. 27. Chapters 3 and 4 examine the dialectics of discipline in the streets of Harlem and Los Angeles as the Nation of Islam looked to build Black united fronts against police brutality from coast to coast in order to combat increasing police surveillance, harassment, and violence.

In 1961, a little-known coalition in Harlem called the Emergency Committee for Unity on Social and Economic Problems was spearheaded by veteran labor and civil rights activist A. Philip Randolph in response to recurrent conflicts between Harlem residents and police. Over the next year, the group undertook an unprecedented attempt to unify the political tendencies of Harlem around a host of community issues, such as housing, jobs, and policing. Chapter 3 explores the disagreements among liberals, leftists, and Black Nationalists over the role of anti–police brutality organizing within the coalition. While historians have largely ignored or dismissed the Emergency Committee as a fleeting or ineffectual attempt at Black unity during the civil rights movement, it offers a rich site to explore the early debates over crime and policing before the rise of mass incarceration. The committee's history suggests that Black Nationalists and the Nation of Islam were central to Black united front organizing during this era. Although these coalitions were tenuous, the debates they engendered were important to future coalition building in the aftermath of the 1964 Harlem uprising and well into the Black Power period.

Just as Muslim prisoners used the courts as sites to testify, the Nation of Islam developed a strategy of courtroom political theater in New York and Los Angeles to recenter state violence. Chapter 4 recounts the NOI's effort to build a broad-based coalition in Los Angeles following Ronald Stokes's murder. In the year between the shooting and the trial, the Nation of Islam worked to maintain this unity despite city officials' attempts to divide Black leadership along lines of class, religion, and politics. The trial coincided with the one hundredth anniversary of the Emancipation Proclamation; the desegregation campaign in Birmingham, Alabama; and a mosque invasion in Rochester, New York, enabling the NOI to draw connections between the southern civil rights movement and Black people's encounters with racism and violence outside the South. Chief Parker and Los Angeles mayor Sam Yorty traveled to Washington, D.C., to meet with Attorney General Robert

Kennedy and demand a federal probe into the Nation of Islam. Meanwhile, the California Advisory Committee for the U.S. Commission on Civil Rights documented the long history of unchecked police brutality in Los Angeles. But calls for police reform were largely ignored until the Watts rebellion of 1965 again highlighted police violence and Black political organizing on a national stage.

The final chapter explores the Harlem and Watts uprisings of 1964–65 and the Attica rebellion of 1971 through the experiences of Muslims in the Nation of Islam. Government commissions studied and defined these revolts as ruptures, marked by their spontaneity and exceptionalism. Such narratives masked the long histories of state violence and resistance to it, which lay behind the rebellions. Putting these uprisings in historical context reveals that they were not aberrant acts of violence but part of a continuum of state violence and Black resistance, showing that mass incarceration and the rise of the carceral state grew from a longer dialectical process. The ideological weapon that legitimized such violence was the same process of state knowledge creation that had produced harmful discourses on the Nation of Islam for decades. By reading Harlem, Watts, and Attica through the actions of Muslim activists, who were crucial prior to, and during, all three rebellions, the closing chapter demonstrates the ongoing centrality of the Nation of Islam during the Black Power movement.

"Those who say don't know" described more than a form of cultural or political ignorance. In addition to being a source of physical harm, the carceral state was engaged in epistemic violence.[55] It created ways of knowing the Nation of Islam that have distorted our understanding of its politics to this day. Prisons and policing have long been central spaces for theorizing, articulating, and enacting critiques of the state. In these crucial sites of politicization, those who envisioned justice and freedom came face to face with those wielding coercive power. Indeed, these visions responded directly to, and grew from, such power. Just as these movements laid claim to the very power structures that oppressed them, we should be mindful of the ways in which earlier generations of activists navigated a dual strategy of demanding state-guaranteed rights while imagining a global vision of freedom that exceeded the boundaries of citizenship and the nation-state. Well-known figures such as Malcolm X, and lesser-known such as Martin Sostre, both suffered the inhumane conditions of imprisonment and lived in a world governed by racial injustice and economic exploitation, yet spoke unyielding truth to power in the name of Black humanity and dignity. The week before he was assassinated, Malcolm urged that the "world see that our problem was no longer a Negro problem or an American problem but a human problem. A problem for humanity."[56] A decade later, Martin Sostre wrote a letter from prison supporting Puerto Rican national independence. He asked, "What is the struggle for freedom if it is not the struggle for human dignity?"[57] Both remind us that movements against the carceral state and the racial capitalism which undergirds it is central to the struggle for Black self-determination.

CHAPTER ONE

The Making of the "Black Muslims"

> You never heard me today refer to myself as a Black Muslim. This is
> just what the press says. . . . This is what the newspapers call us.
> This is what Dr. Eric Lincoln calls us. We are Muslims. Black,
> brown, red, and yellow.
>
> —MALCOLM X, 1963

During the summer of 1942, after the forced removals and mass imprisonment of Japanese Americans in the western United States, the FBI and
police arrested eighty African American "admirers" of Japan in Chicago, with
the FBI claiming that the Nation of Islam was receiving military equipment
from Japanese spies. Among them was Elijah Muhammad, who had already
been arrested once that summer for draft evasion. He was held for over a
month on a $5,000 bond before thirty Muslims wearing "red buttons showing
a 'mystical' white crescent . . . [with] turbans of varying colors worn by the
women and crescent rings on the hands of the men" surrounded the jail for
fourteen hours, demanding that they, too, be put in prison for draft evasion.[1]

The second, more dramatic raid in Chicago was the culmination of months
of coordination between police and the FBI. Federal agents reportedly infiltrated temple meetings in blackface before eventually arresting members and
confiscating materials. After the raid, a federal jury found "hundreds of
books, pamphlets and documents said to advocate overthrow of the white
race by Negroes with the aid of the Japanese," as well as wooden guns and
flags, which the FBI believed were used in "military drills preparatory to the
day when they would take over the government."[2] After "waiting on the go-
ahead from Washington," agents struck in September 1942. In court, Muslim men claimed to be "Asiatic" and explained that their surnames had been
stolen during their ancestors' enslavement. When asked why they had not
registered with the Selective Service, they answered, "I have registered
with Allah."

The NOI's identification with Japan had earned it a place among the groups
targeted by the FBI's new RACON (short for "racial conditions") program. A
young J. Edgar Hoover had designed RACON to investigate "Foreign-Inspired
Agitation among the American Negroes" during the war.[3] By the summer of

1942, the Nation of Islam was among the Black Nationalist groups in the crosshairs. The federal agents' racial anxieties were clear. A Washington FBI field office agent remarked of Muhammad's appearance, "Although he is a Georgia negroe [sic], he looks like a Japanese, having slant eyes."[4] Muhammad was informed that his crime was his public identification with the United States' wartime enemy.[5] He wouldn't be the last.

A year later, an eighteen-year-old Malcolm Little appeared before a local draft board in Manhattan. "With my wild zoot suit I wore the yellow knob-toe shoes, and I frizzled my hair up into a reddish bush of conk," he recalled. In his flowing hipster outfit, similar to one that Chicanos known as Pachucos had been beaten for wearing that same year in Los Angeles by American servicemen, Malcolm started "noising around that [he] was frantic to join . . . the Japanese Army" and intimated to the psychiatrist at the draft board that he wanted to organize Black soldiers to kill whites.[6] Biographer Manning Marable commented that Malcolm's self-presentation "directly repudiated the militant, assertive Black model of his father," who was a Garveyite.[7] Yet Robin Kelley explained that "while the suit itself was not meant as a direct political statement, the social context in which it was created and worn rendered it so."[8] Amid the wartime fabric rationing of the time, sensationalist crime rhetoric about Pachuco zoot suiters, and the internment of Japanese Americans, Malcolm's cultural politics were already signaling the anticolonial global solidarity that he would find and embrace with the Nation of Islam in prison. Both Malcolm and Muhammad saw World War II as a "white man's war" and framed their opposition by identifying with the Japanese cause. In 1950, the FBI opened a file on Malcolm X provoked by a letter he wrote to President Truman from prison in which he identified himself as a Communist who had "tried to enlist in the Japanese Army."[9]

The incarceration of these two men has often stood in for the larger history of Muslims in prison, individualizing an experience which was in fact deeply communal. In April 1942, for example, James Nipper, a window washer for the Department of Agriculture, explained to a judge in Washington, D.C., that he had not registered for the draft because he was taught to "be on the side of our nation Islam, which is composed of the dark peoples of the earth, consisting of the Black, brown, red and yellow people." John Miller and Harry Craighead both testified that they joined the "Islam Nation" in 1940.[10] Frank Eskridge said, "Allah is my keeper and Allah has my card."[11] John X explained that "Anderson is my last name, but that is only a name YOU gave me. Such family names are the names of former slaveowners whose human chattels assumed their masters' names upon regaining freedom."[12] By 1945, as NOI membership dipped below one thousand, nearly two hundred Muslim men had served time in federal prison for draft evasion, constituting the largest group of Black conscientious objectors (COs) during the war.[13]

The Nation of Islam's decision to "register with Allah" brought Muslims into contact with other war resisters who challenged racial segregation, U.S. imperialism, and prison censorship. But incarcerated Muslims were largely regarded by prison officials during this period as "model prisoners" or, as one wrote, as "meek" [but] potentially dangerous." Historians have speculated on the lessons Elijah Muhammad took from his incarceration, citing the self-sufficiency of prison farming and the use of radio broadcasts, both of which were incorporated into the Nation of Islam upon his release. Significantly, prisons became active recruiting grounds for new members. Perhaps most importantly, the near devastation of the Nation of Islam during the war due to FBI surveillance and the imprisonment of high-ranking members made Muhammad profoundly aware of the cost of conspicuous political stands. Part of the Nation of Islam's growth during the next decade relied on its omnipresence in Black communities and its invisibility to white America. All that would change in the summer of 1959 with the television documentary *The Hate That Hate Produced*.

The program sensationally situated the NOI as a "hate group" similar to the Ku Klux Klan by referring to Black Nationalists as "Black racists" and "Black supremacists." It was singularly responsible for launching the NOI into national discussions of race. Mike Wallace (later of *60 Minutes* fame), who was the documentary's narrator, later remarked that it was the "first time that the Black Muslims came to the attention of White America."[14] Within a month, *Time* magazine ran a feature called "The Black Supremacists," which described Elijah Muhammad as a "purveyor of cold Black hatred," who demanded his followers pray toward Mecca five times a day "even if it means falling upon their knees in the streets."[15] For its viewers in New York City, the documentary provided a framework for misunderstanding Black Nationalism and Islam. For law enforcement, it fomented fear and justified repression and surveillance. As Zaheer Ali argues, it was "the first major example of Islamophobia in the mainstream U.S. media."[16]

As word of the Nation of Islam spread like wildfire through the press, C. Eric Lincoln seized on it as the topic for his dissertation at Boston University. When the book was published in early 1961, the phrase he coined— "Black Muslims"—immediately became ubiquitous.[17] Just as *The Hate That*

Hate Produced gave white audiences an intellectual framework to understand Black Nationalism as reverse racism, "Black Muslims" became the lexicon through which the NOI's religious standing could be easily dismissed. Particularly coming at a time when the NOI was attempting to make inroads with emerging anticolonial leaders and respond to other American Muslim groups who challenged Muhammad's claim to prophetic leadership, the "Black Muslims" moniker provided a means for understanding the NOI's practice of Islam as outside the bounds of religious legitimacy.

The book and the documentary offered frameworks for dismissing the organization's relationship to anticolonial politics and orthodox Islam at the precise moment the group was making concerted efforts to engage both. Rather than being recognized as bridging Muslims throughout the world and global Black freedom movements, the Nation of Islam was portrayed as peripheral to the two. The idea of the "Black Muslims" as a hate group, or an example of the emergent falsehood of reverse racism, was facilitated and propagated by carceral officials. It was pliable enough that law enforcement could suppress Muslim practice in prisons and police local mosques by claiming that the NOI was a subversive political group in the guise of religion while offering civil rights organizations the language to dismiss it within the Black freedom struggle. But this suppression and surveillance often helped grow the organization, and Muslims found creative ways to practice Islam and express Black self-determination and anticolonial solidarity, even in the state's most repressive spaces.

The Dialectics of Surveillance and Resistance

Since its founding, the Nation of Islam struggled to define itself against the identities imposed on it by academics, journalists, and law enforcement. As Su'ad Abdul Khabeer points out, "Black Muslims have been monitored by the United States government since the 1930s."[18] In the first academic study of the NOI in 1938, University of Michigan sociologist Erdmann Beynon began, "The Negro sect [is] known to its members as the 'Nation of Islam' or the 'Muslims,' but to the police as the Voodoo Cult." Beynon's article, published in the *American Journal of Sociology* as "The Voodoo Cult among Negro Migrants in Detroit," privileged the latter.[19] Moreover, the entanglement of law enforcement surveillance and academic knowledge production was present at the very inception of scholarship on the NOI. As the FBI later revealed, Beynon and "a detective from the Detroit Police Department who was in charge of the investigation of the group conferred with each other quite frequently and swapped information." Richard Brent Turner observes that this collaboration began a "tradition of scholarly representations of the Nation of Islam that accepted local and national law-enforcement agencies' signification of the organization as a cult."[20]

Before the ubiquity of the "Black hate" paradigm, the NOI was described through a package of Orientalism and African primitivism by the press, police, and Black communities. Non-Muslims' characterizations of the NOI featured phrases such as "cult practices [of] human sacrifice," "sinister influences of voodooism," and a "jungle cult" with women dressed "in long flowing robes of vivid colors reaching below the ankles [and] male members wear[ing] fezzes and other regalia."[21] One journalist described how Muslims entering the temple "uttered the password Ossa lossa lakam" (an attempt to transliterate "As-salaam alaikum"), and a police raid on the Detroit temple found communications with "unintelligible scrawls" written in Arabic. Some called them "Islams," indicating the high degree of bewilderment surrounding the religion.[22] The charge that the group was exploiting uneducated people was common, as Black Christian clergy accused founder W. D. Fard of "prey[ing] upon the more gullible members of their people," and the Black press commented that "leaders shunned contact with the educated Negro."[23]

These early years of the Nation of Islam were marked not only by a struggle over naming and signifying but by intense surveillance and scrutiny by local police and resistance to these practices. Through courtroom theater, marching on police precincts, and refusing to eat pork in jail (described in the press as a "hunger strike"), the dialectics of discipline that would unfold in subsequent decades were already coalescing. The most notable of these was a 1943 raid by police on the NOI's first parochial school, the University of Islam, and a courtroom brawl in Chicago the following year.

When Muslims in Detroit pulled their children out of public schools and enrolled them in their own school in 1943, it aroused suspicion among members of the state board of education. Police and truant officers raided the school on Hastings Street in April of that year, confiscating textbooks and pamphlets. Based largely on reports from police, the *Chicago Defender* trumpeted "Voodoo Is Taught by Leaders."[24] Students David Sharrieff and Sally Allah (seventeen and fifteen years old, respectively) were arrested at the raid, and Elijah Muhammad was charged with contributing to the delinquency of minors and arrested the following day. The raid on the university was the opening salvo in a much more pervasive scrutiny of Muslim family life and education.[25]

While Muhammad and others were held in the county jail, they refused meat and demanded fish and cheese. Days after the arrest, five hundred

Muslims marched to police headquarters. The group was met by fierce resistance, reportedly clubbed and beaten by police as they fought back "desperately with knives, sticks, brickbats, and all similar weapons at their command." Forty-one members were arrested. The next year in Chicago, over forty Muslims accompanied to court a woman charged with breaking another woman's eyeglasses. After the judge refused to issue a warrant, one Black newspaper described an "entire band [which] rose with military precision (such military procedure is a part of their ritual) and started marching to the rear of the courtroom." When they became entangled with other women spectators, the group showed a degree of open defiance, which would become unusual later, especially among women. One woman reportedly told a bailiff to "take off your glasses and I'll whip you," and another sang "Who's Afraid of the Big Bad Wolf." Police fired into the crowd, and a police captain died of a heart attack from the excitement. As Ula Taylor writes, "Clearly the women's belief that it was their duty to support and defend a fellow member, even if that meant fisticuffs, trumped any acquiescence to the dictates of appropriate feminine behavior." Sixteen men were convicted to six months, and twenty-four women served thirty days in jail. In the Detroit trial, a dozen Muslim men held their palms facing up while whites raised their right hands in the common oath given in a court of law. In this way, they demonstrated the deep continuity between courtroom political theater, draft resistance, and faith. As one newspaper noted, the group "does not call itself an organization or a religion, but a nation."[26] And in that nation, as Muhammad later put it, a "Moslem couldn't be a Moslem if he registered [with the United States]."[27] This decision to not register with the Selective Service during World War II would alter the course of the Nation of Islam, the Black freedom movement, and the development of the carceral state.

The War Resisters

As the United States entered World War II, the strategy of seeking fuller citizenship through military service held widespread appeal for many African Americans. Black enlistment rose from 5,000 on the eve of Pearl Harbor to 900,000 by 1945, and a *Negro Digest* poll revealed that 59 percent of African Americans believed that the war would aid the fight for democracy at home. Indeed, it was the foundation of the popular Double V campaign—for victory against fascism abroad and against racism at home.[28] Kevin Gaines notes that although Black participation in foreign wars "would be intensely debated among Blacks in light of the denial of equal protection at home, the race's military service throughout U.S. history would remain a sacred tenet for many, if not all."[29] By the end of 1943, fewer than two hundred Black men had been convicted of draft violations.[30] The majority were Muslims in the Nation of Islam.

While the NOI made up the largest group of Black war resisters, they were a relatively small part of a massive wave of conscientious objectors flooding federal prisons. Over twelve thousand COs served in what was known as the Civilian Public Service (CPS), and another six thousand were incarcerated in federal prisons.[31] The majority were Jehovah's Witnesses, over four thousand of whom protested war and fealty to any government; according to some estimates, they constituted as many as 60 percent of all war resisters.[32] But other COs were experienced racial justice organizers fresh from experiences with the March on Washington Movement (MOWM), the Fellowship of Reconciliation (FOR), and the recently formed Congress of Racial Equality (CORE). Bayard Rustin entered federal prison having just traveled to twenty states, including eight CPS camps, to speak with people about racial justice and nonviolent direct action on behalf of FOR. He began his prison term by singing the antilynching ballad "Strange Fruit" through the vents from solitary confinement at Ashland prison in Kentucky.[33] Others, such as Wallace (Wally) Nelson and Roger Axford, first cut their political teeth in peace movements. Nelson walked out of a CPS camp (which he called Civilian Public *Slavery*) in 1943, penning a seven-page letter on the trend toward totalitarianism and his opposition to all coercive government. In language reminiscent of Muslims' claims to be "registered with Allah," Axford was described by a supporter as "a prisoner of the Lord" and wrote his draft board that he could not "serve God and War."[34]

These war resisters dramatically reshaped prisons. Suddenly, as many as one-fifth of all federal prisoners were objectors.[35] As in World War I, when Leavenworth became what one report called a "University of Radicalism," prisons became laboratories where different social movements intersected.[36] One frequent visitor remarked that prisons "now seem to be information centers to which all news swiftly flies without hindrance."[37] Incarcerated COs shone a spotlight on federal prisons' policy of racial segregation in particular.[38] Black conscientious objectors such as Rustin, Nelson, and Joe Guinn, and white COs such as Axford, David Dellinger, and James Peck, came to prison ready and willing to challenge Jim Crow. While segregation in state and federal prisons continued to be illegal, unspoken and unwritten assumptions about the natural order of white supremacy and its necessity to prison security ensured its prevalence.[39] Whereas the NAACP had previously chosen to contest segregation in prisons through closed-door arbitration, COs were now engaging in nonviolent direct action and civil disobedience. In the most dramatic example, eighteen COs waged a 135-day hunger and work strike at Danbury Prison in Connecticut in 1943 to end racial segregation in the dining hall. Suddenly prisons were filling up with groups of trained activists with experience in peace movements and the tactics of nonviolent resistance, as well as strong networks of supporters outside.

Prison administrators responded by revisiting and reevaluating prison discipline. When eight COs went on a hunger strike at Lewisburg penitentiary to protest segregation in prison cell blocks, James V. Bennett—director of the Federal Bureau of Prisons (BOP)—wrote that "they think their Government discriminates against the negro race, and they are going to reform the whole social structure while they are in prison. I am letting them starve for the time-being and trying to decide what further we should do." He saw the most pressing problem for the BOP as figuring out some way to "rehabilitate" this group. "They are, of course, not criminals, and yet I suppose it is part of our job to try and adjust them to the realistic facts of life."[40] One of those facts was racial segregation.

Sociologist Donald R. Taft, who was temporarily employed as a "technical assistant" to Bennett, believed that COs posed new problems, which invited experimentation and a revision of traditional modes of punishment. After visiting nine prisons in 1943, he submitted his "General Report on CO and JW Policy" to Bennett, which differentiated Jehovah's Witnesses (JWs) from other COs and all COs from other incarcerated men. For Taft, the situation offered "an opportunity to test out for otherwise-similar non-CO inmates the next logical step in the development of Bureau penal policy."[41] The prison's traditional regime of "deprivation of privileges, segregation or isolation, loss of good time, etc.," seemed to him "particularly ill-adapted" when applied to draft resisters. Indeed, Taft explained, "such deprivations tend to increase the feeling of already unjust punishment by the state and to satisfy any desires they may have to play the role of martyrs." He even suggested creating a special prison for COs, where the warden might allow voluntary racial integration. Taft concluded that "'take-it-and-like-it-without-explanation' discipline is still rather prevalent even in federal prisons" and "might well be eliminated."[42] Here he illuminated the dynamic of heightened repression and prisoner activism that constituted the dialectics of discipline long before the Nation of Islam was at the vanguard of the prisoners' rights movement.

But most prison officials shared the tendency to differentiate "traditional" prisoners from this influx of men whom they often regarded as outside the bounds of criminality. Beneath most state musings about the problems posed by COs were assumptions about criminality, race, and class. They saw conventional disciplinary methods as ill-suited for largely white, educated COs, who were, to their mind, not really criminals. Reflecting on the distinction between the general population and political prisoners like himself, Bayard Rustin recalled that "we used to say the difference between us and other prisoners is the difference between fasting and starvation."[43]

In most state-authored accounts, Muslim war resisters are rarely mentioned; if they were noticed at all, they seemed to be regarded with curiosity. Traces of their resistance to the prison regime appear only in the shadows and margins of official narratives of prison activism. Incarcerated Muslims were relatively few, and JWs and white COs attracted most of the state's attention.[44] Unlike COs, who had powerful outside allies and left a robust paper trail through their hunger strikes, work stoppages, and other collective protests, incarcerated Muslim men relied on private correspondence with their wives and families to sustain them and the organization during these years. Clara Muhammad wrote Elijah and her son Emmanuel with verses from the Qur'an, as they were refused access to the holy book and given no official space for worship.[45] Muhammad hosted meetings at Milan federal prison in Michigan on Wednesday and Friday evenings and Sunday afternoons.[46] But the NOI was necessarily cautious during this period; Viola 2X told an undercover FBI informer that the group was "very careful to obey the laws of the United States."[47]

One of the few portraits of Muslim men incarcerated during World War II comes from a 1944 statistical analysis of Sandstone, an isolated federal prison in Minnesota.[48] Like other federal prisons, Sandstone was transformed during the war, receiving 427 Selective Service violators over two and a half years. By 1943, 80 percent of its prisoners were resisters. Muslims constituted 16 percent of its total population and almost half of its Black prisoners.[49] While the study did not document their activities, it reveals how anomalous NOI members were among the war resisters. Nearly all the Muslim men at Sandstone were affiliated with Mosque No. 2 in Chicago. Their age immediately set them apart; Muslims' average age was forty-four, with the youngest man in his mid-twenties, while COs and JWs were, on average, in their late twenties.[50] For example, James 2X (originally from Alabama), Joe X (from Texas), and James X (from Louisiana) were all between forty-nine and fifty-seven.[51] Muslim men also tended to have less formal education and be identified more often as unskilled laborers than their non-Muslim counterparts.[52] Although most Selective Service violators were sentenced to three years or less, 90 percent of NOI members received the full three years, despite a "definite tendency of shorter sentences for offenders in the Conscientious Objector group."[53] Sandstone made national headlines in 1946 for its hunger-striking COs, but Muslims at the prison were "reported to have been their best prisoners in every respect."[54]

When Muslims did protest prison conditions during the war, it was most often over pork served in the dining hall. Albert Bofman was a peace activist who held a bachelor's degree in economics from the University of Chicago and served two years at Sandstone, where he taught Russian and economics in the prison library.[55] During his incarceration, he drafted a report called "Maladministration and Human Relations in a Federal Prison." According to Bofman's account, Nation of Islam members all lived together in one dormitory, which he remarked "may be of their own volition, so as to carry on their religious services, etc. uninterruptedly."[56] Bofman reported that half of all meals served with protein included pork, which he described as "tantamount to deliberate starvation" for Muslims. Beginning in 1944, the prison began substituting a double serving of beans instead of pork, but this change came only after "Muslim Negro objectors liv[ed] on a skimpy diet, refusing pork, for 3 years."[57]

The other prison with a sizable group of Muslims was Milan, where Elijah Muhammad was incarcerated with his son Emmanuel.[58] Taft commented that "the presence of 11 Negro Mohammedians at Milan suggests to me the need for some consideration of their special food needs. Even though as seems apparent they are not genuine Mohammedians but Negroes who have been explo[i]ted by their leaders, nevertheless, their religious views seem to be sincere and I understand they have some difficulty with the food."[59] During one visit to the prison, James Mullin, who was touring the country compiling reports on federal prison conditions in his role as secretary for the Prison Service Committee of the American Friends Service Committee, recorded at least forty-six vegetarians, including "Moslems" and eight other COs.[60] His note that "Moslems have special diets (During Dec. special food and eat at special times)" suggests that Muslims at Milan had managed to secure the right to observe Ramadan, which the NOI celebrated in December.[61]

In 1945, Mullin spent five full days at Milan, speaking with twenty-six COs, including Muhammad, Axford, Nelson, and Guinn. These men all knew one another; at one point Muhammad even took an English course from Axford alongside Nelson.[62] Muhammad told Mullin, "We're trying to give our people the religious basis for knowledge and understanding to return to our own people in Islam."[63] Meanwhile, Nelson, Guinn, and Axford were all being held in solitary confinement. Axford emphasized to Mullin that the "state must not punish men for their religious convictions." Nelson and Guinn were in solitary for protesting racial segregation in the dining hall.[64] Mullin reported that through the steel bars of the single cells, the men talked and "impressed on [him] the richness of the fellowship which had developed among them and what they are learning from each other."[65]

Nelson's and Guinn's solitary confinement was likely retribution for a desegregation petition that had begun circulating in Milan and had garnered thirty-seven signatures its first day. Nelson kept a daily journal in prison, and it took a hopeful tone after a move by Muslims in the dining hall from one table to another appeared to coincide with the petition. But a conversation with James 4X Rowe indicated that it was concern over pork rather than solidarity with the desegregation campaign that prompted the move. Nelson wrote in his diary, "He made me understand that . . . it was their dislike for pork being eating around them rather [than] racism, which is the primary [reason] they requested the table."[66]

Such scattered references to the life and politics of incarcerated Muslims during the war appear in the historical record like light flicking across a page. Bayard Rustin's prison file, which contains detailed notes on his desegregation campaign at Ashland federal prison in Kentucky, includes a brief interrogation by prison staff of "Inmate Bey," likely a member of the Moorish Science Temple of America, who explained that "Rustin had contacted him and endeavored to get him to go along with the hunger strike movement," but Bey did not agree to participate.[67] Nelson's diary also reveals the common misconceptions surrounding the Nation of Islam's beliefs. He wrote that a conversation with "Bro Jacob emphasized another reason [they did not join] two days ago. . . . They believed in and preached Black supremacy like the Bilbos (I think) and Ku Klux Klan [do] white supremacy. Both are equally curious."[68] The parallel made between Black Nationalism and white supremacy would blossom with devastating effects a decade later. Moreover, Taft's assessment of NOI members as "sincere" but not "genuine" Muslims marks the beginning of the long history of prison officials acting as arbiters of religious orthodoxy. As Roger Axford remarked, the prison system "makes pseudo professors out of officials."[69] In Taft's case, it made a pseudo official out of a professor.

When Taft sent James Bennett his "General Report" in 1943, he placed the Nation of Islam in a motley subcategory that included followers of Father Divine, "Israelite Negroes," and "Mohammedan Negroes." But he cautioned that there were "a number of special groups among the CO's which might well be studied separately and I have particularly in mind the rather large group of negro Mohammedans. Possibly this group has already been studied but, if not, someone should do it because there is a feeling which might or might not be well-founded that this apparently meek and ignorant group is nevertheless a part of a movement which may be potentially dangerous."[70] In a discussion among prison officials in the early 1960s exploring brainwashing as a form of prison discipline, the Nation of Islam was raised as a chief concern. There, Bennett made the connection between the COs of World War II and the Nation of Islam decades later. He recalled that "during the war we struggled with the conscientious objectors — non-violent coercionists — and believe me, that was really a problem. . . . We were always trying to find some way in which we could change or manipulate their environment." But he cautioned that "if you pulled out what you thought was the leader and the agitator, you then create a defensive solidarity among all the rest of them and it made it impossible to deal with them as a group."[71] What bridged the so-called model prisoners of World War II and the politicized Muslims whom Bennett and other prison officials were considering brainwashing by the 1960s was a small group of Muslims at Norfolk Prison led by Malcolm X and his co-defendant, Malcolm "Shorty" Jarvis.

Norfolk Prison Colony

In March 1950, Malcolm X (who had converted two years earlier) wrote his brother Philbert from Charlestown State Prison. Although he had been transferred from Norfolk Prison Colony, which he later described as the "most enlightened form of prison that I have ever heard of," to the dark single cells of Charlestown, where he was held seventeen hours a day, he welcomed the solitude.[72] What "more could one desire who wishes to meditate upon the Truth[?] Prison, thanks to Islam, has ceased to be prison." From his cell, Malcolm began a vigorous writing campaign to the prison commissioner. In one letter, he asked rhetorically, "Can the 'laws of this state' deprive one from one's God-given *Rights?* Can it deprive one from the Right to exercise in one's Speech, Thought, and Practise, one's conscientious views concerning one's people, one's God, and one's conception of what constitutes 'a devil,' simply because one is an inmate in a penal institution, and because one's skin is Black? Can it deprive one from discussion, in letters to one's people, the history and religion of one's people? . . . Is there a monopoly on Truth?" He decried the fact that he and other Black prisoners could not access their own history: after requesting books by the pioneering Black historian J. A. Rogers, they were told they could not read "things of that nature." "We spend all of our own time studying, thinking, and speaking with each other about our own people, Black people," Malcolm wrote. "We are seeking the Truth about ourselves, our God, and the devil. Is this against the law? If so, whose law?"[73]

Ironically, one such law was in the constitutional amendment that ended slavery. Embedded in one of Rogers's 1934 *100 Amazing Facts about the Negro with Complete Proof*—that the Thirteenth Amendment abolished slavery—was the so-called exception clause: "Neither slavery nor involuntary servitude, except as a punishment for crime whereof the party shall have been duly convicted, shall exist within the United States, or any place subject to their jurisdiction." This clause gave birth to the convict lease system and enshrined unpaid labor through punitive means. As Dan Berger and Toussaint Losier point out, "The abolition of chattel slavery sanctioned prison slavery."[74] The Fourteenth Amendment furthered the paradox of freedom and unfreedom by barring the vote "for participation in rebellion or other crime" while extending citizenship to formerly enslaved people.[75]

Yet the most sweeping rhetorical equivalence between incarceration and slavery was the Reconstruction-era ruling in *Ruffin v. Commonwealth*. Decided in 1871, just five years after the ratification of the Thirteenth Amendment, the case was named for Woody Ruffin, a Black prisoner who was serving five years for "assault with intent to kill" when he killed someone while escaping a chain gang.[76] The Supreme Court ruled that "a convicted felon has, as a consequence of his crime, not only forfeited his liberty, but all of his personal rights except those which the law in its humanity accords him. He is for the time being a slave of the state."[77]

With the small exception of the 1941 *Ex Parte Hull* decision,[78] which first cracked the walls between the judiciary and the prison by ensuring the right of the incarcerated to seek writs of habeas corpus, the period prior to the 1960s is colloquially known as the "hands-off era." The year after Malcolm's letter to the commissioner, for example, a federal circuit court judge claimed that it "is not the function of the courts to superintend the treatment and discipline of persons in penitentiaries."[79] As James Jacobs wrote, "Prisoners were a legal caste whose status was poignantly captured in the expression 'slaves of the state.' But unlike slaves, prisoners were invisible, except perhaps for occasional riots, when they captured public attention."[80]

Two years after Malcolm X successfully petitioned to be transferred from the Concord Reformatory in Massachusetts to Norfolk to take advantage of its educational opportunities, he and three other Muslims there captured public attention and were transferred back to Charleston for refusing typhoid inoculations.[81] They grew out their beards, refused to eat pork, and demanded cells facing east toward Mecca, threatening to contact the Egyptian consul if that right were denied. They even secured transfer from the foundry after complaining that it was too loud for meditation. The warden at Charlestown "had absolutely no idea who or what converted the quartet" but "pooh-poohed" reports that they were being granted extra religious privileges, noting that the cells facing east were "just regular cells."[82] As one newspaper article concluded, "The four new Moslems enjoyed complete religious freedom—and constant surveillance."[83]

This contradiction of freedom and surveillance came to define the relationship between incarcerated Muslims and prison officials over the next several decades. As Malcolm remarked just days after leaving Norfolk, "All of the opposition was, after all, helpful toward the spread of Islam there, because the opposition made Islam heard of by many who otherwise wouldn't have paid it the second thought." The dialectical relationship between prison repression and prisoner resistance grew from the demands of the four men at Norfolk into the vanguard of the prisoners' rights movement a decade later. As Malcolm wrote to his brother, "The more the devil openly opposed it, the more it spread."[84]

A Bandung Conference in Harlem

Less than a decade after being denied J. A. Rogers's books in prison, Malcolm X shared a stage with him in Harlem. At an African Freedom Day celebration in front of the Hotel Theresa in April 1959, Malcolm X called for a "Bandung Conference in Harlem": "We must come together and hear each other before we can agree. We must agree before we can unite. We must unite before we can effectively face our enemy . . . and the enemy must first be recognized by all of us as a common enemy."[85] The Bandung Conference, held in Indonesia on April 18–25, 1955, marked the first major articulation of the nonaligned movement.[86] It voiced a shared commitment to anticolonialism and self-determination, carving a third path outside the bipolar struggle between the United States and the Soviet Union. Its host, Indonesian president Sukarno, sounded the bell of the Nation of Islam's vision of anti-colonial solidarity from a world stage: "We Asians and Africans must be united."[87]

The success of Asian and African independence movements during the 1950s validated the Nation of Islam's eschatological vision of the end of global white supremacy. The group was encouraged by the emergence of the nonaligned movement, as newly independent nations refused to align with the major power blocs. These early years were marked by gatherings in Bogor (1949 and 1954) and Bandung, Indonesia (1955); Beijing, China (1949); Colombo, Sri Lanka (1958); and Cairo, Egypt (1957 and 1961).[88] In 1957, Elijah Muhammad sent a telegram of support to Egyptian president Gamal Abdel Nasser and the Afro-Asian People's Solidarity Conference.[89] In return, Nasser extended an invitation to Elijah Muhammad, and Malcolm X, serving as his emissary, made his first trip to Africa and the Middle East during the summer of 1959.

This sojourn has been overshadowed by Malcolm's journey to Mecca in 1964, during which he reported praying alongside Muslims "whose eyes were the bluest of blue, whose hair was the blondest of blond, and whose skin was the whitest of white."[90] But Malcolm's first trips to Egypt, Saudi Arabia, Israel, Nigeria, Ghana, Syria, and the Sudan point toward a deepening relationship between the Nation of Islam and emerging nations in Africa and Asia. During the trip, the *Amsterdam News* called Muhammad the "internationally recognized spiritual head of the fastest growing group of Moslems in the Western Hemisphere."[91] There, Malcolm was escorted by Deputy Premier Anwar el Sadat and attaché to the United Nations Ahmad Zaki El-Borai in Egypt, Ahmed Mohamed Nour in the Sudan, and Sheikh Harkon in Saudi Arabia. Writing from the Kandahar Palace Hotel in Saudi Arabia, Malcolm declared: "Africa is the New World—the world with the brightest future—a future in which the so-called American Negroes are destined to play a key role."[92]

Most scholars have pronounced Malcolm the sole architect of this internationalist vision and 1959 as the earliest indication of a commitment to participating in the world community of Islam, or *ummah*.[93] And indeed the trips catalyzed organizational changes that were both cosmetic and substantial. For example, Muhammad announced that Muslim "temples" would be renamed "mosques." His son Akbar Muhammad was sent to study in Cairo at Al-Azhar University, and ministers were encouraged to draw on the Qur'an in their sermons. Arabic, which became known as the NOI's "native" language, was increasingly taught in Muslim schools.[94] Just months after returning with their father, Akbar and Wallace Muhammad delighted a crowd of five thousand at an African-Asian Bazaar in New York as Akbar showed slides and movies of Muslims in Africa and lectured on "the role Islam is playing on the seething African continent."[95] Witnessing the growth of the nonaligned movement and the quickening pace of African decolonization, the NOI incorporated Africa more fully into its religious and political lexicon and became a key progenitor of what Alex Lubin has called the "Afro-American political imaginary."[96]

These changes did not come from nowhere. Throughout the 1950s, the NOI had fostered a relationship to orthodox Islam through a number of Muslim immigrants and scholars, many of whom stumbled across a movement that both intrigued and disturbed them. Mahmoud Yousef Shawarbi, an Egyptian Fulbright fellow in agricultural chemistry, wrote that he "cried tears of joy" when visiting an NOI temple and felt the "real spirit of Islam enveloping them all."[97] Abdul Basit Naeem arrived from Pakistan in 1948 and was also moved to tears while watching Muslim girls at Mosque No. 2 in Chicago recite "passages from the Koran from memory and perform the prayer ritual in a perfect manner . . . using authentic Arab accent." He interpreted what he witnessed as "proof of the now-well-known fact that Islam *is* fast spreading in the United States, especially among Americans of African descent."[98]

These markers of orthodoxy were in large part due to a Palestinian Muslim immigrant, Jamil Shakir Diab. A clerk fluent in Arabic and English who came to the United States in 1948, Diab responded to an advertisement in the NOI paper to teach Arabic at the University of Islam; he taught science and math as well.[99] In the mid-1950s, the school reflected the spirit of Bandung, with classrooms "decorated with large flags of Turkey, Arabia, Pakistan, Morocco, Egypt and other Moslem countries of Asia and Africa."[100] Shawarbi wrote that "the school we found in the heart of Chicago made us feel that we were inside an Egyptian school. . . . Their accurate responses reflected their complete understanding of true Islamic principles and beliefs."[101]

As these emphases on authenticity suggest, immigrant Muslims were concerned about the Nation of Islam's more unorthodox beliefs, especially Elijah Muhammad's position as a prophetic figure. The title *khatam an-nabiyyin* in verse 33:40 of the Qur'an is typically translated as the "Seal of the Prophets," meaning that God's last words were delivered to the Prophet Muhammad. After talking with Elijah Muhammad, Shawarbi suggested that perhaps Muhammad "mistook intuition for a revelation," and he urged other Muslims to work on "correcting [Muhammad's] beliefs and putting an end to his inappropriate behavior and to the spirit of antagonism that he calls for because it distorts the image of Islam in America."[102]

By the late 1950s, the NOI's legitimacy was under attack by other Muslim communities in the United States. Talib Dawud, a jazz trumpeter and proselytizer who eventually founded Muslim Brotherhood USA, published a series of articles attacking the NOI in the *New Crusader*, a Black Chicago newspaper, in 1959. The most scathing was a photograph of founder W. D. Fard, whose national origins remain unclear and was believed to be Allah in person, with the subtitle "White Man Is God for Cult of Islam."[103] The NOI found the article so disturbing that the Chicago and New York mosques purchased and destroyed as many copies of the issue as possible.[104] The following year, Shawarbi and Maulana Muhammad Fazlur Rahman Ansari, president of the World Federation of Islamic Missions, publicly declared that Muhammad was "distorting Islam" and threatened to have both him and Dawud denounced as non-Muslims before the Supreme Council of Islamic Affairs.[105]

Amid these intense debates by Muslims over whether to embrace, denounce, or "correct" the Nation of Islam's heterodox beliefs, the NOI positioned itself within the global Muslim community through Naeem's small journal, *Moslem World and the U.S.A.* Naeem had emigrated from Lahore, Pakistan, to the United States at the age of nineteen, where he enrolled at Western Michigan University and began disseminating information about Pakistan and Islam.[106] After briefly becoming a graduate student at the University of Iowa in 1949 and working at the Pakistani consulate in San Francisco, he moved back to Iowa City and audited classes in magazine production. Naeem worked sixty-five hours a week to fund his journal project, but when his wife, Zuleikha, became ill and could no longer take care of their four children alone, the prospects for *Moslem World* appeared dim. Fortunately for Naeem, a group called the American Friends of the Middle East stepped in to fund the project.[107]

In *Moslem World*'s January 1955 inaugural issue, Naeem described it as the "first authentic, illustrated monthly journal on Islam and Islamic affairs ever published in the United States of America . . . founded to serve as a bridge between America and the far-flung 500-million strong world of Islam."[108] His initial two hundred paid subscribers reflected this global reach: twenty-seven were Muslims in Malaya and Middle Eastern countries; fifty-six were Muslims in the United States; and the rest were individuals, consulates, libraries, and national magazines in and outside the United States.[109] But after publishing only two issues, Naeem took a yearlong hiatus as his family relocated to the vibrant Muslim community of Bedford-Stuyvesant in Brooklyn. The small journal now featured an advisory board and contributing editors, likely a result of connections formed while attending Friday prayers at Shaikh Daoud Faisal's State Street mosque.[110] Although Naeem had been aware of the Nation of Islam since reading about it during his first year in the United States, his decision to visit Chicago and write an article on the "south Chicago Moslems" may very well have been prompted by the recent emergence of the Nation of Islam in Harlem under the leadership of Malcolm X. In fact, it was in *Moslem World* that the young minister published his first editorial in 1956: "We Arose from the Dead!"[111]

Following Naeem's brief article on the Nation of Islam, which stressed its orthodoxy and positioned it as evidence of the spread of Islam in the West, the journal shifted dramatically in character and composition. The article "created quite a sensation in many circles, both in this country and abroad," according to Naeem. "'We would like to know more about these Moslems,' wrote a number of readers."[112] Almost overnight, *Moslem World* was transformed into a vehicle for the Nation of Islam, with editorials by Elijah Muhammad and Malcolm X as well as profiles of NOI members and mosques throughout the country. In fact, the shift was so abrupt that Naeem felt it necessary to clarify to its readers that it was "an independent publication . . . not the property of Mr. Elijah Muhammad."[113]

The strongest addition to the journal's original vision was Pan-Africanism. In an essay titled "The Black Man and Islam," Islam was framed not only as the original religion of the African Diaspora but also as inherently anticolonial. Echoing a refrain common within the Nation of Islam, the anonymous author argued that "acceptance of Islam by a Black man means that he immediately becomes a full-fledged *bona-fide* member of the vast Brotherhood of Believers, and no longer remains in a 'minority group.'" This shift from domestic minority to global majority echoed nineteenth-century thinkers such as the Pan-Africanist Edward Blyden, who positioned Islam as the emancipatory religion of Africans. Accompanied by a map of Africa that linked Islam to African decolonization, the article claimed that "if Islam best suits the needs of Black Africans, it should best suit the needs of the Black men in America as well."[114] A year before Ghana proclaimed its independence, the implication that Islam could liberate nations from the shackles of colonialism had great currency rooted in historical precedent. Five of the eight independent African nations in 1956 were majority Muslim (Egypt, Libya, Morocco, Tunisia, and the Sudan), and Ethiopia had a sizable Muslim minority.

Abdul Basit Naeem (far left), Alhaji Muhammad Wgileruma (second from left), and Malcolm X at Shalimar International, Inc., opening in April 1962. It was described as "America's First Asian African Travel Service." Robert Haggins Collection, Schomburg Center for Research in Black Culture, New York Public Library. Courtesy of Sharon Haggins Dunn.

By the final issue of *Moslem World*, the journal had become almost entirely devoted to the Nation of Islam. During 1957, its final year of publication, Naeem delivered an address at the annual Saviours' Day celebration in which he praised Muhammad for "bringing the so-called Negroes into, or shall I say, *'back into,'* the fold of Islam *en masse.*"[115] That same year, he wrote the introduction to the first edition of Elijah Muhammad's *Supreme Wisdom: Solution to the So-Called Negroes Problem*, a collection of religious teachings and lessons meant to be understood as the perfect wisdom of Allah. Acknowledging that some of the teachings in the book "would not be acceptable to Moslems in the East without perhaps, some sort of explanation by the author," Naeem emphasized that these differences were of "minor importance *at this time,* because these are not related to the SPIRIT of Islam" shared by all Muslims. Naeem declared that "I am in a position to say, most authoritatively, that Moslems under the leadership of Mr. Muhammad have now BEGUN to make a serious study of Allah's Divine Word and to grasp its true meaning. Very soon, I can further state, they will also start receiving instruction in the daily prayers and other Islamic duties."[116]

What had begun as a modest journal in Iowa City had quickly become an organ through which the Nation of Islam placed itself in conversation with global Islam, the nonaligned movement, and African decolonization. *Moslem World* folded later that year, but by its end, the journal had reached a modest circulation of five thousand and played a crucial role in positioning the NOI firmly in conversation with Muslims throughout the world.[117] When *Muhammad Speaks* newspaper began publishing in 1961, Naeem's periodical remained a crucial antecedent. He was soon hired for one-thousand dollars a month to work as a journalist for the paper.[118] And as Malcolm X planned to travel abroad for the first time during the summer of 1959 to develop these connections, Naeem was hired to plan the trip.[119]

The Hate That Hate Produced

In May 1959, a member of the Fruit of Islam stood before a crowd of ten thousand Muslims at Uline Arena in Washington, D.C., and recited the first surah of the Qur'an in fluent Arabic.[120] It was the largest rally the Nation of Islam had ever gathered, with members arriving by bus, train, and plane from seventy cities in twenty states. A white film crew accompanied by Black journalist Louis Lomax filmed the rally for the documentary *The Hate That Hate Produced*, produced by Lomax with Mike Wallace, which aired later that summer. Just after Malcolm met with President Nasser in Egypt on the second week of his trip abroad, the documentary was broadcast on local television in five half-hour episodes. As Malcolm X recalled, "Every phrase was edited to increase the shock mood. . . . In a way, the public reaction was like what happened back in the 1930s when Orson Welles frightened America with a radio program describing, as though it was actually happening, an invasion by 'men from Mars.'"[121]

Footage from the rally was used to emphasize the scale of the movement and fuel hysteria about the growth of "Black hate," while the gathering's opening prayer was omitted from the final version. Its thesis that the Nation of Islam was a racial hate group relied on the erasure of orthodox Islamic practice. As the NOI became a national phenomenon, journalists clamored for a language to describe it within the ideological framework of white Judeo-Christian liberalism. As Claude Clegg observed, the documentary marked a departure in media coverage from the "othering" Orientalist tropes of "voo-doo cults" and rumors of human sacrifice to a discourse of "reverse racism" and "Black supremacy."[122]

Mike Wallace and the production team were clear about the role they saw for themselves in mediating racism.[123] One press release hailed the documentary for "serv[ing] the cause of brotherhood." While it "underscored the viciousness of race hatred," it condescendingly pointed out that "brotherhood is a two-way street." The documentary argued that "racism, among Negroes and whites, remains a grave national problem . . . and showed race hate to be many-faceted." AntiBlackness was thus positioned as only one side of the hostility that marred race relations, and Black people as well as whites were culpable. The documentary was meant to activate both fear and relief among its white viewers. It sensationally warned of a "small but growing segment" calling for "Black supremacy," while consoling whites by suggesting that racism was not just their problem. "Negroes must return the brotherhood they expect from non-Negroes," it scolded.[124]

Louis Lomax was the lone Black voice involved in the production. According to promotional materials, he had "approached Wallace with skeletal evidence that anti-white sentiment among Negroes was on the rise. . . . Then the Wallace-Lomax team began to assemble evidence of the Black supremacists' power in local politics and Negro life in general."[125] The film warned that political figures such as Congressman Adam Clayton Powell and Manhattan borough president Hulan Jack had attended rallies held by James Lawson's United African Nationalist Movement and by the Nation of Islam. The suggestion was that civil rights movement leaders were susceptible to the creeping racial hatred represented by Black Nationalists. Wallace and Lomax invited other movement leaders whom they presented as "sober-minded Negroes" to publicly weigh in on the NOI, including Roy Wilkins and Dr. Anna Arnold Hedgeman.[126] Questions centered on a false equivalency between the NOI and the KKK: If whites were preaching the same thing as the Nation of Islam, would they not also be denounced as preaching hate?

The reductionist analogy between white and Black hate embodied in the title *The Hate That Hate Produced* became the bedrock of most denunciations of Black Nationalism after the documentary was aired. Speaking before a largely Black audience that included Malcolm X, Harvard professor and presidential adviser Arthur M. Schlesinger Jr. stated that "white supremacists and the Black Muslims are two sides of the same coin."[127] A former prison warden claimed before the state of Louisiana's "Un-American Activities" committee that the NAACP called the organization the "Black Ku-Klux-Klan."[128]

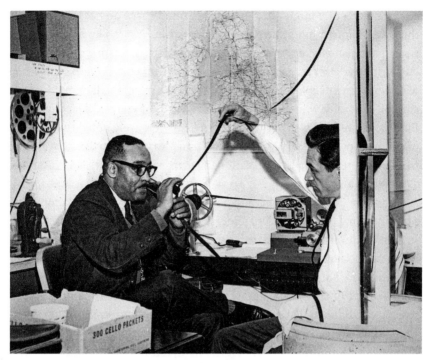

Journalists Louis Lomax (left) and Mike Wallace (right) look over film during the production of *The Hate That Hate Produced*. Box 2, folder 25, Louis Lomax Papers, Special Collections, University of Nevada, Reno. © Wagner International Photos, NY.

Police officer Lee Brown wrote that the movement "can be compared with the Ku Klux Klan; but its philosophy is a reversal of the doctrines postulated by the Klan."[129] Others reformulated or reiterated the title of the documentary. Renowned psychologist Kenneth Clark ended his review of C. Eric Lincoln's book with this: "Hatred, not love, is the child of hatred."[130] Even Lincoln himself called Black Nationalism the "fruit of oppression—the hate that hate produced."[131]

The documentary marked another iteration of national civil rights figures repudiating Black Nationalists, one reminiscent of the heated debates between W. E. B. Du Bois and Marcus Garvey in the 1920s. It also coincided with a fierce debate within the NAACP over the suspension of Monroe, North Carolina, chapter president Robert F. Williams after a May 1959 article in the *New York Times* quoted Williams as advocating meeting "violence with violence." When filmmakers arranged to meet with Roy Wilkins for the documentary, he asked the NAACP's public relations director, Henry Moon, for advice on what he might say, "bearing in mind that I do not wish to inject the NAACP into a full-scale street corner battle." Yet Wilkins's trepidation should not be mistaken for tolerance of the Nation of Islam or its beliefs. He had written a letter criticizing the tradition of "American Negro sympathies with non-white people outside this country" as a misguidedly simple expression of solidarity which offered "an easy (and, of course, deceptive) line: Black v. white."[132] In an earlier letter, he had derisively noted the "surprising number of Abdullahs, Mohammeds, and Messengers [which] have arisen from nowhere" and called the Nation of Islam "violently anti-NAACP as well as violently anti-white."[133]

Despite such Islamophobia and political opposition to Black Nationalism, many national NAACP leaders understood that the NOI posed a real threat to their position as the perceived legitimate voice for Black communities. In a lengthy memo to NAACP leaders, Gloster Current, who was then the field director who worked with local NAACP branches, argued that "mere denouncement of the Nationalist is not good enough." With almost embarrassing candidness, he recounted witnessing a Harlem street corner where the orators dressed and talked like those in the community, using "repetition, alliteration, humorous analogies, [and] biting sarcasm." Current went so far as to suggest that the NAACP purchase its own stepladders to imitate the famous corner orators on 125th Street. Although the memo demonstrates how out of touch national NAACP leadership was with the urban Black working class, it also suggests the anxiety they felt in response to the growth of the Nation of Islam. Wilkins condemned the NOI in the documentary in the very terms the producers suggested: "For years the NAACP has been opposed to white extremists preaching hatred of Negro people, and we are equally opposed to Negro extremists preaching against white people simply for the sake of whiteness."[134] While some, like Current, felt that the NAACP needed to learn from the appeal of Black Nationalists and even imitate their approach to organizing, the organization's high-level leadership opted for outright denunciation.

By the summer of 1961, as C. Eric Lincoln's book circulated and the phrase "Black Muslims" became a lingua franca for marginalizing the NOI's place in global Islam, the NAACP took its boldest step yet at its national convention in Philadelphia. A five-paragraph resolution from the conference entitled "Black Nationalists, Muslims and Other Separatist Groups" announced that the NAACP stood "unalterably opposed to all separatist programs whether advocated by southern segregationists or espoused by non-white racist organizations." It stressed the NOI's separatism, conflating it with White

Citizens' Councils and the Ku Klux Klan and repudiating the use of "hate violence and separatism as instruments of social reform and racial progress."[135] Thurgood Marshall went even further, telling an audience of Princeton students that the NOI was "run by a bunch of thugs organized from prison and jails, and financed, I am sure, by Nasser or some Arab group."[136]

The effect of the *Hate* documentary was to sever the NOI from the Muslim *ummah* and offer up the framework of "Black hate" and "reverse racism." It called on moderate civil rights organizations to denounce Black Nationalism, and the national leadership of the NAACP obliged in the firmest terms. C. Eric Lincoln's book would soon give a language and academic credential to this ideology. Malcolm X later pointed out the parallel between the documentary and the book. "Just as the television 'Hate That Hate Produced' title had projected that 'hate-teaching' image of us, the press snatched at that name. 'Black Muslims' was in all the book reviews, which quoted from the book only what was critical of us, and generally praised Dr. Lincoln's writing." "I tried for at least two years to kill off that '*Black* Muslims,'" he recalled. "Every newspaper and magazine writer and microphone I got close to: "*No!* We are Black *people* here in America. Our religion is Islam. We are properly called 'Muslims!'"[137] The phrase "Black Muslims" became the linguistic shorthand for this dual marginalization.

The Black Muslims in America

After *The Hate That Hate Produced* was broadcast, C. Eric Lincoln, a doctoral student at Boston University, justified focusing his dissertation on the group because of the notoriety it had gained from the documentary, even though relatively little was known about its origins, beliefs, and practices.[138] Lincoln soon wrote the first book-length study on the Nation of Islam, *The Black Muslims in America*.

Lincoln was among a cohort of young Black male academics and journalists who, unlike Naeem, Diab, and Shawarbi, situated the NOI not in the global contexts of Bandung and the Muslim *ummah* but in relation to the burgeoning civil rights movement within the United States.[139] Louis Lomax concluded in 1962 that the "Black Muslims, like the sit-ins and the freedom rides, are part of the Negro revolt." But he dismissed their religious practice, deploring the fact that "rituals and trappings of the faith take up much of their attention."[140] The following year, Nigerian Fulbright scholar E.U. Essien-Udom concluded in *Black Nationalism: A Search for an Identity in America* that "in practice . . . the Nation of Islam is apolitical. . . . Its Zion is not clearly defined."[141] Lincoln, who adopted the viewpoint of the documentary in characterizing the organization as "America's fastest growing racist sect," described the NOI in relation to—yet outside—the bounds of the civil rights movement: its members "engage in no sit-ins, test no segregation statutes, participate in no marches on Washington or anywhere else."[142] Yet more than the others, his book took the NOI seriously as a religious organization.

Upon the publication of *The Black Muslims in America* in 1961, it instantly became the foremost source on the Nation of Islam. Although Lincoln imagined the book as an academic work, he wrote to Muhammad that he hoped it would also "be published . . . for the general public."[143] Neither, however, could have anticipated its immense popularity. In its first six months in print, the publisher shipped over ten thousand copies.[144] Interest came from both within and beyond the United States. Beacon Press publicized the book heavily, sending an incredible forty-three thousand complementary paperback copies to professors in 1962 alone.[145] The book was reviewed in Arabic and translated in an abridged form in German.[146] An in-depth review of the book by Shad Polier, a lawyer who founded the American Jewish Congress, even made its way to the desk of Harris Wofford, who was appointed special assistant for civil rights by John F. Kennedy the same year the book was released.[147]

Lincoln's book was unique not only for its timing and reach but also for its grappling with the question of the Nation of Islam's religious orthodoxy.[148] Pages of his handwritten notes were titled "deviations from Islam," and the book dedicated a chapter to "The Black Muslims and Orthodox Islam." Lincoln's research reflected a dual focus on issues of Islamic orthodoxy and African decolonization that characterized *Moslem World and the U.S.A.*[149] In an anonymous survey, Lincoln asked rank-and-file members if the NOI was "recognized by 'orthodox' Islamic leaders in the U.S.A." He inquired whether Elijah Muhammad relied on international funding and whether Malcolm X was "received" in Mecca during his tour the previous summer.[150] In another survey, a question on the growth of the "Moslem movement" in the United States over the last decade was followed by another, which anticipated that respondents would see its global connections. A separate question asked, "Who do you regard as the major figure in this new period of the re-emergence of the darker peoples of the earth?"[151]

Lincoln compiled most of his research in 1960, during which sixteen countries freed themselves from French, British, and Belgian rule.[152] Responding to both African decolonization and the Nation of Islam's interest in this global development, nearly half of Lincoln's seventeen questions in one survey dealt with Africa and world affairs.[153] Whether or not Lincoln had read the *Moslem World* article "The Black Man and Islam," he had a better grasp than most scholars and journalists of the group's concern with Islam and the importance of its links to African decolonization as well as the Black freedom struggle within the United States.

Yet Lincoln interpreted some of its anticolonial stances through the neocolonial framework of *The Hate That Hate Produced*. For example, his handwritten notes reveal one of the earliest Black critiques of the Israeli occupation of Palestine, made by the NOI. But he simply equated anti-Zionism with anti-Semitism, noting that while Muhammad was not "specifically anti-Semitic," he was "violently anti-white, with 'white' including Jews": "In the last two years, anti-Zionism has crept into his hate campaign. . . . Anti-Zionist doctrine is just now becoming a part of overall temple propaganda. [Egyptian attaché to the United Nations Ahmad Zaki El] Borai and Bashir are working closely with Malcolm X on a long-term project including the importation of a group of dark-skinned Arab-propagandists. Arabs are frequently in touch with E[lijah] in Chicago according to Naeem."[154]

Lincoln missed the meaning of this shift for the Nation of Islam and the Black freedom movement more broadly.[155] Muhammad had long used Jewish Zionism as a key historical precedent for the NOI's vision of nationhood, particularly its claims for land in the United States, and as a model for state building. Lincoln's notes offer a window into the internal debates within the NOI, which were initiated by Arab Muslim advisers and aimed to help develop a settler-colonial framework for understanding Israel's relationship to the Arab world.

Scholars have often pointed to Malcolm X's 1964 essay "Zionist Logic" in the *Egyptian Gazette*, in which he argued that Israel was a "new form of colonialism," as one of the earliest anti-Zionist critiques made from within the Black freedom struggle.[156] There he argued that Zionism had no legal or religious basis but was simply colonialism camouflaged as philanthropy and economic aid to developing nations. He linked Israel to racial capitalism, charging that twentieth-century imperialism was driven by "zionist dollarism," and explored what solidarity with Palestine might look like. Yet understandings of Malcolm's thought after his break with the NOI are often grounded in an erasure of the Nation of Islam from intellectual histories of the Black freedom movement. Lincoln's notes suggest that the NOI had moved toward anti-Zionism as early as the late 1950s.

Ironically, the author with the most nuanced positioning of the NOI within both political and religious domains coined a phrase that marginalized the Nation of Islam from both Black Nationalism and global Islam. In contrast to the documentary, which had simply erased Muslim practice, Lincoln tried to capture the NOI's dual relationship to Islam and the civil rights struggle by calling the group the "Black Muslims." In his dissertation, Lincoln went to great lengths to explain the moniker. It was meant to be "descriptive, definitive, and delimiting": descriptive because all its members are "Black," definitive in that "Muslims" suggested connections to "classical Islam," and delimiting in that it "distinguishes this particular group from all others, here or elsewhere, of whatever religion, and of whatever race or social group." Lincoln made a distinction between "Muslim," which referred only to those in the NOI, and "Moslem," used for "followers of classical Islam," and explained that throughout the dissertation, "'Muslim' refers *only* to an American Negro follower of Elijah Muhammad."[157] But by the time the book was published, this careful parsing had fallen away.

Lincoln's early framings of the Nation of Islam reflected his own precarious position as a Black scholar who was pulled between the Black Nationalism of the NOI and the white liberalism of academia. To his advisers at Boston University, Lincoln described the Nation of Islam in fundamentally negative terms, as a cult that represented the failing of American democracy to achieve racial equality. Echoing the language of *The Hate That Hate Produced*, he framed the NOI as a *"particular* problem" and a "Black cult of hatred." He compared it to the White Citizens' Councils of the South, and one undated manuscript concluded by reproducing the documentary's argument verbatim: "Black Nationalism is the symbol of the hate that hate produced."[158] To Elijah Muhammad and the NOI, in contrast, he positioned himself as a potential ally, an "educator who happens to be Black . . . (and perhaps a more sympathetic one)."[159] Soon after the documentary aired, he wrote Muhammad that it "and the subsequent articles in Time and other magazines, have possibly contributed to rather than clarified the public distortion."[160] "I have had many occasions to speak of Islam, and to dispel many of the popular misconceptions regarding your leadership." He even claimed that he was often "mistaken for a Muslim," adding that "I have felt that many of your goals are not only desirable, but presently attainable, and I have felt constrained to say so whenever the issue has arisen."[161] Although many ministers within the Nation of Islam would later discredit and dissociate themselves from the book, Lincoln made a compelling case to Elijah Muhammad for the significance and integrity of his project. The success of the documentary enabled Lincoln to

C. Eric Lincoln around the time *Black Muslims* was published. The handwritten caption on the back reads: "The Young Professor." Box 319b, folder 383, C. Eric Lincoln Collection, Robert W. Woodruff Library, Archives Research Center, Atlanta University Center.

make appeals both to academics who were skeptical of the movement's importance and to the NOI, which was seeking a more accurate portrayal.

In early 1961, Muhammad went so far as to consider mobilizing the Fruit of Islam to sell Lincoln's book at its next Saviours' Day Convention. If the NOI agreed to purchase five thousand copies, Beacon Press would charge the group just two-thirds of the retail price. Although Muhammad had corresponded with Lincoln throughout his research, he had not read the final manuscript and left the decision to Malcolm. "If the book is not good enough for us to sell to the public, then we will not sell it," Muhammad wrote. "On the other hand, if you think it is suitable for us to back up, the printers have offered a very good commission to the Muslims." Muhammad stressed that the arrangement should remain "top-secret": "THIS IS NOT TO BE MEN-TIONED TO THE PUBLIC." The "main thing for us to remember is that we will not get behind the sale of anything that we might regret in the future, whose contents may prove to be unfavorable for us, but favorable to the enemy."[162]

Whether or not the Nation of Islam ever sold copies of C. Eric Lincoln's work is unclear, but Muhammad's caution reveals the seriousness of the period immediately following *Hate* for the public image of the NOI. As minister Bernard Cushmeer later recalled, "In 1959, the white press, as if on signal, launched a furious attack on Messenger Muhammad and the Nation of Islam."[163] Muhammad's skepticism proved prophetic. He later criticized Lincoln for "show[ing] undeveloped knowledge of just what's what" and charged him with "writ[ing] . . . [to get] on the market."[164] And, as Malcolm X later remarked, "that 'Black Muslims' name never got dislodged."[165]

Lincoln's meteoric ascendance as the foremost expert on the Nation of Islam was accompanied by the adoption of the name "Black Muslims" into the international vernacular. Beyond the academic world, Lincoln's work had a significant impact in three important arenas: policing, prisons, and the courts.

"Muslim Terrorists" and the State

In 1961, law enforcement officials at the National Police Conference in Buffalo, New York, called for the Senate Internal Security Subcommittee to investigate what New York prison inspector Richard Woodward redundantly labeled the "Muslim of Islam movement."[166] That May, Woodward had reviewed what he called a "fine book by Eric Lincoln" for a new monthly memo on the Nation of Islam, which was distributed throughout the state prison system.[167] In a 1962 interview, Los Angeles police chief William Parker commented that he was "reading a book now dealing with an organization of one of these minorities which is totally anti-Caucasian. We have been watching it with concern for a long time."[168] The book was Lincoln's *Black Muslims in America*. Parker was quick to point out that the "Negro author of this book does an apparently objective analysis of this problem." While Parker regularly ignored the structural inequality that caused chronic frustration in the communities of color he policed, he argued that "we ought also to be interested enough in our work to look into some of the causes of these problems. Certainly to pretend the problems do not exist is foolish."[169] The main problem, as he saw it, was the Nation of Islam.

Surveillance of the Nation of Islam by federal, state, and local law enforcement was escalating. Although the breadth and reach of the FBI, especially the Counterintelligence Program (COINTELPRO), has been documented by scholars of the carceral state and the Black freedom movement, the influence and discretionary power of state and local police in surveillance tactics has been underestimated.[170] Tony Bouza, a detective who from 1957 to 1965 was assigned to New York City's Bureau of Special Services (known as BSS, BOSS or BOSSI), described surveillance that was as intense and disruptive as any the FBI had in place.[171] He even called the FBI "peripheral," noting that BOSS had an in-office liaison to pass its surveillance to J. Edgar Hoover. The "real monitor of Malcolm X's behavior was BOSS," he later recalled.[172] In fact, FBI leaders feared that the average agent knew almost nothing of this "especially anti-American and violent cult." To remedy this situation, the federal agency sent a report to seventeen field offices in 1955, including Los Angeles and New York, with instructions that "every Agent now investigating this Cult" should "study and absorb [its] contents."[173]

Law enforcement officials had an insatiable appetite for Lincoln's book, which they characterized as an "objective" portrait of the organization because Lincoln was Black. Soon after *Black Muslims* was released, the Los Angeles Police Department mailed Lincoln a copy of its review in its newsletter with a personal note: "We thought you might like to see our Trainee's review of your book."[174] The book was distributed among criminologists and prison officials as the organization gained a stronger footing in America's prison system. Reuben Horlick of the American Association of Correctional Psychologists invited Lincoln to participate in a panel discussion on the "Black Muslims" at the 1963 convention of the American Correctional Association.[175] Bernard F. Robinson, a sociologist in the Illinois prison system, wrote Lincoln that not "only did I benefit by your very instructive statements regarding the Black Muslim Movement, but my fellow staff members also considered themselves well edified as a result of your correspondence."[176]

The Black Muslims in America served as a touchstone for carceral knowledge production, and Lincoln regularly promoted himself as an expert resource to police and prison officials. When the Georgia Bureau of Investigation requested a copy of his book, Lincoln had one hand-delivered along with a note promising his full cooperation. In 1960, the senior librarian for the LAPD wrote him that she had been "called upon to obtain 'everything available'" on the NOI. Lincoln obliged with over a dozen bibliographical suggestions, while offering to loan the library his notes, literature, and tape recordings. He added that he had "served as a consultant to certain agencies who found the Muslims to be of particular concern" and would do so at no charge.[177] These law enforcement officials all emphasized Lincoln's objectivity. William Carr of the District of Columbia Department of Corrections reviewed the book for *Federal Probation*: "The author narrates with flawless clarity and polished objectivity. . . . The book is absolutely *must* reading for everyone working in the area of human relations . . . particularly correctional personnel who should have considerably more than just a superficial knowledge of the Black Muslim movement."[178] Lincoln not only accommodated law enforcement but promoted himself among prison officials and police. Perhaps motivated in part by anxiety that other books might surpass his own as the authoritative source on the movement, Lincoln's voluntary collusion with law enforcement is evidence of a less sympathetic scholar than he portrayed to the NOI.

Lincoln was not the only collaborator with authorities. The expansion of carceral surveillance during these years included developing relationships between local, state, and law enforcement and the authors of scholarly and journalistic accounts of the Nation of Islam. Nowhere was the interplay between law enforcement surveillance and the production of racist Islamophobia more evident than in the 1963 piece in the *Saturday Evening Post* titled "Black Merchants of Hate." Just six months before Alex Haley signed a book contract with Malcolm X to coauthor his autobiography, the journalist joined Alfred Balk to form an interracial team that would produce the most widely disseminated mainstream account of the NOI since 1959. It aped the prevailing definition of the Nation of Islam as the Black equivalent of White Citizens' Councils while it denied that Black nationalists were under surveillance: "Like counterpart white supremacist groups, the Black Muslims are not on the Attorney General's subversive list."[179] What was most underhanded about this claim is that the authors culled most of their information from government surveillance. Haley and Balk used a seventeen-page report from the Chicago Bureau of Inspectional Services, which was a product of a collaboration between a Black police officer and the FBI.[180] They also relied on Malcolm X's criminal history from his FBI file and a report from the Senate's Fact-Finding Committee on Un-American Activities before the California legislature in 1961. The article ended by quoting Chief Parker, who apocalyptically warned that Muslims "could become the shock troops in a conflict between races."[181] Not surprisingly, as Manning Marable pointed out, by emphasizing a possible rift within the organization and highlighting Malcolm X's potential for leadership, the article did precisely what the FBI had hoped: "foster even greater jealousy and dissent within the NOI's ranks."[182]

That same year, John Drzazga—a retired New York City police sergeant—made one of the earliest rhetorical links in the United States between Islam and terrorism when his sensationalist piece for the right-wing journal *Law and Order* appeared under the headline "Muslim Terrorists." Tellingly, it was placed alongside advertisements for ammunition, discount pistols, military-grade submachine guns, scopes, and police lights. The danger in Drzazga's piece lay as much in its context and rhetoric as in its commonplace argument. Unlike many academic commentators who brushed off the NOI's significance because it professed to be apolitical, Drzazga recognized that the group could sway political power if directed to do so by Muhammad. And with no evidence of violence (other than that *against* the NOI by police) and certainly none of terrorism, Drzazga comfortably echoed the characterization of the Nation of Islam as the "largest 'hate' organization in the county" and made one of the first conflations between Islam and domestic terrorism in U.S. history.[183] As Amna Akbar and Jeanne Theoharis note, "Just as conceptions of Blackness and criminality have been conflated, Muslims and terrorism are seen as inseparable."[184] The Nation of Islam had become susceptible to both.

Perhaps no document more plainly laid out the Islamophobic policing of the NOI than the San Diego Police Department's training bulletin, *The Muslims!!!!!* It suggested clear and programmatic racial and religious profiling of the Nation of Islam. Claiming without evidence that many mosques had gun clubs, it promised to address "a problem that you are going to hear a lot more about in the months ahead." The bulletin reproduced racist stereotypes of innate Black violence by suggesting that "any organization that advocates racial hatred must provide violence and action to satisfy the appetite of its members and to stimulate its program." Most importantly, it claimed that violent encounters with police were inevitable, remarking that an "attack on law enforcement officers may be expected."[185] Such bulletins prepared police officers for the eventuality of violence.[186] They prescribed profiling by outlining the way that members would be dressed and carry themselves, and made it a certainty that these encounters could only end violently.

By the 1960s, carceral officials had created a feedback loop of intelligence gathering and ideological knowledge production justified by its perceived empirical basis.[187] Collaborations between law enforcement officials and academics or journalists constituted the ideological wing of the carceral state's intervention. Just as Black police officers would be hired over the next decade to infiltrate Black activist organizations, Black scholars and journalists were used by the state to conduct a rhetorical war against those same groups.

As the Nation of Islam was increasingly subjected to surveillance and intelligence gathering, it deployed those same tactics against the police. In June 1962, excerpts from *The Muslims!!!!!* were reprinted in *Muhammad Speaks*. The bulletin and an annotated copy of Chief Parker's interview on the Nation of Islam, which are both part of Malcolm X's personal papers, reveal the ways in which policing the police continued to act as a crucial countermeasure to surveillance and as a valuable counterdiscourse to notions of Black criminality. Simone Browne calls this "dark sousveillance": "a site of critique [which] speaks to Black epistemologies of contending with antiBlack surveillance, where the tools of social control in plantation surveillance or lantern laws in city spaces and beyond were appropriated, co-opted, repurposed, and challenged in order to facilitate survival and escape . . . [it] charts the possibilities and coordinates modes of responding to, challenging, and confronting a surveillance that was almost all-encompassing."[188] The NOI conducted its own dark sousveillance. At one Mosque No. 7 meeting, Malcolm X showed an internal FBI intelligence film on the bureau's relationship to local police and its crime lab.[189] The NOI also used photography to identify and share information about law enforcement. A photo from Malcolm's personal collection of a rally at Detroit's Olympia Stadium points out police commissioner George Edwards with a white arrow over his head.

THE PORTRAYALS OF THE Nation of Islam that emerged with *The Hate That Hate Produced* and flourished following the publication of *The Black Muslims in America* were absorbed and interpreted by all levels of law enforcement. Local and state police, prison psychologists and wardens, state commissioners and prison inspectors, the FBI and special service bureaus, and police chiefs all contended that the Nation of Islam was a subversive hate group masquerading under the guise of religion. Although they used these scholarly and popular accounts to gather information, data and interpretive logics flowed in both directions. Journalists leaned on government surveillance for material on the NOI, and scholars like Lincoln offered up their archives and expertise to law enforcement. Together, they constituted a web of knowledge production that created a vast ideological and political project aimed at suppressing an anticolonial and antiracist religious movement by classifying it as "reverse racism," "Black hate," and "Black supremacy" veiled by the façade of Islam.

In 1962, a year after the NAACP passed a formal resolution at its annual conference in Philadelphia denouncing the Nation of Islam as a "hate group," prison officials gathered at the annual conference of the ACA denounced the NOI as an illegitimate religion. It described the group as a "pseudo-religious sect commonly known as the 'Black Muslims' which preaches race hatred and race superiority and segregation." Concluding that the group was rejected by both orthodox Muslims and "responsible leaders among American Negroes," the ACA sought to "call to the attention of the general public, of the courts, and of responsible public officials, that the Black Muslim sect lacks the generally recognized characteristics of religion."[190] The ACA's resolution was sent to the U.S. and state attorneys general as well as prison officials in every state.

After his break with Muhammad, Malcolm described the difficult position the Nation of Islam inhabited due to this dual marginalization. "The movement itself was supposedly based upon the religion of Islam and therefore supposedly a religious movement . . . [but] the government tried to maneuver us and label us as political rather than religious so that they could charge us with sedition and subversion." The result was that the NOI was in both "a religious vacuum" and a "political vacuum." "We became a sort of religious-political hybrid, all to ourselves," he wrote. "Not involved in anything but just standing on the sidelines condemning everything. But in no position to correct anything because we couldn't take action."[191] Malcolm's assessment reflects his disillusionment with NOI leadership and what transpired between the group's entrance into mainstream discourse during the summer of 1959 and his break with the organization in 1964.

In the intervening years, despite the state's extensive efforts to relegate it to the margins, the NOI was deeply involved in global Islam and Black freedom struggles. For just as mainstream America was being introduced to the Nation of Islam through *The Hate That Hate Produced*, prison officials were scrambling to quell the rising numbers of incarcerated Muslims who were initiating the first major organized prison litigation movement in the country's history.

CHAPTER TWO

Shades of Mississippi

> We just can't allow [a Muslim] to parade around the prison yard
> carrying a prayer rug and kneeling on it at least seven times a day,
> facing Mecca, to say his prayers. We haven't got a muezzin in a
> minaret to call the faithful to prayers. Some prisons have towers,
> with guards in them, and calling those of Islamic faith to prayer
> isn't included in their duties.
>
> —NEW YORK COMMISSIONER PAUL McGINNIS, 1960

In October 1962, the *Amsterdam News* ran a shocking photograph of a Black man carrying a stack of books into a courtroom with his arms and legs in shackles. The headline read: "Shades of Mississippi!"[1] A press release with a similar title excoriated the hypocrisy of Nelson Rockefeller and other northern white liberals for publicly criticizing Mississippi governor Ross Barnett while silently condoning the chaining of prisoners in New York: "Sir, do you really think that other Negroes in this state are dumb enough to believe that you and these other white so-called liberals are really for the civil rights of Negroes in the South, while the HUMAN RIGHTS of Negroes here in YOUR state are being trampled underfoot?" If "Ross Barnett is to be blamed for civil rights violations in Mississippi, Nelson Rockefeller must take the blame for human rights violations in New York!"[2] The man in chains was a plaintiff in *SaMarion v. McGinnis*, a case filed by five Muslim prisoners at Attica prison. Nearly a decade before the 1971 rebellion, which would grip the nation and irrevocably alter the course of the prisoners' rights movement and the growth of the carceral state, Deputy Attorney General William Bresnihan captured the case's magnitude: "The whole prison system of the State of New York is on trial here."[3]

The choice of Mississippi for this southern analogy was deliberate. The previous year, Black and white Freedom Riders were held in the notoriously abusive Mississippi State Penitentiary, better known as Parchman Farm. The utility of the phrase "Shades of Mississippi" to northern Black activists was its suggestion that the struggles against incarceration in New York under Rockefeller and in Mississippi under Ross Barnett were more similar than distinct.

A large reproduction of a plaintiff in *SaMarion v. McGinnis* appearing in court carrying legal materials while shackled is displayed behind men protesting outside the New York County Criminal Court building, January 11, 1963. The protest was in response to two men being arrested for selling *Muhammad Speaks* in Times Square on December 25, 1962. Robert Haggins Collection, Schomburg Center for Research in Black Culture, New York Public Library. Courtesy of Sharon Haggins Dunn.

The early 1960s witnessed a significant transformation in the rights of prisoners and their visibility, largely due to the litigation and organizing of the Muslim Brotherhood, as the Nation of Islam was known inside prisons.[4] For almost a century, incarcerated people had no legal claims to constitutional rights. In the eyes of the law, an incarcerated person was still considered "the slave of the state."[5] During this period, known as the "hands-off era," the courts were guided by a dual logic of separating powers of government and the fear that judicial review might intervene in prison security.[6] In 1951, a federal circuit court judge reaffirmed that it "is not the function of the courts to superintend the treatment and discipline of persons in penitentiaries."[7] Yet only three years later, the court puzzled over this balance. "It is hard to believe that persons . . . convicted of a crime are at the mercy of the executive department and yet it is unthinkable that the judiciary should take over the operation of the [prison]."[8]

The wall between the Constitution and incarcerated people held firm until 1961, when Muslim prisoners at Lorton Reformatory in Washington, D.C., and Clinton Prison in New York cited section 1983 of the Civil Rights Act of 1871 (also known as the Second Enforcement Act and the Ku Klux Klan Act) as a means of breaching this barrier. Originally meant to protect freed Black people from the vigilante violence of white supremacists in the South by allowing legal compensation from those acting under state authority through the federal court (rather than through unsympathetic state courts), the act was rescued from a century of obscurity in *Monroe v. Pape*, a case of a Black family beaten and held during a warrantless raid by Chicago police. In the case filed by the American Civil Liberties Union (ACLU), the Supreme Court justified federal intervention when "enjoyment of rights, privileges, and immunities guaranteed by the Fourteenth amendment might be denied by the state agency."[9] Four months later, prominent civil rights attorneys Jawn Sandifer and Edward Jacko hoped that *Pierce v. LaVallee* (a precursor to *SaMarion v. McGinnis*) would set a national precedent for religious rights for incarcerated Muslims. The *New York Times* called it a "widespread legal attack on the state's prison system."[10]

Indeed, just months after the American Correctional Association resolved that the Nation of Islam was not entitled to the constitutional protections of a recognized religion, New York State prison commissioner Paul McGinnis found himself testifying before a federal judge. "All of my contact with this particular sect, my reading, my contact, is the fact it is an organization which preaches hate, subversive activity," he told Judge Henderson in the *SaMarion* case. When the judge asked McGinnis what he had read to reach this conclusion, the commissioner replied, "Many, many newspaper articles, periodicals, magazines, things that have been picked up in our institutions." Henderson pressed, asking McGinnis if he had read "*The Black Muslims in America* by Lincoln." Here, McGinnis faltered: "No, sir, I haven't read it."[11] The judge's question revealed just how authoritative Lincoln's book had become, just a year after its release. But the ambiguity of Lincoln's conclusions regarding the NOI's religious and political views offered state agencies the flexibility to make arguments condemning its legitimacy. For example, in *Sostre v. McGinnis* (1964), the circuit court reversed the judgment of the district court, which had ruled in favor of the NOI by citing Lincoln. "It is obvious from the evidence in the record that the activities of the group are not exclusively religious," the court maintained.[12]

Litigation was just one tool in an arsenal of strategies employed by Muslim prisoners during the late 1950s and early 1960s. They used direct action tactics such as sit-ins, hunger strikes, and occupations of solitary confinement, which anticipated the "Jail, No Bail" efforts of southern civil rights activists, many of whom had been jailed at Parchman. Like the Student Nonviolent Coordinating Committee (SNCC), the Southern Christian Leadership Conference (SCLC), and other groups that filled local jails by refusing to post bail after being arrested for civil disobedience, Muslims in New York incurred disciplinary infractions in order to be sent to, and remain in, solitary confinement until all the cells were filled with protesters. These actions sought not only to neutralize the power of the cell but also to draw public attention to these groups' struggles by eliciting violent reprisals from the state. These two simultaneous streams of activism—appeals to the Constitution and direct-action protest—operated as effective parallel strategies to win protections for prisoners under the law while challenging white supremacy and incarceration more broadly.

The dialectics of discipline took two major forms in New York State prisons during this period. The first was the relationship between state methods of control, such as prison transfers, confiscation of religious literature, solitary confinement, and loss of good time credit, and the responses by Muslim prisoners through hunger strikes, writ writing, and takeovers of solitary confinement. This chapter begins by focusing on the methods of prison discipline at both Clinton and Attica, which were aimed at suppressing Islam. Wardens transferred politicized prisoners between institutions in an attempt to defuse the movement. They confiscated religious literature and disallowed subscriptions to Black newspapers such as the *Los Angeles Herald-Dispatch*, the *Pittsburgh Courier*, the *Amsterdam News*, and later *Muhammad Speaks*.[13] Muslims were denied copies of the Qur'an in Arabic; could not correspond with ministers; were not allowed to have religious medals; and frequently had Muslim publications and even scrapbooks confiscated, censored, and destroyed.[14] They were also disproportionately placed in solitary confinement and lost earned time from their sentences, often serving the entirety of their terms. Prisons' principal system of punishment was through this combination of solitary confinement and good time practices. The two emerged alongside each other as physical and psychological punishments that isolated prisoners while extending their sentences. However, incarcerated Muslims responded to these incursions through protests, hunger strikes, sit-ins, takeovers of solitary confinement, and organized prison litigation. Their activism brought the plight of prisoners before judges and the outside world, ending the judiciary's century-long hands-off policy.

The second dialectic was the interplay between Muslim religious practices and prison surveillance. The politicization and radicalization of prisoners took place in response to these forms of prison discipline, as an emerging web of state surveillance monitored Muslim rituals and daily life. Prison discipline was met with resistance by Muslim prisoners who refused pork, communicated secretly in Arabic, and even performed prayer under surveillance as an act of protest. Yet prison monitoring did more than respond to activism of the Nation of Islam with new modes of repression. It became a central motor for perpetuating a religio-racial formation that justified the suppression of Islam in prisons. Because the state's argument against the NOI in prisons hinged on undermining its religious legitimacy, prison officials emerged as arbiters of religious orthodoxy, determining who was considered authentically Muslim and what constituted legitimate Muslim practice.[15] Throughout the early 1960s, prison workers ranging from guards, wardens, and superintendents to chaplains and psychologists read widely about the growing Muslim movement and presented their thoughts both through monthly internal bulletins and at national meetings, such as the ACA. The academic communities of penology and criminology emerged as an additional arm of the state's developing knowledge production about the "Black Muslims."

One of the greatest structural challenges to prison organizing was physical isolation from the outside world. While prison uprisings such as that at Attica in 1971 certainly publicized prison conditions, litigation also brought about greater visibility. So-called jailhouse lawyers flooded the courts with writs copied and signed by other prisoners and brought prison conditions under the purview of the judicial branch. James Jacobs described this litigation as the "peaceful equivalent of a riot" in terms of voicing prisoners' concerns to a broader audience.[16] Muslim prisoners envisioned the courts as arenas of political struggle, bringing prisons decisively into the Black freedom movement.

This chapter focuses on Muslim prison organizing and litigation in New York State, but we may draw some national conclusions with regard to the prisoners' rights movement and the character of the carceral state. Although activism within the New York State prison system was relatively unusual in its multiracial character, Auburn Prison served as the model for state prison systems outside the South from the 1820s until the 1940s.[17] Clinton and Attica prisons were among the first to witness the wave of

Muslim litigation that drew the attention of the judicial branch to prison conditions, and cases soon came from federal and state prisons across the North, South, and West.[18] Both the demands of Muslim prisoners and the mechanisms of state repression echoed in cases across the country during the 1960s. For example, the use of transfers to isolate and separate politicized prisoners has been documented in states ranging from New York to Texas to California.[19] So, too, have rules governing access to legal materials and writ-writing practices.[20] Indeed, a California Department of Corrections bulletin one year before the first litigation in New York described Muslims as a "management problem" and outlined similar practices of censorship, surveillance, and repression.[21] The experiences of Muslims in New York prisons represent one origin of the modern prisoners' rights movement as well as a piece of a larger mosaic of prisoner activism and carceral response that would ultimately inflect and inform the iconic uprisings at Tombs, Folsom, Attica, and elsewhere a decade later.

Clinton Prison

On December 25, 1959, a small group of Muslims gathered in the Clinton Prison recreation yard for *Jumu'ah*.[22] As one of the prisoners remembered, it "was snowing and it was very cold, but as usual, on Friday we would meet to [do] a short prayer regardless of inclement weather or anything else."[23] Fewer than ten feet from the men was prison guard John Emery Duquette, who was assigned to monitor the congregation that day.[24] It was common for a guard to stand nearby and observe, and the group had routinely met in this designated area for almost a year, drawing anywhere from ten to seventy men.[25] As James X Walker recalled, as "the Muslims grew we began to receive more area."[26] By late 1959, the physical space had grown to fifteen yards long and seventy yards wide and was paved using stones the men had collected from the yard. It featured a stove for cooking and an oven for baking, since the mess halls did not offer halal cooking: "We would all more or less join together to purchase food and things of that nature so that we could cook it ourselves."[27] It also offered a vibrant intellectual life, with a blackboard for illustrations and classes on current events, Black history, Arabic, and readings from the Qur'an on Fridays such as this.[28] As Joseph X Magette later testified, we "were tolerated. I wouldn't say we were admitted, but we weren't denied the right to meet."[29]

Then, Magette recounted, "all of the sudden the situation changed completely. Thereafter we were in complete segregation" (solitary confinement).[30]

Duquette claimed that he heard one of the prisoners say that they were going to take over solitary confinement and filed a disciplinary report using the familiar argument that the group's religious intentions were disingenuous. The men were charged with hosting an "unauthorized meeting under the guise of an assembly for religious purposes."[31] Sammy X Williams, who allegedly made the remark, was locked up immediately, and the other men were soon taken to disciplinary court and moved to a minimum privilege area, which was accompanied by a loss of 360 days of good time.[32] Some of the men remained in solitary confinement until June of the following year.[33]

Clinton, like other prisons across New York, California, Illinois, and Washington, D.C., had become a central battleground for the Nation of Islam by the late 1950s. In 1957, Attica's warden, Walter Martin, wrote to prison commissioner Paul McGinnis that four prisoners at Attica had been identified as Muslim. This "fad for *Qur'an* . . . has been developing over recent months. I have been trying to puzzle out what the 'gimmick' is in this matter but haven't solved it yet."[34] Muslim prisoners requested access to the Qur'an in Arabic, religious literature published in Black newspapers, and correspondence with ministers such as Malcolm X in Harlem and Robert X Williams in Buffalo. They challenged the lawfulness of punishing them for their religious beliefs with such measures as solitary confinement and loss of good time. In many of these cases, the state used the Ahmadiyya Movement in Islam (AMI) to undermine these claims, offering prisoners only English translations of the Qur'an and correspondence with Ahmadi religious leaders. An early precursor to the contemporary "good Muslim/bad Muslim" dichotomy in the United States, which as Mahmood Mamdani points out, pits "good" secular westernized Islam against "bad" pre-modern, radical Islam, was the state's privileging of the AMI over the NOI.[35] The racial particularity of the Nation of Islam's Black Nationalism provided the foundation for the state's argument that the group was insincere in its religious convictions and was merely using Islam as a front for its political agenda.

Muslim prison organizing and litigation in New York joined the first wave of cases that prompted the attention of the courts.[36] No figure was more important in this movement than Martin X Sostre. His parents Saturnino, a Communist merchant seaman, and Crescencia, a cap maker, emigrated from Puerto Rico and settled in New York in 1925, two years after he was born. Sostre was influenced by Lewis Michaux's African National Memorial Bookstore and the stepladder orators on 125th Street in Harlem.[37] He left school in the tenth grade to help his family earn money during the

Great Depression and was drafted in 1942. After being dishonorably discharged in 1946, he was arrested in 1952 for heroin possession. Sostre arrived at Clinton Prison in 1953 and, like many eventual converts, listed his religion as that of his childhood: Catholicism. He later recalled that there were thirty Muslims belonging to "at least four different sects of Islam": AMI, MST, NOI, and Sunni.[38]

Like many before him, Sostre was introduced to Islam through the AMI. He first wrote to the movement in 1958 in an attempt to get a copy of the Qur'an and credited his conversion to another Ahmadi prisoner named Teddy Anderson, who brought his Qur'an from Green Haven Prison. It was the only copy at Clinton.[39] "We would have to consult with him and borrow it from him," Sostre remembered. "He was reluctant to lend it out, naturally, but usually he would loan it out to ones that wanted to peruse it."[40] In this sense, Sostre's conversion was typical of prisoners during the 1950s. Another key organizer, Thomas X Bratcher, later testified that he was raised Roman Catholic but converted to Islam at Auburn Prison in 1959 after receiving teachings on the Ahmadiyya faith. He also described a robust Muslim community at Auburn: "Some were Ahmadiyya, some were Moorish Science Islams, some were Sunni Muslims, some were Wahapi [Wahhabi]. . . . We had a non-sectarian class. That means that we did not lean to the teachings of any so-called sect in Islam." Although the men were introduced to Islam through the AMI, a small but growing community was drawn to the teachings of the Muslim Brotherhood. Citing the state's sanctioning of the AMI, Bratcher asked to write to Elijah Muhammad. "Since permission is granted to the Ahmadiyya Muslims to correspond with religious advisors," he wrote to prison commissioner Paul McGinnis, "I assume similar permission shall be granted to me."[41]

Despite the efforts of prison officials to divert Muslim converts toward the AMI, the Muslim Brotherhood continued to thrive in New York prisons throughout the 1950s. Because they were not given a formal space to hold services within the prison, informal prayers such as those described at Clinton often took place in the prison yard.[42] Men relied on an oral tradition of memorized prayer, and *surahs* were passed from prisoner to prisoner. As William X SaMarion remarked, these prayers were "learned by heart, to be able to speak about."[43] Many of these lessons were based on editorials by Elijah Muhammad and Malcolm X published in Black newspapers in the late 1950s. "Most of us have never seen the inside of a Temple," Thomas Bratcher wrote Malcolm X. "We have had to make up our own lesson from articles appearing in the Los Angeles Herald Dispatch."[44] Newspapers that reproduced these editorials were forbidden at some prisons and monitored at others. In 1958, for example, the California director of corrections notified all wardens and staff that "requests to subscribe to the *Pittsburgh Courier* or the *Amsterdam News* should be screened as possible indications of interest in Muslemism."[45]

The stark contrast between the "tolerance" described by Magette prior to December 1959 and the various punishments levied against Muslim prisoners thereafter points to the state's strategizing to suppress political activism and the spread of Islam in New York prisons. The timing of the response by prison officials was certainly not merely coincidental.[46] Shortly after the airing of *The Hate That Hate Produced*, an entire apparatus of state control, which included local surveillance and a national network of shared information about the Nation of Islam, was erected. Just as the sensationalist miniseries had prompted fear among its largely white viewership and denunciation from moderate civil rights leadership, prison officials who had been puzzling over the growth of the NOI in prisons now took decisive action.

Just two weeks after the *Jumu'ah* raid, "all pens, pencils, paper—anything that could be used to write a writ, was confiscated." "I was told that I could not purchase any more legal paper nor could I have a pen in my possession," Joseph Magette recalled.[47] Walker and Magette were handcuffed together and taken to meet with prison administrators, where Magette claimed he was struck across the face by a prison lieutenant and Walker was told that he must "withdraw this petition and give up this . . . ridiculous idea of a so-called religion."[48] At the time of the Clinton reprisals, Muslim prison litigation was just beginning to be developed as a coherent strategy. Martin Sostre, William SaMarion, James Pierce, and Edward Robert Griffin (who had been paroled by the time of the trial) had submitted what was believed to be the first writ by Muslim prisoners.[49] As the judge later noted at trial, "These complaints were drawn the same day, same thing. Apparently even the wording is practically identical."[50]

The writs from Clinton Prison became the basis for the *Pierce v. LaVallee* case, which was argued by Jawn A. Sandifer and Edward Jacko.[51] Both attorneys were graduates of Howard Law School and protégées of Charles Hamilton Houston.[52] Having won the largest lawsuit against the City of New York on behalf of the Nation of Islam in the Johnson X Hinton police brutality case of 1957, the attorneys were again employed by Elijah Muhammad on behalf of Muslim prisoners at Clinton.[53] Commissioner McGinnis responded to the threat of judicial oversight by extending state surveillance into the daily activities of Muslim prisoners. That summer, he asked wardens to submit monthly reports on all Muslim activities in New York prisons, which the senior prison inspector, Richard Woodward, eventually used to compile a summary that was distributed to each prison administration.[54] As a final measure meant to quell the activities of Muslim prisoners, SaMarion, Sostre, Magette, and Walker (but not Pierce) were all transferred to Attica Prison on June 28, 1960. There they joined an active Muslim community that continued to grow through religious conversions and prison transfers until it included almost sixty members and became one of the most active political communities in the U.S. prison system.[55]

Attica Prison

The transfer of the four men was an explicit, although ineffective, attempt at quelling Muslim activism in the prisons.[56] The practice of transferring prisoners (which were known as "drafts") in order to "break up gangs, separate associates in crime, and prevent disorder" was decades old in New York.[57] In June 1960, a group of officials in the state capital agreed that McGinnis "would attempt to identify ringleaders and upon identification, transfer them to other prisons, pointing out to the receiving warden what to expect. In this way, he hoped to curb their activities in the Cult."[58] When Deputy Warden Albert Meyer sat down with SaMarion during his initial interview at Attica, he told him that he was aware of his disciplinary record at Clinton, which was due to his religious beliefs, and said plainly that "he had been transferred to Attica Prison because the authorities at Clinton felt that he was a leader of a group in that institution."[59]

Like Clinton, Attica had a diverse Muslim community. Meyer later testified that there were "approximately twenty-two of these [Muslims], nine of whom profess to be followers of the Honorable Elijah Muhammad and thirteen of whom profess to belong to other religions—religious groups, Ahmadiyya, Sunni, Shiite. . . . The others are on the list and we suspect or we have reason to believe that they may be Muslims."[60] With James X Pierce separated from his co-plaintiffs, Sostre and SaMarion, administrators at Attica set about regulating the spread of Islam within the prison.

After spending time in reception, where transfers were held before being released into the general population, each of the men had an interview with Meyer. Although a "warden's card" for each prisoner contained his name, number, criminal history, record of disciplinary actions, age, education, and a variety of other information relating to his sentence, William SaMarion recalled telling Meyer, "I had been transferred from Clinton Prison to Attica Prison because of my religious beliefs, and I wanted to know if

I would [be] so persecuted at this prison as I was in the Clinton Prison."[61] Meyer told SaMarion that he could attend Hebrew classes with the part-time Jewish chaplain or write to Khalil Ahmad Nasir of the AMI if he wanted a religious adviser. In an effort to restrict proselytizing, Meyer stressed that any religious literature found outside a cell would be confiscated.[62]

Attica's officials tried to halt the spread of Islam at its source by limiting the dissemination of religious texts. As Magette remembered, Meyer "didn't want us to—in other words—to permit anyone to read literature that we had in our possession dealing with Islam. He wanted us to keep all Islamic materials and periodicals and what-not within the confines of our cells. He didn't want us proselyting in any way."[63] Ironically, just days before Meyer interviewed the men, he had written Attica's warden about the transformative potential of Islam: "It is my feeling that some of these prisoners are really benefiting and have had a decided change in behavior pattern since becoming converts to the religion of Islam. I feel as long as this religion does not interfere with the orderly operation of the institution, we may derive some benefit from it."[64] But Meyer's enthusiasm did not last. Soon after their release into the general population, Magette and Sostre were disciplined as "principal agitators" for distributing hand-printed religious lessons. A number of writs were also being prepared against the warden of Clinton Prison, J. E. LaVallee, and Commissioner McGinnis.[65]

Arthur 2X Johnson and Thomas X Bratcher were already being held at Attica when the other four arrived. They had come to Islam through different paths. Thomas Bratcher was raised as a Roman Catholic in New York City after his parents migrated from the South. His father worked as a driver for the post office before getting laid off in 1962 from the Motor Truck Exchange.[66] Bratcher took an interest in Islam while incarcerated at Auburn Prison in 1959. Just over a year later, he made his profession of faith, or *Shahada*.[67] Arthur 2X converted to Islam during the summer of 1961 after being raised as a Baptist. Johnson had visited the mosque in Buffalo under minister Robert X Williams before his incarceration. "I attempted to embrace Islam then when I was working . . . [but] I wasn't successful in my attempt," he later testified.[68] Although he had not yet officially converted, Johnson's disciplinary record documents the emergence of his faith the previous year. At first all his disciplinary citations were non-religious, but in March 1960 he was charged with having "fanatic religious writings" in his possession.[69] As Johnson recalled, "eleven of us put in writs to the court asking permission, right to religious freedom[,] and later on I read in the paper somewhere where they had passed a law, some other prisoners that were allowed to worship, have congregational services in the institution. . . . Then I began to attend the services of Islam in the yard with the other prisoners that [were] having the classes."[70] It was this combination of litigation beyond the prisons walls and classes and organizing in the recreation yards that eventually led prison officials to develop additional repressive strategies at Attica.

The Muslim Brotherhood was organized around a written constitution outlining its aims and objectives, membership eligibility, organizational structure, meeting dates, and disciplinary measures. Meetings were held regularly on Fridays for *Jumu'ah*. At a monthly conference, guards would report on conditions and duties, and all members would vote on any controversial matters. The monthly meeting also produced a "broad policy and long-range strategy."[71] Like the Nation of Islam outside prisons, the organization operated on a system of internal discipline, whereby a member could be either reprimanded or expelled by trial and vote.[72] As Eldridge Cleaver wrote, each prison featured a "hierarchy patterned rigidly after the structure of the Mosques in the outside world . . . [with a] minister, captain, and Fruit of Islam."[73] The written constitution created a shared community in which each member was responsible to the group, in contrast to the typical prison social formation, which stressed individual rehabilitation and speaking only for oneself.[74] Thomas Bratcher explained that "charges may be brought by any number of the Muslim Brotherhood and placed against another Muslim, because every Muslim's conduct in Attica reflect on every other Muslim."[75]

In some respects, the collective organizing of the Muslim Brotherhood challenged gendered paradigms in prisons. Such organizing and support unsettled some of the singular hypermasculinity of prison life.[76] Dan Berger writes that "NOI study groups and prayer circles facilitated an antiracist collectivity—in the form of consciousness and group action—in an institution governed by divisive individualism."[77] One responsibility was expressed through tithing, and these organizational dues were used for "supplementing the diet of the members and further[ing] the cause of the Brotherhood."[78] SaMarion explained the role of the treasurer as the "one that holds the finances, sees that—if we are short of toothpaste or tooth powder, or the brother has no money and is trying to buy some books, that he has the toothpaste or the tooth powder."[79] This social organization shifted the meaning of what it meant to "do time." Contrary to the social system of cliques outlined by Donald Clemmer in *The Prison Community* (1940), which emphasized the equality of all prisoners, doing one's own time, and the idea that no prisoner could speak on behalf of another, the NOI ushered in a communal solidarity that stressed shared oppression. "The Muslims' definition of their situation as requiring organization, group participation, and communion challenged the basic tenets of traditional penal administration," Jacobs concluded.[80] In other respects, the heteropatriarchal norms that structured NOI life outside of prison were heightened on the inside. The group's constitution explicitly banned membership by gay men. Sexuality and masculinity were significant for all prisoners, particularly men of color. As one prisoner at Attica interviewed after the 1971 uprising said, "Manhood at Attica is intimidated 24 hours a day, 365 days a year."[81] New York prisons during this period intensified heteronormative masculinity by segregating suspected "homosexuals" to different blocks.[82]

Because Muslim prisoners were often denied the space to meet afforded to other religious groups, collective organizing and political and religious education came primarily through classes in the prison yard. SaMarion was in charge of organizing these lessons, and along with Magette and Walker, the group covered a diverse set of teachings, including business, Islam, Arabic, Black history, and law. The "Mufti is known as the one that keeps the peace within the group, discipline," he later explained. "The librarian is the one that has the control of all the literature that we were able to fill our lockers with; literature pertaining to our own kind, Black Man's literature, Black Man's history, mathematics, Arabic, anything we thought would help us in our educational field. . . . The secretary is the one that would record the day's activities, would record the statements of some of the brothers."[83] This community was persistently under threat due to its constantly fluctuating membership base. Short sentences often meant the release of members, and several assistants were appointed for each guard position to ensure continuity.[84] This measure was meant to counter prison officials, who, as Eldridge Cleaver recalled, would "periodically bundle up the leaders of each Mosque and transfer them to another prison, or place them in solitary confinement so that they could not communicate with the other members of the Mosque."[85] Indeed, the two greatest threats to the Muslim Brotherhood came from prison transfers and the "further reduction of our ranks by the implacable enemy through persecutions (solitary confinement)."[86]

Solitary confinement, sometimes referred to as "the box" or "segregation," was the prison's principal tool of security and punishment.[87] As Sostre later put it, "The box is the real barometer of who is a threat to the state."[88] The practice of solitary confinement developed out of the Quaker practice of penitence and solitary reflection, which was codified in the Pennsylvania system and best illustrated at Eastern State Penitentiary in Philadelphia, where prisoners were held entirely alone in $7\frac{1}{2}' \times 12'$ cells with an individual exercise yard. New York's Auburn Prison system augmented this idea by combining solitary living within a system of strict discipline and labor for prison profit, drawing on the nineteenth-century idea that collective work and isolated living would reform prisoners.[89]

By the 1960s, solitary confinement had shed its pretense of reform and become strictly punitive. At Attica, it consisted of fifty individual cells on the third floor of the reception building. The floor made up a gallery of single cells, each with only a bed, a toilet and wash basin, running water, and a light. When assigned to segregation, prisoners were often required to stay for days or weeks in "keep-lock" or a strip cell before moving to the gallery. "Keep-lock" was a single solitary cell, where "your cell doors do not open up any more." The strip cell was bare, with only a bucket and a blanket. As SaMarion described it, prisoners "do an initial twenty days on a concrete floor with only a pair of winter underwear, pair of socks, no sanitary facilities whatever. The only thing you use for calls of nature is a bucket, a defication [sic] bucket." Rations in keep-lock were reduced to half of normal mess hall food and water, with two slices of bread.[90] Magette described keep-lock at Clinton as even more medieval. The "Dark Cell" was completely empty, without even a blanket. He was put there naked, with half a cup of water and one slice of bread three times a day.[91] Asked to compare it to Attica, he described solitary at Clinton as a "solid sheet of steel [door] that has a sliding panel. . . . They have a crack under the door of the block cell about an inch high and through this crack, the cold air comes, and that was the most miserable part of the thing."[92]

Prison officials used solitary confinement as more than a physical punishment. They coupled it with the loss of good time as a way to isolate prisoners while simultaneously extending their sentences. Good time, sometimes referred to as good behavior (often called "earned time"), was a method by which prisoners could shorten their sentence through good conduct. Accumulated losses of good time could be re-earned but often prevented prisoners from shortening their maximum sentence.[93] In the first year the men spent at Attica, thirty-three prisoners were sent to solitary confinement, and four hundred cases of discipline led to 8,525 total days of good time lost over a nine-month period.[94] First, prisoners lost an initial amount of time for the disciplinary matter. For instance, SaMarion lost sixty days for joining a hunger strike, which protested the solitary confinement of another Muslim prisoner. The second loss of time occurred *during* solitary confinement, as each day in solitary earned three lost days. Finally, regardless of prisoners' behavior in solitary, good time could not begin to be re-accumulated until a prisoner had been readmitted to the general population. These practices regarding loss of good time illustrate the vast discretionary powers wielded by prison officials. As SaMarion bleakly noted at his trial, "It is taken at will, you have it one minute, then you don't."[95]

Solitary confinement and the loss of good time were administered to Muslim prisoners for reasons that ranged from possession of religious material and legal papers to "professing religion" or making scrapbooks from clippings not on the approved literature list. In one of the most bizarre instances of arbitrary administrative control, SaMarion was keep-locked for "possessing literature pertaining to [racial] segregation and advocating to other prisoners segregation contrary to the Constitution of the State of New York and the State Administration."[96] The absurdity of this particular charge, which earned SaMarion over a year in solitary, was underscored by the persistence of racial segregation at Attica despite the very state constitution he was charged with violating. Sports teams and barber shops were racially segregated at Attica until the mid-1960s. The guard at the barber shop called first for "white shaves" and then "colored shaves." Although the Fourth of July was the only day of the year that prisoners could roam from yard to yard, segregating ice buckets for cooling off by race was a tradition at Attica.[97] As Bratcher described it, "They bring around two barrels of ice. The first barrel is dumped out on the platform and the guard hollers: 'white ice.' And the white prisoners collect their ice. The next barrel of ice is dumped out on the platform and the phrase is 'colored ice.' The Black prisoners collect their ice."[98] One prisoner said, "I was in Mississippi in the army, in Alabama in the army, and I was all over. I want to tell you something about Attica in 1960. I have never seen so much discrimination in one place in all my life."[99]

A year after the four men had been transferred from Clinton, Attica officials reported that a sit-down strike was being planned to protest Sostre's solitary confinement. At trial, the attorney general pointed to the similarities between the strategies of Muslims in prisons and those of the concurrent civil rights movement outside. "On the 15th day of March, 1962, were you charged with sitting in for the second time after being requested to come out of your initial sit-in?" he asked Joseph Magette.[100] Following the movement in Greensboro, North Carolina, in early 1960, the sit-in had become one of the principal strategies for desegregation in the civil rights movement.

Prison officials responded to the Muslim prisoners' sit-ins by putting them in keep-lock with a loss of ninety days of good time. The group was then broken up and transferred to different blocks with the hope that "after a thirty-day cooling off period and the dispersion of the members of this click[,] [sic] activity will abate."[101] As the state leveraged its three-pronged attack of solitary confinement, loss of good time, and transfers,[102] prisoners continued to develop new strategies of resistance, both large-scale and quotidian, to undermine this system. Unsurprisingly, just as outside organizing centered around the most acute site of state discipline—the jail—for incarcerated Muslims it coalesced around the jail-within-a-jail: solitary confinement.

Prisoners' Resistance

The most common tools of resistance used by Muslim prisoners were hunger strikes, writ writing, and takeovers of solitary confinement. Just as a previous strike had revolved around Sostre's segregation for distributing religious literature, five prisoners planned a hunger strike the following summer "on account of Brother Bratcher . . . [who] was placed on the observation cell or gallery, an excuse by the warden and those to make him seem that he was crazy concerning this trial that was coming up."[103] As Deputy Warden Meyer later told the courts, we "weren't going to permit [SaMarion] to stage a hunger strike; he didn't know the circumstances of the prisoner's being removed and furthermore, it wasn't up to him to question policy of the administration and we weren't going to permit him to do it."[104] Muslim prisoners hoped to gain visibility and public recognition from the hunger strike. 'Woodward reported a man in solitary going on strike saying, "When the 'Man' comes to see you dying from malnutrition then maybe we will win our point."[105]

Several years later, at Stateville Prison in Illinois, the first written demands made by those incarcerated at the penitentiary coincided with a hunger strike and the first violence the institution had seen in thirty years.[106] Although these strikes placed prison officials in a defensive position, they also involved strategic problems for Muslim prisoners in particular. As these examples indicate, striking against solitary confinement and the loss of good time credit was often punished with more of the same. Arthur Johnson observed that Muslims disagreed about whether or not to support a prison-wide strike against loss-of-good-time practices and ultimately decided against participation for fear that they would be "accused of inciting this strike." Just the year before, prison officials and newspapers were quick to blame Muslims for an uprising at California's Folsom State Prison.[107] Johnson later recalled a conversation with Commissioner McGinnis: "'Well,' he said. 'I am a Catholic,' he said. 'I am not prejudiced of any religion,' he said. 'But them follower[s] of Elijah Muhammad,' he say. 'I am going to defeat them.'"[108]

Significantly, Bratcher's confinement preceded the *SaMarion v. McGinnis* trial in Buffalo. Writ writing was a leading justification for prisoners' placement in solitary confinement. As Bratcher recalled, soon after he filed court papers he was quickly "marched to solitary confinement," where he lost ninety days of good time. His disciplinary report read that he had filed a "show cause order, making unfounded statements relating to the management of Attica State Prison."[109] He eventually received his application back from the Supreme Court justice saying that he had mistakenly put Article 77 of the Civil Practice Act instead of Article 88. But by then he was in solitary confinement and could not obtain his legal papers.[110] Not only had Bratcher's writ writing been the justification for his confinement, but being put in solitary then prevented his case from moving forward in the courts.

Litigation hit a nerve among prison officials as the NOI flooded courts across the country with writs. Between 1961 and 1978, there were 66 reported federal court decisions on suits filed by Muslim prisoners.[111] In California, the number of habeas corpus petitions rose from a mere 814 in 1957 to nearly 5,000 by 1965. At San Quentin in 1965, prisoners were churning out almost 300 petitions a month.[112] As one judge realized, these were not "cases where uneducated, inexperienced and helpless plaintiffs are involved. . . . These applications are part of a movement."[113] Prison litigation brought the hidden struggles of prisoners to national attention and catalyzed public support for their cause.[114] The waves of writs coming from incarcerated Muslims moved the courts away from a system of arbitrary and discretionary control by prison officials. As Jacobs argues, the NOI "provided an example for using law to challenge officialdom."[115] Although scholars have duly credited the NOI with launching the first organized prison litigation movement, it is important to explore the actual mechanisms that eventually forced judicial intervention and assured prisoners' constitutional rights.[116]

Martin Sostre was the most proficient "jailhouse lawyer" at Attica, and his writ-writing templates and instructions reveal the measures by which Muslims in solitary confinement were able to coordinate their litigation. By October 1961, three of the four men who had been transferred from Clinton to Attica had joined Bratcher in solitary confinement. Sostre wrote Walker that twenty-two Muslims in the general population were actively preparing writs against the warden and commissioner. These complaints would then be "consolidated into one big mammoth trial."[117] Meanwhile, Bratcher wrote from his segregated cell to Malcolm X and Mosque No. 7 in New York City:

The Grace of Allah has also been upon we Muslims in The New York State Correction System. He has given us several openings in the Federal Courts across the country so that we may seek redress from those in State and Federal authority who seek to regress our Freedom of Religious Worship, rights guaranteed us in the U.S. Constitution. Brothers! We have been persecuted, beaten, marred both mentally and physically, put in "Isolation-Segregation-Protection and Solitary confinement for the past 5 years. But, now, by the Will of Allah, our fight has almost come to an end. Victory is now in sight![118]

Bratcher hoped that Malcolm X would agree to be the key witness in the case in Buffalo the following year and assured him that the prisoners were "still gathering evidence to be used against [the state] at the trial."[119] When the case went to trial, Bratcher and the other plaintiffs routinely checked their diaries for specific dates of disciplinary hearings and regularly produced copies of letters received from Commissioner McGinnis and other prison officials.[120]

Bratcher's letter reveals the importance of jailhouse lawyering in producing organized legal challenges from prison. As Woodward wrote in 1964, although it remained an "indisputable fact that the prisoner's constitutional rights are rather narrow in scope . . . one clear constitutional right which prisoners both state and federal have under the Federal Decisional Law, is the absolute right of access to the courts for appeals and habeas corpus matters."[121] But myriad obstacles prevented cases from reaching trial. To file legal paperwork, a prisoner made out papers and contacted the notary public, who came on designated days of the week. The papers would be notarized and forwarded to the correspondence office to be mailed. Knowing that most prisoners were unable to draw up their own legal challenges, prisons established rules prohibiting legal assistance from jailhouse lawyers. "Rule 21" at Attica stated: "Prisoners are prohibited except upon approval of the warden to assist other prisoners in preparation of legal papers."[122] This ban was part of a national strategy to combat prison litigation efforts. In Texas, writ writers were forbidden from having access to legal materials of a fellow prisoner.[123] In California, it was known as Rule D-2602.[124] Even if a prisoner wanted to use another's paperwork as a template, officials regarded any writ or legal material in a cell not pertaining to that prisoner as evidence of prison lawyering.[125] Thus, when Martin Sostre wrote Walker, he urged him to copy the writ into his notebook but not to "let this lay around. This is dynamite." Calling pens, paper, and notebooks the "most essential weapons in fighting Shaitan (Arabic transliteration of 'the devil')," he emphasized that Walker should then flush the original down the toilet.[126] Sostre's writs were templates on which a prisoner could simply fill in the date and replace the name "James Doe" with his own.

At Clinton and Attica, writ writing developed into one of the most effective tools used by Muslim prisoners to challenge the state. While the Supreme Court had not yet set forth a clear consensus on the NOI's right to religious freedoms in prisons, it strictly forbade any "direct or indirect interference by prisons or state authorities" in prisoners' access to the courts.[127] The writ-writing struggles of Muslims at Attica reveal the ways that prisons attempted to interfere with court access by limiting legal advice, intimidating writ writers, and disrupting the legal process through solitary confinement. Yet Muslims' litigation campaigns were often better coordinated than the authorities' efforts to curtail them, as the strategies of local prison officials and state policy makers were often at odds. In San Quentin, for example, prisoners set up a small office where three of them transcribed writs onto standardized forms that were processed on duplicating machines. Meanwhile, the California Department of Corrections was busy attempting to clamp down on writ writers by prohibiting access to law literature and court decisions.[128]

Prisoners also appropriated solitary confinement, which was the principal mechanism of prison repression, and turned it into a site of organized protest. Recognizing that most of Attica's Muslims were already in solitary confinement, Sostre urged Walker to avoid being sent back to the general population. According to Sostre, they "made a pact not to go down until the religious persecution of the Muslims cease[s]." If Walker were sent back, he was told to threaten to bring contraband literature out of his cell so he would be returned to solitary. They reasoned that each time the warden "snatch[ed] an aggressive Muslim out of population, he would send one down from the box and send another one up from population. In other words, he kept manipulating the brothers like monkeys on a string." Sostre astutely concluded that when "the box ceases to work, the entire disciplinary and security system breaks down."[129] NOI members filled solitary confinement until the box no longer became an effective form of punishment. Wardens then had to decide whether to create hotbeds of activism in segregation or undermine the arbitrary rules they had worked so hard to justify and enforce.

The prisoners' strategy of filling solitary confinement predated the developing civil rights strategy of "Jail, No Bail" in the South.[130] In January 1961, a group of college students who had been staging sit-ins at department stores in South Carolina for a year refused to accept a bond and be released from jail. Instead, the nine students from Friendship Junior College served thirty-day sentences on a chain gang.[131] SNCC, the SCLC, and the NAACP soon joined a local desegregation effort, which targeted transportation, libraries, and lunch counters in Albany, Georgia. One of the defining characteristics of the Albany movement was its strategy of filling the jails. Martin Luther King, Jr. and Ralph Abernathy came to Albany and spent Christmas in a cell. However, Albany police chief Laurie Pritchett had studied the strategies of nonviolent resistance and avoided a national outcry by making mass arrests without the violent reprisals of police dogs and water hoses that etched Birmingham, Alabama, into the national consciousness several years later. As Berger points out, Pritchett had a four-point plan: shield police brutality from public view; arrest all protesters on purportedly color-blind bases; refuse to negotiate with protesters; and "incarcerate, incarcerate, incarcerate."[132] The ultimate strategy, which was perhaps the most effective, was to send protesters to county jails throughout southwest Georgia when the city jails became full.

The prisoners' strategy of taking over solitary dated back to at least 1959, over a year before the Friendship Nine in South Carolina used these tactics. But the temporal order of these two streams of protest is less significant than their mutual theorizing. Both civil rights organizers and prisoners appropriated the mechanisms of local control—jails and solitary confinement—as tools of organized protest. As civil rights organizers in the South and prisoners at Attica undermined forms of state control, the police chief in Albany mobilized a larger network of police and jails, while wardens at Clinton and Attica transferred prisoners to other state prisons when their segregation units became filled with politicized prisoners. Both movements attempted to garner national attention and pressed for federal intervention. For prisoners at Attica, solitary confinement and the loss of good time credit were crucial to their claims in state and federal courts. As Sostre wrote, "We have taken over the box and he is anxious to get us out of the box, especially with the big trial coming soon. So don't let him clean up for we are living proof of the religious oppression complained of in our writs."[133] Filling solitary confinement not only undermined prison security but also built a case for trial and dramatized prisoners' struggles before the courts and the nation.

In both cases, however, the appropriation of tools of state control had consequences. In the case of Muslims at Attica, surveillance intensified statewide, and knowledge production and intelligence sharing on the Nation of Islam in prisons escalated. Despite their similarities, the "Jail, No

Bail" strategy has its place in the annals of civil rights history as a heroic confrontation with southern Jim Crow through nonviolent direct action. Meanwhile, the takeover of solitary confinement by Muslims at Attica has largely remained undocumented.

Albany, New York

While the federal government was no more willing to step into state prisons on behalf of Muslim prisoners than it was in Albany, Georgia to protect nonviolent protesters, the writ writing and activism of the Muslim Brotherhood was met by the construction of an entire state apparatus in the state capital of Albany, New York. Within a month of the raid on religious services at Clinton prison, Commissioner McGinnis called a meeting with assistants to Attorney General Leftkowitz and Governor Rockefeller. There he "reiterated his fears, saying that the Muslim Cult was spreading like a cancerous growth and was becoming a most serious problem." The group determined that the state police would be the "most logical State agency to set up and maintain a file." Guards in the Manhattan subversive unit were sent to Los Angeles, Chicago, Detroit, and East Lansing, where they received "excellent cooperation" from police departments to create a file on the NOI. In May 1960, the New York state police became the primary agency for a broad attack on imprisoned Muslims. McGinnis would turn over arrest records, photographs, and release dates for all identified Muslims in prison, and in return, any information relating to the NOI would be "immediately transmitted to Commissioner McGinnis to assist him in combating this organization's activities."[134]

Writ writing and prison litigation had shone a light on the abusive discretionary powers of the corrections system and invited the courts to scrutinize the system itself. This strategy prompted deep surveillance within prisons and a flood of administrative reports concerning the Nation of Islam. As the group became more prominent in public discussions of race relations and its appeal among prisoners spread more widely, the state developed a framework to justify the continued suppression of Islam in prisons.

Wardens and state prison guards authorized prison surveillance and in some cases even dedicated a staff member to internal supervision of the NOI.[135] This surveillance was meant not only to absorb and report but also to disrupt and subvert. It provided the raw material for the production of state knowledge that could be used to quell prison activism. That the NOI constituted political subversion under the "guise of religion" became a stock phrase among law enforcement and prison officials.[136] Through its intervention, the state assigned political meaning to religious practice, further politicizing incarceration and the practice of Islam within prison walls. The buildup of a carceral state was not simply a top-down response to the gains of outside social movements or a result of federal shifts in political power. The dialectics of discipline between state actors and prisoners often produced these intersecting developments on the ground, which bubbled up to state and national policies.

More accurately than he could have known, Malcolm X wrote in his autobiography that prison officials "monitored what I wrote to add to the files which every state and federal prison keeps on the conversion of Negro prisoners by the teachings of Mr. Elijah Muhammad."[137] Indeed, Commissioner McGinnis requested in 1960 that each prison relay names of all Muslim prisoners to the New York State Police's Criminal and Subversives Section.[138] Within a year, prison inspector Richard Woodward began a series of monthly bulletins highlighting reports from individual prisons, national news on the Nation of Islam, and conference proceedings from the ACA. He then distributed this information to wardens throughout the New York system.

In its earliest form, state surveillance was unidirectional—from prisons to the capital. Disciplinary reports involving Muslims, group associations, names, addresses, and visitation lists were all forwarded to Albany, where they were transcribed and put into individual files with photographs and criminal records. These were in turn sent to the Criminal and Subversives Section. For example, one note from Attica read as follows:

Dear Commissioner:

'A', who was received here by transfer from the Elmira Reformatory and claimed to have no religion.

It has been our experience that prisoners claiming no religion usually gravitate into Muslimism after joining the population.

'C' was received from Greenhaven Prison. He claimed his religion to be Protestant but the record card shows a keeplock for taking part in a large aggressive gathering suspected to be Muslims.[139]

A month after Woodward's bulletins began, he reported that "many clippings have been received on the Muslim activity. They are most welcome."[140] The inspector stressed that "information as to how a situation was handled in one institution may help in other instances."[141]

State surveillance relied most heavily on prison guards, who had daily contact with those imprisoned. One institution devoted a guard to keeping a list of all active members, searching their cells, and confiscating any literature relating to the NOI.[142] Seized materials slowed the spread of conversions while serving as a source for state intelligence. One area of concern was prisoners' use of Arabic. The language not only had a cultural and religious function, but also stymied prison security. For example, Thomas Bratcher gave specific instructions in his letter to Malcolm X: his mother would write him of the minister's reply in red ink with "Three lines of Al-Fatihab" (referring to *Al-Fatiha*, the first surah in the Qur'an).[143] One state report said that it "would seem doubtful if the majority of the prisoners can rea[d] and write Arabic but if notes are picked up that seem to contain no meaning maybe they would bear investigating."[144] Two months later, six pages of Arabic to English and English to Arabic translations were confiscated.[145]

Another surveillance strategy that relied heavily on prison guards was the scrutiny of Muslim eating habits and religious rituals. The refusal to eat pork in prisons dated back to incarcerated Muslims during World War II. At Attica, one prisoner was charged with wasting state food for throwing away his bacon. Bratcher wrote to Warden Wilkins asking for permission to carry food from the mess hall to his cell so he and other Muslim prisoners could eat after sundown during Ramadan.[146] At Milan, where Elijah Muhammad had served time during World War II, prisoners took part in a three-day hunger strike against pork, which eventually resulted in Muslim-prepared food and a separate dining section.[147] In California, the warden of Folsom State Prison wrote Attorney General Stanley Mosk and enclosed surveillance photographs taken by a guard. The correctional sergeant described twelve Muslims holding a meeting in the yard on "benches provided for the purpose of playing chess." As the sergeant approached, apparently snapping photos of the congregation, a prisoner proclaimed, "They want to take our picture, so let's give them a good one." Another suggested that they "face the east and pray to Allah." The group of twelve men then lined up facing east, with their hands raised waist high and palms facing the sky while one prisoner conducted prayer.[148]

Prison officials challenged these actions, quickly seizing on dietary restrictions as a way to assess the legitimacy of a prisoner's religious beliefs. A memo from Attica stated: "In order to check the authenticity of the Muslims, each guard has been required to submit to the principal keeper's office a report on whether or not the particular prisoner in question is eating pork. The members who are eating pork will be . . . included in next month's report."[149] Several months later, another institution counted the Muslims who would not eat when pork was served in the mess hall: "Of the above total [of 70], 30 prisoners either refused their ration or gave it to another prisoner, and [an] additional 16 prisoners took their ration to their cells and only two were actually observed fasting."[150] Prison officials watched and recorded other religious rituals. SaMarion was charged with making "unnecessary noise" and "sloshing water around in the cell" at 5:15 A.M. despite this likely being part of his ablution and morning prayer, or *fajr*.[151] By monitoring prisoners' eating, writings, and literature, prison guards acted as foot soldiers in the state's surveillance and persecution of Muslim prisoners.

Surveillance continued at the state and federal levels long after release. When a Muslim prisoner was paroled, the state police assigned to a subversive unit in that area would be informed "so they could keep track of him." They would also contact the parole guard so they could surveil his "activities in behalf of the Cult, both inside and outside of State institutions." If an NOI member was sent back to prison, the guard was required to immediately notify the commissioner.[152] When Thomas Bratcher was paroled in 1964, agents at both the FBI and the BOSS were alerted and asked to run his name through their systems.[153]

By the mid-1960s, the Nation of Islam had a presence in major prisons from coast to coast, and the network of state surveillance expanded nationally alongside it. California had estimated a little over one hundred Muslim prisoners in the early 1960s, and New York nearly three hundred, with some prisons reporting over a quarter of Black prisoners as Muslim.[154] Just a few years later, this number nearly doubled in New York and quadrupled in California.[155] Some prisons began outlawing membership in the NOI, and one even established a rule prohibiting more than two Black prisoners from congregating together.[156] The emergence of the NOI as a chief concern of prison officials is well documented in the proceedings of the ACA. Donald Clemmer, noted penologist and defendant in the Muslim religious rights case *Fulwood v. Clemmer*, and sociologist John M. Wilson were the first to present on the NOI at the ACA's conference in 1960.[157] Richard Woodward quoted extensively from Clemmer's presentation in his monthly bulletin alongside a review of C. Eric Lincoln's book.[158] By 1963, topics such as "The Black Muslims and Religious Freedom in Prison" and "The Black Muslim in Prison: A Personality Study" had surfaced as well.[159]

The 1960s marked a profound shift from rehabilitative strategies such as "bibliotherapy"—the use of books and education for therapy—to new technologies of violence and psychological warfare. Isolation, sensory

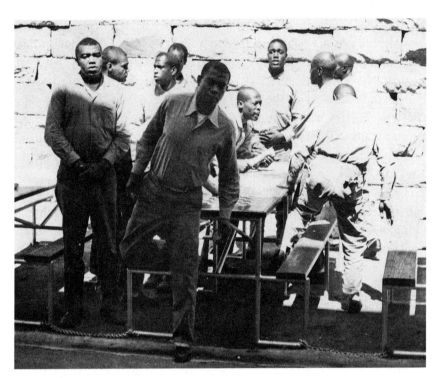

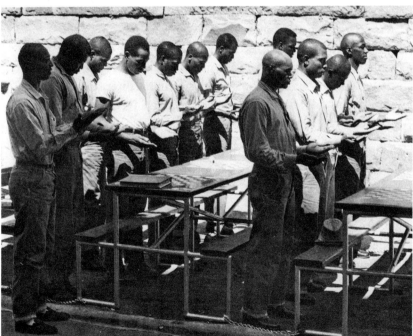

Sequence of surveillance photos taken by prison guard of Muslim meeting at Folsom State Prison, August 26, 1962. Box 173, folder 22, Department of Justice, Attorney General's Office–Division of Criminal Law Records, California State Archives, Sacramento.

deprivation, and brainwashing were all proposed as new forms of control, and Muslim prison litigation helped to "propel this shift."[160] In 1961, Edgar Schein, a professor of psychology at MIT, presented a paper titled "Man against Man: Brainwashing" as part of a symposium sponsored by the Bureau of Prisons called The Power to Change Behavior. The presentations and ensuing discussion were reproduced in the official journal of the Medical Correctional Association. The conversation that followed Schein's talk immediately honed in on the question of "how shall we manage the Muslims."[161]

Protests against racial persecution were analyzed and medicalized. As Jonathan Metzl documented, "psychiatric authors conflated the schizophrenic symptoms of African American patients with the perceived schizophrenia of civil rights protests, particularly those organized by Black Power, Black Panthers, Nation of Islam, or other activist groups."[162] One doctor recounted that while "many of these Negro Muslims were highly intelligent . . . we also found that many of them had characteristics of mental disorder of a minimum degree":

> We started out with the idea that these were people that formed a group of their own and that we could work with them as a group, and we soon learned that this was impossible and that what we were doing was providing a medium for their kind of illness—group illness to grow and to become more cohesive and even more difficult to work with both as individuals and as a group; and we were in a sense feeding their paranoid behavior so that each step in the direction of their goal resulted in additional demands and additional recruits because they showed strain.[163]

Although the psychologist interpreted the Muslims' response to their situation as a form of paranoia, in essence he and the others at the conference were describing the characteristics of the dialectics of discipline, where greater repression of religious practices and political beliefs led to more resistance from those incarcerated. A group that had once been considered "model prisoners" now represented the vanguard of the prisoners' rights movement and the foremost threat in the minds of prison officials. Bertram S. Brown, a staff psychiatrist at the National Institute of Mental Health, ended the discussion by directly addressing the audience of prison officials: "We here in Washington are anxious to have you undertake some of these things; do things perhaps on your own—undertake a little experiment of what you can do with Muslims."[164]

Control units, special housing units, and adjustment centers were all outgrowths of the experimental use of prolonged solitary confinement by prison officials during the late 1950s and early 1960s. Alan Gómez notes that these punishments and techniques, "initially experimented with on Muslim inmates, and later used en masse on political activists, became the model for the entire prison regime."[165] The academic disciplines of penology, psychology, and criminology served as arms of the state's developing knowledge production, which produced new modes of violence waged against incarcerated Muslims. Nearly sixty years later, Schein recalled that when he gave his presentation on the possibilities for brainwashing in the prison setting, he was "struck by how much they said, in effect, we basically already know all this stuff and use it in prison management."[166]

The Courts

When Thomas Bratcher asked Malcolm X to testify as an expert witness in the case of *SaMarion v. McGinnis*, he articulated the relationship between incarcerated Muslims and those outside through the metaphor of war: "The fighting man cannot win a war without the moral support of the home front."[167] Black prisoners saw the courts as a breach in the walls, which allowed them to express their claims before the world outside. Jacobs wrote that "it is as if the courts had become a battlefield where prisoners and prison administrators, led by their respective legal champions, engage in mortal combat."[168] Prisoners used testimony as part of what Berger has called "a strategy of visibility" to make their struggles known.[169] Sostre later described the court as "an arena. It is a battlefield—one of the best. We will use these same torture chambers, these same kangaroo courts, to expose them."[170] Testifying has its political roots in slavery and is central to the Black feminist tradition. As Danielle McGuire argues regarding the struggle against sexual violence in the civil rights movement, "testimony must be seen as a form of direct action and radical protest."[171] Prisoners were fighting on the front lines, with courts as their battlefield, supported by a home front of Muslims on the outside. Writ writing and testimony were what Sostre called their "most essential weapons."

When Commissioner McGinnis took the stand as a defendant before U.S. district court judge John Henderson in October 1962, SaMarion was the only plaintiff from the earlier case of *Pierce v. LaVallee*. The trial differed in several significant ways from the one that had emerged from Clinton two years earlier. The *Pierce* ruling had not brought about the changes the NOI had hoped for.[172] Judge Brennan constantly berated NOI attorney Edward Jacko for trying to expand the case beyond the initial complaint regarding denial of access to the Qur'an, at one point even admonishing him to be a "good little boy."[173] As Brennan saw it, the case had been resolved before it came to trial. He told Jacko, "You are asking to purchase the Koran. Now, the Warden says you can have the Koran. Well, what is there left for me to litigate?" Jacko concluded with dismay, "I think that is the crux of the case."[174] In *SaMarion*, however, the plaintiffs sought weekly congregational services conducted by Buffalo's Robert X Williams, correspondence with and visitation from ministers, and access to prayer books and the *Messenger* magazine. They meticulously documented their losses of good time credit and years in solitary confinement in order to demonstrate religious discrimination.[175]

The *Pierce* case demonstrated the steep challenge for prisoners during the era when the courts followed a hands-off policy. Judge Brennan did not believe the judicial branch should be involved in matters of prison discipline to begin with. "This Court didn't put these men in jail," he opined. "This Court didn't commit the crime for which they were convicted. This Court didn't try them. This Court didn't sentence them. This Court didn't control them, so that you must turn somewhere else to settle those other things."[176] He argued that naming the warden of Clinton had little bearing, since he is "not free to run his prison as he likes," and suggested that if the plaintiffs "wanted something, to get a decision that would bind them, No. 1, you would have to bring in the Department of Correction." Perhaps heeding this advice, the men added Commissioner McGinnis to the *SaMarion* suit.

The state defense attorneys raised the ante by claiming that members of the Nation of Islam were not in fact "true members of the religion of Islam."[177] Calling the tenets of the NOI "preachments of hate [and] race prejudice," Deputy Attorney General Robert Bresnihan outlined what would become the standard argument of the state against the practice of Islam in prisons: that the NOI was a political group acting in the guise of religion and posed clear and present danger to the prison as an institution. He told the court: "It is our position that every activity in a prison must be supervised and it is our position that religion, the guise of religion, does not give a prisoner or anyone else the right to come in and violate those security rules."[178] As court-appointed attorney Richard Griffin later recalled, since religious orthodoxy was taking center stage, it was "clear that I needed an expert witness and [I] decided to contact Malcolm X to see if he would testify."[179] Leading up to the trial, Bratcher wrote Malcolm X optimistically that the "trial promises to be the last one in the Muslims fight for Religious Freedom.

It is taken out in behalf of the 60 Muslims in Attica Prison. This writ covers *all* grievances. We have compounded so much evidence—over a period of two years—against the defendants—Paul D. McGinnis and Walter H. Wilkins—that under its magnitude, these two tyrants must fall."[180] In its breadth, testimony, and implications for future policy, *SaMarion* surpassed previous cases in its capacity to decide the future of the Nation of Islam in prisons.

Bratcher correctly anticipated the state's defense in his letter to Malcolm X a year before the trial. "From the Attorney General's answer to my writ, I can see that his main argument is going to be in the presenting of certain publications out of Books, magazines, and papers about the Muslims. . . . He is going to try and justify the warden's violation of our constitutional rights by submitting these published reports to the court saying that we are preaching 'hate' and we are a fanatical group not recognized by the rest of Muslim World."[181] As the state began to outline its defense that the NOI was an illegitimate religious group that threatened prison security, Bresnihan's questioning of key witnesses revealed its central strategy: to delegitimize the Nation of Islam's religious standing. Recognizing that "this is the only loophole [Bresnihan] has," Bratcher told Malcolm: "I plan to close this hole up forever. The 'Key' wittness [sic] I am depending on to 'seal' our victory is 'You' *Minister Malcolm 'X.'"*[182]

This decision set the stage for a four-day showdown between Malcolm and the state's witness, Columbia University professor Joseph Franz Schacht. While Malcolm admitted openly in court that he had an eighth grade education, had no formal theological training, and could not speak Arabic, Schacht had a "masterly knowledge" of the language, and his book *Origins of Muhammadan Jurisprudence*—which discussed the historical development and sociological implications of Islamic law—was considered a seminal text in the Western study of Islam.[183] Yet Malcolm weaved around the state's probing questions regarding his expertise. When asked if he had a degree in theology, he replied that if "my understanding of the word 'theological' is correct, the study of God, the science that deals with religion and the study of God, I studied theology in that sense under the Honorable Elijah Muhammad about our God." When pressed on the length of his education, he replied, "I am still studying." When interrogated on whether or not he was ordained or had a written certificate permitting him to proselytize, he reminded the court that "Jesus sent his disciples forth with no written certificate or anything but his approval." Malcolm's testimony was so convincing that when Schacht took the stand and listed his memberships in the Royal

Netherlands Academy and the Arabic Academy in Damascus, and his honorary degree in law from the University of Algiers, the judge responded, "I don't think it is quite thoroughly clear at this time to qualify him as an expert."[184]

After establishing his religious credentials, Malcolm used the courtroom as a stage to articulate his political views. Almost a year before delivering his most widely remembered speech, "Message to the Grassroots," Malcolm explained the difference between a "House Negro" and a "Field Negro" to a federal judge. The former, he emphasized, had no support from the Black community. "He is a leader in public relations, but when it comes to actual following among Negroes, he has no following. . . . That is how you can tell him." When asked about the Nation of Islam's opposition to integration, Malcolm pivoted to the difference between racial *separation* and racial *segregation*. "Segregation means to regulate or control," he explained. "A segregated community is that forced upon inferiors by superiors. A separate community is done voluntarily by two equals."[185] The deputy attorney general tried to return to the point that the NOI taught violence and fomented an unsafe environment in prisons, adducing confiscated material that said: "To combat the Negro, convert him or annihilate him is the holiest task of the faithful." This statement, Bresnihan reasoned, was clear evidence of the violent aims of the Nation of Islam. Yet again, Malcolm thwarted the cross-examiner. To destroy the "Negro," he explained, meant to "destroy the stigma that makes this Negro a Negro. By converting him you annihilate, annihilate the ignorance and lethargy and immorality and things of that sort." "No Black person calls himself a Negro except those in America," he continued. "The white man respects the Black man, he disrespects the Negro."[186] Malcolm and the Nation of Islam sought to destroy a denigrated notion of Blackness defined by white society as "Negro" and replace it with an exalted, self-determined definition signified as "Black."

Malcolm's rhetorical sleight of hand was not evasive but didactic. Judge Henderson addressed Malcolm specifically at one point, remarking his changed understanding of the term "Negro": "I was taught in my early life that the word 'Negro' is a mark of respect to the Black man. I learned yesterday for the first time that there is a preferred name, the Black man, I take it. I am not used to that and when I refer to the Negro in my discussions to you, I am not doing it with a mark of any disrespect. I was always taught, and I thought of it as a mark of respect. I want you to understand that." While Henderson had, in effect, apologized for and excused his racism in the same remark, his high regard for Malcolm's opinion shifted the tenor of the trial.

As Griffin recalled, Henderson was "impressed by Malcolm and his testimony" and "respected Malcolm for his clear statements and responses."[187] Bresnihan, likely attempting to curry favor with the judge, then began adopting the phrase "the American Black Man" in his questioning. Malcolm's testimony, which lasted for three days and constituted over 20 percent of the trial transcript, persuaded the judge to rule that the Nation of Islam was a religious organization. Even more importantly, Malcolm's expression of his political views took center stage and fundamentally altered the discourse and scope of the case.

Malcolm's testimony radically expanded the case beyond the issues of religious counsel, correspondence, and access to literature. It articulated the NOI's critique of civil rights leadership and questions of self-determination, citizenship, and racial identity. In Malcolm's own intellectual development, his trial testimonies played a central role in developing his political ideas and rhetoric. Before the October 1962 trial, he frequently used "Uncle Toms" to deride civil rights spokespeople such as Martin Luther King, Jr., Bayard Rustin, and Roy Wilkins. After the trial, he developed the contrast between the "House" and "Field Negro," which drew parallels between slavery and the present in an incisive but more historically rooted analysis.[188] The courtroom served as a space where the NOI articulated its views and developed its broader critiques of the civil rights movement, the prison system, and American racial liberalism. As Malcolm X's three days on the witness stand demonstrated, prison litigation should not be measured in legal victories alone but should be seen as part of a wider arsenal of political strategies, ranging from fighting for constitutional rights through the law to engaging in direct-action protests such as sit-ins, hunger strikes, and takeovers of solitary confinement, which widened the Black freedom struggle during the 1960s.

MALCOLM X'S TESTIMONY in *SaMarion* was so compelling that as another major case—*Cooper v. Pate*—went to appeal, the state hoped to exploit his break with Elijah Muhammad and have him testify *against* the Nation of Islam's religious legitimacy. Having personally experienced Malcolm X's persuasiveness as an expert witness, William Bresnihan wrote to J. Edgar Hoover and J. Walter Yeagley of the Justice Department and implored them to pay to fly Malcolm back from Egypt to testify in the upcoming appeal.[189] In January 1965, the Illinois attorney general's office interviewed Malcolm X in his home for nearly ten hours. Although the assistant attorney general remained hopeful, the FBI was less optimistic, reporting that Malcolm was "seemingly disinterest[ed] in the matter," focusing instead on his interest in bringing the plight of Black Americans before the United Nations.[190]

Malcolm X never testified, and with the ruling in *Cooper*, the Nation of Islam's litigation campaign had successfully brought about the first constitutional legal standing for incarcerated people since the nineteenth century, just four years after the first writs by Muslim prisoners were brought before the courts. The case clearly stated that prisoners have constitutional rights and are entitled to file actions under Section 1983 of the Civil Rights Act, thereby opening the courts to a host of prisoners' rights issues, including freedom of religion and thought, and protection against excessive force and the use of solitary confinement. By the end of the 1960s, federal courts had decided more than two thousand cases citing Section 1983, and that number rose to thirty-nine thousand by the mid-1990s.[191]

The gradual intervention of the courts into the administration of prison discipline was a product of a decade of political strategies, including writ writing, hunger strikes, sit-ins, and takeovers of solitary confinement. In a historical perspective, it is even more significant that the Muslim Brotherhood remade the politics of the prison. As Marie Gottschalk concluded, the Nation of Islam "set in motion a radical transformation in how prisoners viewed themselves and how society viewed them."[192] In his study of Illinois's Stateville prison, James Jacobs found that prisoners who did not join the NOI "nonetheless [came] to define themselves as political prisoners."[193] John Irwin argued that the "altered conception of the prisoner" was the most important legacy of the NOI's prison litigation: "He started as part noncitizen, part nonentity, and part subhuman over whom prison administrators had unlimited power to treat as they saw fit. . . . Now we have progressed to the conception of a prisoner as a citizen in a temporarily reduced legal status."[194] Just as their flood of writs changed the relationship of the courts to prisons, Muslim activism shaped the way that prisoners saw themselves in relationship to the people and places holding them captive.

Although the NOI is often framed as politically narrow or racially insular, its organizing in prisons extended beyond a Black–white binary and was conducted by a large minority of Latinx prisoners, such as Sostre. According to Woodward's reports, over forty prisoners with Latinx surnames joined the NOI during this period, which meant that in the early 1960s, they constituted over 10 percent of NOI membership in state prisons.[195] These prisoners also addressed broader issues of labor and prison conditions, which affected all those incarcerated. In 1962, for example, Black prisoners at Green Haven Prison launched a strike protesting the beating of several Muslims.

White prisoners soon urged that the agenda be broadened to challenge poor food and good-time practices, and a multiracial strike quickly spread to other prisons across New York State.[196] Such demonstrations stand at odds with contemporary and later critiques of nationalist organizations as homogeneous and separatist, suggesting an expansive multiracial activism around an interlocking set of shared oppressions.

The host of strategies brought forth by Muslim prisoners all point to prison organizing—and Black Nationalism more broadly—as central currents in the postwar struggle for Black freedom. These were not post–civil rights struggles but were born out of, and alongside, the broader movement. Similarly, the carceral state was produced through daily, on-the-ground interplay with prisoners' activism, rather than a simple, counterrevolutionary reaction to the gains of social movements through top-down policy changes and electoral shifts. The state responded to basic demands with increased surveillance and an expansion of carceral machinery. The dialectics of discipline that made up the daily interaction between prisoner activism and prison punishment demonstrate the tangled relationship between resistance to the state and its expansion and re-entrenchment.

As Jacobs reflected on the many legacies of the prisoners' rights movement, he argued that the "bureaucratization of the prison" was among the most important. In the early prison litigation brought by the Nation of Islam, prison officials were unable to justify and articulate institutional procedures.[197] Hence, many prison reforms targeted administrative efficiency rather than the principles of punishment. Policy makers reasoned that if prisons and policing could be administered more efficiently, professionally, and equitably (that is, in a color-blind way), they could quell more radical calls for reform and abolition. But efforts to standardize police and prisons often led to greater autonomy for law enforcement, longer and harsher sentences for prisoners, and a more robust and resourced apparatus. This was the carceral state at its most Foucauldian; penal reform meant sharpening the tools and expanding the scope of punishment rather than reconsidering its purpose.

Muslim testimony broke through the long silence around prisoners' constitutional rights. Malcolm X and other Muslim prisoners used the courtroom as a political platform to make broader critiques of American racial liberal democracy. Throughout the 1950s and 1960s, as Muslims were brought to trial in repeated cases of police brutality in New York and California, the courts also became a space for political theater. Just as prison officials had begun a nationwide information-sharing network to construct logics that justified suppression of Islam in prisons, police departments anxiously read *Muhammad Speaks*, profiled and policed the everyday practices of Muslims, and raided mosques without warrants. As defendants rather than plaintiffs, Muslims in the Nation of Islam worked to build local coalitions against police violence and put the state on trial. These Black united fronts were always fraught political projects, yet however short-lived they sharpened coalitions and created new forms of resistance. In New York and Los Angeles, the dialectics of discipline on the streets was another site for the emergence of the carceral state alongside a broad-based anticarceral mobilization by communities of color.

CHAPTER THREE

Whose Law and What Order?

Whose law, one is compelled to ask, and *what* order?
—JAMES BALDWIN, 1964

Throughout the 1950s, the NOI encountered increasing surveillance and harassment from local and state police on the streets as well as inside prisons. This scrutiny was particularly acute in New York and Los Angeles, where the NOI was growing most rapidly. Although New York State Police had taken note of the NOI as early as 1950, units such as the Bureau of Special Services (BOSS) escalated their surveillance in the wake of an impressive silent protest by Muslims outside the Twenty-Eighth Precinct station house in April 1957 following the police beating of Johnson X Hinton.[1]

The scene is immortalized in Malcolm's autobiography: Police intervened in a scuffle and beat Hinton with a nightstick so violently that he eventually needed a metal plate implanted in his skull. After several quick phone calls, the Fruit of Islam assembled in ranked formation outside the station house where he was being held. Malcolm went inside and demanded that Hinton be taken to Harlem Hospital, and as other onlookers joined in, a massive procession marched fifteen blocks down the wide thoroughfare of Lenox Avenue (now renamed in honor of Malcolm X). Assembling around the precinct was a meaningful challenge to the state in its own right, later described by the commander as Harlem's "version of city hall. If they're going to demonstrate against the government, they have to do it here."[2] Once Malcolm had been reassured that Hinton would receive proper medical attention at the hospital, he gave a signal and the crowd silently dispersed. One observer described it as "eerie, because these people just faded into the night. It was the most orderly movement of four thousand to five thousand people I've ever seen in my life—they just simply disappeared—right before our eyes." The scene was punctuated by one police officer's comment to newspaper reporter James Hicks: "This is too much power for one man to have."[3] Even so, much as it may have demonstrated one individual's power, its true threat—one police surely recognized—was its collective power, organized through discipline.[4]

The Hinton case pushed both Malcolm X and the Nation of Islam into the spotlight. And it was not only law enforcement who took notice. In August 1961, after another disturbance brought two hundred police officers uptown, veteran civil rights and labor organizer A. Philip Randolph telegraphed Malcolm X to invite him to an "ad hoc working committee" on a program for Black unity and action in Harlem.[5] Randolph was an elder in the movement: his work stretched back to the founding of the Brotherhood of Sleeping Car Porters and the March on Washington Movement (MOWM) during World War II, which prompted President Roosevelt to issue Executive Order No. 8802, establishing the first Fair Employment Practices Committee. Most recently, he had founded the Negro American Labor Council (NALC) as a response to the American Federation of Labor and Congress of Industrial Organizations' (AFL-CIO) lackluster support of the civil rights movement and its recalcitrance on racial discrimination by unions. Now, despite the impromptu nature of the organization embodied in its name, the Emergency Committee for Unity on Social and Economic Problems represented one of Randolph's most ambitious political projects to date.

Randolph's proposal for an all-Black coalition was hailed as a potential "beacon of light for other communities." Evelyn Cunningham, one of several journalists in the organization, called it an "unprecedented move to rally the opposing forces of the Harlem community."[6] The *NALC Newsletter* heralded the group as "understanding [the] role to be played by the Black working class, and demonstrat[ing] the pressing and urgent need and desire of the people for solidarity."[7] That the Nation of Islam would welcome and participate in such a coalition should not be surprising. In fact, the first documented use of the phrase "Black United Front" came in 1958, when Elijah Muhammad spoke at the NOI's annual Saviours' Day convention at Tabernacle Baptist Church in Chicago.[8] But the Emergency Committee's political breadth was also its greatest challenge: the coalition encompassed liberals, left liberal labor organizers, and Black Nationalists. Cautious observers pointed out that the Emergency Committee was a "finely drawn blueprint which leaves little margin for error."[9] Indeed, just a few years earlier, one of the committee's leaders, Anna Arnold Hedgeman, had been among those civil rights leaders called upon in *The Hate That Hate Produced* to suggest that northern Black Nationalists in the Nation of Islam were as guilty of preaching racial hatred as southern white segregationists.

As Malcolm and other Black Nationalists engaged in concrete debates on the ground with other Harlem organizers, they seemed poised to submerge their political and religious differences in the interest of forming a local Black united front. At its inception in the summer of 1961, the Emergency Committee decided to foreground the "principle of unity which allows for the widest variety of participation and action."[10] Yet unbeknownst to the organizers, this tenuous political alliance was subject to police surveillance from its inception. Listed among the members of the original group was William K. DeFossett of the 369th Infantry Regiment Veterans Association. Covertly, DeFossett was Detective #631 of BOSS, where he had been spying on the Nation of Islam since 1957.[11]

Just three days after Malcolm received Randolph's invitation, a Muslim named Raymond Quarles was arrested and beaten in Queens by two officers. Quarles sold costume jewelry and was carrying two small boxes home when he was questioned and thrown in a police cruiser. He asked to be taken home to verify his story, but when they arrived, officers began searching his home without a warrant. The police, reportedly smelling of alcohol, beat Quarles before he was rushed to Queens General Hospital by other members of the mosque.[12] The Quarles case was at least the fifth violent encounter between police and NOI members in as many years, and the third in New York City.

Police surveillance and brutality had deepened following the attention generated by *The Hate That Hate Produced* and Lincoln's *The Black Muslims in America*. BOSS agent Ernest Latty wrote a full memo on the documentary during the five-part series, and DeFossett reported from a NOI rally a week later that a "great portion of [Elijah Muhammad's] remarks were directed against Mike Wallace and Louis Lomax."[13] But these portrayals did more than intensify police surveillance; they also informed the strategies used by the state. As both ideological frameworks and data sets, the documentary and book became touchstones for police and prison officials to understand the Nation of Islam as a religiously inauthentic and politically subversive organization. A spokesperson for the New York State Department of Corrections spoke for many law enforcement agencies when he concluded: "They attempt to express everything on a religious basis but it is our opinion they are not religiously sincere—that they have ulterior motives."[14]

At the same moment that an alliance of Black Nationalists, liberals, and labor activists was forging an ambitious and sweeping political coalition in Harlem around a platform of Black unity, Black communities nationwide were suffering from unaccountable police violence and surveillance.

And this intensifying assault on Black activism squarely targeted the Nation of Islam. The Emergency Committee would not last long before faltering—yet even though the committee's history was brief, it raises serious and lasting questions about postwar Black social movements and the development of the carceral apparatuses that suppressed them. Borrowing from Robin Kelley's insight that the importance of freedom struggles is not in their success or failure but in the questions they raise and the intellectual legacies they leave, this chapter explores the important questions the Emergency Committee provoked despite, or perhaps because of, its transience.[15] What was the role of organizing against police brutality within the broader Black freedom struggle? What was the place of police violence in catalyzing unified Black political mobilization? Were Black communities calling for more policing or rather for more *just* policing? What roles did Black Nationalism and Black united front efforts play in the Black freedom movement before the emergence of Black Power? Calls for racial unity often explicitly demand that people set aside their religious and political differences while implicitly submerging questions of gender, sexuality, and class. How did such coalitions bury but also sharpen these differences and give birth to new modes and forms of struggle?

Professionalizing the Police

For a full day in August 1957, Los Angeles radio station KMPC celebrated "Chief Bill Parker Day." At a luncheon with city boosters at the Biltmore Hotel, a city councilman pronounced the city's police chief "a model for police and administrators throughout the world."[16] That same month, Parker sat in the law office of attorney George Vaughn to give a deposition—the LAPD was facing a lawsuit for ten cases of police brutality brought by Vaughn's client, the NAACP's Legal Redress Committee. Unfazed, Parker used the occasion to charge Vaughn with "evil intent in this whole situation." He claimed that the committee was trying to "drive the whole Police Department out of the city of Los Angeles" and said that this sort of "unholy harassment" underscored the very necessity of police officers. "We have been getting along fine until you got here," he concluded.[17] Parker's response reflected the mindset of a police department that acted with almost complete impunity yet saw itself as under siege from the communities it terrorized. Without a hint of irony, Parker would later describe police officers as the "greatest dislocated minority in America."[18]

Many of the same surveillance technologies that generated the dialectics of discipline in New York prisons during the late 1950s were being mirrored on the streets of major cities, including New York and Los Angeles. During the postwar years, policing was reshaped by a national impetus toward professionalization led by reformer O. W. Wilson and his protégé, William Parker.[19] In 1950, Parker began what would become the longest tenure of any police chief in Los Angeles, ending only with his death a year after the 1965 revolt in Watts. Kelly Lytle Hernández concludes that by the 1950s, "local activists had gathered enough evidence to categorically describe police violence as a tactical assault on Black life in the city."[20] Los Angeles's notoriety was due not only to the scope and size of the city's policing apparatus but to Parker's role in disseminating it as a model for other cities: "The LAPD's postwar model of policing routinely served as a standard for departments across the country."[21] A master salesman, in Parker's first few years on the job, he gave over a thousand speeches to business groups and civic organizations promoting his ideas about crime and policing, and he is credited with coining the phrases "thin blue line" and "to protect and to serve."[22] Parker justified the violent police occupation of Los Angeles's communities of color through the use of racial crime statistics and masked the department's biases through an aggressive public relations campaign that promoted a modern, professional image.

Police professionalization at its most prosaic meant wrestling autonomy from machine politicians while narrowing the domain and scope of policing to the "expertise" of crime prevention. Police chiefs set about creating universal standards and bureaucratized procedures meant to engender public trust and deter incursions into police discipline from politicians and civilians alike.[23] Significantly, professionalization also meant proactive policing: wiretapping, racial profiling, data gathering, and, of course, discipline. "Perhaps most importantly," Max Felker-Kantor adds, "professionalization ensured the LAPD operated independently from political influence."[24]

No police units were better equipped to do this than the anticommunist Red Squads in cities such as Chicago, Philadelphia, Los Angeles, and New York. Felker-Kantor describes the Red Squads in Los Angeles as a "John Birch Society dream of right-wing, pro-business, white-supremacist politics backed by an all-out attack on progressive social movements and civil rights activists." So palpable was this dream, that some have estimated two thousand Birchers within Los Angeles law enforcement during Parker's first decade as chief.[25] The special squads formed during the Cold War were swiftly expanded to encompass what *The Hate That Hate Produced* had defined as the rise of "Black hate" and "Black supremacy." Indeed, early surveillance reports conflated Black Nationalism and communism, branding them equally "subversive." In 1957, one state investigator for the Bureau of Criminal Investigation (BCI) in New York called the Nation of Islam a "pink organization consisting of colored people."[26] By 1960, after the documentary had aired, the BCI shifted to calling the group a "nation-wide Black supremacy movement."[27]

While the New York Police Department had no figure as iconic or enduring as Parker during the 1950s, its Red Squad police intelligence unit—BOSS—had rescued itself from postwar obscurity and become an evangelist and a model for national counterintelligence programs by the 1960s. Touring as "proselytizers for the cult of intelligence," BOSS was described by one scholar as akin to the Green Berets, a special operative unit that touted itself as the "finest of the finest" and "total professionals." Most importantly, just as monthly surveillance reports from New York prisons radiated outward and modeled national policy, BOSS disseminated information to outside agencies.[28] Tony Bouza, who began his service for the agency the same year that DeFossett first infiltrated the Nation of Islam, recalled an agent who funneled information daily to J. Edgar Hoover and the FBI. In those days, he recalled, "we really rarely got anything from them and they got quite a bit from us."[29]

William Parker was no stranger to police intelligence. When he first joined the LAPD in 1927, he acted as an informant by infiltrating radical groups. Soon after taking office, he declared the files of the Intelligence Division "the property of the Chief of Police."[30] He believed that the effectiveness of surveillance outweighed any infringement on civil liberties. In 1954 he defended surveillance using hidden microphones and recording equipment, and when the California Supreme Court ruled evidence obtained through such unconstitutional means inadmissible, he condemned the decision as "catastrophic" to "efficient law enforcement."[31] Another staple of Parker's department was its autonomy. Although he frequently closed ranks with white politicians during times of crisis, Parker remained insulated from public and government scrutiny: despite long-standing demands for a civilian review board, he was shielded by a city charter that granted the chief of police civil service protection and full power over the discipline of officers.[32]

When Parker laid out his blueprint for the role of the police force in community relations at the 1955 Annual Conference of the International Association of Chiefs of Police, he proudly remarked that *Los Angeles has not experienced an instance of organized group violence in the past twelve years.* He attributed this long period of calm largely to the "professionalization of its police department."[33] His address framed policing through a liberal logic in which diversity was articulated as everyone's *"right* to be different." "We are all minority group members," he told the audience, "any one of which can be, and often has been[,] discriminated against." Parker's justification for the overbearing presence of police in communities of color rested on crime statistics. He explained that the reason for the heavy deployment of police in neighborhoods inhabited mainly by people of color was "statistical—it is a fact that certain racial groups, at the present time, commit a disproportionate share of the total crime." His speech simultaneously defended overpolicing through race-based crime statistics and advanced the pretense of color-blind law enforcement that disregarded race as a meaningful category of analysis.

Parker closed his address by offering an anecdote that embodied his professionalization argument: human relations and community training could eradicate racist policing, if not racist police. He described an "old school" officer, "recruited long before psychiatric examinations were instituted," who walks a beat in this new "racial melting pot" of Los Angeles. Despite carrying with him "the maximum number of racial and religious prejudices one mind can hold," this officer has "memorized every maxim, every scientific fact, every theory relating to human equality." The punchline of Parker's story was that for this "old school" officer, his "intolerance has become a victim of enforced order—habit has won out over belief."[34] In other words, racist police could become disciplined to perform nonracist policing.

The framework for *The Hate That Hate Produced* mapped easily onto this sort of thinking. Parker often justified "the police department's discrimination with reference to *other discrimination*."[35] Just as the documentary portrayed Black Nationalism as a type of racism that inevitably arose in reaction to white racism, Parker understood all groups to be suffering from different types of "minority" status, even—or especially—police. Parker's theories of professionalization as a means to eradicate racist policing were disseminated in LAPD training bulletins. Satirical cartoons illustrated Parker's points, teaching officers that police brutality was not confined to the use of force but that "complaints of so-called 'police brutality' are frequently found to be complaints concerning offensive language or improper attitude."[36] The bulletin used slang directed at police to show that it could be received as hostile when used by outsiders. Parker's outline of human relations training as a means of professionalizing police practices was designed to disguise the specificity of police violence against communities of color by demonstrating that anyone could be a victim of hatred.

Some of Parker's ideas mirrored demands made by the NAACP and other community groups calling for law enforcement reform. His focus on human relations training and a racially diverse police force that could maintain a better rapport with the communities it policed echoed the goals of many in

A cartoon in the Los Angeles Police Department's *Daily Training Bulletin* illustrates the problem with racism through the example of derogatory terms for a police officer. October 22, 1962, box 24, folder 14, Loren Miller Papers, Huntington Library, Pasadena, California.

Los Angeles and New York who were fighting for police reform. But liberal calls for the professionalization of police generally resulted in more police with greater impunity. As later described by Naomi Murakawa, this adhered to the dynamic in which modern police departments and liberal reforms served to cement the notion that police brutality could be solved through more procedures and training, framing "racial violence as an administrative deficiency" rather than a structured and intentional outcome.[37] As Parker contended in his 1955 address, "We are not interested in *why* a certain group tends toward crime, we are interested in maintaining order. . . . Police deployment is concerned with *effect*, not cause."[38] He was content to continue the vicious cycle of overpolicing and racially biased crime statistics, each justifying the other.

By 1960, after the death of a Black teenager at the hands of Los Angeles police the previous summer, the possibility of a police review board had set off a polarizing debate in Los Angeles. The proposal was the product of a multiracial coalition that brought together the ACLU, the NAACP, the California Democratic Council, and what the *Los Angeles Times* referred to as "several Latin or Spanish groups."[39] The proposal called for a five-person board—to be appointed by the mayor with approval from the city council—and allotted $500 each to citizens harmed by police misconduct.[40] The idea of a police review board was invigorated by an onslaught of criticism of Parker for maintaining a department rife with discrimination, the use of excessive force, and racial profiling. His defense rested on a combination of crime statistics, anti-immigration rhetoric, and social scientific notions of racialized criminality. This built on a postwar racial liberalism in which the language of biological racism was often replaced by cultural determinism following the findings of anthropologist Franz Boas. Criminologists and law enforcement officials, as Khalil Muhammad has shown, used crime statistics to refashion Blackness into a "more stable racial category in relation to whiteness" and, in effect, a marker of criminality.[41]

Parker's comments during a two-day hearing before the Federal Commission on Civil Rights in 1960 demonstrate the ways in which cultural notions of race and criminality justified racialized policing. "Flanked by a battery of aides carrying charts," Parker argued that African Americans, Latinxs, and Asians all committed crimes at disproportionate rates compared to their white counterparts (11 times, 5 times, and 3 times, respectively) but neglected to mention the disproportionate policing of the neighborhoods where people of color were concentrated. Demonstrating that he had moved away from discredited notions of innate criminality, he called these statistics a reflection of a "conflict of cultures."[42] Rather than seeing housing segregation as one cause of these disproportionate statistics, the police chief deemed these "dislocations" primarily a problem of "assimilation."[43] In language reminiscent of Progressive-era anti-immigrant rhetoric, Parker claimed that the city had been plagued by people "shipped here by officials of other localities who want to get rid of them."[44] He charged that ultimately the police were the "dislocated minority," complaining that no "one is concerned about the civil rights of a policeman."[45]

The responses of civil rights leaders to Parker's package of social scientific racism and crime statistics also reflect the role that Black sociologists and reformers played in creating a counter-discourse to narratives of Black criminality.[46] NAACP attorney Loren Miller, whom Kenneth Mack described as one of several Black lawyers "well known in their own time but who have been largely lost to history," attended the 1960 meeting and was one such person. Miller was among the most prominent figures in the postwar fight for racial integration in Los Angeles.[47] Early in his career, he was skeptical of law as an engine of social change, believing that it had little effect on race and class inequalities. Miller traveled to the Soviet Union with his friend

Langston Hughes in 1932, disillusioned by the NAACP's reluctance to represent the Scottsboro Boys. Miller was drawn to the communist-affiliated International Labor Defense and was an outspoken critic of prominent attorney Charles Hamilton Houston, particularly for his courtroom theatrics, complaining that the attorney planned to push the new NAACP program "into a mandate for a new orgy of legalistic performances."[48] Miller made a name for himself in Los Angeles by representing Black celebrities in the 1945 "Sugar Hill" housing case, when white residents tried unsuccessfully to oust their affluent Black neighbors from the West Adams neighborhood by citing turn-of-the-century racial covenants. He then worked with Thurgood Marshall on twenty cases against restrictive covenants, which laid the foundation for the Supreme Court's decision in *Shelley v. Kraemer*.[49] It was through such legal victories in the 1930s and 1940s that Thurgood Marshall and the NAACP regained some standing among skeptical Black attorneys such as Miller. As Mack observes, an organization that had "come under fire from a younger generation of Blacks who questioned its lawyers' representativeness once again became a place for lawyers to dream of bigger things."[50]

By 1960, Miller had begun to play a larger role in the NAACP's campaign against police brutality in Los Angeles. He recognized that while a significant portion of Black Angelenos were recent migrants from the South and carried with them a "mental picture of the police officer as an enemy," this view was reinforced by the "underlying policy" of discrimination carried out by Los Angeles police. Miller was joined by Latinx leaders who pointed out that no person of Mexican descent had ever served on a county grand jury.[51] Although he had once criticized courtroom political theater, Miller would soon lead the defense of fourteen Muslims facing forty counts of assault and resisting arrest in Los Angeles in *People v. Buice*, one of the lengthiest and dramatic political trials in city history. It was also the most significant police brutality trial the Nation of Islam had yet faced.

The Trial

> I charge the white man with being the greatest liar on earth. I charge
> the white man with being the greatest drunkard on earth. I charge the
> white man with being the greatest swine-eater on earth. Yet, the Bible
> forbids it. I charge the white man with being the greatest gambler
> on earth. I charge the white man, ladies and gentlemen of the jury,
> with being the greatest murderer on earth. I charge the white
> man with being the greatest peace-breaker on earth. I charge the

white man with being the greatest adulterer on earth. I charge
the white man with being the greatest robber on earth. I charge the
white man with being the greatest deceiver on earth. I charge
the white man with being the greatest trouble-maker on earth.
So therefore, ladies and gentlemen of the jury, I ask you, bring back
a verdict of guilty as charged.[52]

Louis X Walcott, The Trial, 1960

This litany of charges was delivered before a packed room of more than two
thousand on Christmas Eve 1960. In the crowd, Muslim women dressed in
white and men wore suits and bow ties. But this was no ordinary court of
law. The jury and the judge were all Black. The prosecutor was twenty-seven-
year-old Louis X Walcott (later Farrakhan), and the venue was Carnegie
Hall. *The Trial* was always shown with its companion piece, *Orgena* ("A Negro" spelled backwards), and was performed at Afro-Asian Bazaars and other
venues before making its way onto Seventh Avenue. The first witness called
in the on-stage trial was an African character named Jomo Nkrumo.[53] Likely
a composite of independence leaders Jomo Kenyatta of Kenya and Kwame
Nkrumah of Ghana, the character described the process of European colo-
nization and missionizing, chattel slavery, and the plunder of natural
resources in Africa. The second witness called by the prosecution was a Native American character named Charlie Strongbow, who testified to the genocide of indigenous people through disease and the decimation of food sources
before herding "us into reservations to live cooped up like cattle." The trial's
star witness was a character named Thelma X Griffen, who gave accounts of
the middle passage, slave auctions, the rape of Black women, and the lynching of Black men.

In addition to condemning the white man, the play and its characters
chastized the Black middle class and its moderate leadership. Miss Sadie Culpepper of the NAACP and Urban League was a college graduate who worked
as a maid for some "real good white folks" and reminded the jury that the
struggle for integration would be won with patience. In a not-so-lightly-
veiled critique of Martin Luther King and other Black clergy, the character
of Bishop Greene was brought forth as the white man's key apologist. Described as "smug and full of self-righteousness," Greene was broken down
by the prosecutor and revealed as a sellout and "religious bag of wind." The
play reached its climax when the jury found "Mr. White-Man guilty, with no
recommendation for mercy." He was then flung into a lake of fire, with
shouts of "kill the beast, kill the beast" resonating throughout the court.[54]

The play flipped the script of the judicial system by bringing a symbolic white man before an international court of law to be sentenced for his crimes. It framed the struggle of Black Americans through the anticolonial lens of the Global South by featuring an "African-Asian jury"; several African diplomats even attended the performance at Carnegie Hall that evening. This internationalism placed it within a longer history of anticolonial politics and drew on the language of the Civil Rights Congress's 1951 petition to the United Nations: "We Charge Genocide." It positioned Black Americans within a settler-colonial state in dialogue with indigenous freedom struggles, the nonaligned movement, and African decolonization, envisioning a world court—not unlike the UN's Genocide Convention—that would prosecute the United States for human rights violations. Also notable is the play's timing; what is often seen as Malcolm X's important transition from "civil rights" to "human rights" the year after he left the Nation of Islam was already at the discursive center of the NOI half a decade earlier.

The Nation of Islam's model for Black unity was, first and foremost, internationalist. Central to its religious and political beliefs was the idea that believers were not part of a domestic minority but rather belonged to a global majority. The strength of a world community of Islam was an important theme in individual conversion narratives of Muslims in the NOI. Likewise, the NOI's model for building coalitions was the anticolonialism of the nonaligned movement illustrated through the Bandung and Afro-Asian Peoples' Solidarity conferences of the mid-to-late 1950s. The Harlem freedom rallies sponsored by Mosque No. 7 and the united front organizing of the Emergency Committee were an extension of the "Bandung conference in Harlem" that Malcolm called for in 1959.[55] At one such rally, he made the case that just as the "diverse-thinking non-white nations at Bandung increased the stride toward freedom for the Dark People of Africa and Asia, the leaders of America's 20 million so-called Negroes should be able to accomplish the same [feat], with the same display of unity."[56] The NOI applied this global model for Black unity locally in New York in 1961.

By this time, the NOI had experienced cases of police violence, racial profiling, and invasions of homes and mosques in at least six major cities: San Diego (1950); Flomaton, Alabama (1956); Harlem (1957); Queens (1958); Los Angeles (1959); and Monroe, Louisiana (1961). While these cases differed in their contexts and regional specificity, they helped catalyze a set of strategies for dealing with police surveillance, brutality, and subsequent trials in which Nation of Islam members were charged in court despite being the victims of police violence. First, invasions by police into Muslim homes and mosques were condemned as incursions into religious space and violations of Black womanhood. While this charge rested fundamentally on a discourse of male protection, which Ula Taylor termed the "promise of patriarchy" and Farah Jasmine Griffin called the "promise of protection," it offered Black women security often reserved for white women.[57] As Sarah Haley has brilliantly documented in the nineteenth century, Black women were constructed outside normative "womanhood" in the white imagination through gendered racial terror, often by the carceral state.[58] Kali Gross demonstrates how this continued into the twentieth and twenty-first centuries through an "exclusionary politics of protection whereby Black women were not entitled to the law's protection, though they could not escape its punishment."[59] Or, as Saidiya Hartman writes, "Black girls came before the law, but were not protected by it."[60] Just as protecting white women in the postbellum South became a mechanism for "asserting the stability of white manhood in uncertain times," the protection of Black women reclaimed a womanhood denied by white supremacy while reinscribing their acquiescence to Black men.[61]

Second, the NOI used countersurveillance strategies at rallies and in courtrooms by taking photographs of the police to identify and intimidate them and by reading and publishing law enforcement surveillance of the group. Finally, Louis X's play was more than just a cultural product—it showed a way in which political theater could allow the NOI to stage trials in which white supremacy stood trial and Muslim victims were the rightful plaintiffs. While *The Trial* represented an important cultural politics that metaphorically reconfigured the courtroom from a space of legalized lynching to one of Black justice, the Nation of Islam would take its rhetoric and tactics into actual courtrooms to highlight and challenge police brutality.[62] The first major use of this strategy since 1930s Chicago would be employed in 1958, when police violence arrived on Malcolm's doorstep.

Malcolm and Betty Shabazz had been married less than six months when two New York police detectives tried to force their way into the duplex they shared with other Muslims. The home was owned by John X Molette, who lived there with his wife, Yvonne; the tenants included John (later John Ali, NOI national secretary) and Minnie Simmons and other members of Temple No. 7 in Harlem. In addition to living quarters upstairs and in the basement, there was Malcolm's office. The detectives who came to the home that night— Joseph Kiernan and Michael Bonura—falsely identified themselves as FBI agents and asked for Alvin Crosby, who lived in the basement unit. The officers claimed to be looking for Margaret Dorsey, who was wanted for mail fraud. They were met at the door by Yvonne, who informed them that Crosby was at a temple meeting. Kiernan then placed his foot in the door, and the other women rushed to aid Yvonne in resisting his entry. After successfully warding off the police, Yvonne called her husband, who was at the mosque with Crosby and the other male residents.[63]

When the officers returned over an hour later with a postal inspector, they tried to sneak in through a side entrance. This time they met John Molette. When he refused to let the men enter, Kiernan broke the glass and reached in to open the door, cutting his hand on the shards. Yvonne Molette recalled that there "was a crash of glass at the back door and [Kiernan] stuck his gun in the door and fired point blank. I felt the bullet pass my leg. I turned and ran back to get my (four) children out of the way."[64] A glass bottle was thrown from the window above the door as the officer drew his gun and fired shots through the door. He then entered the house as the women blocking the door fled. According to a police report, the detectives then "broke into each room on the upper floor, including the room used by Mr. Little as his office." They eventually found a locked door to a room where Betty, who was several months pregnant, was hiding with Minnie Simmons and her baby. They demanded that the women open the door or they would shoot through it. Outside, John Molette later testified, police "knocked me down and kicked me in the groin and side. They hit me in the mouth and jaw and tore my clothes off."[65] Malcolm told reporters that "Negroes in Mississippi could not have their civil rights as openly violated and stomped upon any worse than has been done here in Queens."[66]

By the time arrests were made and handcuffed NOI members arrived at the precinct station, forty Muslims from the local temple were holding a silent protest outside. Despite having seen a similar demonstration following the beating of Johnson Hinton the previous year, police were "shocked at the speed with which the Moslems had tossed up a picket line."[67] In the immediate aftermath of the home invasion, Malcolm X and the NOI framed the violence as a violation of Black womanhood and religious sanctity. "Officers had fired their guns, not intend[ing] to kill criminals, thieves or bandits," Malcolm told the press, "but to kill our innocent Black women, children and babies."[68] With Betty pregnant with the couple's first daughter, Attallah, and seventeen-year-old resident Audrey Rice also six months pregnant, Malcolm emphasized the white officers' transgressions against Black women and children. In his interview with police, he pointed out that Betty was unable to "put on adequate clothing (it was raining at the time) to be transported to the 114th Pct. Station House." The report also read: "Mr. Little cited as an example the fact that when the detectives arrived on the upper floors of the premises in question, they encountered Mrs. Simmons who was giving her 4 months old child a bath. According to Mr. Little, Mrs. Simmons was not permitted to dress the child, but was ordered downstairs and outside the house by Det. Kiernan. When she protested against taking the naked baby outside she was permitted to leave the child with Mrs. Mary Crosby."[69] While the case in Queens demonstrated the centrality of male protection to the NOI's political framework, it also highlighted its appeal for Black women who were denied the basic security and protections offered to white women.

When the trial opened in early March 1959, attorney Edward Jacko grilled prospective jurors on their religious beliefs and perceptions of American racism. Though he originally framed the case as the right to defend family, life, and home against invasion, he gestured toward the religious, racial, and gendered implications of the case by claiming that a "man's home is sacred and inviolable, and that the Moslems possess Constitutional rights which were violated last May."[70] Malcolm seconded this charge to the press, claiming that the incident "violated the sanctity of their home and religious house."[71] Because of the home office, the defense tried to establish that this was not merely a treading on home and family but also a violation of religious freedom. This emphasis on religion was a marked contrast from the strategy in later cases in Rochester and Los Angeles, which emphasized police brutality as an experience that transcended class, religion, and political affiliation. The combination of racial and religious discrimination in Queens was also distinct from Muslim prison litigation, which focused almost exclusively on appeals to religious rights. In part, the case demonstrated that the NOI's claim to be either religious or political depended on the situation in a given place and time. While appearing as political would jeopardize the group's organizing in prisons, framing the case solely through religion (and Islam in particular) would limit its appeal to a united front against police violence in Black communities.

The courthouse immediately became a battleground. One newspaper wrote that followers "circled May 23, this Friday, on their calendars as 'D-Day,' at which time they will descend upon Ridgewood Felony Court to attend a hearing into the matter of the 'false' arrest of five of their members."[72] With the jury decided, the trial began with a whirlwind of political theater by the NOI.[73] Every day the courtroom was filled in an orderly fashion by NOI members. BOSS watched closely, and one officer noted that the men could be "distinguished by their closely shaven heads, white shirts and scarlet ties" and the women by the "white kerchiefs over their heads."[74] The

NOI brought its own stenographer to record the court proceedings and admitted stacks of evidence, such as photographs, scale drawings of the home
drawn by John Ali, and even the "green door which once hung at the front of
their home and bears the marks of struggle and gunfire."[75] Edward Jacko
produced the police bullet and the torn and bloody clothing worn by John
Molette that night. This use of evidence anticipated the Black Power strategy of physical testimonies to police violence, such as the tours given of
Fred Hampton's West Side Chicago apartment following his assassination
in 1969, revealing a blood-soaked mattress and a bullet-riddled wall behind
his bed.[76]

The testimonies given by the defense witnesses in Queens were not
unlike those in *The Trial*. Yvonne Molette, described as a "tall, handsome
woman whose hair remains neatly tucked beneath a white bandana," gave a
moving description of the police invasion. She recalled that Detective
Kiernan beat her husband and then shouted: "You yellow-bellied bastard,
I should shoot you right now!" Minnie Simmons recounted bathing her
young child and pleading with the police not to force her to bring the naked
child outside in the cold. Jacko was so moved by her story that he stood in
the middle of the courtroom with "tears flowing down his cheeks, unable to
continue his role."[77]

Even more remarkable than their evidence and testimony was the NOI's
disciplined control of the courtroom as a physical space. One newspaper
noted that the flood of members arriving each day displayed a "diligence in
court that has kept all that attend the hearings, both curious and confused."[78]
The NOI brought its own doormen, ushers, and guards and maintained control of the entrances and exits. In one case, a white man curious about the
case in progress attempted to enter the courtroom and was intercepted by a
member of the Fruit of Islam, who turned the man away, telling him it was
not a public trial. The gendered politics of protection played out at the trial
as well. One police officer reported that Detective Kiernan was pushed aside
by an NOI member in the court corridor to allow a Muslim woman to pass.
In the words of the officer, Kiernan "decided to let the incident pass rather
than to worsen an already serious situation." The other strategy of control
and intimidation was the use of photography. All those who entered the
first-floor corridor had their photo taken by three "roving Muslim photog-
raphers [who] patrolled the streets in the immediate area of the court, snapping pictures of any one who met their fancy."[79] The NOI's discipline was so
captivating that one court attendant remarked: "We should put their officers on our payroll. They do a better job tha[n] we do."[80]

FOI captain Joseph Gravitt and Minister Louis X (later Farrakhan) can be seen in the background of a surveillance photo taken by the NYPD outside the 1958 trial. New York City Municipal Archives.

After sixteen days the jury went into deliberation, and nearly four hundred protesters gathered silently outside the courthouse. Three BOSS detectives were assigned to observe and assist in maintaining order. One described what he called a "tense 13 hour vigil by the N.Y. Police Department . . . spent observing and trying to understand what makes this people function." Judge Farrell ordered that spectators not be allowed in the courtroom when the verdict was delivered, and as the crowd swelled outside, it produced a "disturbing calm."[81] In his closing argument, Jacko charged the prosecution with bringing lying testimony to convict four "decent, hard working, home owning, religious people." He then delivered his dramatic final words to the jury: "Free my clients, they are innocent. . . . Free them and live with yourself. And God Bless you in doing so!"[82] In the fourteenth hour of deliberation, at 2:30 in the morning, the jury emerged and fully exonerated Minnie Simmons and Betty Shabazz. Jurors were deadlocked on the issue of whether a person could resist arrest when defending property, so the judge declared a mistrial and set a new trial date for the following month. Jurors were then escorted under guard to the subway as "all of 300 stolid Muslims gathered on the front stairs." Malcolm X stood on the courthouse steps and served what the BOSS officer understood as a "warning on the N.Y. Police Department that they had better be right in dealing with the Muslims." "Any policeman who abuses you," Malcolm told the crowd, "belongs in the cemetery."[83]

As the Molettes and other Muslims from the original trial testified before a civilian complaint review board, which would then forward its findings to police commissioner Stephen Kennedy, the discourse of the case continued to revolve around the protection of Black women. John Ali and Malcolm X were denied an appointment with Kennedy when Malcolm wanted to discuss "incidents of police brutality against Black women" and was "prepared to ask that equal protection be given Negro women as that which is afforded white women." He told the deputy commissioner: "If we can't get justice from the law, then we'll have to seek justice elsewhere [for] we do not intend to let any man, regardless of race, police or otherwise, molest our women."[84] In fact, just two days before the men were stood up by the commissioner, another Muslim couple was attacked by a police officer in Brooklyn and subsequently charged with third-degree assault. The woman was treated for injuries after being allegedly hit in the stomach by the police officer, and the man admitted to holding the officer's billy club "in a menacing manner after she was struck."[85] The case eventually went to trial, and the couple was represented by Edward Jacko, who accused the officer of police brutality. In both cases, the promise of protection remained a salient discourse, as Muslim women remained susceptible to both police brutality and patriarchal purview.

The Queens home invasion was mirrored on the West Coast the following year when the Los Angeles County Sheriff's civil department tried to evict three Muslim families living together. Earl John King, Lillian Bertha King, Andrew J. Caldwell, Henry Morrow, Juanita Morrow, and Alden Earnest Morris were arrested and convicted of disturbing the peace and interfering with a writ of possession after refusing to let police into their home, notifying them that "anyone attempting to come in would be killed." In Los Angeles, the Nation of Islam reproduced the courtroom strategy it had honed in Queens. According to a police report on the trial, 150 Muslims "lined the hall, standing quietly, glaring at the white people passing through the hall. The demonstration was orderly and attained its goal by displaying their militant attitude on Muslim issues." The author bemoaned the "continual barrage of accusations leveled at the Police Department, claiming police brutality and violation of Civil Rights."[86]

By the time of the police beating of Raymond Quarles and the formation of the Emergency Committee during the summer of 1961, the Nation of Islam's political and legal strategy had coalesced. Although members routinely faced charges despite acting in self-defense and the police were never indicted in any of the incidents, the organization's strategy was nonetheless effective. In the well-known case of Johnson Hinton, attorneys Edward Jacko and Jawn Sandifer were able to secure a $70,000 award in damages from an all-white jury, the largest ever paid in a police brutality case against New York City.[87] In Queens, Betty Shabazz and Minnie Simmons were cleared of charges and filed civil suits claiming "false arrest, malicious prosecution, violation of Civil Rights, breaking and entering, assaulting women and property damage" and asking for $100,000 each in damages. The Molettes were also released after a jury failed to reach a decision, leaving the district attorney to call for an adjournment. Malcolm X demanded that the police department investigate the incident and immediately withhold the two officers' badges and guns.[88] The NOI was also successful in pivoting the case toward the issue of police violence by filing a complaint at police headquarters, which led to hearings by the civilian review board. In August, a letter from KKK imperial wizard J. B. Stoner to New York police commissioner Stephen Kennedy was forwarded to the *Amsterdam News* by Malcolm X. In the letter, Stoner reported receiving a report from a Klansman in the NYPD. The paper reprinted the letter in full, and even though the police department said it would "not dignify a letter of this sort with an answer," Malcolm X rattled off the list of police brutality cases, including the Queens home invasion, before concluding that "we feel there is physical evidence to indicate the KKK is very active on the New York police force."[89]

Through the development of a performative politics in the courtroom, the NOI was able to turn these trials into public spectacles, re-centering the issue of police brutality even when Muslims were on trial. The NOI used the courtroom as a political stage that could help it build a Black united front against police violence. Testifying had served a crucial role in the NOI's prisoners' rights cases during the early 1960s, and courts also offered a space to politicize the issue of police brutality. *The Trial* was not simply a metaphorical dramatization in which white defendants were held accountable for their crimes; it was also a model for a performance that challenged all-white

Malcolm X fans out news of victory in the Queens police brutality case covered in the Black press. Circa 1959. Three Lions, Hulton Archive, Getty Images.

juries and judges. Just as the play satirized middle-class Black leadership through the characters of Miss Sadie Culpepper and Bishop Greene, these tensions always hovered near the surface of efforts to sustain Black unity. It would not take long for these political divisions to rise to the surface of the emerging coalition in Harlem.

The Politics of Black Unity

On the eve of New York's primary election, September 6, 1961, over a thousand citizens gathered in front of the Hotel Theresa in Harlem at a mass rally to witness the launching of the Emergency Committee. Evelyn Cunningham wrote that "Harlem almost, but not quite realized the unity it so desperately seeks [at] a strange and unfamiliar kind of rally . . . strange in

the composition of its principal speakers." It brought together Black Nationalists with liberals and left labor organizers. In a speech likely delivered
at this rally, Malcolm X began by stressing Black unity. "I do not stand here
as a politician; not as a republican nor democrat; not as a Mason or Elk;
not as a Christian nor Jew, nor as a Baptist nor Protestant," he emphasized,
"not even as an American. . . . I stand here as a *Black Man*."[90] At one point,
legendary street-corner orator Ed "Pork Chop" Davis quieted a distressed
crowd of nationalists who mistook one of the speakers for white.[91] But, as
Cunningham remarked, despite boos and other distractions, a "fervent appeal for unity" pervaded.

Malcolm's speech urgently situated the issue of police violence within the
broader framework of Black unity at the center of the Emergency Committee's mandate. He condemned white politicians and law enforcement as well
as moderate Black leadership. On the one hand, he pointed out that "Uncle
Tom Negro leaders who condemned the dissatisfaction you displayed at the
UN when Lumumba was lynched by the white man in Africa, have not yet
opened their mouth to protest the attempt by the police to lynch [an]
African diplomat at the 28th Precinct." On the other, he called on city officials to "respect and obey the very same laws they want to enforce upon the
people of our community." In places like Harlem, he contended, only community control of the police could curb the excessive use of force against
Black residents. "As long as white police know that their superiors in the
department and the mayor's office are going to protect them by helping to
white-wash and cover up their brutal acts against the people of Harlem,"
he claimed, "there will always be police brutality, and the tension between
the people and the police will grow until uncontrolled violence explodes."
Pointing out that Harlem had both more police *and* more crime than other
neighborhoods, an argument that subtly undercut and reframed the justifications for racial crime statistics, Malcolm concluded that if they "can't
stop these evils, then we will have to form committees and do so ourselves."
It was the first public event the Emergency Committee held in Harlem, and
Malcolm X's speech positioned police brutality at the top of its agenda.[92]

This forceful statement of police brutality as a principal concern of the
Emergency Committee and the presence of Black Nationalists on the speaker
list should not be mistaken for a commitment to either among those who
initially formed the coalition. A month earlier, a closed-door meeting me-
thodically assessed the causes of racial unrest in Harlem and devised a program to address it. While the group recognized the need to consult with the
Nation of Islam and other Black Nationalists and involve a "cross-section of

community," the two major perceived causes of the unrest in Harlem were telling. The first, economic, predictably pointed to unemployment, poor wages, and dilapidated housing. The second, defined as "racial nationalist chauvinism," targeted the very groups the committee hoped to enlist with three bullet points: "anti-whiteism," "hatred begets hatred," and "violence begets violence." Thus, from its very inception, those forming the Emergency Committee shared the basic premise of *The Hate That Hate Produced*: that Black Nationalism was a form of reverse racism and, along with white racism, bore some responsibility for fomenting racial unrest.

Even more significantly, the group did not cite police brutality as a possible cause of the uprising that had just occurred in Harlem; instead, it stressed "law and order" as a key to achieving better jobs, housing, and schools.[93] Among the group's aims were facilitating better communications among all races in Harlem, preserving freedom of speech and assembly, and achieving a "bigger and better Harlem within the framework of 'law and order.'" Meeting notes reminded members that "with rights, go civic responsibilities and duties, involving compliance with and obedience to the law of the land." Perhaps drawing on one explanation by the *New York Times*—that the conflict began when "nationalist groups had been demonstrating on 125th Street"—the suggestion to shift the "open air forum from street corners to public park[s]" seemed to target Black Nationalist street orators such as Ed Davis, who would eventually join the group's committee on police brutality.[94]

Blaming the unrest on Black Nationalists—and the NOI in particular—reflected press coverage of the disorder that summer, much of which took its cues from local police. The *Pittsburgh Courier* cited worries among police about "cop-hating anti-white tendencies" and named the "Black Muslims." Police sources told United Press International that while the NOI did not initiate the disturbance, it was "definitely involved," and the newspaper described the fifty-member Fruit of Islam as a "tactical command force . . . judo experts, all six feet or taller."[95] So, while the committee invited Black Nationalists in the spirit of a nonpartisan, nonsectarian political coalition, from its inception it positioned these groups not only as potential contributors to the solution but also as sources of the problem.

By the end of August, the Emergency Committee had crafted an action program to deliver to political leaders of both parties before the upcoming primary. A. Philip Randolph trumpeted the breadth of this broad coalition, which included the NAACP, the Urban League, the NALC, Christian and Muslim leaders, Black Nationalists, women's organizations, and the YMCA.

While these groups "approach the problem of liberation differently," he remarked, "I was greatly encouraged by the mutual respect exhibited." Reflecting his priorities as a labor organizer, Randolph ended his call by arguing that "nothing short of a unified leadership, endorsing a crash program for jobs and sound apprenticeship training, can save our communities."[96] When a bipartisan group of mayoral candidates, including incumbent Robert Wagner (D), Attorney General Louis Lefkowitz (R), and Controller Arthur Levitt (D), came to Randolph's office on August 29, they were presented with an action program divided into three major categories: employment, housing, and police enforcement.

Citing the eighty thousand unemployed Black workers in the greater New York area, the group suggested apprenticeship training, a city Fair Employment Practices Committee with enforcement powers, an increase in the minimum wage, and investigations into city contractors and Consolidated Edison (Con Ed) for discriminatory hiring. The program even proposed that, "in light of the Black man's contribution to all modern American music through his development of Jazz," a "Palace of Jazz" be added to the newly proposed Lincoln Center for ballet, symphonic music, and opera.[97] The employment program was followed by a robust eight-point plan for housing, which included more rigorous enforcement of sanitation and health standards, comparative investigations into private rentals in Black and white communities, affirmative action in housing accommodations for families of color, and a relocation program for people displaced by private developers.

Tucked in near the end of the six-page proposal were three recommendations for police reform. Echoing liberal calls for professionalization, the committee demanded a human relations education program on attitudes toward minorities, which would serve as a litmus test for employment on the police force, along with more thorough and efficient prosecution of drug distribution. The committee also suggested that representatives of minority groups should witness and report on the treatment of people of color at police precincts.[98]

Just a week before the primary, candidates fell over themselves to endorse the program.[99] Mayor Wagner wrote Randolph congratulating him on the committee's important service and stating that although injustices could not be eliminated in "one year or even ten," the city had moved faster during his tenure than "any other period of our city's history."[100] Attorney General Lefkowitz, whose representatives had convened with Commissioner Paul McGinnis the previous year to institutionalize surveillance of the Nation of

Seated on platform, from left to right: A. Philip Randolph, Bayard Rustin, and James Haughton lead what was likely an early Emergency Committee meeting, with Malcolm X in attendance, 1961. Box 3, Richard Saunders Collection, Schomburg Center for Research in Black Culture, New York Public Library. Courtesy of Michele Durrant.

Islam in prisons, wrote in a four-page memo that the Emergency Committee has "performed a signal service in presenting a summary of those existing conditions which have worked hardships on many in the City's Negro community."[101] Neither Wagner's letter nor Lefkowitz's report addressed police brutality or the proposed law enforcement reforms.

The ad hoc nature of the group arose from its desire to address the causes of the late July disturbance before the primary election in early September. With support from political candidates in hand, the Emergency Committee went about the task of structuring a more lasting organization. At a meeting chaired by Bayard Rustin and attended by a wide swath of members, including Randolph, Anna Arnold Hedgeman, and James Haughton, as well as Lewis Michaux, Percy Sutton, Ed Davis, and Malcolm X, the group declared: "What is important is action, not structure."[102] Randolph was nominated as chairman and Haughton, his assistant in the NALC, as secretary.

Along with the subcommittees on unemployment, housing, and law enforcement, the group added a fourth on education. But while housing and unemployment were fairly straightforward in Haughton's minutes of the meeting, there were already indications of debate surrounding the scope and purpose of the law enforcement subcommittee. The original committee title of "Police Brutality Enforcement" was crossed out in favor of "Law Enforcement" and eventually "Law and *Order* Enforcement."[103] This change suggested a fundamentally different intention. Most simply, it shifted the accountability for urban unrest and disorder from police violence to the communities themselves. The adoption of the phrase "law and order," which had been used intermittently for over a century to code and signal racist ideas about Black criminality, was a prescient indication of who would shoulder this blame over the ensuing decade. The 1960s marked the emergence of this rhetorical pairing as a salient political tool.[104] By 1972, as President Nixon made it the bedrock of his reelection campaign, the phrase had become a racist and right-wing dog whistle for the policing of dissent and people of color.[105]

A month before a debate between Malcolm X and Bayard Rustin at Howard University, in which Rustin promised to expose Malcolm as a "fraud," with "no political, no social, [and] no economic program for dealing with the Black community," the two made up half of what had become the Law and Order Enforcement Committee, along with Clarence Scott of the NAACP and Ed Davis.[106] Malcolm X's role in the organization quickly expanded. On September 19, the unemployment committee assigned the minister "or another representative of the Muslims" to join a delegation meeting with Con Ed's personnel director as well as Mayor Wagner.[107] Three days later, Malcolm became a member of the committee to draft a proposal for a Forum on Black Liberation.

The forum was chaired by Richard Parrish, a teacher and labor organizer who was a close associate of Randolph in the NALC and would run for councilman-at-large in Manhattan on the Socialist Workers Party ticket in 1963. Joining Malcolm and Parrish was a strong nationalist contingent, which included Michaux, Lawson, Davis, and Alex Prempeh, along with Hedgeman, Haughton, Cleveland Robinson, and Hope Stevens. Citing the "profound and critical need to educate American people in general and the Afro-Americans in particular on the historical struggle of Black people in the United States and Africa," the committee conceived of the forum as a way to create greater awareness of the "historical development of Black people['s] liberation movements changing African and American societies." It was to be held every second Sunday of the month at the Abyssinian Community House or another suitable location, with a lecture and question-and-answer period. The committee planned to invite community organizations as well as university students to the lecture series. The proposed list of speakers featured a breadth and pedigree that would have made the 1963 March on Washington blush by comparison. It included W. E. B. Du Bois, A. Philip Randolph, John Hope Franklin, Kenneth Clark, Elijah Muhammad, Roy Wilkins, Thurgood Marshall, Ralph Bunche, Adam Clayton Powell, Martin Luther King, Mordecai Johnson, James Baldwin, J. A. Rogers, and Leo Hansberry, along with "Three African Leaders."[108] Although the series was formulated under Hedgeman's leadership, with contributions from Cora Walker, a lawyer with her own firm, and Harriet Pickens of the Commission on Intergroup Relations, men monopolized the lectern.[109]

Other divisions cropped up around the forum. Like the meeting notes showing "police brutality" struck out in favor of "law and order," the intrusive hand of an editor who crossed out "Black" and replaced it with "Negro" revealed a deep political fissure beneath the surface of the united front.[110] This internal debate came at a pivotal moment in the eclipse of the term "Negro," and Black Nationalists within the activist networks in Harlem led the movement for change. Before being invited to join the Emergency Committee, Carlos Cooks had called a convention that had "the complete abrogation of that ominous appellation 'Negro'" at the top of its agenda.[111] In 1960, the Committee to Present the Truth about the Name "Negro" met in New York City, bringing as one of its discussants Harlem bibliophile Richard B. Moore, who published *The Name "Negro": Its Origin and Evil Use* that year. Just months before the committee's formation, Percy Sutton used a term that had circulated in 1920s Harlem to characterize the rise of Black Nationalism: the emergence of "a new Negro."[112] And in characteristic rhyming style, Lewis Michaux had this to say of the term: "Use it. Abuse it. Accuse it. Refuse it."[113]

The Nation of Islam had its own deep tradition of contextualizing and condemning the word "Negro," using such terms as "Asiatic Black man" and "so-called Negro" in its place. A classic NOI lecture delivered by Malcolm offered an etymology lesson tracing the origins of "Negro" back to the Greek word for death, *nekro*. This piece of folk etymology pointed not only to the NOI's conviction that 85 percent of Black people were "dead" in the sense that they were "deaf, dumb, and blind" to their own history but also to its contention that the necessary and proximal death of the "Negro" race would lead to the rise of Asiatic "original people." By situating the word "Negro" as a metaphor for Black Americans who were mentally dead, the NOI and other Black Nationalists paved the way for its eventual extinction.

The rhetorical debate about calling this event a forum on "Negro" or "Black" liberation gestured toward a more fundamental controversy about the future of the Black freedom movement. The Emergency Committee was at the ground floor for that debate. The editorial back-and-forth playing out in the margins of the committee's minutes and drafts coincided with Malcolm X's first speeches articulating the difference between the "Black revolution" and the "Negro revolt." In a speech given earlier that year, Malcolm contrasted the American Revolution, the Black revolution, and the Negro revolt. First, while the American Revolution was about white nationalism, the Black revolution was about Black Nationalism. Second, the black revolution was like a forest fire, led by the masses; the Negro revolution was a "backfire," led by "Uncle Toms." The Black Nationalist was a revolutionary "field Negro" and the "Negro integrationist" was a "house Negro."[114] This set of contrasts became the scaffolding for Malcolm's sweeping critique of the March on Washington and the civil rights movement delivered in "Message to the Grassroots" in November 1963.

Malcolm's development of these themes in the context of the Emergency Committee should not be read as a wholesale indictment of Randolph and its other left liberal leaders. Indeed, his speech notes for "Message to the Grassroots" point to Randolph and the NALC as a potential home for an "all-Negro political party and territory and group." Elsewhere, he notes only "minor differences" between them and continues to call for a "United Black Front."[115] It seems clear, however, that the internal debates within the Emergency Committee regarding the Forum on Black Liberation shaped, and were likely shaped *by*, Malcolm's developing ideas about the difference between a Black revolution and a Negro revolt. In other words, the preeminent and lasting critique of the March on Washington did not come from the Nation of Islam's marginal position *outside* the movement but from its central experiences of grassroots organizing *within it.*

In other respects, the Emergency Committee managed to foreground the priorities of Black Nationalists and move forward on its principle of Black unity. The most obvious was its commitment to all-Black membership and leadership. This was a particular point of tension between the Nation of Islam and the NAACP. In 1959, NAACP director of branches Gloster Current called Frank Jenkins after hearing he had made a financial contribution at a NOI rally. Jenkins had headed the Nation of Islam's temple in Troy, New York, but had also been president of the city's NAACP chapter. Although Current was eventually satisfied with Jenkins's defense that he was no longer the acting president of the branch and had made a personal rather than an organizational contribution, he was still troubled by Jenkins's responses to questions about the NAACP's program. When asked if he believed in integration, Jenkins responded negatively: "I'll put it to you this way Mr. Current: how can a white head rule a Black body?"[116] John Ali told Roy Wilkins the following year that the NOI's "greatest regret of your organization is that you do not have a Black man at its head."[117] As Malcolm explained to a predominantly white audience at Wesleyan University, the very "reason we have rejected integration in all forms is that wherever there is Negro-White integration, the Negroes always get run by the whites."[118]

The Emergency Committee also refused to be funded by white interests. Malcolm later explained how white donations jeopardized Black unity: "It's not that there is no desire for unity, or that it is impossible, or that they might not agree with me behind closed doors. It's because most of the organizations are dependent on white money and they are afraid to lose it."[119] As the Emergency Committee carefully navigated its own nascent relationship with Harlem's Black Nationalists, the NAACP waged a similar debate at its national convention in Philadelphia that summer. That controversy arose out of concern among white donors.

As the predominant Black political organization on college campuses prior to the emergence of the Black Student Union, NAACP student chapters had invited Malcolm X to speak at half a dozen colleges and universities in 1960 and 1961.[120] When UC Berkeley canceled Malcolm X's visit, NAACP regional secretary Tarea Pittman found herself in an uncomfortable position when asked by a reporter for the organization's policy regarding the NOI. She wrote Current that "the great damage to NAACP is the belief that NAACP is *sponsoring the group* and is connected with them."[121] Current suggested that regional offices work with student units to ensure that they have received permission before such commitments are arranged. But he, like Pittman, hoped that "some policy decision will be made at the Annual Convention."[122]

As Malcolm X had predicted, behind NAACP officials' concern lay those expressed by its white donors. Edwin Lukas of the American Jewish Committee wrote the NAACP after reading a *Muhammad Speaks* article documenting Malcolm's speech at Queens College. "By itself that would not be newsworthy," Lukas began. "What makes it so is that according to that paper, the appearance of Malcolm X was said to be at the invitation of the Queens College Chapter of the NAACP. If true, I assume the invitation was issued for the purpose of providing the students with a clinical example of extremism."[123] College chapter presidents rarely communicated with the national office and interacted with local adult chapters only sporadically, if at all. But Pittman used the concerns of white patrons like Lukas as ammunition to push for a formal resolution, writing Current that an unnamed contributor to the Committee of 100, a fund-raising group consisting largely of prominent white liberals who supported the Legal Defense Fund, had threatened to withdraw her support because the NAACP seemed to be "sponsoring the Muslims."[124] Senator Joseph Kennedy, Pittman added, felt "so strongly about the adverse newspaper publicity that he has told me he will write the National office about it. This will give you another point of view about the far reaching effects of the [Berkeley] incident."[125]

Several months after the NAACP issued its five-paragraph resolution condemning the NOI, the Emergency Committee supported the NOI's position with regard to white funding. Randolph returned a contribution to Jack Blumstein, the white owner of one of Harlem's largest department stores, with a note reporting that the "committee noted that in the pursuit of its particular objectives it should raise funds by appeals to the people most directly involved."[126] Months later, he gratefully received Joseph Davis's $25 contribution on behalf of the community-based and Black-owned Carver Federal Savings and Loan Association.[127] These decisions to keep the Emergency Committee's membership and funding entirely Black were also at the core of the MOWM twenty years earlier, which had articulated the need to promote racial solidarity and consciousness while preventing white Communist co-optation.[128] As Randolph himself had put it: "If it cost money to finance a march on Washington, let Negroes pay for it."[129]

Despite finding common ground on questions over membership and funding, the primacy of police violence and the role of the subcommittee meant to address it remained unresolved. On October 10, the subcommittee met at Michaux's bookstore and reaffirmed the imperative of dealing with policing. A memo from the meeting reminded the larger committee that it was this crisis that "gave birth to 'UNITY' itself." Referring to itself again as the "sub-committee on police brutality," the memo outlined two immediate actions. First, the subcommittee should "disband at once and give back to the entire body of UNITY the gigantic responsibility of forming an Emergency Committee on Law Enforcement." Randolph should then halt all other committees and have the larger body work solely on policing, headed by "an individual who commands respect from all[,] with some legal background and experience in the field of Law Enforcement."[130] It is unclear whether this directive was ever delivered to the whole Emergency Committee and, if so, how the group responded.[131] But by insisting on placing police violence at the top of the committee's agenda, the largely nationalist contingent of the subcommittee had crystalized the differing priorities and politics within the broader coalition.

Just days later, the law enforcement subcommittee produced its most expansive vision yet for the role that police accountability and reform might play within the Emergency Committee. Now joined by several women, Cora Walker and Harriet Pickens, the group prepared an action plan that foregrounded "police brutality and lack of enforcement of laws against [it]," alongside secondary calls for cracking down on prostitution, gambling, and drug use and sales.[132] The resulting policy recommendations were a mix of liberal professionalization arguments and more progressive calls for limiting police autonomy and making departments accountable to the public and the law.

On the one hand, the group suggested human relations training in the police academy and at the precinct, equitable distribution and hiring of Black personnel, and more minority representation on the bench and in the district attorney's office. Calling for more Black police during an era in which white-dominated forces were occupying armies in communities such as Harlem was a common theme. While in retrospect it might seem obvious why the hiring of individual Black police officers would not produce change within a system fundamentally structured around racist social control, James Forman Jr. points out that there was hardly any data to evaluate whether or not hiring Black officers worked until the mid-1970s.[133] But in places such as Los Angeles, whose police force had been transformed into the most diverse in the country by the 1930s, this strategy had already been shown to not reduce police violence.[134] Felker-Kantor's book on policing in the city "offers a cautionary note to anyone who thinks that more racially inclusive and politically progressive city governments will naturally produce more just law enforcement."[135] Indeed, one of the LAPD's most notable Black hires, Earl Broady, later joined the movement against police brutality as a lead attorney representing Muslim defendants in the 1963 case of *People v. Buice*. And the presence of BOSS agents like DeFossett in the Emergency Committee points to at least one glaring flaw: Black police were often hired with the intent of their becoming "native" informants in Black communities as well as actual informants in the surveillance of Black dissent.

On the other hand, the committee also outlined "precinct community councils" and a civilian complaint review board modeled after that in Philadelphia, both of which would increase the visibility of and accountability for constitutional infringements, racial and religious discrimination, and the use of excessive force. Perhaps most presciently, the committee demanded an end to illegal search and seizures and insisted that officers be educated on the Fourth Amendment. This point not only looked back toward cases such as the Queens home invasion but would prove crucial as such practices expanded several years later through Governor Rockefeller's 1964 "anti-crime" package, which instituted stop-and-frisk policing and "no knock" practices, which allowed law enforcement officers to enter residences without warning or notice.

LESS THAN A YEAR after the Emergency Committee announced its program in Harlem, Malcolm X spoke at a rally sponsored by Mosque No. 7 on the same block. The subject was the most serious incident of police violence the Nation of Islam had yet faced: the shooting of six unarmed Muslims and murder of mosque secretary Ronald Stokes by the LAPD. Malcolm X and the NOI were now working feverishly in Los Angeles to produce a similar Black united front against police brutality that transcended divisions of class, religion, and politics and coalesced around the shared experience of policing and surveillance in communities of color. Although the Emergency Committee would not survive the summer of 1962, both its lessons and its challenges informed the Nation of Islam's attempts to organize all-Black political coalitions against police brutality from coast to coast in the coming years.

Despite the breadth of the participants and scope of the debates during the Emergency Committee's brief existence, scholars have only mentioned it in passing.[136] Michael Fortner suggests that the Emergency Committee offered "alternative conceptions" or "alternative voices within the community," describing the group as an outlier whose "positions on drugs and crime did not represent the views of working- and middle-class African Americans." But the Emergency Committee was intentionally acting as a political cross section of Harlem, rife with its own internal controversies about the form and future of policing in the community. At the same time, many of the ideas about policing offered by the Emergency Committee were *representative* of dominant liberal modes of thinking about crime and harm reduction. Like many Black activists during this period, committee members walked a fine line between advocating for police accountability on the one hand, and what they saw as much-needed policing of drugs, prostitution, and other vice in the community on the other.

But the lessons and impact of the Emergency Committee go far beyond its organizational legacy. The existence of a Black united front that attempted to set aside deep political divisions to address community concerns in housing, unemployment, education, and policing half a decade before the rise of Black Power is noteworthy in itself. While its rejection of white funding and emphasis on all-Black political organizing recalled the commitments of the original MOWM, the strong presence of Black Nationalist leaders marked a distinct moment in the Black freedom movement. The debates that played out in the margins of meeting minutes and draft proposals reflected a fundamental divide over both the causes of and the solutions to racism and urban unrest. Left-liberal Black leadership often shared a flattened vision of Black Nationalists with white liberals and conservatives, which was described at the committee's first meeting as "hate begets hate." Elsewhere, Randolph called Black Nationalism a "ghetto people's defense and offense mechanism against persecution, insult, oppression, and poverty" and said that it "tends to direct its venomous attacks against white people, instead of discriminatory practices of some white people. It is based upon the false assumption of the capacity of Negroes for self-sufficiency in this age of science, industrialism, and technology."[137]

This thinking mapped onto the causes given and solutions offered for police brutality as well. By naming the subcommittee "law and order enforcement" instead of "police brutality," more moderate leaders within the organization shifted to a rhetorical framework that pointed toward pathologizing Black communities and reforming, rather than transforming, policing. Police brutality was simply the most public distillation of violence being enacted against these communities. The Nation of Islam was acutely aware of this situation, as it bore the brunt of police attacks and surveillance. The significance of the Emergency Committee lies not in its success or failure but in the questions it raised and the lines it drew. These would become foundational to the directions these activists took, from the March on Washington to the Organization of Afro-American Unity (OAAU).

By late July 1962, a year had passed since the disturbance in Harlem that brought about the formation of the Emergency Committee. Although the coalition had disbanded, the Nation of Islam sponsored a mass rally, which drew thousands back to Harlem Square around the familiar theme of Black unity. As Malcolm delivered a speech similar to the one he had given at the Emergency Committee's founding rally the year before, Emergency Committee organizers Percy Sutton, Ed Davis, Hope Stevens, Bayard Rustin, Cleveland Robinson, and Anna Arnold Hedgeman all sat behind him. But a flyer advertising the rally points toward a noticeable change from the previous year. Black Nationalists—who, behind closed doors, had been positioned as part of the cause of racial unrest the year before—were now headlining the

Mass Rally For Unity

DEMAND JOBS For New York's
80,000 Unemployed Black Workers

★ ★ ★

INVITED TO SPEAK:

PERCY SUTTON
President N.Y. NAACP

LOUIS MICHEAUX
Nationalist Leader

ANN HEDGEMAN
Civic Leader

V. SIMPSON TURNER
Christian Minister

MALCOLM X
Muslim Minister

CLEVELAND ROBINSON
Labor Leader

A. PHILIP RANDOLPH
Chairman

HEAR . . . A Program for Action NOW!
What YOU Can Do !

★ ★ ★

IN FRONT OF HOTEL THERESA
125th Street and Seventh Avenue, N. Y.

WEDNESDAY, SEPT. 6, 1961 -- 7 P.M.

★ ★ ★

Sponsored by
**EMERGENCY COMMITTEE FOR
UNITY ON SOCIAL AND ECONOMIC PROBLEMS**
A. PHILIP RANDOLPH, Chairman
For further information: 3rd Floor, 217 West 125th Street · Phone: UN 5-8710

**MASS RALLY
at HARLEM SQUARE**
CORNER OF 125th STREET and 7th AVENUE, NEW YORK CITY

SATURDAY, JULY 21st, 1962

From 4:00 P.M. to 9:00 P.M.

"ALL SINCERE SO-CALLED NEGRO LEADERS MUST STEP FORWARD, TAKE
PART IN THIS MASS RALLY, AND LET OUR PEOPLE KNOW ONCE AND
FOR ALL WHERE YOU STAND ON THE MANY PROBLEMS FACING OUR
COMMUNITY."

INVITED GUEST SPEAKERS

MALCOLM X
PRINCIPAL SPEAKER

NATIONALIST LEADERS

CARLOS COOK   JAMES LAWSON
LEWIS MICHAUX   EDWARD DAVIS
              ARTHUR REED

ADAM C. POWELL   BAYARD RUSTIN
ROY WILKINS   HOPE STEVENS
JAMES FARMER   PERCY SUTTON
A. PHILLIP RANDOLPH   PAUL ZUBER
ANNA HEDGEMAN   JOSEPH OVERTON
J. RAYMOND JONES   REV. EUGENE CALLENDAR
Boro. Pres. EDWARD DUDLEY   REV. THOMAS KILGORE, JR.
Welfare Comm. JAMES R. DUMPSON REV. E. L. HARMOND
State Sen. JAMES WATSON   REV. ASAPANSA-JOHNSON
WHITNEY YOUNG   REV. V. SIMPSON TURNER

THEME: MORAL ELEVATION OF OUR COMMUNITY
"LET US FORGET OUR RELIGIOUS AND POLITICAL DIFFERENCES. WE MUST
COME TOGETHER ON THE SAME PLATFORM IN A GREAT DISPLAY OF UNITY."

FREE   ★ ENTERTAINMENT ★   FREE

Two flyers, one from the Emergency Committee in 1961, and the other from 1962 with Black Nationalists at the top of the agenda. James Haughton Papers, Schomburg Center.

list of speakers. Indeed, the names Lewis Michaux, Carlos Cooks, James Lawson, Ed Davis, and Arthur Reed were listed above the names of other invited speakers.

A year later, Malcolm X took the stage at Abyssinian Baptist Church before a crowd of five hundred as part of a ten-part forum sponsored by Rep. Adam Clayton Powell. His speech, "The *Black* Revolution," again openly confronted the forum theme—the "Negro Revolution"—and likely riffed on the themes of "Message to the Grassroots" delivered later that year at the Grass Roots Leadership Conference in Detroit.[138] Attendees included patrolmen Edwin Cooper and Thomas Courtney of BOSS, who reported that a predominantly Muslim audience stood rapt as Malcolm "scored some Negro leaders of betraying their race" while demanding financial support from the government for a back-to-Africa movement or reparations in the form of "'one-seventh' of America's wealth and land."[139] The speaker series (still dominated by men) was advertised as including Jackie Robinson, James Baldwin, James Farmer, and Carlos Cooks.[140] The formal disbanding of the Emergency Committee should not be mistaken for the dissolution of the activist network it constituted and nurtured. The contentious debates over the forum on "Black" or "Negro" liberation and the subcommittee on "police brutality" or "law and order enforcement" were anything but semantic. The forum eventually took form, and when it did, Malcolm was there before a large Muslim audience to point out that the Black revolution and the Negro revolt signaled fundamental questions about the meaning and form of revolution, who would lead it, and whom it would serve.

In March, just three months earlier, when A. Philip Randolph convened a five-person committee and proclaimed that it "was time for the masses of people to move again," Black Nationalists were conspicuously absent.[141] Randolph was joined by many who had drafted the proposal for the Forum on Black Liberation several years earlier, including Parrish, Overton, Robinson, and Hedgeman, to plan another mass display of unity, which they first called the "March on Washington for Jobs."[142] The eventual march on August 28, 1963, was integrated, heavily funded by white interests, and devoid of Black Nationalist representation, and its platform did not prioritize police violence.[143] What it shared with the Emergency Committee was its exclusion of women's voices. But to portray the Nation of Islam and Malcolm X as passive observers watching what Malcolm would call the "Farce on Washington" from the sidelines buries the grassroots organizing by Black Nationalists along with those who eventually conceived of, organized, and excluded them from the march. When Malcolm deemed the expansive gathering on the Washington mall that day a "circus, a performance that beat anything Hollywood could ever do," he did so because it betrayed many of the foundational principles of Black unity that had coalesced in the Emergency Committee: Black leadership, broad-based but all-Black political coalitions, refusal of white financial support, and militancy. These differences were at the heart of how Malcolm distinguished the Black revolution from the Negro revolt.

Just as political cleavages dissolve coalitions, exclusions sharpen organizing and give rise to new alliances.[144] Part of the nature of coalition building is such failure. SNCC organizer Bernice Johnson Reagon once said, "If you're in a coalition and you're comfortable, you're not in a broad enough coalition."[145] When Anna Hedgeman was rebuffed by the NAACP while organizing the March on Washington, she took the opportunity to enlist Dorothy Height of the National Council of Negro Women. Randolph and other male organizers left her off the list of official leadership.[146] The continued exclusion of women from the speakers' rostrum at the march was challenged repeatedly by Hedgeman and civil rights veterans such as Pauli Murray, who proposed picketing Randolph's speech at the National Press Club two days before the march. The masculinism that pervaded the movement was embodied in both Randolph and Malcolm X. In a 1969 interview on Malcolm, Hedgeman pointed out that we must resist canonization and "recognize that Malcolm embraced the chauvinism of Muslimism which places women at the feet of men, that his whole history as a hustler placed women in a position of whores and objects to be used."[147] Partially as a response to such continued exclusions and silences in Black organizing spaces, Murray and Hedgeman joined Shirley Chisholm and Dorothy Robinson to participate in founding the National Organization for Women.[148] Another Emergency Committee member, Evelyn Cunningham, was a founding member of the Coalition of 100 Black Women in 1970.[149]

In the aftermath of the Los Angeles mosque invasion during the summer of 1962, the Nation of Islam continued by building new broad-based local coalitions against police brutality. At a Boston fund-raiser for the family of Ronald Stokes, organizers read a statement from Boston NAACP president Melnea Cass, who was known as the "First Lady of Roxbury," the neighborhood where both Stokes and Malcolm had grown up: "Police brutality has been a concern of the NAACP for a long time. This is as true in Boston as in Los Angeles as in Atlanta or Jackson, Miss." Cass went on: "The NAACP will continue to fight police brutality whenever it shows its ugly head. This will be done by ourselves or in concert with other groups interested and concerned about getting rid of this kind of inhuman treatment."[150] By 1963, condemnations of police brutality echoed from coast to coast. The Rochester NAACP, the Congress of Racial Equality, the Monroe County Non-Partisan League, the United Action Committee for Rufus Fairwell, and the Rochester Civil Rights Committee joined the NOI in demanding police accountability. There, Mildred Johnson—vice president of the Negro Business and Professional Women—paralleled Malcolm X's message of unity by emphasizing that "we are Black folks first!"[151] As local NAACP chapters joined other civic, fraternal, and religious organizations in the Nation of Islam's next attempt at building a Black united front in Los Angeles, organizing against police brutality would become the centerpiece of that tenuous unity.

CHAPTER FOUR

We're Brutalized Because We're Black

> Let us remember that we're not brutalized because we're Baptist.
> We're not brutalized because we're Methodist. We're not brutalized
> because we're Muslims. We're not brutalized because we're
> Catholic. We're brutalized because we're Black people in America.
>
> —MALCOLM X, 1962

For those at Mosque No. 27 in Los Angeles, Elijah Muhammad's visit to the city in April 1961 was a crowning moment, the culmination of years of diligent organizing. Mosque secretary Ronald Stokes and his wife, Dolores, were diligently preparing for the capacity crowd of nearly two thousand that would soon fill the Embassy Auditorium. In 1956, a group of no more than a dozen Muslims had begun gathering weekly in members' homes.[1] Now, five years later, a visit by the Messenger, his son Herbert, and *Muhammad Speaks* columnist Tynetta Muhammad marked its arrival as the most important mosque west of Chicago headquarters. This success also meant the community had become a target for the Los Angeles Police Department (LAPD).

The police anxiously watched the preparations. A surveillance memo described fifty well-dressed FOI members marching from the nearby Pickwick Hotel toward the auditorium "in military fashion" to search and secure the premises several hours before the event. "The area outside the auditorium was well 'policed' by about 125 young male Negroes." Officers watched the disciplined changing of the guard, noting that "at times some marched away from their posts in a military manner. . . . They all moved rapidly and decisively with no discernable signals." The report emphasized that this *"guard force is very well trained and can be considered only as a highly efficient military organization."*[2]

Almost a year later to the day, twenty-nine-year-old Ronald Stokes was shot and killed by Los Angeles police officer Donald Weese while walking toward him with his hands raised. What had begun as two officers questioning Muslim men unloading laundry from the back of a car outside the mosque had ended in a confrontation in which over a half-dozen unarmed Muslims were shot, William Rogers was paralyzed, and Stokes was dead. According to a report by the LAPD's Internal Affairs Division, Weese alone shot five men.[3] In his testimony, Weese described Stokes with "his arms in an outstretched position" with his palms up, repeating a Muslim prayer.[4] When pressed as to why he had shot an unarmed man to death, he bluntly replied, "I am not Hopalong Cassidy. I cannot distinguish between hitting an arm and so forth, sir. I aimed dead center and I hoped to hit."[5] Although no Muslims admitted at trial to chanting in prayer before the shooting, several police recounted having heard a collective call. One said, "Prior to the attack on my partner I did hear a chanting. This is very hard to explain. I guess you could say it was like a song in unison. The group was chanting out something in a foreign tongue and almost immediately upon completion of—well, during this chant the attack on my partner started." Weese's partner, Richard Anderson, remembered the men asking, "Why? Why?" as they were being lined up against the wall and claimed they were shuffling their feet and chanting what "seemed to be possibly three or four words, but it had a basic rhythm." He concluded "that they sounded Arabic."[6] An officer who had been wounded testified that he "heard some other chanting as I came to. When I regained consciousness the second time it appeared to me like 'Allah is the greatest.'"[7] The chant was likely *Allāhu akbar*.[8]

Before the grand jury, the testimony of the trauma surgeon at the central receiving hospital sounded like a casualty list from a battlefield. Monroe Jones: gunshot of the left shoulder. Clarence Jingles: gunshot of the left hip. Roosevelt Walker: gunshot of the testicle, penis, and left thigh. Robert Rogers: multiple gunshot of the left arm, forearm, abdomen, and back. William Rogers: spinal cord completely severed at point. Ronald Stokes: gunshot on the chest, shock. No blood pressure; no pulse.[9] Although it was dubbed a "blazing gunfight" and a "riot" by the *Los Angeles Times*, there was no evidence that any of the men had initially been armed.

This violence was not an aberration but rather an outcome of the policing strategies championed locally by Chief William Parker and embraced nationally as the model of professional and modernized law enforcement. One of the first questions Officer Stanley Kensic asked Monroe Jones and Fred Jingles as they were unloading garments from the back of their vehicle outside the mosque was "if they were Muslims." When asked later why they were suspicious of the men to begin with, Kensic's partner, Frank Tomlinson, noted that the "area is a place where there is a high rate of burglaries" and cited "a possibility of" the clothing "being stolen."[10] As a scuffle ensued between the two men and the police, a Black off-duty police officer named Paul Kuykendall intervened and felled Arthur Coleman, Jr. by slamming a blackjack repeatedly against his head.[11] The violence of this encounter was the end-point of a policing program that used racial crime statistics and profiling precisely to prepare officers for encounters with the Nation of Islam. Liberal reforms like data analysis, community relations training, and racial diversification of the police force would not change this outcome. Indeed, the deadliest case of police violence against the Nation of Islam in its thirty-year history featured all three.

When Los Angeles minister John Shabazz and national minister Malcolm X spoke at the April 1961 rally the previous year in Los Angeles, both men emphasized the need for racial unity. "If you are a doctor or a teacher or whatever you are," Shabazz told the audience, "if your face is Black and you live in America today, you are in bad shape." Malcolm issued a call similar to that delivered at the first Emergency Committee meeting in Harlem: "It doesn't make any difference whether you are a Baptist, Methodist or Catholic. . . . You can still catch hell. You aren't catching hell because you are a Black Catholic, you are not catching hell because you are a Black Baptist. . . . You are catching hell because you are Black. So if you can't get together on the basis of religion you should be able to get together on the basis of catching hell." But his advocacy of racial unity over religious divisions did not stop him from criticizing the NAACP. While he emphasized that the NOI would not be "side-tracked" by fighting the NAACP, CORE, or the Urban League, he contended, "We do think that when you have a Black organization . . . you should have Black leadership." If there were no Black persons qualified to lead the NAACP after fifty years, then the "NAACP has failed to cultivate leadership among our people."[12]

In 1962, the FBI reported that a widowed Dolores Stokes "spoke very bitterly concerning police brutality . . . stat[ing] that all Negroes should forget their religious differences and must protect themselves against the brutality by the white people."[13] Her speech echoed the call that Malcolm X had issued to the one thousand community members gathered at the Park Manor Auditorium in Los Angeles soon after her husband's death. He said, "You're brutalized because you're Black and when they lay a club on the side of your head, they do not ask your religion. You're Black, that's enough."[14] Malcolm had urged the heads of local organizations to organize a unified front: "We must come together against the common enemy. Remember all of us are Black. It's not a Muslim fight. It's a Black man's fight."[15] That summer Elijah Muhammad made a similar appeal in *Muhammad Speaks*: "In these crucial times, we must not think in terms of one's religion, but in terms of justice for us poor Black people. This means a United Black Front for justice in America."[16]

While the Stokes case is one of the most iconic moments in NOI history, scholars and journalists have focused narrowly on Malcolm X and Elijah Muhammad, describing it as a decisive break in their relationship. Peter Goldman referred to the crisis as "a sort of volte-face version of the Johnson parable."[17] Rather than confront police as the NOI had done in Johnson Hinton's case, Malcolm X's delivery of Elijah Muhammad's message to remain "cool, calm, and collected [and] leave it in the hands of God" to a Harlem audience in 1962 did not resound with the same militancy as had the silent protest outside the 28th Precinct in 1957.[18] Journalist James Hicks, who had covered the Hinton case, pointed out that "they lost face" in Los Angeles; "they hadn't fought back, and that aura of don't-touch-a-Muslim diminished a bit."[19] Even Malcolm claimed retrospectively that the NOI's tepid response "caused the Black Muslim movement to be split. Some of our brothers got hurt, and nothing was done about it, and those of us who wanted to do something about it were kept from doing something about it. So we split."[20] But by fixating on internecine struggles within the NOI, these accounts miss the NOI's central role in the formation of a broad-based coalition against police brutality in Los Angeles and the tensions that fractured it. Unity was always tenuous, as it was in the Emergency Committee before. But its strategies and fault lines—and the criminal legal apparatus that opposed it—are instructive for understanding Black freedom struggles against police violence then and now. As Ruth Wilson Gilmore posits, "in scholarly research, answers are only as good as the further questions they provoke, while for activists, answers are as good as the tactics they make possible."[21]

This coalition building comes into focus in the 1963 trial of *People v. Buice*, following a year of organizing after the shooting. Despite killing Ronald Stokes and paralyzing William Rogers, no police officers were ever charged or suspended. Rather, the state brought forty counts of assault and resisting arrest against fourteen Muslims. The NOI operationalized a political strategy at trial that it had been cultivating for years in response to police violence and the legal injustice that inevitably followed. The NOI used the courtroom to stage political theater and put the state on trial. Mosque No. 27 members flooded the court every day of the trial, its men selling *Muhammad Speaks* and its women demanding separate seating from white male spectators. Flyers and newspaper advertisements publicized the trial like playbills, urging the public to demand justice at the courthouse.

Although civil rights historiography has largely focused on the role of the courts in changing federal jurisprudence, the NOI used the courtroom as a political arena to build Black unity on the issue of police violence and across religious and political divides within Black and Latinx communities. Legal scholar Malachi Crawford argues that the "courts became a primary site within which the NOI sought to advance its civil rights initiative."[22] But unlike the efforts of the NAACP's Legal Defense Fund or the cases brought forth by Muslim prisoners, these trials did not seek policy changes or promote civil rights legislation. The NOI sought to shift the discourse of the trial through political theater and community organizing around a united platform against police brutality. Attorney Johnnie Cochran, fresh out of law school and working as an assistant on the *Buice* trial, remembered the lesson of his own first police brutality case several years later: "Those were extremely difficult cases to win in those days. But what [it] confirmed for me was that this issue of police abuse really galvanized the minority community. It taught me that these cases could really get attention."[23]

For its legal defense team, the NOI secured respected NAACP attorneys Earl Broady and Loren Miller, both of whom had impressive local credentials and broad support in Los Angeles. Broady had been in the LAPD, one of the first Black officers in the city to rise to the rank of lieutenant. He left the force in 1944 to attend law school, then worked as a civil rights lawyer before being appointed to the Los Angeles County Superior Court during the summer of 1965, just prior to the Watts uprising. Loren Miller was nearing the end of his career but still occupied a number of significant positions, including seats on the California Advisory Committee to the U.S. Commission on Civil Rights and the NAACP's West Coast legal committee.[24] Although best known for his role in fighting for housing desegregation, most notably in *Shelley v. Kraemer* (1948), Miller had a long-standing interest in reforming policing in Los Angeles. Perhaps most importantly, he owned one of Los Angeles's preeminent Black newspapers, the *California Eagle*. Beyond the Nation of Islam's local ally, the *Los Angeles Herald-Dispatch*, the *Eagle* brought the most sympathetic and comprehensive coverage of the Stokes trial and the Nation of Islam to Black Angelenos.

The trial unfolded as the desegregation campaign in Birmingham, Alabama, was making national headlines. The violence of police chief Bull Connor's forces against nonviolent demonstrators and children broadcast the brutality of southern white supremacy live on televisions across the nation. The Nation of Islam and other Los Angeles activists linked these images to the Stokes murder, debunking the myth of southern exceptionalism. As historian Jeanne Theoharis has pointed out, the "parallels between the racial politics of Birmingham and Los Angeles . . . have been lost to a strict binary between a nonviolent Black movement in the South and the rise of

Black frustration and violence in the North."[25] As these parallel events and movements have been bifurcated by journalists and historians and remembered separately, what has been lost is the tactical deployment of southern analogies by activists outside the South, revealing the ways in which these struggles were synergistic, even when they were distinct.

As the fiftieth anniversary of the Watts rebellion was commemorated, the Stokes case was frequently cited as an example of the pervasive police violence that preceded the uprising in 1965.[26] But as Frederick Knight noted over two decades ago, the "assault on the Los Angeles Muslims had even deeper roots and wider implications."[27] The relationship between the Stokes case and both local anticarceral activism and the national civil rights struggle has gone unrecognized. Most importantly, the years immediately following the *Buice* trial represented another moment of opportunity for the Nation of Islam and other local groups to build a Black united front against police violence across class, religious, and political divisions.

Becoming Mosque No. 27

The Los Angeles temple began in late 1956 under the leadership of Thomas Huff, Ray Cook, Bertha Haynes Johnson, and Leatha and Willie Culton. Every Friday, when San Diego minister Henry Mims got off his job digging ditches, he would drive to Los Angeles and preach until the Sunday afternoon service. Malcolm X arrived the following summer and helped the group find a temporary home at the Maynard Theater before eventually securing a space at Normandie Hall at 1480 W. Jefferson Boulevard. Membership rose from under a dozen in 1956 to seventy-five by 1959. Estimating that between two and eight members were joining a week, police attributed this rapid increase to Malcolm. When Normandie Hall's seating became insufficient, the group rented space at the larger Elks Hall. In December 1958, the Westside temple was officially recognized as the 27th mosque by Chicago headquarters.[28]

The NOI soon won important converts in Sanford and Elizabeth "Pat" Alexander, a Garveyite couple who published and managed the Black weekly newspaper the *Los Angeles Herald-Dispatch*. Sanford Alexander rented the Christ Cosmopolitan Christian Church and began an Eastside branch led by Mims and his young assistant minister, John Morris Shabazz. When Malcolm first came to organize on the West Coast, the paper provided a secretary and office at the *Herald-Dispatch* building at 1431 W. Jefferson, on the same block as Normandie Hall. As Malcolm explained in a letter to Temple No. 7, "The paper in Los Angeles is a very outspoken one. Mr. Alexander, the publisher, has been converted, thanks to ALLAH. . . . That area out there in the West is very fertile territory; we only need some laborers to work it."²⁹ In 1958, he brought aides from New York, six of whom eventually grew into leadership positions in Los Angeles.³⁰

Over two extended visits during those years, Malcolm conducted a membership drive from his base on the 1400 block of W. Jefferson. Following the success of his six-part series in New York's *Amsterdam News* called "God's Angry Men," which coincided with the Johnson Hinton case and led to a serialized weekly column by Elijah Muhammad, Malcolm began a West Coast equivalent under the same name for the *Herald-Dispatch*.³¹ Beginning in July 1957, the column described Islam as "a flaming fire sweeping across the entire Dark World today."³² Malcolm used it to introduce the major religious and political themes of the NOI to its broadest audience at that time. In fact, it was from this column that many incarcerated Muslims— from prisons as distant as Attica—built curricula and learned surahs.

One major theme in "God's Angry Men" was that Black Americans needed to be awoken and politicized to their own history. "Yes, we who were once dead (morally, mentally, socially, politically and economically), lying at the rich white man's feet here in the grave of ignorance, are being raised today from this 'death' being made upright," Malcolm wrote. He argued that second-class citizenship was no citizenship at all. Without a flag and a nation of their own, Black people had been duped into working, fighting, and dying for a white man's country. Malcolm brought these ideas of citizenship and mental and spiritual death together by arguing that "when a person is deaf; and dumb and blind, that person is the same as DEAD. When one is lost from one's own kind, that one is DEAD. When one doesn't enjoy civil rights (Citizenship) that one is DEAD." Such moral, mental, and social death ultimately led to civil death. "We don't have full citizenship (CIVIL RIGHTS) here in America, and therefore the word 'American' can't rightfully be applied to us to designate our NATIONALITY, so our slavemaster calls us NEGROES, and Messenger Elijah Muhammad teaches us that the word 'Negro' means something that is DEAD, LIFELESS."³³ For these reasons, when the Emergency Committee debated whether to organize a forum on "Negro" or "Black" liberation years later, Muslims in the Nation of Islam would have seen "Negro" liberation as an empty signifier. "Negro" identity signified social and civil death, so to be liberated on those terms was no liberation at all.

Building on these insights, Malcolm made a remarkable claim for formal political engagement in 1957: "In this great drama, the NEGROES play the leading role, and thereby pose a serious problem. The position they occupy is both STRATEGIC and UNIQUE, for although the NEGROES are deprived of most of their voting power, yet their "diluted" vote will swing the balance of power in the Presidential (or any other) election. What would the "role" and "position" of the NEGROES be if they had a full voting voice? No wonder the freedom (EQUAL RIGHTS) of the NEGROES is so greatly feared by their enemies."[34] Malcolm's 1964 "The Ballot or the Bullet" speech at Cory Methodist Church has long been taken as evidence of his first major ideological shift following the split from the Nation of Islam.[35] But Malcolm's embrace of electoral politics, or at least his recognition of voter registration as a useful weapon in the arsenal of democracy, was not the sharp departure that historians have assumed.[36] By 1963, Elijah Muhammad had declared that the future of Black Americans "lies in electing our own." A front-page article in *Muhammad Speaks* stated that there "will be no real freedom for the so-called Negro in America until he elects his own political leaders and his own candidates." It promised that the NOI would soon "enter the political arena on the side of candidates with programs designed to alleviate the deplorable conditions under which Negroes are forced to live . . . [and] may portend a giant coast-to-coast registration drive in preparation for the 1964 national elections."[37] The germ of this strategy, which is often described as evidence of Malcolm's "evolving" political thought after he left the NOI, can be found in the late 1950s in Los Angeles.

The bulk of Malcolm's columns were dedicated to castigating white liberals and the Black church. He chastised an editorializing preacher whom he assumed was white, only to double down the next week after he learned the preacher was Black. "He fooled me completely!" Malcolm wrote. "This NEGRO PREACHER wants to set himself up as the lawyer for the white race."[38] Calling Black clergy puppets, parrots, and tools of white supremacy, he blamed churches for divisiveness within the Black community and contended that they "were not interested in the welfare of the people but only wanted wealth and power for themselves."[39] In one of his most fiery columns, Malcolm attacked both targets at once: "Your time is up white man. You have fooled the world long enough. The best thing you can do now is be quiet. You may get a few of these Negro puppets and Uncle Toms who are yet intoxicated with your pallid skin to side with you . . . but the majority of our people are awakening."[40]

As Malcolm's words found their way from Los Angeles to prison cells in New York, he began a series of popular lectures on Friday evenings and Sunday afternoons.[41] In his speeches at Normandie Hall, Malcolm emphasized building Black unity even while openly criticizing the most formidable institution in the Black Angeleno community. One *Herald-Dispatch* article carried the headline: "Moslem Leader Scores Preachers as Misleaders."[42] At Elks Hall, Malcolm lectured on the theme of unity and urged the Black community to drive out white businesses and patronize their own. But he also wrote that the "number one tool of the white slavemaster was the NEGRO Preacher."[43] These attacks on the Black church alienated local clergy. Three preachers reportedly "hotfooted" it out of a standing-room-only meeting after Malcolm challenged Black churches to put their congregations' money to work "for the members" instead of for themselves and white interests. He charged that the money raised by churches was "dead capital" being used for segregated housing and loans to white businesspeople who served Black customers.[44]

Malcolm made deliberate efforts to carry a message of unity beyond W. Jefferson Boulevard to the far reaches of the city's Black and brown communities.[45] He warned Black college students not to "think because you are studying at UCLA that they won't hang you."[46] Continuing to develop the NOI's relationship with the pan-Arab world, Malcolm and Elijah Muhammad participated in a Pakistan Republic Day celebration at the University of Southern California (USC), where Malcolm shared the stage with prominent Iraqi Shi'a Dr. Mohammad Mehdi.[47] These connections built a Black Nationalist organization that was not narrow and homogeneous but expansive, multiracial, and multiethnic. By the early 1960s, Benjamin X Perez, who was connected to migrant farm labor activists and César Chávez and was one of the first Muslims of Mexican descent in the NOI, had become an assistant minister to John Shabazz. Malcolm's comments to students at USC affirmed the relationship between the NOI's internationalist and local visions. Malcolm admonished them to "consider the liabilities as well as the assets" of American democracy and to study the plight of Black Americans, "whose wretched condition is the by-product of the hypocrisy which is skillfully cloaked in the disguise of Western Democracy."[48] Behind these efforts at unity, however, criticisms of the church and Black clergyman left festering wounds that reemerged in the aftermath of the Stokes shooting.

Although Malcolm frequently criticized the NAACP, the national organization had formally joined the struggle against police brutality in Los Angeles before the NOI did. In 1961, Roy Wilkins made national headlines by characterizing the LA police as "next to those in Birmingham, Alabama." He condemned Chief Parker for running as a rogue force without oversight from the mayor and other elected officials. "This system allows the Police

Minister John Shabazz speaks at a press conference a month before going on trial in *People v. Buice*. Assistant minister Benjamin X Perez is seated to his right; Edward Shabazz is to his left. Perez, who had connections to Cesar Chavez and migrant farmworker activists, was one of the first Muslims of Mexican descent to join the Nation of Islam. Fang Family San Francisco Examiner Photograph Archive Negative Files, BANC PIC 2006.029:138149_02-NEG, box 1403. © The Regents of the University of California, The Bancroft Library, University of California, Berkeley.

Department to be the judge and jury of its own personnel without having to pay any attention to the public."[49] The following year, just months before Ronald Stokes was killed, the NAACP's Legal Redress Committee issued a twelve-page report documenting ten major cases of police harassment and brutality. It concluded that Black residents "never know where or at what hour may come blows from the guardians of the law who are supposed to protect them but from whom they are helplessly unprotected."[50]

The NOI's initial half decade of organizing in Los Angeles was productive but hard fought. One historian estimated that membership had grown to three hundred by the late 1950s, a figure supported by police reports.[51] While small compared to established mosques in Chicago or New York, Mosque No. 27 remained an important outpost in newly charted territory. By 1960, the Westside and Eastside mosques were finally merged under John Shabazz's leadership after receiving an order to "straighten out all internal conflicts within the Temples in the Los Angeles area."[52] Malcolm X returned to Los Angeles the next year for another fund-raising drive and two weeks of classes and lectures. He hosted a series of talks at the Garden of Prayer Baptist Church on the question of "Integration or Separation" and debated Los Angeles NAACP president Edward Warren at Los Angeles State College.[53] Yet Malcolm stated that his second visit had not "been the success he had thought it would be" and reportedly called "Los Angeles . . . one of the worst places in the United States to convert people to Islam."[54] Whatever the challenges, it was clear from the scope and content of the NOI's organizing efforts in Los Angeles that cultivating leadership and building broad-based unity were its primary goals.

The Los Angeles police were less likely than Malcolm to see the NOI's local organizing as a failure. Instead, they watched with mounting concern, even fear. As C. Eric Lincoln wrote, "The Los Angeles Police openly worry about 'what it's going to take to light the fuse.'"[55] In 1961, the first full year that *Muhammad Speaks* was distributed as the official organ of the Nation of Islam, police accosted Muslims selling the newspaper outside a Safeway supermarket. Officers claimed that Muslims selling their paper had been blocking the doorways of the grocery store for almost a year. But when the case went to trial, the store manager signed an affidavit acknowledging that he had given his permission to the defendants. The six men arrested were acquitted by an all-white jury, and the NOI filed a million dollar lawsuit against the grocery store chain.[56] Yet photos such as the one published in the *Los Angeles Times* following the arrest, showing a police officer reading the headline "Muslims Set for Christian Attack," demonstrated that policing the paper had joined mosque raids among the tactics now used by local law enforcement against the NOI. By targeting vendors and surveilling the paper's content, police harangued local Muslims while continuing to cull knowledge about NOI activities.

This pattern of policing, which positioned Muslim newspaper vendors as loiterers and trespassers on private property, emerged across the country. On Christmas Day the following year, two FOI selling papers were arrested

Men protest the December 25, 1962, arrest of two Muslims in Times Square in front of police outside the New York County Criminal Court building on January 11, 1963. Robert Haggins Collection, Schomburg Center for Research in Black Culture, New York Public Library. Courtesy of Sharon Haggins Dunn.

for blocking a subway entrance, leading to a large public demonstration in Times Square by the NOI during their trial in 1963. Perhaps more significant, at least three of the men eventually tried in *People v. Buice* had been accosted by Los Angeles police for selling *Muhammad Speaks* on the UCLA campus the same week that Stokes was murdered.

On the Monday before the mosque shooting, about ten men from the mosque drove to the UCLA campus to sell the paper near Royce Hall. While there, they were hassled by several police officers who asked whether they were students and demanded their identification. Accounts of the event diverge widely. According to Officer Joseph Moreton Jr., he spotted two men selling papers while two others acted as lookouts. When he asked for identification, Arthur Coleman Jr. replied, "You have taken away my name." Moreton claimed that Coleman brushed past with his shoulder, so Moreton pinned the man's arms behind him to "prevent further violence." Campus police officer Jack Gustafson added that Coleman had "fists clenched" and that he heard the men say, "Let's get these dirty cops. There's no better way to die. Now is the time. Give us the word." Coleman testified that an officer had tried to purchase a paper from him, which he declined, claiming it was his last. He was then told to hand over his draft card, a form of identification loaded with implications during the early years of the Vietnam War, especially given the NOI's historic refusal to register with the Selective Service.

Police testimony registered the familiar combination of fearful awe regarding the FOI's discipline. Gustafson recalled that "all of a sudden I heard a whistle. I didn't see who had done the whistling, but about four or five others joined the group. . . . They converged on this area from different directions." This incident ended with Coleman and others heading to the dean's office to talk about selling the newspapers on campus. But four days later, after traveling once again to the UCLA campus, this time to accompany minister John Shabazz to an invited class lecture, Coleman would have his head lacerated by a gun butt and be shot in the chest and the base of his penis by Donald Weese. Following the gunfire, Coleman was handcuffed and left lying on the ground, bleeding, next to Ronald Stokes and William Rogers. Policing the paper was part of a more quotidian surveillance and profiling strategy that served as the foundation for the dramatic violence of evenings such as April 27, 1962.[57]

Black Unity on Trial

As Ronald Stokes was laid to rest, attorney Loren Miller offered his own eulogy in the *California Eagle*. Stokes and Miller had belonged to the same college fraternity, and Miller compared him to Benjamin Davis, the former Black city councilman from Harlem who was serving a five-year sentence for violation of the Smith Act because he belonged to the Communist Party. Miller remarked that despite the "long distance between Muslim belief and Communist thinking," two middle-class men from educated backgrounds had rejected the moderation expected of their standing. Miller invoked a Du Boisian double consciousness in which one must go "to war with himself" and decide whether to pledge allegiance to a "political system which condones discrimination, and to organizations, such as the NAACP, designed to reform that system" or to rebel and embrace a "hostile doctrine which declares there is no hope within the framework of American democracy."[58] For Miller, who had been enamored with the work of the International Labor Defense and the nationalism of the Communist Party's "Black Belt" thesis before becoming a prominent NAACP attorney, the essay was a personal reflection on a path not taken. This dilemma of reforming American democracy or revolting against it embodied the struggle many Black leaders in Los Angeles would soon face as they attempted to simultaneously condemn police brutality while distancing themselves from the Nation of Islam.

Despite Miller's longtime affiliation with the NAACP and his support for desegregation, his writings from the year of the Stokes case display his movement away from liberalism and toward support for all-Black political organizing. His "Farewell to Liberals," published in the *Nation* in 1962, articulated the frustration of many Black leaders with the slow pace of reform. Miller argued that white liberals would never cede control and supported the new militancy within the Black freedom movement, which called for nothing short of Black-led political parties and organizations. "Rejection of liberal leadership does not mean that Negroes do not want, and expect, continued liberal aid," Miller clarified. "But they want it on their own terms and they are too sophisticated to believe that liberals can resign a battle involving fundamental equalitarian issues out of pique at the rejection of their leadership." He observed that Muslims were "drawing substantial urban support" through a similar critique of liberalism and concluded that it was time for white supporters to re-enlist in the struggle as "foot soldiers and subordinates in a Negro-led, Negro-officered army under the banner of Freedom Now."[59]

Miller's article was well received among both moderate and left civil rights activists. Robert Carter of the NAACP circulated the article among his colleagues and told Miller that the essay "aptly describes what I regard as the realistic position of the Negro vis-à-vis white northern liberals today."[60] The NAACP even reproduced and distributed the article.[61] Miller was among a growing group of the civil rights old guard who were increasingly critical of American liberalism. Psychologist Kenneth Clark, whose famous doll studies with his wife Mamie provided much of the evidence on the psychological damage inflicted on Black children by racial segregation cited in the *Brown* decision, wrote in *Commentary*: "I must confess that I now see white American liberalism primarily in terms of the adjective 'white.' And I think one of the important things Negro Americans will have to learn is how they can deal with a curious and insidious adversary—much more insidious than the out-and-out bigot."[62] Although Miller's decision to take the *Buice* case was no doubt swayed by the considerable retainer offered to him and Broady by NOI headquarters, he was among the growing number of civil rights leaders whose arguments had much in common with the NOI's critique of racial liberalism.

There were others who came out in support of the NOI as well. Celes King III, a special consultant for the NAACP's Legal Redress Committee and a longtime bail bondsman in Los Angeles, put up over $160,000 in bail bonds to secure the release of all fourteen Muslims despite his close relationship with Mayor Yorty and threats from Los Angeles police.[63] As he remembered decades later, he knew both John Shabazz and Captain Ed Sherrill. "These were people that were viable out here in our community. So I didn't look at it in the same way. And the Muslims did not hesitate in terms of where they were and their support of me whenever it was needed."[64]

Roy Wilkins also offered a show of solidarity from the NAACP's national office. In a telegram reprinted in *Muhammad Speaks*, Wilkins urged the organization's Los Angeles branch to stay involved. "Never in its history has the NAACP withheld condemnation of and action against police brutality because of race or religion, and it will not do so now."[65] The NAACP demanded an investigation be launched by California attorney general Stanley Mosk and U.S. attorney general Robert F. Kennedy.[66] "Paced by a strong statement from Roy Wilkins," the *California Eagle* reported that the Black community "is coming down overwhelmingly on the side of the Muslims."[67]

Attorney Hugh Manes, chairman of the Citizens Committee for a Police Practices Review Board, argued that despite the "misgivings the Black Muslim has stirred in the white community, we should not lose sight of the widespread respect and sympathy—if not support—which he commands in the Negro community."[68] Indeed, at a meeting called by the district attorney, a group of over thirty Black leaders—including the Citizens Committee, the NAACP, and its Legal Redress Committee—expressed concern over the state's tactic of pitting other Black groups against the Nation of Islam. Mayor Yorty, "his voice trembling with anger at times, scored local officials . . . while he praised the NAACP on the national level." Local leaders, he claimed, "are bringing about the very condition they are complaining about."[69] Yet they refused to condemn the NOI. At this critical juncture, Mayor Sam Yorty, Sheriff Peter Pitchess, and Chief Parker traveled to Washington, D.C., to meet with Attorney General Robert F. Kennedy as Black leadership in Los Angeles held a series of rallies to protest police brutality.

The efforts by city leaders to scapegoat the NOI only fueled the argument for the necessity of a Black united front. For two consecutive Sundays in May 1962, unity prevailed in Los Angeles. A Citizens Protest Rally was held on May 13 at the Second Baptist Church.[70] Although the church made it clear that it was opposed to the NOI (even comparing it to the KKK and White Citizens' Councils), the rally was cosponsored by the Nation of Islam, the

Spectators jam the courthouse corridor, with the Fruit of Islam selling *Muhammad Speaks*. Herald Examiner Collection, Los Angeles Public Library.

Community Civic League, and the recently formed Citizens Protest Committee. The rally explicitly called for the national office of the NAACP to continue to support the local branch's efforts and "disregard the efforts of those who would drive a wedge between the local branch and the national office."[71]

Wendell Green of the Citizens Protest Committee echoed the NOI's call for a united front.[72] "This is not a political rally. Neither is it a religious rally," he told the assembled twelve hundred concerned citizens. "If there is one thing that our community stands united on, it stands united against unlawful police violence and abuse of police power." The police shooting could have just as easily happened in front of the Elks lodge or Shriners Auditorium, Green argued. All you had to be "was Black and moving within sight and range of a shooting policeman's weapon." Like Miller, he critiqued the use of statistics to generate and mask police violence. "The Negro community is over-policed. Why? The Los Angeles Department is statistic happy. . . . These unnecessary arrests build the statistics that the police department uses to poison the minds of the public and the policemen giving a gross misrepresentation of our community."[73] Although he was not scheduled to speak,

Malcolm X took the opportunity to second this call for unity, stating that because the NAACP had backed the NOI, the police department was now mad at both organizations.[74]

Two days later, Malcolm delivered another rousing call for Black unity at the Park Manor Auditorium before a crowd of over one thousand, who waited outside to pour into the auditorium. The minister called for a mass protest march on city hall and congratulated Black leaders, in particular the NAACP, for coming together on the issue of police brutality.[75] One of the attendees was Ron (Everett) Karenga, later Maulana Karenga of the US Organization and the founder of Kwanzaa. A year after writing C. Eric Lincoln, requesting an advanced copy of his book to help advance his study of the "Black Muslim Brotherhood," Karenga wrote in the *Herald-Dispatch* that "this rally, being neither religious nor political is to bring together all people with the same problem and to find a solution."[76]

But concern was growing among NAACP officials about what this budding coalition might mean. That "the NAACP is supporting the rights of the Muslim[s], without embracing their doctrine[,] is shaking everybody up," one organizational report noted. Field secretary Althea Simmons "is getting a considerable amount of calls about it." Simmons wrote to Gloster Current that "the Muslim situation has almost gotten out of hand as far as NAACP is concerned in that in Mr. [Edward] Warren's T.V. appearances and statements to the press the NAACP's participation has not been clearly confined to the issue of police brutality and therefore, we now have the Muslims embracing the NAACP and stating that NAACP supports the Muslims unqualifiedly." A year after its conference resolution to condemn Black Nationalists in Philadelphia, Simmons again asked for clarification so that "we would know the details of the position of the National Office."[77]

The NAACP was not alone in its discomfort. The unity of early May began to falter when Reverend H. H. Brookins and other Black clergy came away from protest rallies feeling that Malcolm had made "irresponsible statements" and that the Black unity espoused by the NOI did not adequately distinguish between the group and their churches.[78] More than two hundred ministers from all denominations gathered in late May at the First AME Church to draft what became known as the "Ministers' Manifesto." The ministerial alliance was unconvinced by Malcolm's argument that this was "an attack on the Black people, who incidentally were Muslims, but who were Negroes first."[79] The president of the Western Christian Leadership Conference complained that a "handful of Muslims is attempting to represent themselves as spokesmen for 500,000 Negroes in the Los Angeles community."[80]

The Ministers' Manifesto denounced police brutality while calling the Nation of Islam "separate and distinct" from this struggle. Brookins called the group "anti-law, anti-race and anti-God." The meeting was even halted at one point to ferret out and remove suspected Muslims. The manifesto used language eerily close to that which the state used in prisoners' rights cases: "We suspect the Muslim movement wears the garb of religion, but in reality is just another nationalistic movement."[81]

For Parker and Yorty, this division between the NOI and Black churches was opportune. The mayor quickly thanked the ministers for the "sturdy, realistic—and Christian—statement of their position."[82] Brookins remembers that the mayor's approval quickly faded as soon as they raised the issue themselves. "When we came back to articulate the issue of police brutality, we were then called . . . irresponsible leaders, these preachers catering to the big Communist lie, and that you cannot trust these few people out here who propose to speak for their people."[83] Some in the Black community saw the manifesto as a sellout that shattered the united front. At another mass rally, spectators called the ministers "Uncle Toms" and "handkerchief heads." Earl Walter, chairman of Los Angeles CORE, argued that it was "unwise and unprofitable for segments of the minority community to begin attacking each other at this time."[84]

The Ministers' Manifesto was a product of old resentments and new political liabilities. Poor relations between the NOI and Black clergy had long preceded the Stokes murder. In Malcolm's Los Angeles lectures in the late 1950s, he had criticized the Black church for wasting financial resources and providing promises of heaven after death while offering few solutions in life. When the People's Independent Church of Christ refused to let the NOI use its facilities for an anti–police brutality rally, it cited a vote it had taken two years earlier forbidding the organization from renting the building.[85] Any show of support for the Nation of Islam also brought risk of repercussions from agents of the state. As Celes King recalled, after posting bail for Muslims in the Stokes case, he received threats and was told he "would not be posting any more bonds in this town."[86]

Nonetheless, Malcolm and the NOI continued to emphasize the importance of a united front in Los Angeles. After the issuance of the Ministers' Manifesto, Mosque No. 27 minister John Shabazz personally invited all the ministers to the second mass protest at Park Manor in the "interest of Community Solidarity and complete understanding."[87] At the national level, Malcolm wrote an open letter urging that a "united front by the five Negro Congressman against the injustice of police brutality . . . would go far towards creating a United Front of 20 million Black people behind the 'example' set by your 'congressional' unity." He stressed that the public outcry against Jim Crow atrocities in the South would "mean nothing so long as the HUMAN RIGHTS of Negroes here in the North also can be trampled underfoot by white savages disguised as police officers."[88] Although the Ministers' Manifesto revealed a deep fissure within the Black community, the *Pittsburgh Courier* maintained that the NOI received "a good deal of sympathy in the Negro community despite the public denouncement."[89]

The Trial

By the start of the trial a year after Stokes's death, the profile of the national civil rights movement had been elevated by two events, one historical and one current. First, 1963 marked the one hundredth anniversary of the Emancipation Proclamation, offering an occasion to take stock on the progress that had been made and how much remained to be done. Then, on Palm Sunday 1963, the day before jury selection began in *People v. Buice*, Reverends A. D. King (Martin Luther King's brother), Nelson Smith, and John Porter led a march in Birmingham, Alabama, which began a monthlong push to end racial segregation in the city's public accommodations. The political backdrop of Birmingham added to the national significance of the trial. Each day of courtroom coverage in Los Angeles shared the front page with horrifying acts of police brutality against nonviolent protesters in Birmingham. As Stephen Ward argues, 1963 was "the 100th year of Black emancipation and the first year of the Black Revolution."[90]

The political coalition that had shown promise the year before was reinvigorated in the months leading up to the trial. In February, minister John Shabazz participated in a discussion at the First Unitarian Church alongside Benjamin Davis of the Communist Party, outgoing president of the San Francisco NAACP Terry Francois, and Daniel Gray of CORE. The event was billed as "Alternative Paths to Negro Freedom."[91] Shabazz then served as master of ceremonies at a forum called "A United Negro," sponsored by the African-Asian Businessmen, which was likely affiliated with the NOI.[92] There, Malcolm X shared the stage with the former NAACP chapter president, Edward Warren, and community leader Dr. Marcus McBroom. Although both men had once debated Malcolm publicly over the strategies and aims of the civil rights movement, they now came together to denounce police brutal-

Twelve of the fourteen defendants, from left to right: John Morris, Randolph Sidle, Louie Buice, Arthur Coleman, William Rogers (seated), Robert Rogers, Roosevelt Walker, Monroe Jones, Fred Jingles, Nathaniel Rivers, Troy Augustine, and Raymond Wiley. Not shown are Charles Zeno and Elmer Craft. Box 88, folder 54, Amsterdam News Photograph Collection, Cornell University.

ity.[93] The *New York Times* reported that the coalition's "implications locally transcend the very limited Negro separatist movement, since the central issue of alleged 'police brutality' is something the entire Negro community has long been aroused about."[94]

As calls for a Black united front echoed from Los Angeles to Rochester, Gloster Current finally set about resolving what he described as the NAACP's "*difficult public relations problem*"—a national position to which local chapters would be bound. Like the church leaders who drafted the Ministers' Manifesto a year earlier, Current saw the problem as "how to protest police brutality and not appear to be supporting the Muslims on their program *per se*, a position into which Malcolm 'X' wants to push us." He agreed with Roy Wilkins that the organization could not forsake its condemnation of police brutality but nevertheless cited the resolutions at the last two annual conventions denouncing the Nation of Islam. Current laid out a five-step directive for local organizers when protesting police brutality alongside the NOI:

1. *Issue a statement* protesting the incidents of police brutality, but at the same time make clear the Association's position on the Muslims. *Quote the text of the 1962 resolution in your statement.*

2. If a community-wide mass protest meeting called by the NAACP involves other groups, *avoid*, if at all possible, having Muslim speakers at your rally. Public meetings are, of course, open and the possibility is that Muslims will attend, ask questions and seek to get their viewpoint across. NAACP spokesmen should reiterate our position, stating clearly that in fighting police brutality we are *not* supporting the Muslims.

3. *Avoid at all costs any inference* of a Unity Movement or that NAACP is calling for a "common front." Point out clearly wherein our programs differ, although we uphold all citizens' constitutional rights.

4. *NAACP spokesman should chair such meetings*, make the introductory statements and rebut any distorted statements.

5. When called upon for TV or radio appearances in connection with Muslim or Black Nationalist rallies or statements, make clear and definitive statements of NAACP opposition to all segregationist programs; that we oppose bigotry; that our program is affirmatively seeking to eliminate the causes of racial discrimination and prejudice—poor housing, discrimination in employment, denial of educational opportunities and civil rights. The NAACP spokesman should speak vigorously and determinedly in favor of ending all forms of discrimination.[95]

Current's uncompromising directive suggests the success of the NOI in garnering local support on both coasts around a message of Black unity but also illustrates the tensions between local and national-level organizing. The nation's oldest civil rights organization had now crafted an edict specifically forbidding coalitions with the Nation of Islam centered around the issue of police violence.

When jury selection opened at the superior courthouse in Los Angeles, the scene was a familiar one. One hundred seats were filled with prospective jurors, and the remaining two hundred occupied by men "dressed in neat dark suits, and . . . women in ankle-length, flowing dresses and white or pastel colored scarves."[96] NOI members sold *Muhammad Speaks* in the corridors and passed out leaflets signed by Elijah Muhammad asking: "Can we allow innocent Negroes to be murdered in cold blood by the Los Angeles police?"[97] Despite the NOI's formidable presence, jury selection—like the grand jury inquest—had a predictable outcome. After a total of 239 jurors had been excused over thirteen days of questioning, an all-white jury of eleven women and one man remained.[98] The state prosecutor defended the process by arguing that he had only excused Black jurors who had admitted to reading newspaper articles that alleged police brutality. Of course, this excluded anyone in Los Angeles who read a local Black newspaper, all of which were closely covering the trial. Although Broady and Miller contemplated an appeal to the state supreme court for a mistrial due to discriminatory jury selection, the case moved forward.[99]

On only the second day of the trial, attorneys and bailiff gathered around the judge to discuss the legality of the NOI's courtroom strategy. One female juror was approached during a court recess by a man selling *Muhammad Speaks* who asked, "Sister, are you biased or prejudiced?" The bailiff reported to the judge that "she was somewhat on the—a little bit on the scared side." Pedestrians outside the courthouse complained of the constant presence of Muslims selling newspapers, but authorities admitted that they could only intervene if sales took place inside the courtroom.[100] Not only was the Nation distributing *Muhammad Speaks* at the courthouse, but the paper was reporting the trial in depth, with editorials being written by defendants such as minister John Shabazz. Judge Coleman remarked that this was unprecedented. "I have never tried a case in which a defendant was writing stories about the trial while it was in progress," he told Loren Miller, who responded, "I have never been in one either."[101]

The NOI advertised the upcoming trial as if it were a public performance, not unlike *The Trial* at Carnegie Hall. Flyers asking "Who Hates Who?" and "Does the Negro Get Justice?" were distributed like playbills, urging people to come to the courthouse on North Hill Street and see for themselves.[102] Other flyers, such as one advertising a mass unity rally sponsored by "all local organizations concerned with human rights," urged people to protest the "Terror in Birmingham" and "Police Brutality in Los Angeles" while uniting for the common goal of freedom and justice.[103] Enclosed in *Muhammad Speaks*, a subscription flyer put Los Angeles in conversation with the southern civil rights movement and African decolonization. Calling the new newspaper the *"third dimension"* in national and international news, the advertisement recognized that "people want to know *more* than what happened in Greenwood, Miss., or Angola, S.W. Africa, or Los Angeles."[104]

As Boston prepared for a fund-raiser for Stokes's family at Boston Arena in late July, flyers drew parallels between Algeria and Los Angeles.[105] Publicity and protest rallies transformed the *Buice* trial into a stage, which brought together the southern wing of the civil rights movement, the struggle against police brutality in New York and Los Angeles, and anticolonial struggles as three acts of a global play.

Activists during this period were cognizant of the salience of southern bigotry and frequently deployed analogies to demonstrate the prevalence and depth of racism outside the South. Several years earlier, Roy Wilkins had described Los Angeles police as being as bad as those in Birmingham, just as the phrase "Shades of Mississippi" had highlighted the persecution of Muslim prisoners in Attica, New York. In early 1963, Mildred Johnson called Rochester the "Mississippi of New York State."[106] Malcolm X sent a telegram to President Kennedy claiming that "the City of Rochester has become worse than Oxford and Jackson, Mississippi combined."[107] He also emphasized that Stokes's murder in Los Angeles occurred in a purportedly liberal city. As Malcolm told radio host Dick Elman immediately after the shooting, "This happened in Los Angeles last Friday night, in the United States of America, not South Africa or France or Portugal or any place else or in Russia behind the iron curtain, but right here in the United States of America."[108] By drawing analogies between the atrocities of the U.S. South, apartheid South Africa, and the urban West, Malcolm was tracing global systems of racial violence before Black Power–era concepts such as "internal colonialism" were circulating.

While the NOI worked to highlight connections with Birmingham, many whites in Los Angeles countered the organization's efforts by crafting a color-blind narrative that distanced Los Angeles from the racism of the South. As one juror recalled, we "jurors did not consider or make an issue in our deliberations of what was happening in the south or back east. This was our state's problem." The same juror assured the press after the trial that "race, religion, color or creed never entered our minds or thoughts during our deliberations. We simply tried the Black Muslim defendants as individuals and considered the police officers as individuals."[109] Many Black Angelenos were also not ready to see Birmingham and Los Angeles as two sides of the same coin. Community interviews after the trial revealed that while most followed the Stokes case in the press alongside the developments in Birmingham on a daily basis, some were resistant to such analogies. "There are problems here," one man explained, "but how can anyone say—as one of our leaders has said, to my knowledge—that 'Los Angeles is as bad as Birmingham?'"[110]

While we must heed the caution of Robert Self, who urges that it is not "historically sound to frame all forms of Black struggle in terms of their relationship to the southern variant," police brutality in Los Angeles was being linked to the southern wing of the movement by activists themselves.[111]

As trial testimony opened in late April, a group called the Hollywood Race Relations Bureau picketed the courthouse and denounced the NOI as "defy[ing] the respectful and peaceful approaches . . . toward total desegregation."[112] Another picketer at the Elks lodge rally was punched in a scuffle before a backdrop of signs reading "Those 6-year-old children in Birmingham have more guts than you have." Malcolm X calmly told the press that the NOI would "not be responsible for anything that happens to these pickets."[113] Yet other picketers emerged in support of the NOI, carrying signs that read "Arms to the Oppressed in Alabama" and "We Support the Muslims." As the trial continued to be understood in relation to an emerging national civil rights movement, the obstacles to a Black united front in Los Angeles were again rising to the surface.

Inside the courtroom, the issue of racial segregation so central to the Birmingham movement became the trial's main story. A confused *Los Angeles Times* reporter wrote, "An unusual problem in seating of spectators arose Tuesday when women members of the sect refused to accept seats alongside white persons." Using the Fruit of Islam as its enforcers, the NOI challenged the discourse of racial segregation by successfully petitioning to have a section of the courtroom cordoned off for Black women. But most reports did not make the distinction between "segregation" and "separation" that was central to the NOI's Black Nationalist politics.[114] When the court eventually reversed its policy, it was described in the press as "desegregation" by court order.[115] This issue revealed the fragility of the coalition between the local NAACP and the NOI, as it appeared that Judge Coleman's reversal was partially in response to NAACP president Christopher Taylor's remark to a reporter that he must oppose any form of racial segregation, regardless of who initiated it.[116] More importantly, however, it showed how the separate gender spheres typically regarded as evidence of the NOI's conservatism nevertheless opened a space for women to challenge the state. While this was always embedded in the discourse of male protection, it challenged white supremacist notions of who could legitimately seek that protection and in what spaces.

The NOI continually broadened the scope of the trial and exerted control over its proceedings. Police officer Donald Weese horrified the audience with his frank testimony. Meanwhile, Malcolm X sat in the audience with a camera around his neck taking photos of him. He told the press, "Do you know

Women seated separately in the courthouse at the *People v. Buice* trial. Bill Walker, Herald Examiner Collection, Los Angeles Public Library.

who I'm taking a picture of? I'm taking pictures of a murderer."[117] As in Queens, the NOI used photography as a way to control the trial. In newspaper photographs, Malcolm X is often seen with the camera, taking sympathetic portraits of Muslim defendants or images that could be used to identify Los Angeles police.

Earl Broady used his cross-examinations to emphasize the racist language used by police—both in the trial and during the arrests. Just days after Weese's disturbing testimony, Broady stopped during the middle of a cross-examination after he objected to the use of the term "male Negroes" by the witness as prejudicial: "Your Honor, I believe these defendants should be referred to exactly the same as if they were Caucasians. This officer wouldn't refer to two male Jews. He wouldn't refer to two male Irishmen. He wouldn't refer to two male Swedes. He wouldn't refer to two male Caucasians, and I think this man should be admonished that this constantly referring to race, there is no reason for it and it is highly prejudicial to continue in the presence of this all-white jury, to continue to refer to them as Negroes."[118] Broady became so incensed at the repeated use of such descriptors by police that he told the judge, "I'm not ill. I just thought I might lose my temper . . . this man referring to male Negroes. I thought I might pull a Muslim."[119] Despite the judge's ruling that the witness used the term "Negro" only for identification, Broady's critique of the term was reminiscent of Malcolm's explanation to Judge Henderson in the Buffalo trial of Muslim prisoners the year before. Yet his use of the phrase "pull[ing] a Muslim" conjured the image of a militant, or even violent, organization in a trial in which the group stood accused of police assault.

Throughout the trial, defendants testified that police at the scene had called them "niggers" on the night of the 27th. Soon after Weese had opened fire outside, shooting at least three men before killing Ronald Stokes as he emptied his revolver, men inside the mosque were being lined up against the wall and searched for weapons.[120] During this lineup, Troy Augustine recalled one officer saying, "'We ought to shoot these niggers. We got them lined up. We ought to shoot them in the back and kill every one of them. . . . We just killed some of your brothers out in front and we ought to kill you.'"[121] Others testified they were called "Nigger Muslims" while being told of the slaughter outside. "'Line up. Don't turn your heads, you Black nigger Muslims,'" Robert Buice remembered hearing. "'We just killed six of your brothers out there.'"[122]

At the intersection of racial epithets inside and the shooting outside was another display of police power. Lined up against the wall in his place of worship, Randolph Sidle heard an officer say, "Let's tear the suits off of these niggers."[123] Every defendant inside the mosque during Weese's shooting testified that their suits were torn up the back and down the seam of the groin.[124] Augustine had his suit jacket torn up the back and thrown over his head before his pants were pulled down and he was kicked between his legs.[125] Nathaniel Rivers also had his jacket snatched over his head and forcibly slashed. His pants were "jerked and they were ripped also down the front and the back."[126] The men were all made to walk out of the mosque and over the handcuffed and bleeding bodies of Arthur Coleman, William Rogers, and Ronald Stokes with their pants at their ankles.[127]

The Fruit of Islam prided themselves on their starched white shirts and immaculate bow ties. Key to the Nation of Islam's redemption of Black womanhood and manhood was its strict dress code for members of the Muslim Girls Training class and the Fruit of Islam. The practice of violently stripping men of their signifying clothing recalled the Zoot Suit Riots of 1943, when Los Angeles police stripped baggy zoot suits from young Pachucos. The tactic was again used in the 1970s at Attica following the prison uprising and in

Philadelphia as police made Black Panthers stand against the wall in their underwear while handcuffed during a raid of their headquarters. It was "an embarrassing position," Sidle testified. "It wasn't to see if we had any weapons. They did it out of vengeance."[128] A raid that began on April 27 under the pretext of searching a trunk full of suits ended in their deliberate and violent shredding to humiliate the men who proudly wore them.[129]

Broady and Miller spent much of the trial working two interrelated angles: to acquit the men of the charges they faced as defendants while expanding the scope of the trial to questions of excessive force, implicit bias, and outright racist state violence. The attorneys repeatedly charged that the men were not being tried on the basis of their actions but rather on public misconceptions about the NOI's beliefs. Loren Miller commented that people have "been schooled into seeing evil in the Muslim movement where there is none." He and Broady asserted that "these men were not prosecuted so much for what they *did* as for what they *are*."[130] Not unlike the claims of Muslim prisoners, the defense was suggesting that these men were political prisoners, tried on the faulty grounds of public perception and political ideology rather than on their alleged crimes. In order to illustrate this injustice, Broady asked the all-white jury to imagine a "hypothetical case . . . where there are a number of white men being tried before a Negro judge and prosecuted before a Negro jury by Negro lawyers."[131] Whether he knew it or not, Broady was describing the premise of *The Trial*.

In late May, two months after jury selection began, Broady and Miller presented their concluding arguments. Broady reportedly held "the packed courtroom in Superior Court spellbound as he probed, accused and outlined point after point."[132] Miller urged the jury to consider the "irreparable effect" that a conviction would have on the defendants and ended by calling Los Angeles police "vigilantes . . . acting like judges, jurors and executioners."[133] The jury deliberated for eighteen anguishing days. Malcolm X and other supporters held vigils outside the courthouse, while two hundred deputy sheriffs, many with nightsticks and helmets, patrolled around them.[134] In the end, the jury found eleven of the fourteen defendants guilty, most of assault and resisting arrest.[135] Although he was among those acquitted, Minister John Shabazz declared that he was not satisfied. "These are my brothers, and we all stand together," he told the press. He then joined others in a "military precise march from the courtroom." Herbert Rogers, whose son William was found guilty of assault while sitting in a wheelchair, paralyzed from the waist down by police bullets, summed up the trial most succinctly: "You can't get a fair trial in a white man's court."[136]

Robert and William Rogers. William remained paralyzed from the waist down and attended the entire trial either in a wheelchair or on a stretcher. Box 88, folder 54, Amsterdam News Photograph Collection, Cornell University.

THE DAY AFTER jurors went into deliberation at the Stokes trial, Los Angeles hosted its largest civil rights rally ever. Over thirty thousand people heard Martin Luther King Jr. speak at a fund-raising "Rally for Freedom" at Wrigley Field to support the Birmingham campaign. Reverend Brookins, who had led the denunciation of the Ministers' Manifesto, was the master of ceremonies, and Christopher Taylor, who had decried the "segregation" of the courtroom in the Stokes trial just weeks earlier, spoke of the parallels between Birmingham and Los Angeles. "We are here to help the people of Birmingham," he told the crowd, "but I would be remiss in my duty if I did not mention certain problems we have in Los Angeles." The first issue he named was police brutality. A week later, a group calling itself the United Civil Rights Committee (UCRC) held its inaugural meeting. As the *Chicago Defender* put it, the battle against Jim Crow had gone west, but as with the

March on Washington, it had set aside the lofty goal of Black political unity set forth by the Nation of Islam in the aftermath of the Stokes case. The freedom rally at Wrigley Field ushered in a new form of coalitional politics that differed from the Black united front proposed by Malcolm X and John Shabazz in Los Angeles and the Emergency Committee in New York.[137]

Although it emerged in part from the political coalitions against police brutality that had existed since 1962, Althea Simmons wrote that the UCRC was "mostly an outgrowth of the Freedom Rally held for the benefit of SCLC."[138] Headed by Taylor, the group's leadership was drawn from a wide swath of civil rights organizations, such as the NAACP, CORE, the Urban League, and SNCC; labor associations, such as the AFL-CIO and the UAW; and religious and ethnic organizations, including the American Jewish Congress. Much like the Emergency Committee, its five standing committees addressed housing, education, employment, direct action, and police practices.[139] One of its first four demands was for a report on the "establishment of a procedure for presentation of citizens' greviances [sic] against law enforcement agencies to independent citizens' review boards."[140]

California assemblyman Mervyn Dymally, acting on his campaign promise, soon introduced a six-bill package that included establishing police review boards in all cities with more than fifty thousand residents and offering redress for those harmed by police misconduct, a demand that the New York Times was quick to note had grown "after the April 1962 riot between the police and Black Muslims."[141] The recently formed UCRC and the NAACP called on Stanley Mosk to convene a statewide meeting with law enforcement officials.[142] Although the Los Angeles police department had agreed to stop using crime statistics as a defense of racist policing, the central issue continued to be whether or not the city would establish a citizen review board.[143] Despite garnering support from the NAACP, the ACLU, and the California Democratic Council, review boards still faced vehement opposition from the white majority. The Los Angeles Times complained that a civilian review board would hurt morale in what it judged to be "very probably the best metropolitan police department in the nation."[144] The idea that police officers would be demoralized by citizen oversight was taken a step further by the Fire and Police Protective League, which followed Chief Parker's lead in suggesting that police were the "smallest and most oppressed minority" and were being stripped of their civil rights and due process protections.[145] Others remained unconvinced. The Assembly Committee on Criminal Procedure voted for a two-year study of the potential impact of Dymally's bill.[146] Despite endorsing review boards in the first month of its existence, the UCRC was reportedly reconsidering its proposal by August.[147]

The most obvious difference between the UCRC and the Black united fronts in New York and Los Angeles that had included the Nation of Islam was that the UCRC was interracial. While there were early reports that the "Mexican-American community" would be involved, the coalition was largely biracial. In fact, a newspaper reported that at one protest there were so many white picketers in front of an all-white housing tract that "residents have questioned whether the campaign is supported by Negroes." The composition of the group's leadership and activists reflected its fundamental political difference from all-Black organizations committed to self-determination. Taylor declared, "We mean it when we say that we want integration now."[148] Yet it was not immediately apparent what the framework of integration meant for addressing police brutality.[149]

In Los Angeles, as in New York, integrationist political coalitions moved forward without the Nation of Islam. But these coalitions did not resemble the Black united fronts that had briefly coalesced between 1961 and 1963 in New York City, Los Angeles, and Rochester. They were biracial efforts that employed the strategies and language of integration central to the southern nonviolent wing of the movement. There were certainly differences between organizing in Harlem and organizing in Los Angeles, notably the absence of New York's deep Black radical tradition on the West Coast and the unanimity of white political power in Los Angeles. However, despite these different political milieus, the NOI's coalitional efforts to organize against police brutality came to similar ends in 1963. In both cities, all-Black mobilizations that arose out of crises of police violence had ended in biracial liberal coalitions that focused their attention on issues outside the one that originally brought about their birth: police brutality. To defer this question meant that while the uprisings in Harlem and Watts in the upcoming years were not inevitable, they could hardly be a surprise. Studies in the aftermath of the Stokes case by attorney Hugh Manes, police officer Lee Brown, and the California Advisory Committee for the U.S. Commission on Civil Rights proposed different causes and solutions to the simmering crisis of policing in Los Angeles in 1963 but agreed on one thing: there would be further unrest if policing was not addressed.[150] The failure of these Black united front efforts to foreground and address police violence were another such indication.

Over the next two years, the Harlem and Watts rebellions transformed the civil rights movement and the future of policing and prisons. National attention suddenly moved outside the South, where urban communities were misleadingly portrayed as destroying themselves. The Watts uprising became the iconic moment when the civil rights movement "moved north." As Theoharis points out, in historical memory Watts often "serves as the introduction to the northern racial landscape, the dividing line between the heroic southern freedom struggle and the civil rights movement's militant and northward turn."[151] These narratives of a southern movement shifting northward rupture the historical continuities in the turn from civil rights to Black Power. The organizing of the Emergency Committee in the early 1960s was apparent in the activism following the Harlem uprising. Likewise, networks established during Black united front efforts in Los Angeles after Ronald Stokes's murder were activated after Watts. The state used narratives of aberration, disorganization, and spontaneity to characterize these revolts and blamed communities of color as pathological sources of crime and disorder. Yet the NOI's organizing before, during, and after these uprisings suggests a continuity of resistance that disrupts justifications of force and the construction of a more expansive carceral state.

CHAPTER FIVE

The State the State Produced

> One day I was sent to Segregation for a fight, year later they asked
> me if I wanted to go to inmate population, I said no, I like it in the
> box and most of the followers of Hon. Elijah Muhammad was
> there. . . . I may not have any constitutional rights, but let me
> tell you I have Islam. "Allah is the greatest." I have no fear.
>
> —GILBERT SPRINGER TO GOVERNOR NELSON ROCKEFELLER,
>   January 28, 1967

On February 21, 1965, Malcolm X was assassinated at the Audubon Ballroom in the Washington Heights neighborhood of New York City. He was set to unveil the new program of the Organization of Afro-American Unity (OAAU), the revolutionary Pan-Africanist organization he helped organize after leaving the Nation of Islam the year before. There was a disturbance as a man in the audience yelled "get your hands out of my pockets!" As the crowd's attention shifted to this diversion, another man sitting in the first row stood up and shot Malcolm at close range with a sawed-off shotgun. In a full-page spread in *Life* magazine called "The Violent End of the Man Called Malcolm X," three photographs document the frantic scene immediately following.[1] The photos display Malcolm's shirt torn open, bullet wounds clearly visible, a different person huddled over him in each photo. In one, it is his wife, Betty Shabazz. Another features OAAU member Yuri Kochiyama. The last shows a man known affectionately within the organization as "Brother Gene" attempting mouth-to-mouth resuscitation. Gene Roberts was one of Malcolm's bodyguards—but he was also an undercover police officer with the NYPD's BOSS.[2]

Only one of the conspirators, Talmadge Hayer, was detained at the scene of the crime. Yet some eyewitnesses recalled a second person being arrested that day. OAAU Liberation School teacher Herman Ferguson remembered a police car pulling up alongside the ballroom with a man "obviously in great pain." Thinking that the injured man was one of "our guys," he watched as the cruiser sped away and disappeared across the Hudson River. The Associated Press reported the day after the assassination that "two men were taken into custody."[3] Yet no one at the scene that day besides Hayer was ever brought forth and tried. The NYPD soon arrested two more members of Mosque No. 7 in Harlem: Norman 3X Butler (later Muhammad Abd Al-Aziz) and Thomas 15X Johnson (later Khalil Islam). Both men, with the corroboration of key witnesses who knew them well, denied that they were at the ballroom that day. Yet Hayer was reluctant to exonerate his co-defendants at the 1966 trial by naming other accomplices, and all three were sentenced to life in prison.

Histories of the Nation of Islam are often told through Malcolm's life and thus end with his death in 1965, creating an artificial rupture that walls the NOI off from the larger story of Black Power. Rather than position Malcolm's assassination as an end, this chapter emphasizes the continuities between these evolving forms of Black Nationalism, including what emerged after his split with the NOI. Muslim activism has largely been erased in historical accounts of Black Power, absent from the major uprisings in Harlem (1964), Watts (1965), and Attica (1971) that defined the era. As earlier chapters have documented, the NOI organized and participated in broad-based movements against state violence in all three places where these uprisings occurred. In Harlem just three years before the 1964 revolt, Malcolm X joined the Emergency Committee for Unity on Social and Economic Problems with other community leaders around an agenda to address police brutality, despite their internal contentions. After the murder of Ronald Stokes in Los Angeles, the NOI used the trial to mobilize a united front against police violence. When Watts erupted in 1965, many activists in the local civil rights movement viewed the 1962 police killing as one of its essential preconditions. And at Attica in 1971, where Muslim prisoners had gone on hunger strikes, filled solitary confinement, and launched the first prison litigation movement a decade earlier, many of the key organizers—including Richard 2X Clark and Herbert X Blyden, as well Thomas 15X Johnson—were Muslims in the Nation of Islam. These connections, when noted, have often been mistakenly treated as coincidental rather than foundational.

In most histories of Black Power, as the Black Nationalist, anticolonial, and anticarceral frameworks developed by the NOI throughout the civil rights period shifted from margin to center, the NOI inexplicably recedes from view.[4] But highlighting the continuity between these ideas, formations, and strategies and the period in which they flourished and spread belies state narratives of nihilism, rupture, and disorder, which served to justify further carceral buildup.

In March 1965, the OAAU reconvened for the first time since Malcolm's assassination. According to Kochiyama, the meeting's purpose was to "establish stability from this crisis." A Japanese American whose family was incarcerated in internment camps during World War II, Kochiyama had first met Malcolm at a Congress of Racial Equality (CORE) protest in 1963 and was among the graduates of the OAAU's first and only Liberation School cohort the following year.[5] She regularly took detailed notes of these sessions, and March 6 was no different. Circled at the bottom of the page was the identity of the second man: "Ray Woods is said to have been seen also running out of Audubon; was one of two picked up by police. Was the second person running out."

Although Kochiyama may not have known it then, Woods was likely another undercover BOSS officer named Raymond A. Wood. He had begun his career the year before by infiltrating the Bronx CORE chapter and the Detroit-based Freedom Now Party under the name Ray Woodall. There he posed as a twenty-seven-year-old graduate of Manhattan College studying law at Fordham. He was soon named CORE's housing chairman and oversaw a voter registration project. Wood earned his activist bona fides by getting arrested with two others at city hall while attempting a citizen's arrest of Mayor Wagner for allowing racial discrimination on a public construction project.[6] Tony Bouza a former BOSS lieutenant, recalled that Wood "never set foot in any police installation during the first months of his career as a policemen except as a person to be booked."[7]

By 1965, Wood had been reassigned to infiltrate a group calling itself the Black Liberation Front (BLF). There he was credited with foiling an alleged bomb plot by the BLF that targeted the Statue of Liberty and other national monuments just four days before Malcolm X's assassination. As was typical in these cases, Wood played the role of an agent provocateur, delivering an army field manual on explosives to the group at the request of his police superiors.[8] One of the four arrested in the plot was Walter Bowe, co-chair of the OAAU's culture committee. For his work on the BLF case, Wood was promoted to detective second grade. Although his name and a photo of the back of his head circulated throughout the press in the days leading up to Malcolm X's assassination, the NYPD reported that he was put back to work because his "face is still a secret."[9] Wood's close association with an OAAU member and the Freedom Now Party makes it likely that others at the Audubon that day would have recognized and perhaps named him at the March meeting. Wood and Roberts parlayed their credentials to entrench themselves deeper within the movement.[10] Tony Bouza later wrote that an "undercover agent gains legitimacy and acceptance by drifting in and out of groups that permit evaluation of their intent."[11] Wood went on to infiltrate the Revolutionary Action Movement and both he and Roberts ultimately provided testimony as the state's key witnesses at the Panther 21 trial in 1969–1970.[12]

Talmadge Hayer eventually recanted his testimony implicating Butler and Johnson. Radical attorney William Kunstler, who met Hayer while acting as an official observer during the Attica uprising in 1971, helped persuade him to sign two affidavits in an attempt to reopen the case and try the four accomplices he was now willing to name.[13] Despite this new evidence, those named by Hayer were never tried, and Butler and Johnson remained incarcerated until 1985 and 1987, respectively. Both have always maintained their innocence.

Malcolm X was dead, two Muslim men served decades in prison for a crime they likely did not commit, and the factional war between Malcolm and Muhammad loyalists that had been fomented by law enforcement for years was launched full-scale. It was both a culmination of decades of surveillance and disruption and a foreboding of what was to come — the scaling up of such strategies. Histories of state violence during the Black Power era focus on the development of the FBI's COINTELPRO and its role in infiltrating and destroying groups such as the Black Panther Party in part by fueling internal dissension and exacerbating political disagreements into insoluble conflicts. But the constellation of local, state, and federal law enforcement strategies that constituted COINTELPRO was a coalescence of those that had suppressed Islam in Black communities inside and outside prisons for decades. COINTELPRO is best understood as a refinement, extension, and escalation of a set of state tactics that had been developed to combat the Nation of Islam since its inception. State violence was not new, but it was ascendant.

In the summer of 1964, two weeks after the nation's first stop-and-frisk policing program went into effect in New York City, a Black ninth grader named James Powell was shot and killed by a police officer in front of his classmates in Brooklyn. Students protested and CORE chanted "stop killer cops," demanding a civilian review board, the suspension of Officer Thomas Gilligan, and the resignation of Police Commissioner Patrick Murphy.[14] A week later, Governor Nelson Rockefeller sent the National Guard to quell a rebellion in Rochester, New York, marking the first deployment of federal troops in a northern city since the Civil War. The following summer, the Watts neighborhood of Los Angeles was on fire, under curfew, and invaded and occupied after another case of police violence. Newark and Detroit followed in 1967, and another one hundred cities revolted after Martin Luther

King Jr.'s assassination in 1968. As Elizabeth Hinton points out, these large-scale revolts were part of a more widespread rebellion, which included over two thousand smaller uprisings in almost one thousand cities from the beginning of 1968 until the end of 1972, most of which involved Black residents responding to police violence.[15]

When incarcerated men at Attica revolted in 1971, the state saw it as a continuation of these urban uprisings. Government-appointed commissions tasked with locating the root causes of these rebellions often pointed to deep-seated structural racism but nevertheless argued that these were spontaneous, rather than organized, responses to omnipresent state violence. In U.S. Senate hearings on these types of events in 1967, mayors' reports routinely described "spontaneous" triggers.[16] A 1970 study of 820 urban uprisings between 1961 and 1968 funded by the Office of Economic Opportunity concluded that 341 (42 percent) had "spontaneous" origins.[17] And despite over one thousand prisoners quickly assembling a multiracial coalition with a platform of well-formulated demands, the McKay Commission's report on Attica concluded that the "highly organized inmate society in D block yard developed spontaneously, after a period of chaos."[18]

By framing uprisings as outbursts of nihilism rather than expressions of a longer Black freedom struggle, these reports sought to suggest that state violence in response to them was likewise exceptional.[19] But the previous chapters on Attica, Harlem, and Los Angeles have shown that state violence, and organized resistance to it, was typical, not aberrant. Nikhil Singh has argued that "far from being irrational, inexplicable phenomena, [the uprisings] were the result of well-established patterns and recurrent racial conflict."[20] Orisanmi Burton describes the escalation of prison rebellions as a tactic of "organized disorder."[21] Such ongoing state violence requires an ideological apparatus to legitimize it. Distinctions between legitimate forms of violence (such as capital punishment, police force, and military power) and illegitimate forms (such as looting and organized self-defense, including judo and rifle clubs) provided one discursive ballast for the carceral state. Another was narratives of spontaneous eruption versus sustained political response. Through such narratives, the carceral state justified itself. It was the state the state produced.

The *state* the state produced gestures to both meanings of the word: a set of conditions as well as a political terrain and coalescing of power. The carceral state entered a period of unprecedented expansion built on its own rhetoric of limited state power, which Craig Gilmore and Ruth Wilson Gilmore have termed the "anti-state state." It is constructed on its discursive terms: a state that "*grows* on the *promise* of shrinking."[22] As Wilson Gilmore writes, "We simultaneously make places, things, and selves, although not under conditions of our own choosing."[23] Dan Berger notes that the prison "does not eliminate politics but rather seeks to control its emergence and shape its form."[24]Muslim activists during the Black Power era encountered a carceral state that was not totalizing in its power, but profoundly constricted and shaped their choices as well as our ability to describe them.

In Harlem, Watts, and Attica, Muslims were targeted by law enforcement and a revanchist state using violent reprisals to reestablish territory in jeopardy. In the months leading up to the Harlem rebellion, journalists, politicians, and police attempted to link the rise of a "violent anti-white gang" they called the "Blood Brothers" to the NOI. Amid a moral panic about roving Black teenagers killing whites and speaking Arabic, the New York Police Department was granted its most extensive discretionary power yet.[25] Similarly, in Watts, just as the curfew was lifted and violence had waned, Los Angeles police and the National Guard again raided Mosque No. 27. A hundred police officers descended on the mosque, showering the place of worship with over five hundred rounds. Police found no weapons but nevertheless arrested over fifty Muslims and seized files and membership rolls.[26] And before the uprising at Attica, a group of men calling themselves the Attica Prison Liberation Faction drafted a set of demands known as the July Manifesto. The list drew heavily from a strike at Folsom the previous year and Tombs jail before that.[27] Richard Clark, one of the elected leaders of the Attica rebellion, explained that although "we knew it was gonna happen. . . . we never planned for it."[28] When Attica was retaken, the National Guard tear-gassed prisoners from helicopters before indiscriminately opening fire and killing thirty-three incarcerated men. They then beat, tortured, and humiliated prisoners—Muslims in particular.

As these rebellions demonstrate, the dialectics of discipline between the Nation of Islam and the carceral state endured and expanded in the Black Power era. Black united front organizing against police brutality and multiracial prison activism were foundational before, during, and after the uprisings. And law enforcement and penal regimes responded by drawing on a repertoire of tactics they had cultivated against the NOI. Racist and Islamophobic narratives about violence and "terrorism" legitimized state violence in the form of religio-racial profiling and mosque raids. The traditional use of solitary confinement, good-time-lost practices, and prison transfers was refined through the late 1960s and developed into harsher isolation units and brainwashing, for which Muslim prisoners were the experimental subjects.

Histories of this period that do not mark the longer continuities of dialectical struggle between activists and the carceral state risk reproducing the state's narratives by suggesting that these rebellions marked a decisive shift toward spontaneous violence and urban nihilism, thereby justifying a robust repressive response. While a swelling and violent carceral state was successful in dividing and conquering organizations and caging key activists (many to this day), the dialectical nature of struggle meant that a broader base was politicized and organized alongside it. As organizers in Los Angeles recalled, "The fire had not yet died out and the smoke was still in the air when some of the people of Watts talked about the tomorrow they would build."[29] This final chapter offers a counternarrative through the lens of the Nation of Islam, showing how the rebellions in Harlem, Watts, and Attica grew out of previous coalitional organizing and ultimately mobilized even more people than before.

Harlem

New York Governor Nelson Rockefeller outlined his legislative blueprint in January 1964, affirming his commitment to civil rights legislation while simultaneously promising a "major anti-crime program."[30] Two months later, ignoring the din of civil rights groups denouncing its unconstitutionality, he signed into law the first explicit "stop-and-frisk" policing program in the United States. Street stops and interrogations had long been policing tactics, but Rockefeller's anti-crime bill was the first to officially sanction these practices. The stop-and-frisk policy enabled police to legally detain anyone "reasonably" suspicious and identify and search them, while its "no-knock" policy permitted police with a search warrant to enter a residence without notification. As attorney Paul Zuber joked, "A lot of us folks in Harlem thought that was the law already because they've been doing it that way for years."[31]

Harlem activists and residents mobilized against the bill. The NAACP, CORE, the Harlem Lawyers Association, and the Emergency Committee for Public Schools all opposed it, and two other emergency groups—the Ad Hoc Committee for Fair Police Practice and the Committee on Police-Community Relations—quickly formed to sponsor a protest rally. Another ad hoc group offered free legal counsel to those targeted by the new policies. The New York State Bar Association argued that the legislation likely violated the Fourth and Fourteenth Amendments and suggested that "nowhere in the history of Anglo-Saxon jurisprudence have we so closely approached a police state as in this proposal."[32] The following week, three thousand demonstrators marched on the state capital, including several hundred Puerto Ricans protesting the bill.[33]

Among the groups opposing Rockefeller's proposal was Malcolm X's newly formed Organization of Afro-American Unity. Although the OAAU was not formally unveiled until June 28, 1964—the same week the legislation went into effect—the group had developed through clandestine meetings earlier that year, when Malcolm was still part of the Nation of Islam. Its charter members decided that "immediate action is necessary in Harlem. The 'No Knock' law and police brutality are prime issues." Despite its later reputation for an internationalist vision, the OAAU concluded that it should "start work at [the] local level." Months before the law went into effect, the group determined that "the 'No Knock' law should be the main and immediate project of this organization." Members began training in self-defense and planned to establish public safety committees throughout Harlem. Their action program included setting up a twenty-four-hour hotline for victims of the law, distributing leaflets at rallies, and staging a silent funeral march from 145th to 125th streets, with participants dressed in black carrying a casket symbolizing their "intention to bury" the law.[34]

A grassroots Pan-Africanist organization, the OAAU imagined Harlem as a local model for an internationalist human rights movement.[35] In its earliest stages, charter members decided to choose a concrete issue "that the community is concerned with most and wage a resolute struggle around it—in order to galvanize the masses and raise their level of consciousness."[36] Honing in on the anti-crime bill as the issue capable of mobilizing the community, they focused on political education, reducing the excessive police force in Harlem, and assisting victims of police violence. Anyone in the New York area who had expressed interest in Malcolm X would be informed about the "essentials of the Anti-Negro 'No Knock' and 'Search and Seizure' laws" and "educated to defend those who are arrested resisting" them.[37]

As the OAAU outlined its plan to combat the bill, the mainstream press stoked a moral panic focused on Harlem. On April 17, 1964, teenagers in Harlem who knocked over a fruit stand were brutalized by officers stationed at a special police unit nearby. When a Black bystander intervened, he was beaten so badly he eventually lost an eye. Weeks later, when two white store owners were stabbed and one died, the boys associated with the "Little Fruit Stand Riot" were taken into custody, charged, and eventually convicted of first-degree murder and sentenced to life in prison. Soon after the arrests, the *New York Times* concluded that there was a connection between the "Fruit Stand" boys and what it described as a roving, anti-white gang trained to "maim and kill" white people. Indicating the rapid spread of this panic, the *New York Times* described a gang that was "making traditional street warfare in Harlem obsolete. . . . The new gang has no turf—no territory—to protect, and its target knows no geographical limitations: it is the white man."[38]

The reporting on what became known as the "Blood Brothers" gang borrowed heavily from the discourse of *The Hate That Hate Produced*: false equivalencies with white supremacy, denouncements from mainstream civil rights figures, and desperate attempts to link the group to the NOI. The *Times* reported the emergence of the gang as "chilling news . . . as indefensible as the Ku Klux Klan" and called for the gang to be "firmly repressed by the police."[39] Civil rights leaders such as John Morsell of the NAACP came forth to denounce these "Black racists" for their similarities to white ones: "We have consistently opposed inflammatory denunciations of white people by spokesman for Black Nationalist groups and we have pointed out their similarity to the racist utterances of such Southern segregationists as former Governor Ross Barnett of Mississippi and Governor Wallace of Alabama." While the Nation of Islam had called attention to the similarities between Barnett and Rockefeller by describing prisons in New York as "shades of Mississippi," Morsell pointed those similarities back at the NOI. "Just as we hold that the Barnetts and the Wallaces bear some of the responsibility for the bombings and murders of Negroes by weak-minded white people, so today we find reckless anti-white pronouncements contributing to acts of terror against whites. If there's any sense of responsibility left on the part of either the white or the Black racists, they are under the sternest obligation to stop now," he chided.[40]

DRIVEN BY INTERVIEWS and intelligence from police, journalists went to absurd lengths to link the fictitious Blood Brothers to Malcolm X and the Nation of Islam (largely neglecting their recent split). "Although they do not admit being affiliated with the Black Muslim sect, they greet one another with 'Salaam alekim,'" one article read. Malcolm X's close associate, James 67X Shabazz, was described by one police spokesperson as the gang's "unofficial legal adviser." The group supposedly repeated such phrases as "blue-eyed devils" and "the chickens are coming home to roost."[41] The *New York Times* reporter responsible for "breaking" the Blood Brothers story, Junius Griffin, was later fired by the newspaper.[42] By fall, BOSS had conducted an investigation which determined that "there is no evidence . . . to indicate the presence of any large scale, formally organized, group in existence."[43]

Speaking about the Blood Brothers at the Militant Labor Forum the same day he was interviewed by the FBI (while surreptitiously audiotaping them) about his possible connections with these youths, Malcolm X reflected on the lessons of *The Hate That Hate Produced*:

> I recall in 1959 when everybody began to talk about the Black Muslims. All the Negro leaders said no such group existed. In fact, I recall on the Mike Wallace show, Roy Wilkins was asked about the Black Muslims, he said he'd never heard of it, and then they flashed the picture of him on the screen shaking hands with me.
>
> One of the mistakes that our people make. They are too quick to apologize for something that might exist that the power structure finds deplorable or finds difficult to digest. And without even realizing it we try to prove that it doesn't exist.[44]

Malcolm's statement importantly acknowledged the possibility of multiple truths: that the state fed misinformation to journalists in order to foment white fears and justify carceral expansion, and that there were Black people who were prepared to meet it with revolutionary violence.

The Blood Brothers panic provided cover for an expansive policing infrastructure at the very moment the NYPD had been granted its broadest powers yet. Mayor Wagner allocated an additional $5 million for policing and declared what the *Washington Post* called an "all-out war on roving Negro terrorist gangs" and "hoodlums." More than forty Black undercover police officers were whisked to Harlem, and Commissioner Murphy assigned dozens to investigate the NOI's influence on the Blood Brothers.[45] Marshall England of New York CORE pointed out that this moral panic was "an indication of how far the white press will go to create hysteria" in order to generate "a climate of support for the vastly unpopular 'No Knock' and 'Search-and-Seizure' laws recently enacted by the State Legislature."[46] At a moment when some Black activists were calling for more representation on the Harlem police force, one police official remarked, "It is essentially more Negro undercover men we need at this time."[47] The NYPD appeared willing to recruit Black officers—though this was more often about infiltrating and subverting activist groups than about mitigating against discriminatory policing in Black communities.

That summer, following a week of protests in Harlem and Brooklyn, police, journalists, and civil rights leaders continued to point to the Nation of Islam. Rev. Richard Hildebrand, president of the New York NAACP, blamed Communists and Black Nationalists and named the NOI one of "100 such hate units" in Harlem. A five-month investigation by police and the FBI allegedly revealed what the *Los Angeles Times* called "Red and Racist": "an unholy alliance" of financial support for the NOI by Communists and southern white supremacists.[48] Reporters peddled a discourse of nihilism and criminality, claiming that the climate in Harlem had been poisoned by Malcolm X and "other fringe radicals." Another pair of reporters claimed that activists were now "joined by the Black Muslims and a group of dope-pushers and thugs who cared nothing about political theory, but plenty about the profit to be made in looting." In a list of eight uprisings across the country, one report mentioned the NOI in nearly half, suggesting that although the riots "started spontaneously," the NOI had "created a climate of resentment against authority."[49]

Harlem mobilized in the face of these attacks. Just five days after James Powell was killed, nearly seventy members representing over thirty Harlem organizations gathered at the Upper Manhattan YWCA to form the United Council of Harlem Organizations (Unity Council). Like the Emergency Committee of 1961, it featured a remarkable political breadth, including representatives of the NAACP, the NALC, the Urban League, Harlem Youth Opportunities Unlimited (HARYOU), the Nation of Islam, and a parent-teacher association.[50] Although one journalist proclaimed that "never before have these groups worked together in round-table conference," many of the members of the Unity Council—including its chair, Joseph Overton—had been members of the Emergency Committee. A former president of the local NAACP currently affiliated with the NALC, Overton was described as "acceptable" to ten of the nearly twenty Black Nationalist groups represented.[51] At the group's first public rally, held during the 11th Annual Marcus Garvey Day celebration in Harlem, he praised the Black Nationalist groups associated with the Unity Council and promised that "we will weed out those Blacks who do not know they are Black. We will weed out those Blacks who want to be white. And we will move with unity."[52]

Like the Emergency Committee, the Unity Council originated as a direct community response to police violence. But unlike the debates in the Emergency Committee over the primacy of police brutality or whether to frame it as an issue of "law and order," the council unanimously declared policing its central concern. At its initial four-hour meeting at the YWCA, the group agreed on three principal demands: Gilligan's immediate suspension, the creation of a civilian review board, and an end to the ban on public gatherings and the police occupation of Harlem.[53] Later demands would again focus on the recruitment and hiring of Black police captains in Harlem, leading to

Lloyd Sealy being named the first Black police captain of a Harlem precinct. Much like William Parker's model of police professionalization in Los Angeles, reforms tended to focus narrowly on training programs that, as Commissioner Murphy put it, aimed to ensure that "each and every man on patrol is a public relations man." A "police speakers' unit" was formed to send police into the community, one of the earliest iterations of what would become known as "community policing." Still, calls for a civilian review board remained unanswered.[54]

The Unity Council and the Organization of Afro-American Unity both emerged during the summer of 1964 and shared visions of Black unity, self-determination, and community control. OAAU secretary Lynne Shifflett, described by the FBI as "running the OAAU while Malcolm X is in Africa," sent 165 invitations to a roundtable moderated by Ossie Davis and Clarence Jones (attorney for Martin Luther King, Jr.). Among those invited were Overton and the Unity Council. Shifflett described the OAAU's purpose as uniting "Afro-Americans and their organizations around a non-religious, non-sectarian constructive program for human rights."[55] Of the dozen or more who agreed to participate, most were former members of the Emergency Committee, including Anna Arnold Hedgeman, Bayard Rustin, Percy Sutton, Cleveland Robinson, Hope Stevens, and a similar Black Nationalist contingent of Lewis Michaux, James Lawson, Carlos Cooks, and Ed Davis.[56] Yet Shifflett also appeared frustrated that the Unity Council had not invited the OAAU to recent gatherings. She wrote Overton that "it is the understanding of the Organization of Afro-American Unity that all organizations in the community involved in the human rights struggle . . . are at least to be present as observers at all meetings of the Harlem Unity Council." The OAAU had assigned two representatives, which Shifflett refered to in her note: "We do hope that in the future they will be admitted freely to all meetings of the council."[57]

While such tensions recalled similar dynamics that had haunted the Emergency Committee, it was notable that these two coalitions coexisted at all, given the hostile political climate of Malcolm X's departure from Mosque No. 7. Malcolm's life was threatened routinely during his intermittent return visits to the United States, yet OAAU members likely attended Unity Council meetings alongside members of the Nation of Islam. Other developments since the debates within the Emergency Committee suggested the growing influence of the NOI and other Black Nationalists. The fierce debates over "Negro" and "Black" which had played out in the margins of committee proposals and meeting minutes were now being openly discussed. "Black Muslims, for example, object to the word 'Negro,' saying it is a 'slave name' given to the colored man by whites," one article noted. "The council tries to use a vocabulary which will not offend them, or others." Even Reverend Hildebrand admitted being surprised to find common ground with Black Nationalists: "When I sat down at the first meeting with the leaders of the more extreme groups—nationalists, Muslims, and so on—I realize that I had grown aloof from them. . . . When I began talking with them, I found many of them with good minds, discussing the issues calmly and sensibly."[58]

The most notable development was that the Unity Council defined itself in explicit opposition to singular charismatic leadership and espoused coalitional politics instead. Its strength was its religious and political diversity. As one founder, Livingston Wingate of HARYOU–ACT, explained: with Malcolm X and Adam Clayton Powell both absent during the uprising, the "Council was formed to step into this leadership vacuum." Overton declared that the "day has gone when any one Negro can, by the sheer force of his example, lift up the Negro people. . . . We need organization, planning, groups of Negro leaders working together."[59] In this way, the Unity Council reflected both the Emergency Committee and the unity rallies that Malcolm X and the NOI organized after the committee's dissolution in 1962.[60] Even the council's guiding principle, "responsible militancy," attempted to bridge this political divide. After a delegation met with Mayor Wagner at Gracie Mansion, one delegate emphasized that this was the first time the mayor had met "such a diversified representation from the Harlem community."[61] Yet when asked if he would continue to meet with the group, Wagner joked: "I don't know how long this council will hold together."[62]

The OAAU was notably led by Black women in Malcolm X's absence. A month after its public debut, the group was described by the FBI as having "six women and one man" working at its headquarters in the Hotel Theresa.[63] Lynne Shifflett was executive secretary; former schoolteacher and NOI member Ethel Minor was secretary; Sara Mitchell was in charge of membership; and Nanny Bowe, who had been a member of the group On Guard for Freedom, chaired the cultural committee.[64] Artists such as novelist Paule Marshall, singer Abbey Lincoln, and children's author (and Shifflett's college roommate) Muriel Gray contributed to its cultural wing. Maya Angelou had returned from Ghana with plans to move to New York and begin her work with the OAAU just days before Malcolm X was assassinated.[65] Yet while the Unity Council had replaced singular with collective leadership, it still failed to afford women equal representation in leadership positions. The same few women invited to participate in the Emergency Committee—Anna Arnold Hedgeman and Cora Walker in particular—were again enlisted as a small minority in the Unity Council. Nonetheless, as James Farmer reflected, however "shaky and ultimately ineffective the Council may turn out to be, the very nature of the attempt is significant."[66] Like the preceding attempts at creating broad Black united front coalitions in Harlem and Los Angeles, the success of the Unity Council may not have rested in its longevity but in the experiment itself.

Watts

On August 11, 1965, Marquette Frye and his brother Ronald were pulled over for suspected drunk driving. As the two brothers and their mother were beaten by California highway patrolmen, bystanders began throwing rocks and bottles at the officers. Over the next six days, a nearly fifty-square-mile area would erupt and be invaded by the National Guard and placed under curfew. By the time it was over, thirty-four people were killed, a thousand were injured, and four thousand were arrested. White observers feigned shock and expressed outrage. California governor Edmund Brown claimed, "Nobody told me there was an explosive situation in Los Angeles." But those in Watts were less surprised. Between 1962 and the time of the uprising, police had killed sixty African Americans; twenty-five were unarmed, and twenty-seven were shot in the back.[67] In a 1967 survey, 70 percent of Black respondents believed police brutality to be a cause of the uprising, compared to fewer than 20 percent of white respondents.[68] As Ruth Wilson Gilmore argues, the "Watts Rebellion was a conscious enactment of opposition (even if 'spontaneous' in a Leninist sense) to inequality in Los Angeles, where everyday apartheid was forcibly renewed by police under the unabashedly white supremacist Chief William Parker."[69]

Many traced the accumulating grievances and precipitating events back to the police murder of Ronald Stokes two years earlier. To many activists, Stokes was a martyr. The dedication in the first issue of the Berkeley-based Black radical journal *Soulbook* positioned Stokes alongside assassinated anticolonial Black freedom fighters such as Félix-Roland Moumié, Ruben Um Nyobé, Medgar Evers, and Patrice Lumumba.[70] Ruth Robinson, a Black teacher and victim of police violence who had unsuccessfully tried to sue the city for years, recalled joining the fight in 1962 after Stokes was killed. "I became a member of the Citizens Protest Committee and we tried in every way to do something about police malpractice." Like others, she felt that the Watts uprising could have been prevented if the city had responded to their recommendations.[71] Journalists also pointed to the 1963 report by the California Advisory Committee (CAC) to the U.S. Commission on Civil Rights as offering an essential explanation of what later happened in Watts. Largely ignored when it was published, it was now hailed as "required reading. . . . Anyone who reads this two-year-old civil rights document in the backdrop of the ugly recent riots will, we guarantee, be angered at the 'all's well with us' attitude of petty politicians."[72]

But Chief Parker and other state officials pointed to these continuities as proof that the Nation of Islam was again responsible for urban unrest. In April, the California attorney general released a report titled *Para-Military Organizations in California*, which listed the Nation of Islam alongside white supremacist and right-wing terrorist organizations such as the Minutemen, the California Rangers, the National States Rights Party, and the American Nazi Party. It cited the murder of Ronald Stokes and the police beating of Johnson Hinton in New York as "samplings [which] serve to illustrate the highly explosive emotional level to which the Muslims are keyed." Mobilizing state narratives about the use of Islam as a duplicitous garb to mask "deep racial hatreds," it charged that the NOI "combines religious fervor with race hatred in generating fanaticism in the most extreme degree." The Nation of Islam was considered a "continuing source of concern to the law enforcement agencies of this state," one which posed "a potential, present and future danger."[73] The LAPD continued to surveil those distributing the NOI newspaper. In May 1965, the Board of Police Commissioners met to discuss an eight-minute film gathered by officers "surreptitiously photographing" the FOI selling *Muhammad Speaks*.[74]

With Watts still under curfew and occupied by the National Guard, on Sunday, August 15, the LAPD would receive word of one of its greatest fears. Marquette Frye—one of the victims of police violence whose beating set off the rebellion—appeared as a guest speaker at Mosque No. 27. Although John Shabazz denied that Frye was Muslim, he described his appearance as "part of a general awakening."[75] The joining of the NOI with the most visible figure in the Watts uprising so alarmed local authorities that news of the meeting quickly made its way to the White House and Attorney General Ramsey Clark.[76] A day later, a spokesperson for Chief Parker suggested that although the department had been too busy quelling violence to investigate the causes of the uprising, "there are several things which point very definitely to Black Muslim participation." One piece of evidence cited was the cover of *Muhammad Speaks*, which read "Stop Police Brutality!" Another was a radio statement by a Muslim that asserted that "this is war and all Black men should rally." Police believed their calls were being intercepted and conveyed over walkie-talkies, although there was no mention of NOI involvement in that spying operation.[77] On August 17, Minister John Shabazz described the uprising as war and linked it to the violence in Vietnam, with the "Black man being an Asiatic, fighting an Asiatic war."[78]

It did not take long for the LAPD to retaliate. The morning after Frye's appearance, just after midnight, an unidentified caller reported weapons being carried into 5606 South Broadway. Police radios across Los Angeles were advised that this was the address of the Muslim mosque, and more than twenty police cruisers soon arrived. Officers reported "flashes" of gunfire from the second floor before riddling the building with over five hundred rounds of ammunition, while National Guardsmen threw tear gas into sewers they believed to be escape routes. Officers then arrested nineteen Muslims, four of whom later needed medical care for scalp lacerations (no police were injured). A police sergeant proudly announced that the mosque looks "like a Swiss cheese."[79] Although police found no guns, ejected casings, secret exits, or hidden passageways, they eventually arrested over fifty Muslims on charges of suspicion of assault to commit murder and suspicion of conspiracy.[80] Three of the men arrested—Troy Augustine, Clarence Jingles, and Robert Rogers—had already been beaten and tried in the 1963 case of *People v. Buice*.[81]

The event was a familiar mix of police violence, confiscation, and surveillance. In photographs taken at the scene, one officer held up a bloodied Muslim star and crescent flag, and another smugly sported a confiscated Elijah Muhammad button pinned to his uniform. A third photograph showed an officer posed with a shotgun in one hand and *Muhammad Speaks* in the other.[82] The evening ended in the burning of the mosque after police had removed its membership rolls. Around 2:00 A.M., the fire department received a call that the mosque was on fire; a second was reported at 2:42 A.M. An investigative report by Councilman Billy Mills determined that the incendiary device would have had to "travel through a window, across a room, over a hallway, into the center of another room, change direction, and land against the east wall with no fire evidence left in its wake" to reconcile the contradictory police accounts of the fire. Since law enforcement officers were the only ones inside the building and had it completely surrounded, this raised "a damaging question."

Mills's report concluded that the invasion was an "unwarranted, unjustified, and irresponsible use of police power."[83] Robert Reynolds, one of the officers involved in the 1962 shooting, later described it as "stupid" and confirmed it was based on the belief that the NOI was trying to "organize *all* the

LAPD officer holds a bloodied star and crescent flag following the August 18, 1965, raid on Mosque No. 27. Herald Examiner Collection, Los Angeles Public Library.

Black radicals."[84] In 1971, a former informant for the LAPD who also infiltrated the Black Panthers revealed that he had made the anonymous phone call about weapons being loaded into the mosque.[85] "The police department came to the conclusion that the Black Muslims 'were getting too big, too powerful,'" Louis Tackwood later confessed. He called on behalf of the Special Investigation Section in return for immunity from prosecution.[86]

Several weeks after the raid, Elijah Muhammad recorded a statement pleading with Black people across the country to "open your eyes to the brutality of the American police force." As people in Watts were being described in animalistic terms and even characterized by Chief Parker as "monkeys in a zoo," Muhammad inverted this racialized language by denouncing "bloodthirsty white policeman" who came "upon us like swarms of wild beasts from the jungle, and ran in[to] our Mosque shooting down every unarmed Muslim that they met with."[87] He linked this police violence with the growing numbers of Black people in prison, arguing that there was no sense trying to reason with those who are "stamping you under their feet, beating you down in the streets, hauling you into their prison houses all over the country and outright shooting you for nothing."[88]

As in Harlem, Watts activists formed an emergency coalition. The Temporary Alliance of Local Organizations (TALO) described itself as "a confederation—a coalition of many diverse groups who form a functional whole" and reportedly represented a wide range of groups, from "churches to the Communists; Nationalists to the NAACP; social clubs to society matrons."[89] A year before armed Black Panthers began following police in Oakland, TALO launched a volunteer Community Alert Patrol, which monitored police behavior over two-way radios.[90] As with previous coalitions, Black Nationalists—including Ron Karenga and Hakim Jamal—broke with the group the following summer, and it eventually focused largely on reforms directed at police professionalization, such as reviewing police academy curriculum and hiring practices.[91] It is unclear whether, or how deeply, Mosque No. 27 was involved in the united front.

After enduring a decade of mosque raids and the wounding and killing of unarmed Muslims, Elijah Muhammad offered a remarkable concession to police departments across the country through a press release giving them permission to "conduct an orderly search" of any mosque where Muslims are accused of carrying arms.[92] By 1965, police repression and violence against the NOI had grown so pervasive and costly that Elijah Muhammad condoned a practice not unlike the controversial "no-knock" bill in New York in its most sacred space. Unfortunately, this invitation did not stop police from raiding Newark's Mosque No. 25 in December of that year, prompting what *Muhammad Speaks* called an "almost unprecedented unity [of] Black civic, fraternal, religious, and community organizations."[93]

A study conducted by the U.S. Commission on Civil Rights in the aftermath of Stokes's murder had predicted further unrest if police violence remained unaddressed.[94] Loren Miller, who had recused himself as chair of the advisory committee for the report while acting as the NOI's attorney, ominously forecasted a year before Watts that "violence in Los Angeles is inevitable. Nothing can or will be done about it until after the fact."[95] Now he regretted that his "melancholy predictions came true" and only hoped his next prediction would be wrong: that a commission would be appointed and "do no more than damn law enforcement officials and civil rights leaders alike."[96]

Several months later, the advisory committee quipped that Miller was "in error only to the extent that the McCone Commission failed to levy the criticism against Chief Parker which was so obviously called for." Instead, it praised Parker as a "capable Chief who directs an efficient police force that serves well the entire community."[97] Much like the more influential Moynihan Report published that same year, the McCone report placed the onus on Black communities and civil rights leaders rather than on violent policing and intransigent white supremacy.[98] It concluded that no "amount of money, no amount of effort, no amount of training will raise the disadvantaged Negro to the position he seeks and should have within this community—a position of equality—unless he himself shoulders a full share of the responsibility for his own well being." The report neither investigated previous cases of police violence nor made any recommendations to avoid future incidents. The paltry section on law enforcement was subtitled "The Thin Thread," a reference to the "thin blue line" Parker had popularized a decade earlier as the barrier between law and order on one side and chaos on the other. It opined, "Maintenance of law and order is a prerequisite to the enjoyment of freedom in our society. Law enforcement is a critical responsibility of government."[99] The McCone report endorsed the LAPD's decade-and-a-half reign of terror under William Parker. It also revealed how effectively he had created an entire mythology of policing, which was now circling back to protect him.

Loren Miller and the CAC published a searing rebuttal titled "The McCone Commission Report—a Bitter Disappointment."[100] They were shocked by its omission of previous reports, such as their own. Worse still, "We were assured by the McCone Commission that it considered the Muslim Temple episode of substantial significance and that it would treat it fully. Nevertheless, the report of the McCone Commission fails to contain a single word concerning the Muslim Temple incident. This, we do not understand."[101] Yet even from its inception, one of the members of the McCone Commission had publicly stated that he wanted the commission to avoid "extremist" accounts, which he clarified to mean "racists, Muslims, etc."[102] He did, however, want the NOI's influence within the community examined. In other words, the commission hoped to gather intelligence about the NOI and its influence while ignoring the reasons for its standing. Ultimately, Miller's advisory committee concluded that the McCone report "prescribes aspirin where surgery is required."[103]

The only group that was neither disappointed nor shocked by the outcome was the Nation of Islam. Shortly after the McCone Commission was announced, a cartoon in *Muhammad Speaks* satirized a group of white men in overcoats inspecting the rubble of Watts. Two Black women looked on and repeated a variation of the familiar adage: "If you have to ask, you'll never know."

Whether in Harlem or Watts, the state performed a delicate dance in which law enforcement planted stories of spontaneous and disorganized violence capitalized on and fueled by the Nation of Islam. A state-appointed commission would then exclude these "extremist" voices and conclude that a spontaneous trigger had ignited a powder keg of "perceived" discrimination. These narratives emphasized violence, nihilism, and political naiveté in Black communities while asserting the exceptionalism of the state violence that both precipitated and followed such uprisings. As prison uprisings joined urban rebellions by the late 1960s, the state reproduced this formula, all of which came to a head at Attica in the summer of 1971.

Attica

Shortly after the Watts mosque invasion, Robert Buice filed a lawsuit from San Quentin against the state for violating his religious rights; due process and equal protection; and freedom of speech, association, and the press. One of the victims of the 1962 raid on Mosque No. 27 and the defendant named in *The People of California v. Buice*, he was now the plaintiff in *Buice v. The People of California*. The case came on the heels of the U.S. District Court of Illinois's ruling in *Cooper v. Pate*, which finally granted constitutional rights to prisoners, finding that they could legitimately challenge religious discrimination under the Civil Rights Act. By 1974, the Supreme Court had declared no "iron curtain drawn between the Constitution and the prisons of this country."[104] Much of this was due to litigation by the NOI around the constitutional right to religious freedom in prisons.[105]

Yet in New York in 1967, William SaMarion, Thomas Bratcher, Joseph Magette, and James Walker all remained plaintiffs in a Supreme Court hearing. There, Judge William Lawless finally put the state's assertion that the "Black Muslims" were not a legitimate religion to rest. He ruled that Commissioner McGinnis's policies had been "unreasonably and unduly broad so as to effectively exclude all Muslim inmates from the exercise of every religion service" and considered them a "vehicle for suppression of the Black Muslim religion."[106] Also significant, Lawless suggested that the "word 'Muslim' and 'Muslimism' be used without prefixing the word 'Black.'"[107] Five years after hearing Malcolm X and incarcerated plaintiffs testify in *SaMarion v. McGinnis* in Buffalo, the courts finally recognized the Nation of Islam, in the most basic sense, as Muslims.

The years between Harlem and Watts and the Attica rebellion represented one of the most organized periods of prison activism. Formerly incarcerated

Chicano poet Raúl Salinas described 1968–72 as the "prison rebellion years."[108] In part, this shift mirrored the militancy of the Black Power movement outside and its growing attention on the criminal legal system. The editor of *Freedomways*, Jack O'Dell, wrote in 1966 that "one of the most important of all the obligations confronting our Freedom Movement . . . is to mobilize political power sufficient to effect a far-reaching reformation of the prison-system in this country, as well as a revolution in many of the concepts upon which it is founded."[109] The following year, he connected the Vietnam War with "policemanship as a style of government" in cities such as New York and Los Angeles. While slavery used the plantation as the primary mode of confinement, he argued that post-emancipation confinement was defined by the ghetto, which he called the "urban plantation." Now a third form of confinement had emerged to incapacitate and warehouse African Americans: the prison. Loïc Wacquant calls this relationship between urban space and prison a "carceral continuum."[110] But as O'Dell's writings suggest, this was a relationship theorized by activists as it unfolded. Berger points out that the "Black Panthers' dictum to organize the 'brothers on the block' was . . . understood to apply simultaneously to both the cell block and the city block."[111] *Muhammad Speaks* described California's prisons "as if you had taken Harlem or Watts, put a wall around it and erected gun towers outside."[112]

Robert Buice's case illuminates this continuum of policing and confinement. Wrongfully incarcerated after being the victim of police violence in the 1962 raid on Mosque No. 27, he now challenged the carceral state from prison. Perhaps no one better represents the transition in prison organizing during the 1960s than Martin Sostre. Like Eldridge Cleaver and many other incarcerated Muslims, Sostre was forced to choose between Malcolm X and the NOI in 1964. New York prison inspector Richard Woodward described Muslims as "in [a] somewhat confused state," and one prison took the time to distinguish between those who were loyal to Malcolm and those who stuck with Muhammad.[113] Cleaver wrote that the assassination had created a "profound personal crisis in my life and beliefs, as it did for other Muslims."[114] Martin Sostre, whom state police described as a "rabid Muslim," left the NOI.[115]

By the time of Malcolm's assassination in 1965, Sostre had moved to Buffalo. He saved money while working at the Lackawanna steel mill and opened an Afro-Asian bookstore, which acted as a community space for college students and young people in the neighborhood to gather and read books by Robert F. Williams, Malcolm X, and Chairman Mao. He gave out free pamphlets and let people come back every day to sit and read the same book until it was finished. During the 1967 Buffalo uprising, police raided Sostre's bookstore and charged him with narcotics possession, arson, and assault. The state's key witness, who had originally testified that Sostre sold him $15 worth of heroin, eventually signed an affidavit recanting his story and explaining that he had framed Sostre in return for his own freedom. Sostre remained in prison until his sentence was commuted in 1975 by Governor Hugh Carey in response to political pressure from Amnesty International and Martin Sostre Defense Committees throughout the country. Yet during his second prison term, Sostre criticized Muslims as "model prisoners and cooperators. You don't find them in Solitary any more." They were "so alienated from the Black masses, I gave it up."[116]

Although Sostre regarded the NOI as insufficiently radical, the state still saw Muslim prisoners as a threat. By 1964, James Bennett was in his thirty-seventh and final year as director of federal prisons. He described incarcerated Muslims as "much like our former prisoner, Bayard Rustin, now apparently a moving force in the Civil Rights movement."[117] While Muslims had been considered "model prisoners" during World War II, when Rustin waged hunger strikes and dining hall sit-ins, the NOI had fulfilled sociologist Donald Taft's warning to Bennett in 1943 and become "a movement which may be potentially dangerous." During the Black Power era, as prison populations grew younger and predominantly Black and Latinx, the NOI competed with the Black Panthers, the Young Lords, and the Five-Percent Nation (Five Percenters) — a group founded by former NOI student minister Clarence 13X Smith in Harlem in 1964 — for recruits inside.[118]

State surveillance had grown more sophisticated and wide-reaching to accompany this burgeoning political mobilization. The days of Richard Woodward's mimeographed reports on Muslim activity across the country were long gone. Individual wardens intensively monitored incarcerated Muslims. Each warden would report to the commissioner monthly on their correspondence, visitations, disciplinary infractions, and legal actions.[119] One correspondence log noted letters to Mosque No. 2 in Chicago along with non-affiliated mosques in Switzerland, Brooklyn, and Berkeley.[120] In another example of this broadening dragnet, between 1969 and 1970 monthly "Muslim" reports were suddenly renamed "Muslim–Black Panther" reports.[121] Sometimes the two were conflated without missing a beat.[122] Prison surveillance that had monitored Muslims absorbed these new groups into its interpretive frameworks and ever-expanding apparatus.

When Richard 2X emerged as one of the leaders of the Attica rebellion in September 1971, he and other Muslim activists had already helped organize prison uprisings in New York and California the previous fall. As Clark remembered, "The brothers who were in the know feel that Attica started long before September 9." The rebellions and manifestos produced at Folsom and Auburn prisons and Tombs jail in late 1970 laid the groundwork for the notorious uprising at Attica.[123] A criminologist told the McKay Commission, "You might well view Attica as merely a continuation of the Auburn riot. . . . Find out how many prisoners from Auburn were at Attica, and perhaps, how many prisoners from the Tombs riots were in Attica."[124]

Herbert Blyden was instrumental in these uprisings at Tombs in September and October 1970 and became one of the Tombs Seven, charged with over seventy counts, including kidnapping and riot in the first degree.[125] The next month, a work strike including prisoners affiliated with the NOI and Black Panthers was declared in the Auburn yard after their request for a Black Solidarity Day was denied. They briefly took control of the main yard and the PA system, making speeches for six hours before being threatened with an armed assault by state troopers.[126] The prisoners took hostages and drafted a list of demands, including many that were repeated the following year at Attica: courses in Black history, better medical care and sanitary conditions, more Spanish-speaking staff, improved law library and "good time" programs, and protection from reprisals. Yet over one hundred men were eventually placed in solitary confinement, and six faced criminal charges. As Heather Thompson noted, "Word that the Auburn protesters had surrendered peacefully but had still been beaten, placed in segregation, and charged with crimes quickly spread throughout the prisoner grapevine." This communication was facilitated by prison officials themselves, who transferred the Auburn Six to Attica while they were awaiting trial. So, as Commissioner Oswald admitted, "The focus of our anxieties moved from Auburn to Attica."[127]

In the fall of 1970, a group of Black Nationalist organizers at California's San Quentin had begun developing what became known as the Manifesto of Demands and Anti-Oppression Platform. Muslims had been active in the prison for over a decade, and Eldridge Cleaver was once a minister there. The activists were soon transferred to Folsom, where they organized a nineteen-day strike with over two thousand incarcerated men. The Folsom manifesto included twenty-nine demands as well as a fifteen-point prisoners' bill of rights. It became a framework for the future demands at Attica, including the right to organize a labor union within the prison, to maintain sexual relationships with their partners outside, to communicate without censorship, and to obtain legal access and representation.[128] Finally, in July 1971,

Herbert Blyden joined Donald Noble and Carl Jones-El of the Moorish Science Temple, along with Peter Butler and Frank Lott, to form the Attica Liberation Faction and issue the July Manifesto, a list of twenty-eight demands that included religious freedom for incarcerated Muslims.[129]

In the weeks before the Attica uprising, the nearly fifty Muslim men at the prison carried on their normal well-disciplined routines of study and religious practice. Clark recalled that "Islam in prison was study time. . . . Basically, it was reading, which put you at odds with the institution."[130] Much of the literature available may have been ordered through a mail-in catalog from Mosque No. 7 run by the young minister Larry 4X Prescott (also known as Akbar Muhammad). Among the belongings that survived the uprising was a catalog for Books and Things, which specialized in Islamic literature and Black history and included a wide range of books, including the Ali edition of the Qur'an with Arabic text; back issues of *Muhammad Speaks*; books by James Baldwin, Langston Hughes, Richard Wright, Frantz Fanon, W. E. B. Du Bois, and J. A. Rogers; and an entire section of "Marxist Literature."[131]

Scrapbooks confiscated in the aftermath of the rebellion again demonstrated the countersurveillance and monitoring of the state in order to protect incarcerated Muslims from repression. Richard Clark's role as lieutenant captain was described as serving "security, investigation and intelligence."[132] The mosque secretary was responsible for bimonthly reports on lecture discussions, individual profile cards, accurate copies of lessons, and biweekly reports given by the FOI assistant secretary in each of the prison's four blocks.[133] A page titled "Orientation Class" emphasized the following: "We are taught in a military way and must act like a soldier, which instills discipline."[134] Henry X described the Fruit of Islam as an army "ready to fight when it is organized, equipped and trained. . . . Training in discipline is the most important phase of training, this is required by constant drilling; this forms the habit of obedience."[135]

The day after George Jackson was murdered in California, Minister Louis Farrakhan visited Attica and spoke to incarcerated Muslims on the theme "The Fall of America."[136] Although only sparse notes likely taken by the mosque secretary remain, the phrases "as thou has done, so shall it be done unto you" and "Babylon, the Great, is Fallen" sketched on a notepad were ominous reminders of the Nation of Islam's eschatology that judgement was imminent and the end of white supremacist rule was near. Just weeks later, many of the same men helped outline the first six demands of the rebellion, one of which was the presence of outside negotiators, including

Minister Farrakhan and Joe Walker of *Muhammad Speaks* newspaper.[137] The morning the rebellion began, Clark frantically searched the yard for ministers Norman X Butler and Thomas X Johnson in D block (Clark was in A) to receive instructions.[138] Blyden recalled pandemonium in the yard. "Looking at this madhouse, we had to put an end to it by bringing the Muslim piece into play and, setting up the negotiating table with a clearer head." About thirty-five Muslims formed two circles around the forty-two blindfolded hostages and linked arms.[139] As prison guard Mike Smith remembered, "They were instructed to protect us to the death with their own life."[140] Clark later put it, "We need to organize to let them know that we're civilized and to help ourselves because these people gonna come in here, and they gonna kill us."[141] He found Blyden, Noble, Lott of the Attica Liberation Faction, Mariano Gonzalez of the Young Lords, Tommy Hicks of the Panthers, and Sam Melville of the Weathermen gathered at a central table. They decided to hold an election whereby two men from each block would represent the entire group in D yard. Clark was elected for A block and Blyden from B block.

The process of building a list of demands was also democratic. As proposals were yelled out, votes were tabulated by "the [decibel] point or the octave of the voices of the yard, the brothers in the yard, yea or nay." A list that had swelled to almost fifty demands was eventually narrowed to thirty-two.[142] These were then condensed into fifteen "practical proposals," many of which reflected Muslim prison organizing: religious freedom, an end to newspaper censorship and solitary confinement, and a request to "stop feeding us so much pork."[143]

The issue of amnesty was at the center of negotiations between prison officials and the men at Attica. Black assemblyman Arthur Eve, publisher of Buffalo's largest Black newspaper and one of the observers sent in to monitor the process, described how previous organizing informed decisions about amnesty. "These guys were totally together. Some of them had been through the Tombs and Auburn rebellions. They knew that promises were made before and never kept. And that they were punished more than before. And there were reprisals, reprisals, reprisals!"[144]

Still facing charges for his participation in the Tombs rebellion, Blyden explained to D yard the day before the massacre why he would only accept transportation to a "non-imperialist" country. Clemency, he argued, would still mean the death penalty for the two hundred men serving life sentences. "Man, I'm not trying to scare you. All of these things are going to be said and promised on T.V. and you're gonna still die, some of us."[145] Decades later, he recalled feeling that "amnesty on its face meant no more than the emancipation of slaves during Lincoln's days. Just mere words by the White man."[146]

During the rebellion, unity and solidarity prevailed inside. Marco Cisco Solo Jr. sent a message to "all my brothers and sisters in Brooklyn. Please, we must get organized." Another spoke "to the oppressed people all over the world, we have the solution. The solution is unity." John Adrini tied this unity to discipline: "I was in the Marines and not even in the Marines have I ever seen such discipline and such unity." Even one of the prison guards emphasized the unity they saw around him: "White brothers, Black brothers, Puerto Rican brothers, all you people show that you have got yours together. . . . We all wish we could be home. By 'we,' I don't mean 38 of us; I mean all of us, all 1,538 of us."[147] He was describing a multiracial unity not only among prisoners but also between the hostages and those they typically held captive. This solidarity was dangerous. Clark later recalled that before the rebellion, he was not able to walk in the yard with a white person as a member of the Nation of Islam because guards labeled him a racist. But he knew the real reason was "because it's a sign of solidarity, and they didn't want the prisoners to have any kind of sense of solidarity."[148]

As it became clear that Governor Rockefeller would not come to Attica to negotiate, some guards began to recognize that the real violence to fear was not from those holding them hostage but from the state. Mike Smith, a white guard who was being held hostage, told *New York Times* journalist Tom Wicker, who was serving as an observer, that "we are not scared of any of you people," indicating the prisoners. "We know it's not you hurting us, but the people outside, the Governor, the people that elected the Governor and all the people in the United States."[149] After the massacre, the president of the Correction Officers Association in New York acknowledged with shock that Muslim men were responsible for saving hostages' lives. Arthur Eve was exasperated: "I have tried to tell you for two years to let people practice their own religion. And here is a man who is saying that those who believe in the Messenger and the Holy Qur'an have displayed such knowledge and feeling for human life that they in the final analysis did not commit murder."[150]

On Sunday, September 13, a day described by Blyden as a "blue Monday . . . rainy, overcast, damp, just a weird day," the National Guard dropped tear gas on the prison from helicopters flying overhead.[151] Hundreds of New York State Police officers and prison guards armed with rifles and gas masks fired into the smoke and entered the prison. As Thompson remarked, they were "accountable to no one."[152] A total of forty-three people—ten guards and thirty-three prisoners—were killed during the uprising. All but four were killed by the state during the massacre that day. As one incarcerated man said before the attack, "if the lives of the hostages and inmates are lost, in the final analysis it is going to prove that the animals are not in here but the animals are out there running this government and this system." Eve later reflected that they "understood the system and the mentality of the people governing the state better than I did. . . . The credibility of the state and system was exposed by the men at Attica better than it ever has been before."[153] As Martin Sostre wrote from his solitary cell at Auburn, "Attica defrocked the vicious outlaw murderers who were passing themselves off as lawful authorities."[154]

In the aftermath of Attica, incarcerated men suffered the revanchist violence of the state. The Muslim men who had protected hostages from violence throughout the rebellion were now subject to brutal reprisals by other prison guards. In a suit brought by the victims at Attica, which took decades to adjudicate, Muslims testified to being shot, sodomized, forced to run through a gauntlet of officers, and play Russian roulette. Lead plaintiff Herbert Scott Dean (Akil al-Jundi) was shot multiple times, including through his hand, which required sixteen operations to reconstruct. As he watched another Muslim, James Richey, being jabbed in his wounds with rifles, he began to chant in Arabic from his stretcher. Guards then beat him. He was later brought out of his cell, put in a hole at a remote spot of the prison, and tortured for days. An officer taunted that "Allah would not help him." He was eventually released to a hospital. Most of the men reported lifetime struggles with flashbacks, nightmares, and PTSD. As Melvin Dunlop Muhammad put it, "Attica is always there."[155]

Although New York journalist Joe Walker and *Muhammad Speaks* were not represented on the observers' committee, the paper offered some of the most critical and extensive coverage of the rebellion in the months that followed. Walker's seven-page day-by-day account of the uprising was based on extensive interviews with Arthur Eve and marked an important counternarrative to the state's false accusation that prisoners slit guards' throats.[156] The paper reprinted the full demands of the Attica Liberation Faction.[157] Many women used it as a space to memorialize and mourn, to honor victims and relay stories from survivors. Sandra 17X visited her husband Clifford 8X in late September, shortly after he was transferred from Attica, and recounted his story in the paper. She described the leadership of Richard Clark and such details as their five o'clock prayer on the morning of the massacre. "They were doctors, carpenters, peace-makers and guards," she wrote. Clifford interpreted his survival as a sign from Allah that there was "some greater task for me."[158] Others eulogized their lost loved ones. Helen Williams received a terse telegram informing her of her husband's death. Her husband, Alfred, had a photographic memory that helped prisoners write legal challenges, and one relative commented that it was "like he had finally found himself" through his work as a "jailhouse lawyer." Brenda West believed that her husband had "found so much inner peace. . . . They knew that they were going to die, but they were willing to die, I would imagine, for all the people of the world." The lesson she took from the uprising was "unity and love of one another that the brothers demonstrated there."[159] Prisoners who could not access the paper directly used *Muhammad Speaks* as a conduit to the world outside.[160] Herbert Blyden sent a letter to Joe Walker through the ACLU on behalf of the men at Attica, calling the massacre "My Lai Two" and drawing attention to proposals to construct a prison for experimentation in "behavioral technology."[161]

The year after Attica, the editorial staff at *Muhammad Speaks* announced a new weekly column, "Prison News in Black," which consolidated many of these threads of testimony, advocacy, and policy reform efforts. Journalist Samuel 17X promised that the column would keep readers abreast of specific cases of abuses against Black prisoners as well as their civil suits and organizing: "We will run excerpts from various court cases affecting Muslim and other inmates. We will also carry writings from inmates around the country." Interest in the column was so strong, he warned, that space limitations would mean "many times we will only be able to run excerpts from inmate writings."[162] The section also acted as a legal resource. Some articles cited legal precedents at length, listing the various cases that appealed to the First Amendment's right of religious freedom and the Eighth Amendment's guarantees against cruel and unusual punishment.[163] "Prison News in Black" formalized the newspaper's commitment to the voices and struggles of incarcerated people. While other prison newsletters sometimes offered more radical critiques of the prison, *Muhammad Speaks* became the most widely circulated outlet for the writings of Black prisoners during the 1970s.

Meanwhile, the McKay Report on the Attica uprising followed the script of other state narratives following urban rebellions by distilling years of organized political resistance to state violence into "a spontaneous burst of violent anger . . . [that] was not planned or organized in advance."[164] But those such as Sostre recognized that the rebellion was an expression of a longer tradition of radical prison organizing to which he had been instrumental, tracing a direct line from late-1950s Muslim prison litigation to the Attica rebellion. The "struggle to exercise a First Amendment 'preferred' right (freedom of religion) took from 1958 till 1971, thirteen years of torture, suffering and death at the hands of racist outlaw savages who recognize no law except that of force, violence and murder."[165] He located the origins of this movement in a "six-year spiritual, physical and legal struggle led by three determined prisoners . . . [that] commenced in Clinton Prison during 1958." Just as state commissions on urban rebellions and prison uprisings papered over the deeper roots of everyday violence and resistance, the revanchism of the state—whether police in Watts or prison guards at Attica—demonstrated its capacity for violent reprisals with impunity, especially against Muslims. The Nation of Islam had not disappeared in prisons and Black communities during the Black Power era, nor had the state that opposed it.

AT THE FIRST annual meeting of the American Correctional Association after the Attica uprising, an audience of penologists, criminologists, wardens, and chaplains packed into a room to hear a panel on "a topic which causes deep concern and alarm": the rise of the "political prisoner."[166] One panelist charged prisoners with using the term too loosely. Another suggested providing remedies in prisons that would preempt such prisoners from developing. Yet they all acknowledged the dramatic changes that had taken place in prison demographics over the last decade and readily cited names like Angela Davis and Eldridge Cleaver, who, along with "too many other unknown John Browns and Jane Does," had ushered in this new radicalism.[167]

At the same time, locked in solitary confinement at Auburn State Prison, Martin Sostre was theorizing this "new prisoner." "Do you not see that we've converted your prison camps into revolutionary training camps for cadres of the Black liberation struggle?" he warned. "More important, your prisons have become ideological crucibles and battle grounds. Soon you shall reap the harvest."[168] The conversion of prisons into revolutionary schools recalled the Muslim strategy of taking over solitary confinement, a larger repurposing of the site and the tools of repression into spaces and weapons of resistance.

Sostre declared that "we are all political prisoners regardless of the crimes invoked by white racist oppressors to legitimize their kidnapping us from the ghettos and torturing us in their cages."[169] Despite being added to Amnesty International's "prisoner of conscience" list after Justice Constance Motley ruled that he had been punished "not because of any serious infraction of the rules of prison discipline but for legal and political activities and beliefs," Sostre traced a longer trajectory of activism, which had shifted from the politic*ized* prisoner to the political prisoner.[170] The idea that all Black and brown prisoners were political prisoners was widespread, and endorsed by the NOI as well.[171] In a letter to the editor published in *Muhammad Speaks*, Brother Al Morris wrote that George Jackson's death shows that "America itself is a prison and we Black people are the prisoners."[172] Although, or perhaps because, they were the most narrowly and forcibly confined, incarcerated people were crucial to theorizing the widest extent of Black confinement. As Sostre reasoned, the country was a minimum-security prison; those inside were simply under maximum security.[173]

By this definition, Malcolm X's convicted killers—Norman 3X Butler, Thomas 15X Johnson, and Talmadge Hayer—were also political prisoners. Some might consider such a judgment fraught political terrain. Yet these contradictions have much to tell us about the nature and form of state violence. At its heart is the difficulty of capturing the relationship of the oppressed to their oppressor, of state violence to its subjects, through the terminology generally ascribed as "justice." The prison files of Thomas Johnson, Norman Butler, and Thomas Hayer contained mug shots and notes emphasizing that they had killed Malcolm X. But innocence and guilt are fictions of the state, which shield its culpability. What is at stake is not individual condemnation or redemption but our understanding of the conditions of struggle. As Marx wrote: "Men make their own history, but they do not make it as they please; they do not make it under self-selected circumstances, but under circumstances existing already, given and transmitted from the past. The tradition of all dead generations weighs like a nightmare on the brains of the living."[174] Just as history acts as an invisible motor of the present, the state shapes and obscures the terrain of struggle and our ability to describe and respond to its outcomes in ways both glaring and ghostly.

Through Malcolm X's assassination, the carceral state forcibly and dramatically intervened in the lives of countless people. It also transformed the course of the Black freedom movement at a critical juncture in the ascent of Black Power. Stories in the aftermath of Malcolm's death emphasized what has now become a familiar trope in shielding the violence of the state from scrutiny: "Black-on-Black" violence. Journalists' ambivalent eulogies for Malcolm reiterated a moralistic "live by the sword, die by the sword" narrative. Headlines like "Malcolm X Lived in Two Worlds, White and Black, Both Bitter" and "Malcolm Fought for Top Power in Muslim Movement, and Lost" emphasized internecine violence without investigating its causes.[175] Civil rights leaders distanced themselves even further from Malcolm in death than

Mug shot of Thomas 15X Johnson (later Khalil Islam). On the back is a note that he "killed Malcom [*sic*] X." Such notes were often attached to the files and photos of Johnson, Talmadge Hayer, and Norman Butler. Box 47, Non-Criminal Investigation Case Files (NCICF), New York State, Division of State Police, New York State Archives.

in life. Even Elijah Muhammad chimed in that "Malcolm X got just what he preached." Such narratives cemented Malcolm as a violent figure while masking the violence of the state. Self-defense "by any means necessary" was conflated with the sorts of fictitious unprovoked, violent attacks of the "Blood Brothers" gang or the BLF bomb plot that pervaded the press. Yet at the same time, other acts of state violence in Harlem, Watts, and Attica were legitimized. Malcolm's assassination was presented through the discourse of a fatal fight between street gangs in the ghetto. Deaths that should have implicated law enforcement were used to evidence stereotypes about inherent Black violence and criminality.

The same story was told about urban rebellions: narratives of rampant "crime" and of Black communities destroying themselves obfuscated state violence. Elizabeth Hinton points out that "a proper understanding of sixties-era urban rebellion depends on our ability to interpret it not as a wave of criminality, but as a period of sustained political violence."[176] In Harlem, Watts, and Attica, the violence of the carceral state was laid bare. Its otherwise quotidian nature was now belied by its exceptional visibility. But the commission reports that followed emphasized spontaneity, violence, and rupture over organizing, self-defense, and continuity. By ignoring the longevity of social movement organizing and its ideas as well as the fundamental violence of policing and prisons, investigations of the uprisings licensed further carceral growth in response to rebellion misperceived — or misrepresented — as nihilism and political naiveté.

Yet Black Nationalist organizing resisted and escaped the totalizing coercive power of the state in the sites of its greatest violence: the prison and the "urban plantation." Berger reminds us that "the prison cannot be victorious because walls, bars and guards cannot conquer or hold down an idea."[177] Dialectics are ongoing and therefore never won or lost; out of these struggles new questions and possibilities are created. The prison continued to develop as a mode of Black confinement, and police and prison guards remained the unrepentant foot soldiers of the carceral state. But the anti-imperialist, antiracist, and anticarceral organizing of the Nation of Islam acted as a crucial challenge to the state. Organizations are never static. They are always waxing and waning, shifting and changing with the influx of new people and ideas. But it is not organizations, but organizing, that creates opportunities for collaborative thinking and collective action. It is through that dynamic process that we can best understand the legacy of the Nation of Islam to the Black freedom movement.

Epilogue

On July 8, 2016, the Dallas Police Department's SWAT team used a remote controlled robot with a bomb attached to kill Micah Johnson, who had just murdered five Dallas police officers in retaliation for ongoing police violence against African Americans. Less than two weeks later, Gavin Long was immediately killed after fatally shooting three officers in Baton Rouge on the same street where African-American Muslim activist Blair Imani and members of the New Black Panther Party had protested after the killing of Alton Sterling. That year, according to the *Guardian*, at least one thousand and ninety-three people were killed by police. Two hundred and sixty-six were Black, twice their representation in the U.S. population.[1] Johnson's death marked the first lethal use of a robot by police, although similar robots have also been used in endless wars against predominantly Muslim countries over the last decade.[2] For many, this raised new ethical and moral questions while marking ominous possibilities for techno-policing.[3] But the Johnson and Long cases were as deeply rooted in the past as they were signs of a dystopic future.

News outlets immediately gravitated to Johnson's middle initial, X, to suggest a possible affiliation with the Nation of Islam. One newspaper went as far as to state that he was "named after Malcolm X."[4] In fact, his middle name was Xavier. Despite Long's insistence that he was not associated with any movement, commentators linked him to the NOI, the Moorish Science Temple, and the Washitaw Nation based on previous statements he had made on YouTube. The Southern Poverty Law Center (SPLC) cited pages Johnson liked on Facebook to connect him with organizations it classifies as "Black separatist hate groups," including the NOI.[5] Soon, several of the families of the officers killed filed lawsuits against groups ranging from Black Lives Matter to the Nation of Islam asking for damages and citing these alleged connections.[6] Less than a year later, the FBI's Counterterrorism Division disseminated a memo to local and federal law enforcement that used Johnson and Long as evidence of the rise of a "Black Identity Extremist (BIE) movement."[7] Here, just as Black Nationalism had been portrayed as *The Hate That Hate Produced*, Black identity was framed as necessarily anti-white, extremist, and violent.

Just five days after the FBI circulated the memo internally, the SPLC published an article titled "Return of the Violent Black Nationalist," indicating that the story may have been sourced from the very same memo, or government sources familiar with it.[8] In fact, its author Daryl Johnson was a former high-ranking official in the Department for Homeland Security.[9] Like the FBI, the article categorized these men as part of a broader movement, often conflating Black Nationalism with terrorism and white supremacy. While Johnson noted that Black Nationalism is "categorically different than white nationalism," he cited more equivalencies than differences. For example, he characterized Black Nationalists' demand for a separate state as "similar to white nationalists who argue for a white homeland in the Pacific Northwest." He also described Black Nationalism's appeal in prisons as part of an effort to "recruit inmates into their extremist cause." Both the FBI and the SPLC located the origins of the so-called rise of Black extremism today in the 1960s and 1970s. Yet the real historical continuity was the natural collaboration between liberal think tanks, media outlets, and law enforcement to stoke public fears and justify the surveillance and repression of Black dissent.

For surveilled and over-policed communities, the leaked FBI memo quickly became regarded as "COINTELPRO 2.0."[10] Like terms such as "Black supremacy" and "Black hate," which had little salience prior to *The Hate That Hate Produced*, the phrase "Black Identity Extremists" was created almost out of thin air. *Foreign Policy* reported in October 2017 that only five instances of the term showed up online, all beginning with the memo that August. As one former official with the Department of Homeland Security acknowledged, "This is a new umbrella designation that has no basis."[11] Both false equivalencies and the information sharing between law enforcement and journalists recall *The Hate That Hate Produced* and other portrayals of the Nation of Islam during the 1960s. As Mike Wallace later remembered, the very meaning of the documentary was "there is hate, hatred, suspicion, whatever, *on both sides*."[12] President Donald Trump famously used this equivalency to conflate antiracist protestors and Nazis in Charlottesville, Virginia in 2017.[13]

Of course, as Malcolm X pointed out just weeks before his death, white people's accusations of hate and violence were designed to mask their own role as purveyors of both. "He won't say he didn't do it, because he can't. But he'll accuse you of teaching hate just because you begin to spell out what he did to you."[14] Despite the fact that domestic white supremacists pose the largest terrorist threat, international terrorism is prosecuted more vigorously and the demonizing rhetoric of "radical Islam" pervades our public discourse.

A review by the *Intercept* revealed that "the Justice Department applied anti-terrorism laws against only 34 of the 268 right-wing extremists prosecuted for such crimes in federal court since 9/11. In the same period, they used those laws against more than 500 alleged international terrorists."[15] The Anti-Defamation League also found that despite the focus on "Islamic extremism" by pundits and politicians, right-wing terrorism and violence accounted for seventy percent of politically inspired murders from 2007 to 2017.[16]

Conflations between Black Nationalism and white supremacy target Black activism while shielding the state from scrutiny. In 2011, Manning Marable's biography of Malcolm X named the assassins alleged in Talmadge Hayer's 1977 and 1978 affidavits and reinvigorated calls to reopen the case.[17] The Department of Justice declined, responding that the "matter does not implicate federal interests sufficient to necessitate the use of scarce federal investigative resources into a matter for which there can be no federal criminal prosecution."[18] One possible remaining avenue for reopening the investigation was the Emmett Till Unsolved Civil Rights Crime Act of 2007 (known colloquially as the Till Bill). When signed into law, the bill was envisioned as a way to address "racial injustices before they become permanent scars on our democracy."[19] It promised sustained, well-funded investigations of "racially-motivated" murders occurring prior to December 31, 1969 and assigned a representative within the Department of Justice and the FBI to work together to identify civil rights era cold cases and lead successful prosecutions, authorizing the Attorney General to assign up to $13.5 million annually. But the Till Act was never a priority for the Justice Department. In fact, the FBI's first step was not to look within its own expansive records, but rather, to ask the SPLC for the names of cold cases from the civil rights era.[20]

A major barrier for reopening Malcolm X's assassination under the Till Bill has been the requirement that the murder be "racially motivated." As the NAACP noted, the Justice Department opened only two cases over a three-year period, but closed 89, many of which were due to a perceived lack of racial motivation (despite the Ku Klux Klan being involved in many).[21] Rather than reopen a case and evaluate whether or not race was a motivating factor, agencies have relied on the original prosecution to determine racial motivation. In the case of Malcolm X, this means understanding the murder as the work of the three men convicted for the crime in 1965. This stands in the face of substantial historical evidence and multiple affidavits by Hayer indicating that four other unprosecuted men were involved. But most importantly, the "racial motivation" clause has not been interpreted to include the motivations of a white supremacist state, which enables the state to disregard the significant role that Black police and FBI informants play in surveilling and infiltrating activist groups. They not only gather evidence and disrupt organizing, but also provide ongoing cover for the state. The racial motivation stipulation of the Till Bill narrowly interprets "civil rights murders" as vigilante white supremacists killing Black people, and thereby shields state culpability. Here, the mobilization of the trope of "Black-on-Black" violence, whose emergence David Wilson traces to the 1980s, extends both back to the assassination of Malcolm X and forward to more recent attempts to reopen it.[22] It justifies over-policing while deflecting blame from structural causes and state forces. Nowhere is this more manifest than in the rise of mass incarceration.

In 2016 and 2018, tens of thousands of incarcerated people across the country launched widespread work stoppages on the anniversary of the Attica uprising.[23] Their demands were a mix of broad calls such as the "end to prison slavery" and more specific policy measures such as the repeal of the Prison Litigation Reform Act (PLRA). They echoed many of the demands of the 1971 rebellion at Attica, as well as the struggles begun there by Muslim prisoners a decade earlier. The PLRA in particular repealed the gains initiated by the Nation of Islam's organizing. Signed into law by President Bill Clinton in 1996, it required that prisoners exhaust all remedies through intra-prison administrative means before accessing the courts. It signaled a return to the "hands-off" era that had protected prison from the judiciary for nearly a century prior to the organized prison litigation of Muslims during the 1950s and 1960s. In the year after the passage of the PLRA, as the jail and prison population soared above 1.6 million, the number of civil rights filings by incarcerated people dropped by almost half: from nearly 40,000 to slightly over 25,000. It continued to decline over the next decade as the incarcerated population swelled to exceed 2.2 million. Margo Schlanger documents filings per 1000 prisoners dropping from 24.6 the year before the law to 9.6 in 2007.[24] In addition to rolling back prisoners' access to the courts, the PLRA's distinction between worthy and unworthy suits echoes the state's condemnation of the religious sincerity and political legitimacy of grievances brought forth by incarcerated Muslims in the Nation of Islam.

In 2017, Amna Akbar and Jeanne Theoharis urged us to understand the Islamophobia of Donald Trump's Muslim ban in the context of national security infrastructure assembled during the previous Bush and Obama administrations, underscoring the "widespread surveillance of Muslim life and politics; paradigms of preemptive prosecution and radicalization enabled by capacious material support bans to root out would-be terrorists; the use of inhumane conditions of confinement and secret evidence that defendants are precluded from seeing before trial; and targeted assassinations."[25] They also pointed to the rationale embedded in arguments to close Guantánamo Bay, which have "often been predicated on the idea that the offshore base is an exception to the fairness of our domestic legal process." But nearly all of these conditions apply to cases documented in this book as the state responded to the growth of the Nation of Islam in the immediate pre- and postwar United States. Torturing Muslim political prisoners by putting them in solitary confinement without due process has been a central feature of the carceral state since the Second World War. The now obligatory denunciations of Louis Farrakhan demanded by white liberals of Black and Muslim communities which has become a staple of modern politics, was forged during the heart of the Cold War as the Nation of Islam became one of the first Black American groups to denounce Israel as a settler colonial state.[26]

As Detroit activists and philosophers Grace and Jimmy Boggs emphasized, "revolution and counter-revolution both involve social upheaval, but they are not equal opposites." While revolution anticipates and builds the future, counter-revolution is aimed at maintaining the present and restoring a mythic past. Counter-revolution is thus "invariably anti-historical," in that it obfuscates struggles for power and coercion by the state to create a new social order shrouded in historical mythology.[27] Many of the themes of this book conjure post–civil rights, post–9/11, and contemporary social justice struggles. The organizing against policing and prisons sometimes described as the "civil rights movement of our time" has been a crucial, although often forgotten, tradition of Black political struggle. Its erasure is due in part to the anti-historical nature of counter-revolution. But it also reveals the deep contestation within Black freedom movements over the primacy and urgency of such organizing.

In late 1949, Malcolm X took the stage at Norfolk Prison Colony as the second speaker in a debate on the "Abolishment of Capital Punishment." He delivered this opening line: "the whole history of penology is a refutation of the deterrence theory, yet this theory, that murder by the state can repress murder by individuals, is the eternal war cry for the retention of Capital Punishment."[28] Malcolm never explicitly advocated the abolition of prisons: in his *Autobiography* he wrote, "I am not saying there shouldn't be prisons, but there shouldn't be bars." Yet his support for the abolition of the death penalty gestured toward a foundational fault line running through the history of U.S. penology. Deterrence, he argued, could only be achieved by "mandatory death penalties, almost perfect detective forces, incorruptible police and judiciary, juries unswayed by human emotions and a stern pardoning power." If our criminal legal system did somehow meet these unattainable standards, he concluded, it would "result in such a large number of executions that the defenders of the death penalty would stand aghast." Malcolm X did not describe a criminal legal system which was broken, but one which, if it worked to perfection, would incarcerate and execute unimaginable numbers. That same year, an editorial in the Norfolk Prison newspaper, *The Colony*, predicted that "Prisons in time will be abolished and students will read of our age as we do now of the Dark Ages. Prisons and crime have grown to such proportions that they are now almost out of hand. If allowed to continue at the present rate crime then prisons will soon become one of our top enterprises."[29]

In early 2019, Domineque Hakim Marcelle Ray was executed by the state of Alabama while an imam watched from behind the glass. The U.S. Supreme Court had allowed the execution to move forward over an appeal to determine whether the prison had violated the Establishment Clause of his First Amendment rights in not permitting his spiritual counsel to be present.[30] Surveillance, policing, and incarceration of Muslims—in particular, but not exclusively, those in the Nation of Islam—was a central feature of the carceral state during the Black freedom movement and remains so today. Embodied in the phrase "Those who say don't know, and those who know don't say" was both the historical erasure and epistemic violence of the state on one hand, and the strategic silences of anticarceral and antiracist Muslims on the other. The NOI's challenge to policing and prisons was integral to the twentieth-century Black freedom movement. Islamophobia and criminalization have deep roots in the repression of Black religious and political expression throughout the postwar period. The interplay between law enforcement and the NOI's activism are the groundwork for the modern carceral state as well as the contemporary abolition movements that oppose it.

Acknowledgments

One of the best-kept secrets of single-authored books is that they're actually collaborative projects produced by, and which in turn produce, communities. In the span of nearly a decade working on this project, I have accrued a great deal of debts, none of which can be repaid simply by listing my gratitude here. As I asked questions and favors, succeeded and stumbled, I found and formed a community of scholars and activists who ask critical questions of the past and dream of a more just future. To them I am profoundly grateful, and hope that I offer as much as I receive in return.

This project started many years ago through the gracious mentorship of Manning Marable. It arose from the lingering questions and archival silences after three intensive years working closely on the Malcolm X Project and his biography, *Malcolm X: A Life of Reinvention*. While the questions I asked, and the conclusions I came to, depart in many ways from his, he would have eagerly engaged and debated them with me. Outside of my parents and my partner, I have never experienced such a resolute belief in my potential. I feel great sorrow that I cannot share the final product of this work with him, but his commitment to black history as a political praxis speaks through this manuscript and continues to influence my thinking and doing every day. While I often feel his absence as a mentor, I just as often feel his presence. I owe so much to Leith Mullings, who has continued the warm mentorship and friendship of her late husband. I hope to do justice to their tremendous influence on me.

In the course of researching for this book, I consulted nearly forty university, public, and government agency libraries and archives. Contrary to the clichés of "hidden," "lost," or "forgotten" papers, these documents were all previously catalogued and retrieved by librarians and archivists, many of whom graciously scanned and emailed me materials so I would not have to travel across the country on a whim or a hunch. I have tried to maintain a list over the years and apologize to those I may have missed: Jennifer Allison, Susan Gilroy, and Addie Owens the Law School Library, College Library, and Interlibrary Loan at Harvard University respectively; Okezie Amalaha at the Auburn Avenue Research Library on African American Culture and History; Shelley Barber and Adrienne Pruitt at the John J. Burns Library at Boston College; Brooke Black at the Huntington Library; Robyn Carlton at the Appellate Division Law Library in Rochester, New York; Wendy Chmielewski and the entire staff at the Swarthmore College Peace Collection; Sigrid Cornell, Alexa Pearce, and Julie Herrada at the University of Michigan Library and Labadie Collection; Ikumi Crocoll at the Newberry Library in Chicago; Donnelyn Curtis at the University of Nevada at Reno Ethnicity and Race Manuscript Collection; Rebecca Darby-Williams, Lorna Kirwan, and Kathi Neal at the University of California at Berkeley Bancroft Library; Jennifer Fauxsmith at the Massachusetts Archives; Jim Folts at the New York State Archives; Jessica M. Herrick at the California State Archives; Tim Hodgdon at the University of North Carolina at Chapel Hill Louis Round

Wilson Special Collections Library; Stacy Jones, Amber Anderson, Derek Mosley, and Kayin Shabazz at the Atlanta University Center Robert W. Woodruff Library; Shola Lynch, Michael Mery, Mary Yearwood, and the staff at the Schomburg Center for Research in Black Culture; Haley Maynard and Amanda Weimer at the National Archives in College Park; Nan Mehan and Tim Noakes at Stanford Special Collections; Bill Offhaus at the University Archives at the University of Buffalo; Charlene Boyer Lewis and James Lewis made me feel at home pursuing history at Kalamazoo College and Andy Mozina always supported my creative writing and my well-being, especially during some rough patches when I needed it most. My heart will always be at the Institute for Research in African American Studies (IRAAS) at Columbia University. My IRAAS family has sustained me through it all. Thank you May Alhassen, Zaheer Ali, Megan French-Marcelin, Farah Jasmine Griffin, Sharon Harris, Elizabeth Hinton, Liz Mazucci, Shawn Mendoza, Russell Rickford, and Courtney Teague. At the University of Michigan, this project was developed with the help of a wonderful cohort without whom I could not have survived graduate school: Lloyd Barba, Jasmine Kramer, Jenny Kwak, Katie Lennard, and Eric Shih. I am thankful for the tremendous support of our directors of graduate studies: Stephen Berrey and Kristin Hass. Thank you Marlene Moore for being an advocate and an ally, and for always making everything as simple as possible. Thank you to the faculty who offered encouragement along the way: Sandra Gunning, Martha Jones, Susan Juster, Mary Kelley, Matt Lassiter, Gina Morantz-Sanchez, Margo Schlanger, and Rebecca Scott. Matthew Countryman chaired my committee, supported my student organizing, and demonstrated the meaning of engaged pedagogy. Sherie Randolph and Stephen Ward were like the big sister and brother I never had. Sherie, despite your insistence that "you are not my friend," I am happy to call myself yours. Stephen (and your beautiful family, Sekai and Chaney), you have never wavered in your belief and have been so generous with your time. Thank you to Penny Von Eschen, whom I have known since before this project began, and to Heather Ann Thompson, for joining my committee and helping to develop this project without hesitation. Thank you Elizabeth James in DAAS for your unwavering commitment to students.

As Robin D. G. Kelley writes, "social movements generate new knowledge, new theories, new questions." Many new questions grew out of organizing and co-founding the United Coalition for Racial Justice (UCRJ) in 2013–2014. Thank you to those who labored all those long hours to address the desperate need for racial justice at the University. I especially appreciate Tiya Miles for supporting our organizing, and Barbara Ransby, upon whose shoulders we stood and whose support meant so much to us then, and continues to this day. I met Austin McCoy during my first semester on campus and so much of my thinking and organizing has been shaped by our conversations over the last decade. I cannot imagine getting through graduate school or those difficult years without him.

When I moved to Portland, Oregon in 2014, I was met with friendship and comradery from Reiko Hillyer and Anoop Mirpuri in particular. Reiko's willingness to co-teach a Malcolm X class at Columbia River Correctional Institution changed the trajectory of my life, and she and Anoop both offered critical feedback on article drafts and job talks. I also appreciate Mark Burford and Margo Minardi involving me in the intellectual life at Reed College, as well as the entire Reed library staff, who greeted me kindly for years as I marched by their desk each morning with the same coffee thermos to the same desk to write my dissertation. Portland was home in so many ways, none more than my Liberation Literacy family. I still cherish a photo of our original group—Nash, Marika, Mihir, Paul, Hen, Joshua, Quandrell, Karl, Sandy, and Shane—with the white board behind us reading: "group name?" We were supported during those early years by many gracious comrades. Robin Kelley sent us the first handful of books for the Freedom Library, which now has more books than the prison can hold. Dan Berger, Elizabeth Hinton, Walidah Imarisha, Walter Johnson, Ibram X Kendi, Scott Kurashige, Khalil Muhammad, Tef Poe, and Stephen Ward all volunteered their time to visit or Skype to discuss their books.

There are many to whom I owe a great deal for intellectual support as this project transitioned from dissertation to book. Keisha Blain, Ashley Farmer, and the AAIHS community offered me the chance to experiment with and develop many of the ideas of this book through blogging for what later became *Black Perspectives*. The bulk of this book was written during my fellowship year at Harvard's Warren Center for Studies in American History. There I received thoughtful, incisive, and nurturing feedback from an incredible cohort of scholars of the carceral state: Elizabeth Hinton, Julilly Kohler-Hausmann, Rebecca Lemov, Toussaint Losier, Lisa McGirr, Donna Murch, Susan Reverby, Stuart Schrader, Micol Seigel, Timothy Stewart-Winter, and Heather Ann Thompson. Thank you to Melissa Castillo-Garsow, Chris Clements, Tej Nagaraja, and Juliet Nebolon for allowing me to be an "honorary" post-doc. I am also grateful to Elsa Hardy, Sonya Karabel, Monnikue McCall, Arthur Patton-Hock, Elizabeth Ross, and Kaia Stern for their help and support with the Beyond the Gates conference and to Walter Johnson for always being in our corner.

Research for this monograph was also funded by the National Endowment for the Humanities, and the Schomburg Center for Research in Black Culture's Scholar-in-Residence Program. There, I was fortunate to learn from another brilliant cohort— Denisse Andrade, Gaiutra Bahadur, Adrienne Brown, Jasmine Johnson, and Chris Wolloughby—led by Brent Hayes Edwards. Any views, findings, conclusions, or recommendations expressed in this publication do not necessarily represent those of the National Endowment for the Humanities.

There are so many scholars, activists, editors, and friends who have supported various forms of my work and without which I would likely not have a career. Dan Berger, Nathan Connolly, Farah Jasmine Griffin, Elizabeth Hinton, Robin Kelley, Jullily Kohler-Hausmann, Khalil Muhammad, Premilla Nadasen, Barbara Ransby, Stuart Schrader, Nikhil Singh, Micol Seigel, David Stein, Ula Taylor, and Heather Ann Thompson, have all been resources and sources of support through this process. Jessie Kindig, Brandon Proia, and Katy O'Donnell in particular have worked with me to get books inside prisons in various ways and students at Harvard—Salma Abdelrahman, Trevor Ladner, Nick Wyville, Amisha Kambath, Zoë Hopkins—have been willing to marshal their resources and time to make projects happen. Others read drafts and gave invaluable feedback, particularly Zaheer Ali, Dan Berger, Ori Burton, and John Woodford. Zaheer, Dan, and Elizabeth have been strong supporters, resources, comrades, and friends, all of which I am intensely grateful for. Although not everything made the book, thank you to those who shared their recollections, memories, and stories with me, such as J. Herman Blake, Ned Block, Tony Bouza, Richard Fallenbaum, Ernest Green, Richard Griffin, Charles Keil, Lucy Komisar, Shahid Naeem, Gay Plair, and Michael Winston.

When I arrived at the University of Mississippi, I found a supportive and generous community of colleagues who are great people as well as great scholars and teachers. Thank you to James Thomas, Shennette Garrett-Scott, and Jessie Wilkerson for organizing with me before we even met in person; Jodi Skipper and Rhondalyn Pairs for fighting for Ida with me; Patrick Alexander and Otis Pickett for warmly welcoming me into the Prison-to-College Pipeline Program; and to Zack Guthrie, Becky Marchiel, and Afton Thomas for being spirited friends and supporters from the jump. The rest of the U.S. caucus, Mikaëla Adams, Shennette Garrett-Scott, Eva Payne, Jarod Roll, Ted Ownby, Darren Grem, and Chuck Ross, many of whom hired me, have been both patient with my delay and welcoming upon my arrival. I am particularly indebted and thankful to my chair Noell Wilson for her ability to see the connections between my scholarly and activist work, and to support both with enthusiasm. The endowment of the Arch Darlymple III Department of History provided needed and necessary funds and the Dean of the College of Liberal Arts, Lee Cohen, and the UNC Press Authors Fund helped underwrite this book.

It is an honor to be a part of the Justice, Power, and Politics Series expertly shepherded by Heather Ann Thompson and Rhonda Y. Williams. I had the editorial dream team. Grey Osterud taught me how to write a book. Our conversations over breakfast were as much about social movement theory as they were chapter and paragraph structure. She is one of the most brilliant and generous people I have ever met and I am grateful to Sherie Randolph for making the connection. Brandon Proia and I met when this book was a dissertation prospectus and we have been conspiring ever since. Brandon is a talented editor who advocates for his authors and whom I consider a dear friend. Many thanks to Tamara K. Nopper for her indexing and proofreading. I was also fortunate to have two incredible scholars, Elizabeth Ross and Elsa Hardy, help me with research and editing. Hilda Johnson, Hannah Ontiveros, and Jay Driskell all aided by photographing and scanning archival materials from afar.

I owe so much to my friends and family. To have my book cover designed by one of my oldest and closest friends, Zachary Norman, is an amazing privilege. I have roped Zach into almost every project from college to the present and I am grateful that he has never once said no. Ernie and Phil have always been there for me to listen and encourage. Ngina, you ground me and remind me to laugh. Robin, Bud, Mackenzie, Zane, and Zeb, I feel so lucky to have you as my family. Christine, Kiefer, Nick, and Randy welcomed me with open arms and I have enjoyed every moment of growing alongside and among this beautiful family. Thank you to my mother, Lynette, and father, Steven, for raising me right. My father gave me his sardonic sense of humor, without which life would be an onerous and bleak endeavor. My mother has read nearly as many drafts as I have written of this book, offering invaluable insight along the way. She was the first in her family to graduate from college, earned her PhD, inspired me to teach, and showed me what it is to be a true lover of books. Margaux, you are the most beautiful, kind, supportive, thoughtful human on this earth. They haven't yet made words for you. Those who have been lucky enough to spend a day with you know what I mean. I am fortunate enough to get a lifetime. Julian, my little moonchild, you are the other sweet joy of my life. I hope the world shines as brightly for you—and you for it—as you do for the two of us.

Notes

Abbreviations to Notes

ABP	Albert Bofman Papers, Swarthmore Peace Collection, Swarthmore College
ABPN	Alfred Balk Papers, The Newberry Library, Chicago, Illinois
ACIF	Attica Commission Investigation Files, New York State Archives
ACLU	American Civil Liberties Union, National Committee on Conscientious Objectors, Bayard Rustin Papers, Swarthmore Peace Collection, Swarthmore College
ACLU-SC	American Civil Liberties Union of Southern California, Charles E. Young Research Library, UCLA
ADLL	Appellate Division Law Library, Rochester, New York
AFSC	American Friends Service Committee, Swarthmore Peace Collection, Swarthmore College
AID	Attica Inmate Documents Seized, 1971, #22421, New York State Archives
ANC	Amsterdam News Collection, Division of Rare and Manuscript Collections, Cornell University Library
APRP	A. Philip Randolph Papers, Library of Congress, Washington, D.C.
BOP	Records of the Bureau of Prisons, Record Group 129, National Archives and Records Administration at College Park, Maryland
CCOH	Columbia Center for Oral History, Rare Book and Manuscript Library, Columbia University
CCW	Center on Conscience and War, Swarthmore Peace Collection, Swarthmore College
CELC	C. Eric Lincoln Collection, Robert W. Woodruff Library, Archives Research Center, Atlanta University Center
CSA	Subject Files, Muslims, Division of Criminal Law, Attorney General's Office, California State Archives
HMP	Hugh R. Manes Papers, Charles E. Young Research Library, UCLA
JHP	James Haughton Papers, Schomburg Center for Research in Black Culture, New York Public Library
JLC	Joseph A. Labadie Collection, University of Michigan Special Collections Library
JWNP	Juanita and Wallace Nelson Papers, Swarthmore Peace Collection, Swarthmore College
LBP	Lee Brown Papers, Woodson Research Center, Rice University
LLP	Louis E. Lomax Papers, Ethnicity and Race Manuscript Collection, University of Nevada–Reno
LMP	Loren Miller Papers, The Huntington Library, San Marino, California

MMC Margaret Meier Collection of Extreme Right Ephemeral Materials, Department of Special Collections, Stanford University
MWC Marvin Worth Collection, Howard Gotlieb Archival Research Center, Boston University
MXB Malcolm X BOSS File, in author's possession
MXC Malcolm X Collection, Schomburg Center for Research in Black Culture, New York Public Library
MX-FBI Malcolm X FBI File
MXP Malcolm X Project Records, Rare Book and Manuscript Library, Columbia University
MXPF Malcolm X Prison File (#22843), Massachusetts State Archives
NARA National Archives and Records Administration at College Park, Maryland
NARA-KC National Archives and Records Administration–Kansas City
NARA-NYC National Archives and Records Administration–Northeast Region, New York City
NCICF Non-Criminal Investigation Case Files, New York State, Division of State Police, New York State Archives
NOI-FBI Nation of Islam FBI File, National Archives and Records Administration at College Park
OAAU-FBI Organization of Afro-American Unity FBI File, National Archives and Records Administration at College Park
PJFK Papers of John F. Kennedy, John F. Kennedy Presidential Library and Museum, Boston, Massachusetts
PNAACP Papers of the NAACP, Library of Congress
RDJ Records of the Department of Justice, National Archives and Records Administration at College Park, Maryland
TBP Taylor Branch Papers, The Southern Historical Collection at the Louis Round Wilson Special Collections Library, University of North Carolina–Chapel Hill

Introduction

1. "'Muslims' Riot: Cultist Killed, Policeman Shot," *Los Angeles Times*, April 28, 1962. See Knight, "Justifiable Homicide, Police Brutality, or Governmental Repression?," 182–96.

2. Grace E. Simons, "I Killed Stokes, Says Officer," *California Eagle*, May 17, 1962.

3. Robert A. Heinze to Stanley Mosk, January 8, 1963, box 173, folder 22, CSA.

4. Blain, *Set the World on Fire*, 3.

5. A similar dynamic is explored in the work of Alan Eladio Gómez, who describes the 1960s–1970s as a "dialectic of prison rebellions and repression." See Gómez, "Resisting Living Death at Marion Federal Penitentiary," 60. Also see Max Felker-Kantor, *Policing Los Angeles*, 160.

6. Michel Foucault writes that the "prison and police form a twin mechanism; together they assure in the whole field of illegalities the differentiation, isolation, and use of delinquency." Foucault, *Discipline and Punish*, 282.

7. All men in the Nation of Islam belonged to the Fruit of Islam.

8. *SaMarion v. McGinnis* (Civil 9395), trial transcript, 172, NARA-NYC. The case bundled a number of cases against Commissioner McGinnis, including Civil 9398, Thomas Bratcher Jr.; Civil 9454, James Walker and Joseph Magette; Civil 9455, Joseph Magette and James Walker; and Civil 9838, Arthur Johnson; SaMarion v. McGinnis, Civ. 9395, slip op. at 10 (W.D.N.Y. Oct. 14, 1963).

9. W. Haywood Burns, *Voices of Negro Protest in America*, 73.

10. Representative of this critique is Gilroy, "Black Fascism," 70–91. For more on the way Black Nationalism and white nationalism have been flattened as mirrored images, see Garrett Felber, "Black Nationalism and Liberation," *Boston Review*, August 30, 2016.

11. The distinction between carceral state and nation state may be itself overly semantic. As Micol Seigel argues, for example, "*Police* and *state* are differentiated by degree: police are the human-scale expression of the state." "Criminal justice," Lawrence Friedman adds, "is, literally, state power." Anthropologist James Ferguson points to the ways that the state is more a "way of tying together, multiplying, and coordinating power relations, a kind of knotting or congealing of power." Similarly, Stuart Hall and others, building upon Italian Marxist philosopher Antonio Gramsci, describe the state "not so much an entity, or even a particular complex of institutions, so much as it is a particular site or level of the social formation." As critical geographer Brett Story summarizes, the carceral state can be "conceived less as a *thing* and more as an *organizer*." See Micol Seigel, *Violence Work*, 9; Lawrence Friedman, *Crime and Punishment in American History*, quoted in Ruth Wilson Gilmore, *Golden Gulag*, 174; James Ferguson, *The Anti-Politics Machine*, quoted in Seigel, *Violence Work*, 18; Stuart Hall, et al, *Policing the Crisis*, quoted in Brett Story, *Prison Land*, 16.

12. Malcolm made this speech at an Organization of Afro-American Unity rally held at the Audubon Ballroom on January 24, 1965. Malcolm X, "Malcolm X on Afro-American History," in *Malcolm X on Afro-American History*, 11–72.

13. Summary report, New York, November 17, 1959, 23, MX-FBI.

14. Singh, *Black Is a Country*, 6.

15. Dan Berger notes that for incarcerated people "the courtroom was more a site of public intervention than of legal wrangling." Berger, *Captive Nation*, 178.

16. Lincoln, *Black Muslims*, revised ed., 274.

17. See Blain, *Set the World on Fire*; Farmer, *Remaking Black Power*; Randolph, *Florynce 'Flo' Kennedy*; Spencer, *Revolution Has Come*; Taylor, *Promise of Patriarchy*; Ward, "Third World Women's Alliance." See also Blain, Leeds, and Taylor, "Women, Gender Politics, and Pan-Africanism." For more on the role of women in the NOI, see Taylor, *Promise of Patriarchy*; Gibson and Karim, *Women of the Nation*; Jeffries, *Nation Can Rise No Higher Than Its Women*; West, "Revisiting Female Activism in the 1960s."

18. Blain, Leeds, and Taylor, "Women, Gender Politics, and Pan-Africanism," 139.

19. Taylor, *Promise of Patriarchy*, 5.

20. Griffin, "'Ironies of the Saint,'" 214–29.

21. Taylor, *Promise of Patriarchy*, 89. This echoed patriarchal white supremacy in the nineteenth century. According to James W. Messerschmidt, one lynching was accompanied by a sign that read, "We Must Protect Our Southern Women." As he writes,

"Violence against alleged Black rapists earned white men positions of superiority over white women as well as over African American men; thus lynching equated the preservation of the race with passive femininity." Messerschmidt, "'We Must Protect Our Southern Women,'" 88, 90. For men in the Nation of Islam, protecting Black women from white men was the means by which they claimed masculinity. In both cases, women were the passive currency that defined masculinity, yet Black masculinity needed to be proved in part due to the violent framework of white masculinity.

22. "2 Negroes Maul Chief in Flomaton," *Pensacola Journal*, February 23, 1957.

23. Summary report, New York, April 30, 1958, 2–3, 14, MX-FBI. A detailed analysis of this event is given in Taylor, *Promise of Patriarchy*, 86–90.

24. "2 Negroes Maul Chief."

25. Griffin, "'Ironies of the Saint,'" 216.

26. Abdul Khabeer, "Islam on Trial," forum response, *Boston Review*, February 27, 2017.

27. Platt, *Beyond These Walls*, 61.

28. Amna Akbar and Jeanne Theoharis, "Islam on Trial," *Boston Review*, February 27, 2017.

29. I use the term "double jeopardy" here to gesture toward Frances Beale's powerful articulation of the "both/and" intersectionality of Black womanhood. See Beale, "Double Jeopardy: To Be Black and Female."

30. Foucault, *Discipline and Punish*, 21 and 27.

31. Abdul Khabeer, "Islam on Trial."

32. "Black Nationalists, Muslims and Other Separatist Groups," resolution adopted by the 52nd Annual Convention of the NAACP, 11, July 15, 1961. Annual Convention File, 1961 Resolutions, Group III, Series A, Administrative File, Annual Convention, PNAACP.

33. "Black Muslim Sect," resolution adopted at the Annual Business Meeting of the American Correctional Association, September 20, 1960, enclosed in E. R. Cass to Attorney General of the United States; the Governor and Attorney General of all states; correctional administrators, October 3, 1962, box 173, folder 22, CSA.

34. Curtis, *Black Muslim Religion in the Nation of Islam*, 6.

35. Lincoln, *Black Muslims in America*, 3rd ed., 91, 262. Lincoln records the order differently each time. This is a variation of the proverb by Chinese philosopher Lao Tzu, "Those who know do not speak. Those who speak do not know."

36. For example, the *Los Angeles Times* reported that "Inspector John Powers, assistant commander of the police patrol bureau, is an authority on the Muslim Movement." "Muslim Hatred Called Threat to Community," *Los Angeles Times*, May 7, 1962.

37. Malcolm X, "The Oppressed Masses of the World Cry Out for Action Against the Common Oppressor," in *February 1965*, 46–65; quote on 61.

38. Malcolm X, "Not Just an American Problem, but a World Problem," in *Malcolm X: The Last Speeches*, 172–73.

39. Weisenfeld, *New World A-Coming*, 5.

40. Turley, *American Religion*, 390. See also Turner, *Islam in the African-American Experience*, 71–108.

41. Beynon, "Voodoo Cult among Negro Migrants in Detroit," 894–907.

42. Comment by James V. Bennett, director of Bureau of Prisons, "The Power to Change Behavior: A Symposium Presented by the United States Bureau of Prisons," *Corrective Psychiatry and the Journal of Social Therapy* 8, nos. 1–4 (1962): 101.

43. Berg, *Elijah Muhammad and Islam*, 40; Essien-Udom, *Black Nationalism*, 70. Claude Andrew Clegg III estimates that during the late 1950s, Chicago and Washington, D.C., had the largest memberships, between 400 and 600, and that New York was the fastest growing, at around 350. See Clegg, *Original Man*, 114.

44. "Nation of Islam, Locations of Some of the Temples, Mosques, and Affiliated Groups throughout the United States," October 11, 1962, box 9, folder 326, ABPN.

45. Malcolm X, "Twenty Million Black People in a Political, Economic, and Mental Prison," in *Malcolm X: The Last Speeches*, 51.

46. This is also the basis behind the Five Percent Nation, or the Five Percenters. See Michael Muhammad Knight, *Five Percenters*.

47. Dick Woodward to Lieutenant, box 24, items 990–999, NCICF. Emphasis added.

48. I borrow the term "prison organizing" from Berger, *Captive Nation*.

49. For more on *Ruffin v. Commonwealth*, see Dennis Childs, *Slaves of the State*.

50. James Jacobs, "The Prisoners' Rights Movement and Its Impacts," 434, 440.

51. Berger, Captive Nation, 78.

52. Michael Brown, *Working the Street*, 290, cited in Murakawa, *First Civil Right*, 90.

53. Schrader, "More Than Cosmetic Changes," *Journal of Urban History* (April 2017): 19.

54. For an excellent treatment of policing in Los Angeles under Parker and its legacies, see Felker-Kantor, *Policing Los Angeles*.

55. For more on epistemic violence, see Spivak, "Can the Subaltern Speak?," 24–28.

56. See Malcolm X, "Not Just an American Problem," 175–76.

57. Sostre, *Letters and Quotations*, 35, JLC.

Chapter One

1. Evanzz, *Messenger*, 135–37; "FBI Holds Moslem Chief on Draft Evasion Charge," *Afro-American*, May 16, 1942; "'Islamites' Camp Outside Jail That Holds Their Draft-Dodging Leaders," *Cleveland Call and Post*, June 13, 1942; "Islamites Camp Outside Prison," *Atlanta Daily World*, June 9, 1942.

2. "U.S. Jury Studies Cult Case," *Cleveland Call and Post*, October 17, 1942. The *Amsterdam Star News* reported that "colored officers aided in the arrest of members when the FBI cracked down on them after several months of investigation during which Federal agents donned dark makeup to get on the inside." See "Accused Cultists Preyed on Ignorant," October 3, 1942.

3. In the conclusion to the FBI's RACON survey, the bureau listed the following groups as having "pro-Japanese ideas and attitudes, as well as anti-white sentiments": Universal Negro Improvement Association, Society for the Development of Our Own, Pacific Movement of the Eastern World, Peace Movement of Ethiopia, Ethiopian Pacific Movement, Moorish Science Temple of America, Colored American National Organization (also known as Washington Park Forum and Brotherhood of Liberty for the Black People of America), Allah Temple of Islam, African Moslem Welfare Society

of America, Addeynu Allahe Universal Arabic Association, and International Reassemble of the Church of Freedom League, Inc. See Hill, *FBI's RACON*, 407. For more on Black anticolonial solidarity with Japan, see Allen, "When Japan Was 'Champion of the Darker Races'"; Lipsitz, "'Frantic to Join . . . the Japanese Army'"; Gallicchio, *African American Encounter with Japan and China*; Kearney, *African American Views of the Japanese*; Plummer, *Rising Wind*; Blain, "'Confraternity among All Dark Races.'"

4. Evanzz, *Messenger*, 137.

5. A government official allegedly told him: "That's all we are putting you in jail for, to keep you out of the public." See Clegg, *Original Man*, 89–90.

6. DeCaro, *On the Side of My People*, 70–71; Malcolm X and Haley, *Autobiography of Malcolm X*, 121–22.

7. Marable, *Malcolm X*, 60.

8. Kelley, *Race Rebels*, 166.

9. Summary report, Boston, May 4, 1953, 3, MX-FBI.

10. "Members of D.C. Moslem Sect Charged with Draft Violation," *Washington Post*, April 2, 1942.

11. Crawford, *Black Muslims and the Law*, 24.

12. David Orro, "Seek Indictments of Sedition Suspects," *Chicago Defender*, October 3, 1942.

13. Statistics on Black draft resistance vary by source. According to a study by pacifists at the end of the war, a total of 6,086 conscientious objectors went to prison for refusal to register with the Selective Service. The majority of these (4,441) were Jehovah's Witnesses. However, 3 percent of imprisoned COs were Black and described by researchers as "Moslems." Gordon, *Spirit of the Law*, 109. In 1943, with over 6,000 men convicted of violating the Selective Service Act, the *Pittsburgh Courier* reported that fewer than 2 percent were African American. Of the 73 Black draft resisters, 54 were Muslims in the Nation of Islam. "Negroes Represent Less Than 2 Per Cent of Draft Dodgers Jailed," *Pittsburgh Courier*, September 11, 1943. The U.S. government estimated a slightly higher number in 1943, finding that 167 Black men had been convicted of draft violations. *Selective Service Conscientious Objector*, vol. 1 (Washington, D.C.: Government Printing Office, 1950), 261, 264–265, cited in Stanford, *If We Must Die*, 146.

14. Wallace interview by Blackside, Inc.

15. "Black Supremacists," *Time*, August 10, 1959.

16. Zaheer Ali, "Islamophobia Did Not Start at Ground Zero," *Root*, September 7, 2010.

17. A Proquest newspaper search revealed no instances of the phrase "Black Muslims" the year of *The Hate That Hate Produced*, 113 in the year of the book's release, and over 600 by 1963. Others acknowledged Lincoln's coinage but were less attuned to the NOI's critiques. Louis Lomax wrote that "the term 'Black Muslim' was coined by Dr. Eric Lincoln while he was preparing his Ph.D. dissertation. . . . They do not use the term when speaking of themselves. They call themselves 'Muslims.' However, they do not object to the term employed by Lincoln." Lomax, *The Negro Revolt*, 164n1.

18. Abdul Khabeer, "Islam on Trial."

19. Beynon, "Voodoo Cult," 894.

20. Turner, *Islam in the African-American Experience*, 163.

21. Taylor, *Promise of Patriarchy*, 23; "Grand Jury Is Probing," *Atlanta Daily World*, September 28, 1942.

22. "80 Negroes Held as Jap Admirers," *Washington Post*, September 22, 1942.

23. Taylor, *Promise of Patriarchy*, 23–27; "Accused Cultists Preyed on Ignorant," *Amsterdam Star-News*, October 3, 1942.

24. Russell Cowans, "Seize 13 in Raid on Islam' Cult," *Chicago Defender*, April 21, 1934.

25. See Taylor, *Promise of Patriarchy*, chap. 3, "Allah Temple of Islam Families: The Dillon Report," 31–43, for fuller discussion of the Dillon Report.

26. Taylor, *Promise of Patriarchy*, 25, 28–29, 51–52.

27. James P. Mullin, "Secretary's Report on Milan," September 11, 1945, 3 (DG 002), Prison Visits of James Mullin: Reports and Notes, Prison Service Committee, AFSC.

28. For a fuller debate on the role of World War II in the Civil Rights Movement, see Kruse and Tuck, *Fog of War*. On the role of Black GIs in wartime politics, see Guglielmo, "Martial Freedom Movement."

29. Gaines, *Uplifting the Race*, 27.

30. Stanford, *If We Must Die*, 145–47. This number grew over the following three years, however, and by 1946, over two thousand Black men (an estimated 18% of all draft violators) had been imprisoned for Selective Service violations. See Gill, "Afro-American Opposition to the United States' Wars of the Twentieth Century."

31. Bennett, *Radical Pacifism*.

32. Bennett, *Radical Pacifism*; Gordon, *Spirit of the Law*, 106.

33. D'Emilio, *Lost Prophet*, 45, 80.

34. Ruth Isabel Seabury to "Dear Friend," August 22, 1944, and Roger Axford, "Statement to Local Draft Board No. 1," December 28, 1943, Part I, Series E, 2, Roger Axford, CCW.

35. D'Emilio puts it at one in six. See *Lost Prophet*, 73. John Wood's estimate is 20 percent; see Wood, "Wally and Juanita Nelson and the Struggle for Peace, Equality, and Social Justice," 77. According to one federal report, the total number held in federal prisons in a given year before World War II rarely exceeded eighteen thousand. Langan, Fundis, Greenfield, and Schneider, *Historical Statistics on Prisoners in State and Federal Institutions*, 5–7.

36. Heatherton, "University of Radicalism."

37. Report of Secretary's Visit to the U.S. Penitentiary, Lewisburg, PA," April 30–May 3, 1945, box 31, Series D, ACLU.

38. By the end of the war, violators of the Selective Service Act represented almost a quarter of all federal prisoners. Over a six-year period, the BOP classified over twelve hundred prisoners as COs. See *Federal Prisons*, 1946, 8, 12–14.

39. James Bennett wrote the Committee against Race Discrimination in the War Effort: "You ask whether or not there is any Federal law or regulation segregating Negro prisoners from other prisoners in federal institutions. There is no such law." King, *Separate and Unequal*, 142–44.

40. James Bennett to Donald Taft, May 31, 1943, box 79, Central Administrative File, Prisoners: General, BOP.

41. "Memorandum No. 3 on CO and JW Policy," August 4, 1943, box 37.

42. Donald Taft to James Bennett, "General Report on CO and JW Policy," August 30, 1943, box 6.

43. D'Emilio, *Lost Prophet*, 85.

44. As a 1943 federal report observed, aside from the JWs, "the only other religious sect represented in any considerable number were members of a Negro 'Moslem' cult, of whom there were 100." Those classified as having a "purely philosophical basis" for their objection to military service totaled 167. DOJ Report, August 27, 1943, box 87, Part I, Series B, CCW.

45. When Muhammad requested a copy of the Qur'an while awaiting trial, he was denied access and told "that is what we put [you] in prison for." See Clegg, *Original Man*, 91, 96.

46. Clegg, *Original Man*, 94–97.

47. Taylor, *Promise of Patriarchy*, 71. Although records of Muslim women's experiences during the war are even scarcer, Taylor does a remarkable job of chronicling their leadership; see 70–73.

48. Charles Palmer's Report on Visit to Sandstone, Minnesota, n.d., Part I, Series B, Prisons/CO Prisoners: COs in Sandstone Federal Correctional Institution (MN), CCW.

49. There were 65–67 Muslims and a total of 132 Black prisoners at the prison. "Final Report on a Statistical Study of SSA Violations: Federal Correctional Institution, Sandstone, Minnesota," 45, Appendix, Table 23, box 80, Central Administrative File, BOP.

50. "Final Report on a Statistical Study of SSA Violations."

51. See Weisenfeld, *New World A-Coming*, 214.

52. Three quarters of Muslims were listed as unskilled laborers, compared to only 8 percent of COs and 31 percent of JWs. The rest of the NOI members were skilled or clerical workers, and none was a professional. The majority of COs and JWs were agricultural laborers. Only fifteen Muslims showed any formal education; all categories except Muslims and "Negligent Violators" were classified at eighth grade level or above. See "Final Report on a Statistical Study of SSA Violations," 41–42, 61, Table 38. Because the report only tabulated war resisters, it is impossible to compare Muslims with other Black prisoners.

53. JWs' sentences averaged thirty-nine months, and 49 percent were given three years, compared to only 22 percent of COs. "Final Report," 22–25.

54. Winslow H. Osborne to James Mullin, December 4–7, 1944, Part I, Series B, Prisons/CO Prisoners: COs in Sandstone Federal Correctional Institution (MN), CCW. For more on the Sandstone hunger strike, see memo for Mr. Loveland and Mr. Alper, September 17, 1946, re: Hunger Strike at Sandstone, box 92, Central Administrative File, BOP.

55. It is possible that Bofman was largely responsible for this statistical analysis, which had "joint sponsorship of the Medical, Educational and Social Service departments . . . [and was] supervised by the Educational Department." See "Final Report on a Statistical Study of SSA Violations." According to the Chicago History Museum, Bofman worked from 1938 to 1942 as a "field advisor for the Illinois Department of

Unemployment Compensation, a research assistant for the Illinois Tax Commission, and a price inspector for the Office of Price Administration (OPA)."

56. Albert Bofman, "Maladministration and Human Relations in a Federal Prison: A Report Based on the Federal Prison, Sandstone, Minnesota, 1943–1945," November 1948, ABP.

57. Albert Bofman to Holley Cantine, July 25, 1948; Bofman, "Maladministration and Human Relations," ABP.

58. "Milan: Actions by the United States Parole Board," June 9, 1944, Part I, Series B, Prisons/CO Prisoners: COs in Milan Federal Correctional Institution (MI), CCW; Evanzz, *Messenger*, 149. The other known Muslim men were Benjamin Mitchell, Karriem Allah, Leonard X, Lamlus X, Lester X, Robert X, and James 4X and Willie 2X Rowe.

59. "Memorandum No. 3," 16.

60. James Mullin, handwritten notes, n.d. (DG 002), Prison Visits of James Mullin: Reports and Notes, Prison Service Committee, AFSC.

61. Prison Visits of James Mullin: Reports and Notes, Prison Service Committee, AFSC. Ramadan was introduced in December by Fard and Muhammad as one of the shortest months of the year for first-time fasting, as well as a counter to Christianity and Christmas. Muslims were encouraged to eat only fish and vegetables and avoid land animals. I am grateful to Zaheer Ali for pointing this out to me.

62. Evanzz, *Messenger*, 148.

63. Mullin, "Secretary's Report on Milan."

64. The NAACP reported that "two Chicago Negroes, both of whom are religious conscientious objectors to the war," were holding a silent protest against racial segregation and had been joined by several white prisoners. CORE press release, July 21, 1945, NAACP Discrimination Complaint Files: Bureau of Prisons, 1942–1946, Part 15, Segregation and Discrimination, Complaints and Responses, 1940–1955, Series A: Legal Department Files, PNAACP. Later that year, CORE announced that racial segregation at federal prisons like Milan had finally been abolished. See *Race Relations: A Monthly Summary of Events and Trends*, 263.

65. Mullin, "Secretary's Report on Milan."

66. Rowe most likely converted to Islam two summers earlier, in July 1943. See "Report of Disposition of Criminal Case," October 18, 1944, box 48, Record Group 60, Central Files, Classified Subject Files, Correspondence, Litigation Case Files, RDJ; Wallace Nelson, diary entries July 1–4, year unknown, (DG 262), Series B, JWNP. Theodore Bilbo was a Democrat who served as governor of Mississippi and U.S. senator, filibustering in support of white supremacy.

67. L. J. Watson to the Central File, relating to "Inmates Rustin #2905 — Bey #3482, June 11, 1945, box 39, Notorious Offenders Files: Rustin, Bayard, BOP.

68. Nelson, diary entries July 1–4.

69. Seabury to "Dear Friend."

70. Taft to Bennett, "General Report on CO and JW Policy."

71. "The Power to Change Behavior," 101.

72. Malcolm X and Haley, *Autobiography*, 160.

73. Malcolm X Little to Commissioner MacDowell, June 6, 1950, MXPF.

74. Berger and Losier, *Rethinking the American Prison Movement*, 20.

75. Berger and Losier, *Rethinking the American Prison Movement*, 21. Ironically, it included former Confederate military commanders and officials as well as freed people.

76. Andrea Armstrong, "Slavery Revisited in Penal Plantation Labor," 870.

77. *Ruffin v. Commonwealth*, 62 Va. (21 Gratt.) 790, 796 (1871).

78. In *Ex Parte Hull*, the Supreme Court struck down a Michigan statute that prohibited prisoners from filing legal papers that were not found to be "properly drawn" by the parole board. It ruled that "the State and its officers may not abridge or impair petitioner's right to apply to a federal court for a writ of habeas corpus." Ex Parte Hull, 312 U.S. 546, 594 (1941).

79. *Stroud v. Swope*, 187 F.2d 850 (9th Cir. 1951).

80. Jacobs, "The Prisoners' Rights Movement," 433.

81. Malcolm to Philbert, March 26, 1950, box 3, folder 1, MXC.

82. "Local Criminals in Prison, Claim Moslem Faith Now: Grow Beards, Won't Eat Pork; Demand East-Facing Cells to Facilitate 'Prayer to Mecca,'" *Springfield Union*, April 21, 1950; "Moslem Converts Get Concessions," *Dunkirk Evening Observer*, April 20, 1950.

83. "Moslem Converts Get Concessions."

84. Malcolm to Philbert, March 26, 1950.

85. "Malcolm X Calls for Bandung Conference," *Los Angeles Herald-Dispatch*, April 23, 1959.

86. The term "non-alignment" was first used in 1953 at the United Nations. As Vijay Prashad summarized, "At Bandung, the representatives of the formerly colonized countries signaled their refusal to take orders from their former colonial masters; they demonstrated their ability to discuss international problems and offer combined notes on them." Prashad, *Darker Nations*, 131.

87. Prashad, *Darker Nations*, xvii.

88. For more on previous significant gatherings of anticolonial women, such as the Conference of the Women of Asia in Beijing in 1949, see Elisabeth Armstrong, "Before Bandung."

89. "Mister Muhammad's Message to African-Asian Conference," *Pittsburgh Courier*, January 18, 1958.

90. Malcolm X and Haley, *Autobiography*, 391. Passages such as this have been cited as evidence that Malcolm was moving away from Black Nationalism toward a sort of color-blind radical humanism. The 1964 trip is the subject of an entire chapter, while the 1959 trip receives only a passing mention. While in Saudi Arabia in 1964, however, he wrote in his diary, "Our success in America will involve two circles. Black Nationalism and Islam. It will take Black Nationalism to make our people conscious of doing for self and then Islam will provide the spiritual guidance. Black Nationalism will link us to Africa and Islam will link us spiritually to Africa, Arabia and Asia." Travel diaries, April 23, 1964, box 5, folder 13, MXC.

91. "Malcolm X Off to Tour Middle East," *Amsterdam News*, July 11, 1959.

92. Malcolm X, "Arabs Send Warm Greetings to 'Our Brothers' of Color in U.S.A.," *Pittsburgh Courier*, August 15, 1959.

93. *Ummah* means "community" or "nation" and is used to refer to a community of believers or the unity of Muslims worldwide. Biographer Louis DeCaro concluded that "it was Malcolm's own dream to build such bridges into Africa and Asia; Muhammad merely benefited from Malcolm's zealous advances into the Islamic world." Edward Curtis suggested that when faced with the choice between "abandoning parts of his particularist vision or risking his Islamic legitimacy among non-movement Muslims, [Muhammad] chose the latter, entrenching himself even more deeply in his own prophetic authority." See DeCaro, *On the Side of My People*, 138; Curtis, *Islam in Black America*, 64; Marable, *Malcolm X*, 120–21.

94. Marable, *Malcolm X*, 69. See also "Race Doctrines," handwritten notes, n.d., box 136, folder 8, CELC.

95. "Muhammad's Son at Bazaar Saturday," *Amsterdam News*, April 9, 1960, and "Muhammad's Sons at African-Asian Bazaar," *Amsterdam News*, April 16, 1960. Although known as African-Asian bazaars at the time, these bazaars became known simply as African bazaars beginning in 1963. Flyers advertising these bazaars, which had once featured the pyramids and Sphinx of North Africa, now also depicted West African drums and an outline of the full continent, all indications of the impact that African decolonization had on the Nation of Islam's racial imaginary. For example, see flyers in box 11, folder 9, MXC. In 1964, Malcolm X recalled that "prior to 1959, many of us didn't want to be identified with Africa in any way, not even indirectly or remotely." See "Speech to Peace Corps Workers," December 12, 1964, Subseries XII, box 20, MXP. For more on this shift among Black Americans, see Meriwether, *Proudly We Can Be Africans*.

96. Lubin, *Geographies of Liberation*.

97. Alhassen, "Islam in America," 259.

98. Naeem, "The South Chicago Moslems," 22–23.

99. Allen, "Religious Heterodoxy and Nationalist Tradition," 13.

100. Naeem remarked that this was "in sharp contrast to the situation in Cedar Rapids." Naeem, "Rise of Elijah Muhammad," 25.

101. Alhassen, "Islam in America," 259.

102. Alhassen, "Islam in America," 260.

103. "White Man Is God for Cult of Islam," *New Crusader*, August 15, 1959. For an extensive inquiry into Fard, see Morrow, *Finding W.D. Fard*.

104. DeCaro, *On the Side of My People*, 148.

105. "Moslems Denounce US 'Muslims,'" *Amsterdam News*, October 22, 1960. Just weeks later, Shawarbi did an about-face and was the surprise guest at an African-Asian bazaar in New York, where he called the Nation of Islam "pioneers in building up understanding between the U.S. and Africa." See "Moslem from Cairo Lauds Muslims Here," *Amsterdam News*, November 5, 1960. He nevertheless continued to focus on "correcting" the NOI's heterodox practices.

106. Naeem spoke as a guest of the International Relations Club, whose goal was "fostering a growing interest in the relationships of the United States and other countries." See "International Relations Club," *Brown and Gold*, 1949, 98.

107. "Has Magazine for Moslems," *Iowa Quest*, June 1, 1955; "Luck Finally Changes for Abdul Naeem," *Des Moines Register*, January 15, 1955. The American Friends of the

Middle East (AFME) was a private group with ties to the CIA. Although there is no evidence to directly suggest that Naeem was aware of this relationship, there are lingering questions as to whether or not Naeem informed on the NOI. For example, a report on Malcolm X's 1959 trip in his BOSS file is attributed to Naeem, but it is unclear whether he provided it to the police knowingly. See Abdel Basit Naeem's account of Malcolm X's visit to Egypt, August 5, 1959, MXB. For more on AFME and the CIA, see Wilford, "American Friends of the Middle East."

108. Naeem, "Editorial," 2. Naeem's name for the journal seems to draw on his 1951 article "Pakistan and U.S.A." for the *Muslim World*. See Naeem, "Pakistan and U.S.A.," 227.

109. "Has Magazine for Moslems."

110. Curtis, "New York City," 431. Among them were international figures such as Maulana Ansari and staff artist Bilal Abdurahman, part of a rich musical community in Bed-Stuy that produced innovative mixes of jazz, African, and Middle Eastern sounds. See Hosein, "Dr Maulana Fazlur Rahman Ansari, His Life, Works and Thoughts." Abdurahman recorded albums alongside childhood friends Randy Weston and Ahmed Abdul-Malik. Abdul-Malik's 1958 album *Jazz Sahara* is considered the first to combine jazz and the sounds of the Middle East. See Kelley, *Africa Speaks, America Answers*.

111. Malcolm X, "We Arose from the Dead!," 24–27, 36. This essay was republished in the *Pittsburgh Courier* several months later as Malcolm X, "We Have Risen from the Dead," *Pittsburgh Courier*, December 28, 1956.

112. Naeem, "Rise of Elijah Muhammad," 19.

113. "Mr. Elijah Muhammad and the MOSLEM WORLD AND THE U.S.A.," 8. Brenda Plummer asserts that the NOI subsidized the journal. See Plummer, *Rising Wind*, 265.

114. "The Black Man and Islam," 11.

115. Naeem, "Moslem World and the U.S.A. Editor-Publisher's Brief Address," 23.

116. Naeem, introduction to *Supreme Wisdom*, 5.

117. Circulation figures in 1957 were reported to be 5,500. International distribution of the journal is difficult to estimate. *Ayer and Sons Directory of Newspapers and Periodicals*, 1386.

118. Elijah Muhammad to Abdul Basit Naeem, April 12, 1962, box 11, folder 14, MXC.

119. "Malcolm X As Nasser's Guest," July 23, 1959, MXB.

120. One 12-inch reel (unlabeled) in brown film canister labeled "Sound" and "Uline Akene, CBS—APR." 16 mm, box 1, MXC. I am grateful to Zaheer Ali for noting this.

121. Malcolm X and Haley, *Autobiography*, 273–74.

122. Clegg, *Original Man*, 127.

123. In a 1998 interview, Mike Wallace explained that the producers viewed the Nation of Islam as racist. In recounting the reasoning behind the documentary's title, he said, "They were racists. They were separatists. They wanted, they wanted to separate, separate the Blacks from the Whites in this country. Ah, if they felt that hatred it was in reaction to the hatred that they felt had been directed against them. Therefore, 'the hate that hate produced.'" Mike Wallace, interview by Blackside, Inc.

124. Untitled and undated promotional materials, box 2, folders 24–25, LLP.

125. Untitled and undated promotional materials, box 2, folders 24–25, LLP.

126. When Wallace was later asked who these "sober-minded Negroes" were, he said, "the entire Black leadership" before naming Wilkins. Mike Wallace, interview by Blackside, Inc.

127. "Harvard Professor Had Called Muslim Racists," *Pittsburgh Courier*, February 4, 1961; Summary report, New York, May 17, 1961, 14, MX-FBI. That same evening, in a smaller Q&A discussion, Malcolm X confronted Schlesinger from the audience about his analogy between the NOI and the KKK and White Citizens' Councils. Malcolm identified himself only as a Muslim.

128. Hearing, Joint Legislative Committee on Un-American Activities, State of Louisiana, November 27, 1962, 28, box 23, folder 10, MMC.

129. Lee Brown, "Black Muslims and the Police," 119.

130. Kenneth Clark, "Needed: Antidote to Hatred," *Saturday Review*, May 13, 1961, box 175, folder 1, CELC.

131. C. Eric Lincoln, "Extremist Attitudes in the Black Muslim Movement," paper presented at the annual meeting of the American Psychological Association, September 1, 1962, 12–13, box 136, folder 14, CELC.

132. Roy Wilkins to Henry Moon, May 20, 1959, General Office File, Black Muslims, 1958–1960, Part 24: Special Subjects, 1956–1965, Series A: Africa-Films, PNAACP.

133. Roy Wilkins to Joel Judovich, August 25, 1958, PNAACP.

134. Quoted in Shapiro, *White Violence and Black Response*, 465.

135. "Black Nationalists, Muslims and Other Separatist Groups." See also Summary minutes of the 52nd Annual Convention, July 10, 1961, 9, Annual Convention, 1961, Minutes, Part 1: Supplement, 1961–1965, PNAACP.

136. "Calls Moslem Leaders 'Thugs': Feels Cult Threat to FBI, NAACP," *Chicago Defender*, October 31, 1959.

137. Malcolm X and Haley, *Autobiography*, 284.

138. C. Eric Lincoln to Professor Walter G. Muelder, October 8, 1959, box 70, folder 1, CELC.

139. Lincoln, *Black Muslims*, 1st ed.; Lomax, *The Negro Revolt*; Burns, *Voices of Negro Protest*; Essien-Udom, *Black Nationalism*.

140. Lomax, *The Negro Revolt*, 177.

141. Essien-Udom, *Black Nationalism*, 250.

142. Lincoln, *Black Muslims*, 1st ed., 3–4. By the second edition in 1973, the phrase "fastest growing racist sect" had been replaced with "foremost Black nationalist movement."

143. Lincoln to Muhammad, July 27, 1959, box 175, folder 12, CELC.

144. "Royalty Statement," April 30, 1962, box 54, folder 1, CELC.

145. Mary Lou Thompson to C. Eric Lincoln, February 7, 1962, box 54, folder 2, CELC.

146. Review of *The Black Muslims in America* in Arabic, box 175, folder 4; F. Manasseer to Lincoln, April 6, 1961, box 70, folder 3; and "Die Black Moslems in den USA," box 134, folder 10, CELC.

147. Shad Polier, memo, American Jewish Congress, March 2, 1962, White House Staff Files of Harris Wofford, Alphabetical File, 1956–1962, Miscellaneous, 1962: February–April 7, PJFK.

148. For example, in the introduction, Lincoln wrote that his dissertation was concerned with a "social movement which has certain religious or theological aspects pertinent to its description." See chapter 1: introduction, 9, box 134, folder 12, CELC.

149. The journal and other writings by Naeem are among the surviving materials from Lincoln's book, most of which were destroyed in a fire at his home. For example, see Abdul Basit Naeem, "Malcolm X's Cordial Reception in Cairo," 1959, box 278, folder 28, and *Moslem World and the U.S.A.* 1, no. 6 (October–November–December 1956), box 285, folder 3, CELC.

150. Questionnaire, October 27, 1959, box 70, folder 1, CELC. Lincoln distributed this survey and collected responses in written form.

151. Questionnaire, n.d., box 134, folder 15, CELC.

152. From 1945 to 1960, forty countries and 800 million people won independence from European colonialism. Von Eschen, *Race Against Empire*, 125.

153. Questionnaire, n.d.

154. "Race Doctrines," handwritten notes, n.d., box 136, folder 8, CELC.

155. As Robin D. G. Kelley points out, "When Israel was founded in 1948, Black leaders and the Black press, for the most part, were jubilant." Kelley, "Yes, I Said, 'National Liberation,'" 146.

156. Malcolm X, "Zionist Logic," *Egyptian Gazette*, September 17, 1964. See, for example, Kelley, "Yes, I Said," 148–49. Malcolm defined "Zionist dollarism" as a process by which "European imperialists wisely placed Israel where she could geographically divide the Arab world, infiltrate, and sow the seed of dissension among African leaders, and also divide the Africans against the Asians." This global capitalist vision undermined Nasser's call for "African-Arab Unity under Socialism."

157. C. Eric Lincoln, chapter 1: introduction, 10–12, box 134, folder 12, CELC.

158. "Black Muslims in America, Part 1: The Spectre of Black Protest," n.d., box 134, folder 9, CELC.

159. C. Eric Lincoln to Elijah Muhammad, February 27, 1959, box 175, folder 12, CELC.

160. C. Eric Lincoln to Elijah Muhammad, August 25, 1959, CELC.

161. C. Eric Lincoln to Elijah Muhammad, July 27, 1959, CELC. In fact, Lincoln was an ordained Methodist minister with a degree from the Chicago Divinity School, and his PhD was in social ethics. His later research focused on the Black church.

162. Elijah Muhammad to Min. Malcolm X (Little), March 23, 1961, box 3, folder 8, MXC.

163. Cushmeer, *This Is the One*, 39–40, cited in Lincoln, *Black Muslims*, 3rd ed., 174.

164. Clegg, *Original Man*, 178.

165. Malcolm X and Haley, *Autobiography*, 284.

166. Richard Woodward, bulletin, October 1961, items 487–505, NCICF. The Senate Internal Security Subcommittee, known as the McCarran Committee, was authorized in 1950 to investigate subversive activities such as espionage, sabotage, and other threats.

167. Woodward, bulletin, May 1961, box 22, items 381–390, NCICF.

168. "The Police," an interview by Donald McDonald with William Parker, 1962, box 12, folder 1, MXC.

169. "The Police," box 12, folder 1, MXC.

170. For example, the *Indianapolis News* reported that "the cult has earned itself a fat file in Indianapolis police headquarters, as it has in South Bend and four dozen other cities in 21 states." See "Cult Preaches Hate for Whites at Rituals Here," *Indianapolis News*, February 20, 1961, White House Staff Files of Harris Wofford, Alphabetical File, 1956–1962, Martin, Dora Rogers, February 27, 1961, PJFK.

171. According to Bouza, in August 1955, the Bureau of Special Services and Investigations (BOSSI) dropped "Investigations" and became known simply as BOSS, but many continued to refer to it as BOSSI. In this book, I use the acronym BOSS unless describing a period prior to the change. Bouza, *Police Intelligence*, 24. I am grateful to Ori Burton for pointing this out to me.

172. Tony Bouza, phone interview with author, December 23, 2014. See also his 1976 book *Police Intelligence*.

173. Special Agent in Charge Letter No. 55-43, June 28, 1955, NOI-FBI.

174. *The Monthly Bulletin of the Association for Professional Law Enforcement*, April 1961, 8, 10, box 175, folder 1, CELC.

175. Reuben Horlick to Lincoln, May 23, 1963, box 70, folder 12, CELC. It is unclear if Lincoln accepted, but Horlick eventually presented at the conference on the need to understand the "latent aggression in the Negro personality and the hate of the Muslim." See Horlick, "Black Muslim in Prison," 360.

176. Bernard F. Robinson to Lincoln, September 5, 1962, box 70, folder 10, CELC.

177. Constance Martois to C. Eric Lincoln, October 4, 1960, and Lincoln to Martois, October 8, 1960, box 70, folder 2, CELC.

178. William E. Carr, "The Black Muslim Movement and Its Rationale, *Federal Probation*, March 1964, box 175, folder 1, CELC.

179. Alex Haley and Alfred Balk, "Black Merchants of Hate," *Saturday Evening Post*, January 26, 1963, 68–75.

180. "Muslim Cult of Islam," n.d., box 9, folder 326, ABPN. The report is identical to one credited to the Bureau of Inspectional Services, Chicago Police Department, May 24, 1962, in *Shaw v. McGinnis*, Respondent's Appendix, A123–A149.

181. Haley and Balk, "Black Merchants of Hate."

182. Marable, *Malcolm X*, 231.

183. Drzazga presumably meant that if the NOI engaged in electoral politics, Muhammad could greatly influence elections. Drzazga, "Muslim Terrorists," 38–41, 56–57, quote on 38.

184. Akbar and Theoharis, "Islam on Trial," *Boston Review*, February 27, 2017.

185. *The Muslims!!!!!*, San Diego Police Department training bulletin, n.d., box 12, folder 1, MXC.

186. The press was also complicit in this narrative of inevitability. For example, a 1961 exposé in the *Indianapolis News* that called the NOI a "Hate Cult" ended by pointing toward the next installment: "Police watch and wait." See "Newcomer's Frisked at Hate Cult's Rites," February 21, 1961, White House Staff Files of

Harris Wofford, Alphabetical File, 1956–1962, Martin, Dora Rogers, February 27, 1961, PJFK.

187. Brown, "Black Muslims," 119.

188. Browne, *Dark Matters*, 21. Quoted in Dan Berger, "Mapping Resistance to Surveillance," Black Perspectives (blog), African American Intellectual History Society, March 29, 2019, https://www.aaihs.org/mapping-resistance-to-surveillance/.

189. FBI headquarters was predictably concerned that its eighteen-minute color film, *A Day with the FBI*, which was used internally to illustrate crime detection and lab work, had been compromised. The director wrote to the New York office and demanded that agents be interviewed to determine whether this was the same film and what administrative action should be pursued if it were not. Summary report, New York, May 17, 1960, 34–35, and memo, director to New York, June 1, 1960, MX-FBI.

190. "Black Muslim Sect" ACA resolution, in E. R. Cass to Attorney General of the United States, October 3, 1962, box 173, folder 22, CSA. The previous year, finding an estimated 114 Muslims in California state prisons, the State Advisory Committee on Institutional Religion affirmed the Department of Correction's decision that the NOI not be entitled to religious rights in prisons. "Black Muslims in Prison," 1482n19. See also Lee Helsel to Laurence Stutsman, January 25, 1961, reproduced in Morrison, "Religious Legitimacy and the Nation of Islam," appendix, 76–77. The committee wished to avoid going on the record, judging that "groups of this kind thrive on notoriety."

191. Malcolm X and Haley, *Autobiography*, 173–74.

Chapter Two

1. "Shades of Mississippi! Muslims Chained in N.Y. Courtroom," *Amsterdam News*, October 27, 1962.

2. "Negroes Chained in N.Y. Courtroom," undated press release, box 11, folder 19, MXC.

3. *SaMarion v. McGinnis*, Civ. 9395, slip op. at 10 (W.D.N.Y. Oct. 14, 1963), trial transcript, 28, NARA-NYC.

4. This should not be confused with the Muslim Brotherhood in Egypt.

5. *Ruffin v. Commonwealth*.

6. Vogelman, "Prison Restrictions—Prisoner Rights," 386; John Fliter, quoted in Berger and Losier, *Rethinking the American Prison Movement*, 65. Fliter writes that "the hands-off policy was not mandated by the Supreme Court in any formal sense and not all courts followed it, but throughout this period, the Court encouraged a policy of nonintervention." In *Coffin v. Reichard*, for example, the Court of Appeals for the Sixth Circuit had ruled that a "prisoner retains all the rights of an ordinary citizen except those expressly, or by necessary implication, taken from him by law." Coffin v. Reichard, 143 F.2d 443 (6th Cir. 144), *cert. denied*, 325 U.S. 887 (1945).

7. *Stroud v. Swope*.

8. United States v. Shaughnessy, 112 F. Supp. 143 (S.D.N.Y. 1953), cited in Vogelman, 395n77.

9. Quoted in Berger and Losier, *Rethinking the American Prison Movement*, 62.

10. Lawrence O'Kane, "Muslim Negroes Suing the State," *New York Times*, March 19, 1961; Berger and Losier, *Rethinking the American Prison Movement*, 61–63.

11. Exchange between Federal Judge John O. Henderson and N.Y. State Corrections Commissioner Paul D. McGinnis, Buffalo, N.Y., October 30, 1962, 30, box 11, folder 19, MXC.

12. Sostre v. McGinnis, 334 F.2d 906 (1964). The passage cited from *The Black Muslims in America* read: "Although the Black Muslims call their Movement a religion, religious values are of secondary importance. They are not part of the Movement's basic appeal except to the extent that they foster and strengthen the sense of group solidarity." See Lincoln, *Black Muslims*, revised ed., 29.

13. For example, in 1958 the California Director of Corrections sent a bulletin to all wardens and staff that "requests to subscribe to the *Pittsburgh Courier* or the *Amsterdam News* should be screened as possible indications of interest in Muslemism." See Robert McGee, "Administrative Bulletin No. 58/16—Special Procedures for Muslim Inmates," February 25, 1958, reproduced in Morrison, "Religious Legitimacy," 72–73.

14. New York assistant attorney general Manuel Murcia said at trial in 1960, "We particularly object to their communicating with the Moslem Temple in Harlem which is run by a fellow by the name of Malcolm." Pierce v. LaVallee, 212 F. Supp. 865 (N.D.N.Y. 1962), trial transcript, 46, NARA-KC.

15. Scholars such as Mai Ngai and Margot Canaday have suggested that the state does not merely react to social identity but works to construct it as well. Canaday calls this process "state-building from the bottom up" and constructs "a social history of the state." Canaday, *Straight State*, 5. See also Ngai, *Impossible Subjects*.

16. Jacobs, "The Prisoners' Rights Movement," 459–60.

17. McLennan, *Crisis of Imprisonment*, 12. Prison activism in Texas and California was also often multiracial.

18. The other two were Lorton Reformatory in Virginia and Folsom State Prison in California. In 1966, a survey reported the highest activity of incarcerated Muslims in states with "large Negro populations concentrated in urban areas," including California, Illinois, Indiana, Kansas, Michigan, Missouri, New Jersey, New York, Ohio, and Texas. Caldwell, "Black Muslims behind Bars," 204. See also Report of Security Section, Intelligence Division, Bureau of Inspectional Services, Chicago Police Department, May 24, 1962, in Shaw v. McGinnis, 14 N.Y. 2d 864 (1962), Respondent's Appendix, A127-A128, ADLL.

19. Chase, "Civil Rights on the Cell Block," cited in Colley, "'All America Is a Prison,'" 13. In 1967, Eldridge Cleaver described a similar situation when Muslims, sentenced following a confrontation with police in Los Angeles, arrived in California prisons: "Officials separated them by sending each man to a separate institution. They did this because Black Muslim inmates looked upon these men as heroes in that they were political prisoners who had fallen in the line of duty, not for committing petty crimes." See Cleaver, *Post-Prison Writings and Speeches*, 16.

20. Larsen, "Prisoner Looks at Writ-Writing," 356; Chase, "We Are Not Slaves," 73.

21. See McGee, "Administrative Bulletin No. 58/16."

22. For an account on the case at Clinton through the lens of constitutional law, see Gordon, *Spirit of the Law*, 117–26.

23. *SaMarion v. McGinnis* transcript, 712–13.

24. *SaMarion v. McGinnis*, 1145–59.

25. *SaMarion v. McGinnis*, 433, 711.

26. *SaMarion v. McGinnis*, 477.

27. *SaMarion v. McGinnis*, 744. James Walker explained to Judge Henderson, who thought this was a garden plot: "No, sir, to cook on, whatever activities you wish. It was actually in the recreation yard. . . . They had a section there, what we call a hill, it is up high." Quote on 478.

28. *SaMarion v. McGinnis*, 432–33.

29. *SaMarion v. McGinnis*, 711.

30. *SaMarion v. McGinnis*, 708.

31. *SaMarion v. McGinnis*, 1157. James Walker remembered this language in his testimony: "That was the time that we were taken to the principal keeper and charged with holding unauthorized meetings under the cloak and guise of a religion" (432).

32. *SaMarion v. McGinnis*, 712–13, 721.

33. *SaMarion v. McGinnis*, 721.

34. *Attica: The Official Report.* Ironically, the warden's puzzlement over how Islam constituted some sort of hustle is reminiscent of Malcolm X's own initial confusion over converting to Islam as told in his autobiography. When his brother Reginald told him not to eat pork or smoke cigarettes and that he'd show him how to get out of prison, Malcolm's "response was to think he had come upon some way I could work a hype on the penal authorities. . . . I was aching with wanting the 'no pork and cigarettes' riddle answered." Malcolm X and Haley, *Autobiography*, 180–83. The time frame for the rise of Islam in New York corresponds with the activism found by James Jacobs at Stateville Prison in Illinois. There, disciplinary reports identified Muslims beginning in 1957 and listed nearly sixty members by 1960. Jacobs, *Stateville*, 60.

35. Mahmood Mamdani, *Good Muslim, Bad Muslim*.

36. *Pierce v. LaVallee* and *SaMarion v. McGinnis* followed and coincided with cases in Virginia (*Fulwood v. Clemmer*, 295 F.2d 171 [1961] and *Sewell v. Pegelow*, 291 F.2d 196 [1961]) and California (*In re Ferguson*, 55 Cal. 2d 663, 361 P.2d 417, cert. denied, 368 U.S. 864 [1961]). Significant research on the Nation of Islam's influence in Illinois and California prisons has been produced, but organizing at Lorton Reformatory in Virginia is still understudied. See Cummins, *Rise and Fall of California's Radical Prison Movement*; Jacobs, *Stateville*; Losier, "'. . . For Strictly Religious Reasons.'"

37. Schaich and Hope, "Prison Letters of Martin Sostre," 284.

38. *Pierce v. LaVallee* transcript, 18. Further evidence of the breadth and contentiousness of the Muslim community in New York prisons came at the *Shaw v. McGinnis* trial, in which a fight between Saki [likely Zaki] Abdullah and James Walker was reported over "a difference in the two branches of Muslimism." Abdullah was listed elsewhere as a leader of the NOI at Auburn Prison. See W. B. Surdam to Inspector W. F. Driscoll, February 4, 1960, box 19, items 11–20, NCICF.

39. Anderson was also persecuted as a Muslim at Clinton. He was listed as "one of the leaders of the Moslems" at Clinton and was transferred to Auburn in May 1959.

Earlier that year, he was placed in solitary confinement "because he started an agitation about the Moslem Religion among the prisoners." See Surdam to Driscoll.

40. *Pierce v. LaVallee*, 143, 150.

41. *SaMarion v. McGinnis*, 558, 602. Malcolm X later explained when testifying in the case, "Just as a priest is not acceptable to a Protestant or a Protestant clergyman is not acceptable to a Catholic, although both of them are Christian, neither is Ahmadiyya acceptable to us." Martin Sostre gave a similar explanation in *Pierce v. LaVallee*, telling the judge that he would not want any of the four interpretations of the Qur'an listed as acceptable for the "same objection a Catholic wouldn't use a Protestant book." See *SaMarion v. McGinnis*, 85; *Pierce v. LaVallee*, 188.

42. See Frankino, "Manacles and the Messenger," 38, 50.

43. *SaMarion v. McGinnis*, 376.

44. Thomas X Bratcher to Malcolm X, n.d, box 4, folder 9, MXC. The state even brought forward confiscated material from the *Pittsburgh Courier* as evidence in the *Shaw v. McGinnis* trial several years later, including a 1958 article by Elijah Muhammad called "Separation Solves the Problem." See *Shaw v. McGinnis*, Respondent's Appendix, A71.

45. McGee, "Administrative Bulletin No. 58/16."

46. Although the timing of the disciplinary action on Christmas Day seems as if it were a reactionary response to Islamic practice on a Christian holy day, no evidence or claims were given at the trial to suggest that either the plaintiffs or the defendants believed this to be a motivation.

47. *SaMarion v. McGinnis*, 722.

48. *SaMarion v. McGinnis*, 430–31.

49. "Moslems Hurl Charges at State Prison Rule," *Amsterdam News*, November 7, 1959.

50. *Pierce v. LaVallee*, 102.

51. The fourth plaintiff, Edward Robert Griffin, was paroled before the case went to trial, so the judge dismissed his case against LaVallee. See *Pierce v. LaVallee*, 21. For a good legal summary of the *Pierce v. LaVallee* and *SaMarion v. McGinnis* cases and their significance, see Crawford, *Black Muslims and the Law*, 65–90.

52. For more on Jacko's legal career and the influence of Charles Hamilton Houston, see Crawford, "Neo-Houstonian Studies."

53. Marable and Felber, *Portable Malcolm X Reader*, 82. There was much dispute at the beginning of the trial over whether Sandifer and Jacko represented the men. All three plaintiffs had written letters to the judge claiming they had not heard from their counsel, and Jacko explained that he and Sandifer were "asked to appear here by the Moslem Mosque No. 2 of Chicago, Illinois." *Pierce v. LaVallee*, 15–17.

54. *Attica: The Official Report*, 123; *SaMarion v. McGinnis*, 1183.

55. Thomas Bratcher testified that there were roughly sixty Muslims at Attica before he was placed in segregation. *SaMarion v. McGinnis*, 612.

56. *New York State Commission of Correction Annual Report, 1960*, 78.

57. *Attica State Prison*, 7. The McKay Commission, established to report on the Attica rebellion in 1971, cited New York prisons under McGinnis as trailblazers of this strategy. But it was not unique to New York. Robert Chase points out that the Texas

Department of Correction distributed Muslims throughout state prisons to limit their influence in any given place. See Chase, "Civil Rights on the Cell Block," cited in Colley, "'All America Is a Prison,'" 13. *Attica: The Official Report*, 121.

58. Lieutenant G. W. Craig to Superintendent Arthur Cornelius, Jr., April 28, 1961, box 19, item 145, NCICF.

59. *SaMarion v. McGinnis*, 1013.

60. *SaMarion v. McGinnis*, 1211.

61. *SaMarion v. McGinnis*, 1024.

62. *SaMarion v. McGinnis*, 333, 338. Attica had two full-time chaplains (Protestant and Catholic) and one part-time Jewish chaplain. They all offered weekly services, hospital and segregation visits, and personal consultations. They also assisted with correspondence to relatives and lectured on "successful living." See *New York State Commission of Correction Annual Report, 1960*, 85–86. For more on Khalil Nasir, see Turner, *Islam in the African-American Experience*, 125.

63. *SaMarion v. McGinnis*, 764.

64. Albert Meyer to Walter Wilkins, July 1, 1960, *SaMarion v. McGinnis*, 1187.

65. Attica report on Muslim activities, September 1, 1960, *SaMarion v. McGinnis*, 1191.

66. Lofton J. Bratcher, "Jobless," *Amsterdam News*, December 1, 1962.

67. *SaMarion v. McGinnis*, 598–601. It is unclear whether Muslims in the NOI would have called it the *Shahada* at this particular moment.

68. *SaMarion v. McGinnis*, 503.

69. *SaMarion v. McGinnis*, 1078.

70. *SaMarion v. McGinnis*, 534.

71. Muslim Brotherhood Constitution, 34A, box 11, folder 19, MXC.

72. *SaMarion v. McGinnis*, 33A–34A. Thomas Bratcher's constitution for D Block at Attica also read: "If the brother accused denies the charge, a trial is to be had." *SaMarion v. McGinnis*, 608.

73. Cleaver, *Post-Prison Writings*, 14.

74. See Jacobs, "Prisoners' Rights Movement," 435.

75. *SaMarion v. McGinnis*, 608.

76. As Berger observes, while similar organizing was "a staple of women's resistance, such an emphasis on collectivity in men's facilities belied some of the hypermasculinity of the constant calls to arms that celebrated the power of a heroic individual." Berger, *Captive Nation*, 175.

77. Berger, *Captive Nation*, 58.

78. Muslim Brotherhood Constitution, 31A.

79. *SaMarion v. McGinnis* transcript, 406–8.

80. Jacobs, "Prisoners' Rights Movement," 435.

81. See *Attica: The Official Report*, 119.

82. At Clinton, for example, the prison reported that "forty-three homosexuals were segregated in F-Block" in 1960. Attica reported having fifty-two prisoners in segregation for mental reasons, protection, or those "suspected of having homosexual tendencies." See *New York State Commission of Correction Annual Report, 1960*, 105; *New York State Commission of Correction Annual Report, 1963*, 85.

83. *SaMarion v. McGinnis*, 406–8.

84. Muslim Brotherhood Constitution, 32A. The constitution noted that by using "this method our organization is indestructible; shall always maintain its continuity; and shall frustrate the enemys [*sic*] attempts to destroy it, since as soon as a member is drafted to another prison it is his duty to organize there a Muslim Brotherhood upon the same lines as the present organization, thereby spreading the unifying and awakening force of Islam among all the brother prisoners in all the N.Y. State Prisons." This passage was noted with great concern by Senior Prison Inspector Richard Woodward, who wrote that it "might be a good thing in the institutions to find out the leaders and their assistants." See Richard E. Woodward, bulletin, April 1961, box 21, items 340–49, NCICF.

85. Cleaver, *Post-Prison Writings*, 14.

86. Muslim Brotherhood Constitution, 32A.

87. Prison officials insisted on calling solitary confinement "segregation." In one case, William SaMarion wrote to his lawyer, and the warden charged that he was writing lies. "I asked the warden specifically what was untrue in the letter [to Jacko], and he made reference to I should change the 'solitary confinement' to 'segregation.'" See *SaMarion v. McGinnis*, 371. This emphasis on language was reflected in California as well. At San Quentin, incarcerated people were forbidden from writing about prisons, being critical of American society, or even referring to themselves as prisoners. See Cummins, *Rise and Fall*, 83.

88. Nadle, "Martin Sostre Up Against the Wall."

89. Oshinsky, *"Worse Than Slavery,"* 6.

90. *SaMarion v. McGinnis*, 364–66, 613.

91. *SaMarion v. McGinnis*, 718.

92. *SaMarion v. McGinnis*, 718.

93. As Deputy Warden Meyer described it, "Good time is tentatively assessed. It is assessed for misconduct, the prisoner may earn back some of this good time if he conducts himself in a manner conforming to the rules and regulations. However, the final disposition of good time is made by the prison board and the prison board in the final analysis determines all good time." *SaMarion v. McGinnis*, 1035.

94. *New York State Commission of Correction Annual Report, 1961*, 79–89.

95. *SaMarion v. McGinnis*, 363, 462, 586.

96. *SaMarion v. McGinnis*, 362.

97. *Attica: The Official Report*, 33, 80.

98. *Attica: The Official Report*, 626. John Domino described his introduction to racism at Attica in 1969, after "white ice" was brought out in five-gallon buckets and "Black ice" was pushed out in wheel barrels and dumped into the sand for men to wash off as it melted. Domino, *Attica: A Survivors Story*, 57.

99. *Attica: The Official Report*, 80.

100. *SaMarion v. McGinnis*, 771.

101. *SaMarion v. McGinnis*, 1203. A monthly report noted that on May 27, 1961, "prisoner Martin Sostre, 17019, was apprehended, having in his possession in the corridor certain inflammatory Muslim literature, including many of the recent writings of Elijah Muhammad. This is in direct violation of institution rules

concerning Muslims. Sostre was confined to segregation." *SaMarion v. McGinnis*, 1248.

102. Eldridge Cleaver wrote of a similar combination of strategies in California's prisons: "In 1963, when I was transferred from San Quentin to Folsom for being an agitator, they put me in solitary confinement. The officials did not deem it wise, at that time, to allow me to circulate among the general prisoner population." See Cleaver, *Soul on Ice*, 33.

103. *SaMarion v. McGinnis*, 417.

104. *SaMarion v. McGinnis*, 1045.

105. Richard E. Woodward, bulletin, November 1961, box 22, items 487–505, NCICF. SaMarion lost sixty days of good time for planning the action. See *SaMarion v. McGinnis*, 425.

106. Jacobs, *Stateville*, 61–62.

107. See "Muslim Cult Blamed in Prison Strife," *San Bernardino Sun*, March 5, 1961; "Riots Force Segregation at Prison," *Washington Post*, March 5, 1961.

108. *SaMarion v. McGinnis*, 497–98.

109. *SaMarion v. McGinnis*, 581.

110. *SaMarion v. McGinnis*, 582–83.

111. Jacobs, "Prisoners' Rights Movement," 434.

112. Cummins, *Rise and Fall*, 80.

113. O'Kane, "Muslim Negroes Suing the State."

114. Jacobs, "Prisoners' Rights Movement," 433, 460.

115. Jacobs, "Prisoners' Rights Movement," 433.

116. As Jacobs argues, the NOI succeeded in part by "provid[ing] an example for using law to challenge officialdom. Jacobs, "Prisoners' Rights Movement," 433. See also Gottschalk, *Prison and the Gallows*, 175. For more on Muslim prison litigation and the prisoners' rights movement, see Smith, "Black Muslims and the Development of Prisoners' Rights."

117. *Shaw v. McGinnis*, Respondent's Appendix, A108–9.

118. Bratcher to Malcolm X, n.d.

119. Bratcher to Malcolm X, n.d.

120. For example, see *SaMarion v. McGinnis*, 574.

121. Richard Woodward to Richard Sampson, memo, May 20, 1964, box 24, items 850–59, NCICF.

122. *SaMarion v. McGinnis*, 1,237.

123. Chase, "We Are Not Slaves," 73.

124. Larsen, "Prisoner Looks at Writ-Writing," 356.

125. See Meyer's testimony, *SaMarion v. McGinnis*, 1055.

126. *Shaw v. McGinnis*, Respondent's Appendix, A109.

127. Woodward to Sampson, memo, May 20, 1964.

128. Cummins, *Rise and Fall*, 80–81.

129. *Shaw v. McGinnis*, Respondent's Appendix, A120–21.

130. For more on the connections between imprisonment and the civil rights movement, see Colley, *Ain't Scared of Your Jail*; Berger, *Captive Nation*, 20–48.

131. Felder, *Civil Rights in South Carolina*, 99.

132. Berger, *Captive Nation*, 46.

133. *Shaw v. McGinnis*, Respondent's Appendix, A121.

134. Craig to Cornelius Jr., April 28, 1961.

135. Craig to Cornelius Jr., April 28, 1961.

136. This language appeared both in a hearing on Un-American Activities in Monroe, Louisiana, and in the disciplinary report on the prisoners at Clinton Prison. See Hearing, Joint Legislative Committee on Un-American Activities, State of Louisiana, November 27, 1962, 28, box 23, folder 10, MMC.

137. Malcolm X and Haley, *Autobiography*, 211, 197.

138. In *Attica: The Official Report*, 123. Eventually this category included anyone who listed "no religion" as well, which likely resulted in inflated figures. However, since the majority of Muslim prisoners converted while in prison, it is also likely that many members went undetected by the state's system. Many would have come, like Thomas Bratcher and Arthur Johnson, from a Christian background and listed their denomination upon entry.

139. *Attica: The Official Report*, 123.

140. Woodward, bulletin, April 1961.

141. Richard E. Woodward, bulletin, March 1961, box 21, items 336–39, NCICF.

142. Richard E. Woodward, bulletin, September 1961, box 22, items 487–505, NCICF. Some of these guards may have been undercover. The report stated that "a member of the guard force was placed in a cell adjacent to a Muslim and recorded information of a subversive nature resulting in the prisoner's being placed in segregation."

143. Bratcher to Malcolm X, n.d.

144. Woodward, bulletin, April 1961.

145. Richard E. Woodward, bulletin, June 1961, box 22, items 381–90, NCICF.

146. *SaMarion v. McGinnis*, 1324, 571–73.

147. Lester X Anthony, "How Faith Surmounted—Trials of Prison," *Muhammad Speaks*, October 25, 1963.

148. Robert A. Heinze to Stanley Mosk, interdepartmental communication, January 8, 1963, box 173, folder 22, CSA.

149. Attica prison report, March 1, 1961, SaMarion v. McGinnis, Civ. 9395, slip op. at 10 (W.D.N.Y. Oct. 14, 1963), trial transcript, NARA-NYC, 1195.

150. Richard E. Woodward, bulletin, May 1961, box 22, items 381–90, NCICF.

151. *SaMarion v. McGinnis* transcript, 1043–44.

152. Craig to Cornelius Jr., April 28, 1961. For an example, see Marcelino Rodriguez, parole report, November 27, 1963, box 23, items 775–84, NCICF.

153. Thomas Bratcher, parole report, February 2, 1965, box 24, items 980–89, NCICF. This was also true in California, where the "associate warden or associate superintendent shall notify, through channels, the department chief records guard of the release date of any person listed as a Muslim [*sic*]." See McGee, "Administrative Bulletin No. 58/16."

154. *Shaw v. McGinnis*, Respondent's Appendix, A127.

155. Richard E. Woodward, "History of Muslims Presented to Uniformed Supervisors Association of the New York State Department of Correction," February 5,

1964, 7, box 24, items 831–39; NCICF and Caldwell, "Survey of Attitudes toward Black Muslims in Prison," 238n4. The California Department of Corrections estimated in 1966 that there were between four hundred and five hundred Muslims imprisoned in the state.

156. Irwin, *Prisons in Turmoil*, 70.

157. Clemmer and Wilson, "The Muslim in Prison."

158. Richard E. Woodward, bulletin, n.d., box 22, items 381–90, NCICF. Perhaps most disturbing in Woodward's use of Clemmer's findings was that he made no distinction in his report between his voice and that of the author. His memo shuffles effortlessly between his own conclusions and Clemmer's, notably that the most "disturbing phenomena of the Muslims in prison is their nonconformance and their bitter racial attitudes. In these respects they demonstrate an ethnocentrism, —that is a catering to ones one race and [ethnic] group, as chief interest or end."

159. Sheehy, "Black Muslims and Religious Freedom in Prison"; Horlick, "Black Muslim in Prison."

160. Gómez, "Resisting Living Death," 62.

161. Schein, "Man against Man," 98.

162. Metzl, *The Protest Psychosis*, xiii. Also see Thuma, *All Our Trials*, 11 and 58.

163. Schein, "Man against Man," 100–101.

164. Gómez, "Resisting Living Death," 62–63. See also "The Use of Psychiatry as an Instrument of Repression," February 19, 1968, in McCubbin, *Martin Sostre in Court*, 6–10, JLC. Brown was appointed special adviser to President Kennedy in 1961 and served as director of the NIMH from 1970 to 1977.

165. Gómez, "Resisting Living Death," 59–60, 79. Cummins noted that in "this prison-within-a-prison [San Quentin's AC unit,] inmates received far fewer treatment programs, not more." See Cummins, *Rise and Fall*, 92.

166. Edgar Schein, email correspondence with author, April 23, 2018.

167. Bratcher to Malcolm X, n.d.

168. Jacobs, "Prisoners' Rights Movement," 429.

169. Berger, *Captive Nation*, 6.

170. Quoted in McCubbin, *Martin Sostre in Court*, 13.

171. McGuire, *At the Dark End of the Street*, 228.

172. Perhaps because of these shortcomings, NOI headquarters did not invest lawyers in the *SaMarion* trial.

173. *Pierce v. LaVallee*, 117.

174. *Pierce v. LaVallee*, 48–49, 53, 55–56.

175. Deputy Meyer at one point threatened to destroy one of two notebooks that William SaMarion kept for the purpose of documenting his persecution. However, he agreed to let SaMarion keep them after SaMarion threatened to have them subpoenaed. See *SaMarion v. McGinnis*, 373.

176. *SaMarion v. McGinnis*, 258.

177. *SaMarion v. McGinnis*, 22.

178. *SaMarion v. McGinnis*, 27.

179. Richard Griffin, letter to author, July 21, 2014. Griffin represented William SaMarion and Thomas Bratcher. Clark Zimmerman represented Joseph Magette,

Arthur Johnson, and James Walker. Jacob D. Hyman and Wade Newhouse of the University of Buffalo Law School also served as court-appointed attorneys. See *SaMarion v. McGinnis*, 28; and "Muslims Battle State," *Amsterdam News*, October 20, 1962.

180. Bratcher to Malcolm X, n.d.

181. Bratcher to Malcolm X, n.d.

182. Bratcher to Malcolm X, n.d. Richard Griffin recalled traveling to the Harlem luncheonette frequented by Mosque No. 7 in order to meet with Malcolm X and convince him to testify in the case. Richard Griffin, phone conversation with author, June 6, 2014.

183. Jeanette Wakin, "Remembering Joseph Schacht," Islamic Legal Studies Program, Harvard Law School, *Occasional Publications* 4 (January 2003): 29.

184. *SaMarion v. McGinnis*, 788. Malcolm gave testimony on October 17, 18, and 23, 1962, which can be found on pages 45–285 and 642–704 of the trial transcript.

185. *SaMarion v. McGinnis*, 172, 220.

186. *SaMarion v. McGinnis*, 147–50.

187. Griffin, letter, July 21, 2014. Griffin represented only William SaMarion and Thomas Bratcher. Clark Zimmerman represented Joseph Magette, Arthur Johnson, and James Walker, and Jacob Hyman and Wade Newhouse of the University of Buffalo Law School were also appointed by the court. See *SaMarion v. McGinnis*, 28; and "Muslims Battle State."

188. As Berger points out, Malcolm's analogy relies on an erasure of the roles that enslaved people who lived and worked in the house played in gathering information and organizing acts of resistance and even mass uprisings. "Metaphors make compelling polemics but lousy history: house slaves were often central to slave resistance precisely because of their proximity to the master's family." See Berger, *Captive Nation*, 60.

189. William Bresnihan to J. Walter Yeagley and J. Edgar Hoover, October 16, 1964, MX-FBI. In response, Hoover said that the bureau "doubt[s] he has defected from the beliefs of the Muslims or that there is any great ideological separation. . . . I would be surprised if Malcolm X would be of any value to you as a witness if he were called." His letter reveals the shallowness of the FBI's understanding of Malcolm's activities abroad. Despite knowing some dates and places, Hoover wrote that the "best we can determine is that he is traveling in Africa." J. Edgar Hoover to William Bresnihan, October 27, 1964, MX-FBI.

190. Chicago to the director, February 18, 1965, MX-FBI; Chicago to the director, February 18, 1965, OAAU-FBI. The OAAU file does not redact the names of Freidman and Decker, whereas Malcolm's file does. In the FBI's summary of the interview with Malcolm, he did not mention the Cooper case. He informed the men that he was invited to the upcoming Bandung Conference to be held in Indonesia and, according to the FBI, stated that he was "now an Orthodox Moslem and believed in the brotherhood of all mankind including the whites."

191. Berger and Losier, *Rethinking the American Prison Movement*, 64.

192. Gottschalk, *Prison and the Gallows*, 174.

193. Jacobs, *Stateville*, 10.

194. Irwin, *Prisons in Turmoil*, 105.

195. Woodward, bulletin, March 1961.

196. "Religious Persecution in New York Prisons," box 11, folder 19, MXC.

197. Jacobs wondered, "Is it better or worse that today's prison is more fully bureaucratized than the prison of a decade ago?" Jacobs, "Prisoners' Rights Movement," 458 and 463.

Chapter Three

1. Chief Inspector Thomas Nielson urgently requested information from police departments and prisons in Michigan and Massachusetts regarding Malcolm X's criminal background within weeks of the Hinton protest. See five messages from Nielson, all dated May 15, 1957, MXB.

2. Quoted in Flamm, *In the Heat of the Summer*, 82.

3. DeCaro, *On the Side of My People*, 113.

4. As Malcolm put it, "Surely you must realize that anyone who can assemble so many well-disciplined young Negroes together as swiftly as we, should never be underestimated as a force to be recognized and reckoned with here in Harlem's community affairs and conferences." See Malcolm X, "Muhammad Will Support All Community Efforts," *Los Angeles Herald-Dispatch*, January 30, 1960, box 175, folder 15, CELC.

5. A. Philip Randolph to Malcolm X, August 11, 1961, box 3, folder 13, MXC. Reports on the cause of the disturbance varied. Police and journalists cited excessive and sustained heat, drinking, a fight, and a pedestrian hit by a bus; others suggested demonstrations by the Nation of Islam and other Black Nationalists as the cause. See Philip Meagher, "Violence in Harlem Brings 200 Police," *New York Times*, July 29, 1961; "Muslims Pushed Harlem Riots, Police Report," *Atlanta Daily World*, August 1, 1961.

6. Evelyn Cunningham, "Randolph, Muslims Cooperate on Curbing Riots," *Pittsburgh Courier*, August 12, 1961. From the beginning, headlines signaled that the group was concerned with "curbing riots" rather than police reform. For more on Cunningham's incredible career as a journalist, see Herb Boyd, "Grande Dame of Black Journalism, Evelyn Cunningham, Passes at 94," *Amsterdam News*, April 12, 2011.

7. Quoted in Jones, *March on Washington*, 144.

8. Lee Blackwell, "Off the Record," *Chicago Daily Defender*, February 19, 1958.

9. Harold Keith, "Leaders Bury Differences, Merge," *Pittsburgh Courier*, October 7, 1961.

10. Jim Haughton, Planning Committee Report, n.d., box 19, Emergency Committee for Unity on Social and Economic Problems, APRP.

11. His first report was titled "Activities of the Members of the Temple of Islam," William K. DeFossett to Commanding Officer, Bureau of Special Services, June 3, 1957, MXB. DeFossett graduated from DeWitt Clinton High School in the Bronx in 1932 and served with the 369th Regiment and the 4th Marine Division as a chief warrant officer in World War II. He joined the police department on February 1, 1949. During the 1950s and 1960s, he also worked as a special agent for BOSS. He later became the first Black security agent for the U.S. State Department.

12. "Muslim Charges Police Brutality," *Amsterdam News*, August 19, 1961.

13. William DeFossett to Commanding Officer, July 27, 1959, and Ernest Latty to Commanding Officers, July 16, 1959, both in MXB.

14. "Prison Sect Incited State's Negro Cons," *Daily News*, October 31, 1959, box 19, items 31–40, NCICF.

15. Kelley, *Freedom Dreams*, ix.

16. Domanick, *To Protect and Serve*, 143–45.

17. "Police Chief Parker Appears, Refuses Some Questions," *NAACP Newsletter* 3, no. 1 (September 1957); "Policemen, Chief Parker Sued for Half Million," *NAACP Newsletter* 2, no. 12 (August 1957), Printed Matter, Newsletters, Part 25: Branch Department Files, Series C: Branch Newsletters and Printed Materials, 1956–1965, PNAACP.

18. Sides, *L.A. City Limits*, 136. For the most thorough discussion to date of William Parker and policing in Los Angeles, see Felker-Kantor, *Policing Los Angeles*.

19. Lee Brown, whose idea of "community policing" eventually became the next major wave of police reform in the 1970s, recalled reading Wilson's classic *Police Administration* during officer training in the 1960s. Lee Brown, phone conversation with author, January 5, 2018.

20. Hernández, *City of Inmates*, 159.

21. Felker-Kantor, *Policing Los Angeles*, 14.

22. Kraus, "William Parker," 1321–23; Gooch, "Illegal Search and Seizure, Due Process, and the Rights of the Accused," 87.

23. Brown, *Working the Street*, 39–51.

24. Felker-Kantor, *Policing Los Angeles*, 21.

25. Felker-Kantor, *Policing Los Angeles*, 141 and Platt, *Beyond These Walls*, 100, 107.

26. Report, Bureau of Criminal Investigation (BCI), box 19, items 1–10, NCICF.

27. "Muhammad's Temple of Islam" to Chief Inspector Martin F. Dillon, BCI, February 19, 1960, box 19, items 21–30, NCICF.

28. Donner, *Protectors of Privilege*, 49, 155.

29. Tony Bouza, phone conversation with author, December 23, 2014.

30. Donner, *Protectors of Privilege*, 249.

31. Gooch, "Illegal Search and Seizure," 88–89, 92.

32. As Max Felker-Kantor explains, "The structure of municipal government limited the mayor's direct power over the police department and granted the police chief civil service protection, while Section 202 of the city charter conferred all power of discipline over officers to the chief." See *Policing Los Angeles*, 115.

33. W. H. Parker, "The Police Role in Community Relations," Annual Conference of the International Association of Chiefs of Police, October 3, 1955, 6, 13, 22, box 24, folder 14, LMP.

34. Parker, "The Police Role in Community Relations," 17.

35. Parker, "The Police Role in Community Relations," 17.

36. "The Officer and the Public–III," *Daily Training Bulletin* 5, no. 7 (October 22, 1962): 11, box 24, folder 14, LMP.

37. Murakawa, *First Civil Right*, 18.

38. Parker, "Police Role in Community Relations," 23.

39. Gene Hunter, "Police, Fire League Hits at Proposed Review Board," *Los Angeles Times*, April 19, 1960. While it was unclear whether the Japanese American Citizens

League was part of this coalition, the group had worked alongside the Legal Redress Committee throughout the 1950s. See "Legal Committee Program Working," *Los Angeles Branch NAACP Newsletter* 2, no. 10 (June 1957): 2, 4, Part 25: Branch Department Files, Series C: Branch Newsletters and Printed Materials, 1956–1965, PNAACP.

40. Hunter, "Police, Fire League."

41. Muhammad, *Condemnation of Blackness*, 5.

42. "Parker Angrily Denies Racial Discrimination," *Los Angeles Times*, January 27, 1960.

43. Bill Becker, "Police Brutality on Coast Denied," *New York Times*, January 27, 1960.

44. "Parker Angrily Denies Racial Discrimination."

45. Becker, "Police Brutality on Coast Denied." Parker would later charge that "a dangerous custom has arisen in America wherein the hapless police officer is a defenseless target for ridicule and abuse from every quarter." Quoted in Felker-Kantor, *Policing Los Angeles*, 49.

46. Muhammad, *Condemnation of Blackness*, 229, 269.

47. Mack, *Representing the Race*, 9. For a more comprehensive look at Miller's political life, see Hassan, *Loren Miller*.

48. Mack, *Representing the Race*, 9, 181–82, 186.

49. Kurashige, *Shifting Grounds of Race*, 232.

50. Mack, *Representing the Race*, 189, 204, 206.

51. "Parker Angrily Denies Racial Discrimination"; Becker, "Police Brutality on Coast Denied."

52. *The Hate That Hate Produced* transcript, July 23, 1959, 1–2, box 6, LLP.

53. The name is sometimes recorded as Jomo Nkrumwah. See "Meet 'The Devil' and 'Bishop Green,'" *Muhammad Speaks*, Special Edition 1, no. 6 (1961).

54. "The Trial Becomes Broadway Smash Hit," *Muhummad Speaks*, December 1960. According to *Muhammad Speaks*, the "white man/Devil" was played by Frank X of the Boston mosque, who did "such a superb job imitating the white man throughout ORGENA, most of the audience believe the Black Muslims have hired a white actor to play this part." See "Meet 'The Devil' and 'Bishop Green.'"

55. Curtis, "Islamism and Its African American Muslims Critics," 687.

56. "Muslims Plan 6-Hour Freedom Rally May 28," *Amsterdam News*, May 21, 1961.

57. See Taylor, *Promise of Patriarchy*; Griffin, "'Ironies of the Saint.'"

58. She writes that the "practice of gendered racial terror worked to crystallize the position of the Black female subject outside of the normative category 'woman.'" Haley, *No Mercy Here*, 57.

59. Gross, "African American Women, Mass Incarceration, and the Politics of Protection," 25.

60. Hartman, Wayward Lives, Beautiful Experiments, 29.

61. Haley, No Mercy Here, 56.

62. The NOI drew on the political theater of the Communist Party and the National Negro Congress decades earlier. Erik Gellman writes of a mock trial for police brutality that demonstrated the "new-style tactics of the NNC: with the theatrics in front of a large public audience, the mock trial showed how the District ought to protect citizenship rights through democratic governance." See Gellman, *Death Blow to Jim Crow*, 119.

63. Malcolm was in Boston at the time.

64. "Moslems' Ten Day Trial," *Amsterdam News*, March 21, 1959.

65. See William K. DeFossett to Commanding Officer, May 27, 1958, MXB.

66. "Moslems' Ten Day Trial."

67. "Moslems Charge False Arrests in N.Y.," *Pittsburgh Courier*, May 24, 1958.

68. Summary report, New York, May 19, 1959, 48, MX-FBI.

69. DeFossett to Commanding Officer, May 27, 1958.

70. Al Nall, "Moslem Trial Begins," *Amsterdam News*, March 7, 1959.

71. "Moslems Plead 'Not Guilty,'" *Amsterdam News*, October 18, 1959. Jacko's and Malcolm's charges were nearly verbatim, as the former claimed that the invasion represented both a "violation of their civil rights, as well as violations of privacy of their home and religious house." See Al Nall, "The Moslem Trial," *Amsterdam News*, March 28, 1959.

72. "Moslems Charge False Arrests."

73. The jury was composed of three Black men and ten white men, described by one reporter as majority "Hebrews." See Al Nall, "The Moslem Trial."

74. Ernest B. Latty, Report on Trial, March 27, 1959, MXB.

75. Al Nall, "Moslems Accuse Cops; Bring Their Own Steno to Court," *Amsterdam News*, March 14, 1959.

76. Haas, *Assassination of Fred Hampton*.

77. Al Nall, "Moslems Go Free," *Amsterdam News*, March 21, 1959. Jacko was fully quoted as saying, "Those shots were not to get criminals, thieves and bandits, but to kill women, children and babies." The FBI reported that Malcolm said virtually the same thing when quoting a *Los Angeles Herald-Dispatch* article on March 26, 1959. Because of the timing, it is most likely that either Malcolm adapted Jacko's line from the courtroom or that the FBI misquoted the news article.

78. Nall, "Moslems Accuse Cops."

79. Latty, Report on Trial.

80. "Moslems Ten Day Trial."

81. Latty, Report on Trial.

82. Nall, "Moslems Go Free."

83. Latty, Report on Trial.

84. "Cops Quiz Moslems; New Hearing Slated," *Amsterdam News*, May 2, 1959.

85. "Arrest Moslem Woman," *Amsterdam News*, June 20, 1959.

86. Memo, Sgt. J. N. Dershimer to Chief Inspector Martin F. Dillon, BCI, New York State Troopers, February 27, 1960, items 41–50, NCICF.

87. "City Gives Muslim $70,000 Award," *Amsterdam News*, July 1, 1961.

88. Al Nall, "Moslems Confer with Top Cop," *Amsterdam News*, April 11, 1959; "Cops Quiz Moslems."

89. "Say NY Cops KKK Members," *Amsterdam News*, September 12, 1959.

90. Malcolm X, address on police brutality, undated and untitled, box 5, folder 2, MXC. There are several indications that this is the September 6 rally. For example, he says that "just recently we read where the white police had severely beaten an African diplomat here in Harlem." This occurred on August 26, 1961. He ends his speech with "great respect for APR [A. Philip Randolph]."

91. Evelyn Cunningham, "Panel Will Continue: Malcolm X and Randolph Spark Rally in Harlem," *Pittsburgh Courier*, September 16, 1961.

92. William Jones and Manning Marable both focus on the more conservative elements of Malcolm's speech, noting that he criticized police for allowing crime and violence in Harlem while opposing a mass march on the 28th Precinct. See Jones, *March on Washington*, 145; Marable, *Malcolm X*, 192–93.

93. The actual cause of the disturbances remained unclear. Police and journalists reported excessive and sustained heat, drinking, a fight, and a pedestrian being hit by a bus, along with the Harlem Black Nationalists, as potential causes. See Meagher, "Violence in Harlem."

94. Meagher, "Meeting concerning Crisis of Racial Violence in Harlem," August 2, 1961, box 19, APRP.

95. "Cops Beaten in Harlem Rioting," *Pittsburgh Courier*, August 5, 1961; "Muslims Pushed Harlem Riots."

96. A. Philip Randolph to "Dear Friend," August 24, 1961, box 19, APRP.

97. Later iterations of this proposal included the mandate for Black workers in all stages, including administrative, technical, and service areas. Unfortunately, it would take until 1987 for Jazz at Lincoln Center to be realized and until 2004 for a physical space to be created to honor jazz amid these other Eurocentric art forms. See Proposals for a Unity Action Program, box 2, folder 5, JHP.

98. "Economic and Social Demands, Presented to New York City Officials and Those Candidates Running for Office," August 29, 1961, box 2, folder 5, JHP.

99. "3 Mayoral Candidates Agree on Harlem Move to Aid City's Negroes," *New York Times*, August 30, 1961.

100. Robert Wagner to A. Philip Randolph, September 5, 1961, box 19, APRP.

101. Attorney General Louis J. Lefkowitz's Report to A. Philip Randolph Group, delivered September 1, 1961, box 19, APRP.

102. Haughton, Planning Committee Report, Subject Files, Emergency Committee for Unity on Social and Economic Problems, APRP.

103. These debates show up routinely in the Emergency Committee's founding documents. A draft of the Action Program presented to political leaders on August 29 shows a significant shift from the original category of "Hostile Police Enforcement" to simply "Police Enforcement" (potential replacement adjectives "problem" and "difficult" were scribbled in the margin). See Proposals for a Unity Action Program. Emphasis added.

104. A Proquest newspaper search, for example, shows 34 uses of "law and order" in the 1950s compared to 412 in the 1960s and 808 during the 1970s.

105. In the decade between 1962 and 1972, its use quadrupled. See Google Books Ngram Viewer data. For more on "law and order" in American political development, see Murakawa, "The Origins of the Carceral Crisis."

106. Bayard Rustin interviews with Ed Edwin, November 1984–June 1987, 217, CCOH; Haughton, Planning Committee Report.

107. The exchangeability of Malcolm for another representative of the Nation of Islam likely indicates the minister's hectic schedule. But it also demonstrates that the Emergency Committee did not see Malcolm as somehow "outside" the NOI.

Unlike contemporary historiography, which often reads his split with the NOI in 1964 backwards and positions Malcolm as politically distinct from the organization for which he spoke, organizers more likely saw Malcolm as a representative of the larger movement. As the recently appointed national spokesman of the NOI, Malcolm was perceived as the voice of the movement rather than in tension with it.

108. "Draft Proposal for a Forum on Black Liberation," n.d., box 2, folder 5, JHP; "Draft Proposal for a Forum on Negro Liberation," n.d., box 19, Emergency Committee for Unity on Social Problems, 1961–1962, APRP.

109. According to William Jones, Randolph delegated much of the responsibility for organizing the Emergency Committee to Hedgeman. See Jones, *March on Washington*, 144.

110. This played out most prominently in two different documents found in Haughton's and Randolph's personal papers. In the handwritten draft in Haughton's papers, it is called a "Forum on Black Liberation." In the typed version in Randolph's papers, "Black" is crossed out in favor of "Negro." In the "Unity Action Plan" in Haughton's papers, "Negro Ministers" is crossed out in favor of "Black Ministers." In Randolph's papers, it reads "Negro Ministers of the Community." In "Draft Proposal for Forum on Black/Negro Liberation" and "Unity Action Plan" in box 2, folder 5, JHP, and box 19, APRP.

111. Randolph's original telegram on August 11, 1961, inviting members to be part of an ad hoc committee included "Corliss Cooke" of 315 Lenox Ave. This was a misspelling of Carlos Cooks, whose group, the African Nationalist Pioneer Movement, shared that address.

112. Robert Teague, "Negroes Say Conditions in U.S. Explain Nationalists' Militancy, *New York Times*, March 2, 1961.

113. Quoted in Flamm, *In the Heat of the Summer*, 135.

114. Although the speech notes are undated, the combination of Malcolm's reference to the Bay Area and thanking Donald Warden make this likely a talk delivered on May 7, 1961, at either Mosque No. 26 in Oakland or the Fillmore Auditorium in San Francisco. See "Speech Notes: The Black Revolution," box 10, folder 4, MXC.

115. "Speech Notes: The Black Revolution," box 10, folder 4, MXC.

116. Conversation of Gloster Current with Frank Jenkins, July 27, 1959, 3–4, General Office Files, Black Muslims, 1958–1960, Part 24: Special Subjects, 1956–1965, Series A: Africa-Films, PNAACP; J. F. Finn to Everett C. Updike, "Muslim Cult of Islam," box 19, items 1–10, NCICF.

117. John Ali to Roy Wilkins, June 30, 1960, General Office Files, Black Muslims, 1958–1960, Part 24: Special Subjects, 1956–1965, Series A: Africa-Films, PNAACP.

118. "Black Muslim Malcolm X Calls for Racial Separation in US," *Wesleyan Argus*, February 7, 1962.

119. Marlene Nadle, "Malcolm X: The Complexity of a Man in the Jungle," *Village Voice*, February 25, 1965.

120. These included (in chronological order): Queens College, Yale University (twice), Howard University, UC Berkeley, and Rutgers. For more on these college lectures and their impact, see Felber, "'Integration or Separation?'"

121. Tarea Pittman to Gloster Current, May 9, 1961, General Office File, Black Muslims, 1961–1965, Part 24: Special Subjects, 1956–1965, Series A: Africa-Films, PNAACP.

122. Gloster Current to Tarea Pittman, June 8, 1961, General Office File, Black Muslims, 1961–1965.

123. Edwin Lukas to John Morsell, July 27, 1960, General Office File, Black Muslims, 1961–1965. For more on the relationship between the AJC and the NAACP, see Cohen, *Not Free to Desist*, 383–89.

124. For more on the Committee of 100, see Jonas, *Freedom's Sword*, 47.

125. Pittman to Current, May 9, 1961, General Office File, Black Muslims, 1961–1965.

126. A. Philip Randolph to Jack Blumstein, September 12, 1961, box 19, APRP. In 1964, Blumstein's Department Store was purported to employ almost 85 percent Black workers. See Theodore Jones, "Harlem's Heart Beats Message on 125th St." *New York Times*, February 8, 1964.

127. A. Philip Randolph to Joseph A. Davis, November 14, 1961, box 19, APRP.

128. See "Minutes of Sub-Committee Meeting on March to Washington held in NAACP Office," April 10, 1941, cited in Lucander, "'It Is a New Kind of Militancy,'" 303.

129. Garfinkel, *When Negroes March*, 4.

130. Statement from Sub-Committee on Police Brutality, October 20, 1961, box 11, folder 18, MXC.

131. The memo, likely written by Malcolm X, was dated the same day as the next major meeting of the Emergency Committee. There, all five subcommittees were set to report on their progress.

132. Harriet Pickens, Minutes, Meeting of Subcommittee on Law and Order Enforcement, October 23, 1961, box 19, APRP.

133. Forman, *Locking Up Our Own*, 78–118. Beryl Satter's history of the Afro-American Patrolmen's League in Chicago is an important counternarrative to consider. See Satter, "Cops, Gangs, and Revolutionaries in 1960s Chicago." See also Pihos, "Policing, Race, and Politics in Chicago."

134. Hernández, *City of Inmates*, 159. For the longer history of efforts to diversify the police force in Los Angeles, see pages 184–89.

135. Felker-Kantor, *Policing Los Angeles*, 256–57.

136. Manning Marable's biography of Malcolm X interprets the committee's significance through the book's principal character: "The importance of Malcolm's role on the Emergency Committee is central to interpreting what happened to him after he broke with the NOI in 1964." See Marable, *Malcolm X*, 193. Jennifer Scanlon and William Jones also offer a brief account of the Emergency Committee's rise and fall. See Scanlon, *Until There Is Justice*, 156–57; Jones, *March on Washington*, 143–44.

137. A. Philip Randolph, quoted in Lightfoot, "Negro Nationalism and the Black Muslims," 4.

138. Emphasis added.

139. Patrolman Edwin Cooper to Commanding Officer, June 24, 1963, BSS #294-M, Municipal Archives.

140. "Powell Plans Racial Forums," *New York Times*, June 20, 1963.

141. Scanlon, *Until There Is Justice*, 156.

142. Jones, *March on Washington*, 163.

143. One memo from just before the march did, however, list "An End to Police Brutality Now" as an approved slogan for signs. See Bayard Rustin and Cleveland Robinson. "March on Washington for Jobs and Freedom, Organizing Manual No. 1," 1963. Box 30, Folder 1. Bayard Rustin Papers, Manuscript Division, Library of Congress, cited in Stein, "Fearing Inflation, Inflating Fears," 151. I am indebted to David Stein for pointing this out to me.

144. For example, see Sherie Randolph's biography on attorney and organizer Florynce "Flo" Kennedy, who worked within dual spaces of marginalization—from the Black Power movement and the predominantly white women's movement—to build coalitions and bridges between the two. As Randolph writes, "Seeking to make connections where others saw divisions, Flo extended Black Power outside Black radical circles into primarily white feminist spaces." Randolph, *Florynce "Flo" Kennedy*, 125.

145. Abbreviated quote in Gilmore, *Golden Gulag*, 232.

146. Hedgeman later said, "As usual, the men must have discussed the matter in my absence, and when the first leaflet was printed, I was embarrassed to find that I was still the only woman listed." Quoted in *Florynce "Flo" Kennedy*, 166.

147. Memo, Arnold Perl, "Discussion with Anna Hedgeman," October 17, 1969, box 60, folder 11, MWC.

148. Jones, *March on Washington*, 175, 242.

149. Boyd, "Grande Dame of Black Journalism."

150. "Black Muslims to Hold Rally Here Sunday," *Boston Globe*, July 26, 1962.

151. Laura Warren Hill, "'We Are Black Folks First,'" 164.

Chapter Four

1. "Muhammad's Temple of Islam," memo to Chief Inspector Martin F. Dillon, Bureau of Criminal Investigation, February 19, 1960, Box 19, Items 21–30, NCICF.

2. W. C. Lovelock to Robert E. Denman, "Muslim Activities in the Los Angeles Area," June 6, 1961, 3, box 22, items 401–10, NCICF.

3. See drawing of crime scene by Internal Affairs Division. It reports five men shot by Donald Weese's six bullets and another two by Lee Logan. Box 4, Records of the Commission on Civil Rights, NARA.

4. *The People of the State of California v. Louie R. Buice, Arthur Coleman, Elmer Craft, Fred Jingles, Monroe Jones, Robert Rogers, William Rogers, Roosevelt Walker, Charles Zeno*, trial transcript, 21, folder 188, TBP.

5. "Top New York Muslim Says L.A. Is on Trial," *Los Angeles Times*, May 4, 1963.

6. *People v. Buice*, 429–30.

7. *People v. Buice*, 115.

8. Malcolm X later mentions the men saying *"Allāhu akbar"* as they held hands on the sidewalk after being shot. See speech delivered at Park Manor Auditorium on May 5, 1962.

9. See testimony of Partev Manasjan, *People v. Buice*, 4–17.

10. *People v. Buice*, 10.

11. Branch, *Pillar of Fire*, 9.

12. Transcript of Malcolm and John Shabazz at Embassy Auditorium, April 16, 1961, in "Muslim Activities in the Los Angeles Area," box 22, items 401–10, NCICF.

13. Summary report, New York, March 21, 1963, 8, Leon Ameer FBI File, box 9, subseries VI.3, MXP.

14. Summary report, New York, November 16, 1962, 20, MX-FBI. See also "Second Mass Protest Rally . . . to Eliminate Police Brutality," May 20, 1962, box 11, folder 18, MXC.

15. Summary report, New York, November 16, 1962, MX-FBI.

16. "Muhammad Calls for United Black Front!," *Muhammad Speaks*, June 1962.

17. Goldman, *Death and Life of Malcolm X*, 97.

18. Bagwell, *Malcolm X: Make It Plain*.

19. Goldman, *Death and Life of Malcolm X*, 100.

20. Breitman, *Last Year of Malcolm X*, 17. Others, such as Hakim Jamal, also split from the NOI over its response to the Stokes case. See Jamal, *From the Dead Level*.

21. Wilson Gilmore, Golden Gulag, 27.

22. Crawford, *Black Muslims and the Law*, xii.

23. Pendergast, *Contemporary Black Biography*, 48.

24. He recused himself from the Advisory Committee during a 1963 investigation and report, prompted by the killing of Ronald Stokes, because he was acting as the Nation of Islam's legal representation.

25. Theoharis, "Hidden in Plain Sight," 51.

26. See Jeanne Theoharis, "50 Years Later, We Still Haven't Learned from Watts," *New York Times*, August 11, 2015; Robin D. G. Kelley, "Remember What They Built, Not What They Burned," *Los Angeles Times*, August 11, 2015.

27. Knight, "Justifiable Homicide," 183.

28. "Muhammad's Temple of Islam."

29. Malcolm X to Beatrice X Clomax, December 22, 1957, box 3, folder 3, MXC.

30. Correlation summary, August 22, 1961, 20, MX-FBI.

31. "Young Moslem Leader Explains the Doctrine of Mohammedanism," *Los Angeles Herald-Dispatch*, July 18, 1957.

32. Summary report, New York, April 30, 1958, 39–43, MX-FBI.

33. Summary report, 97, 107.

34. Summary report, 102.

35. As Manning Marable argued, his suggestion that voter registration could change the political balance of power indicated that he had shed "the old Nation of Islam claim that participation in the system could have little effect." Marable, *Malcolm X*, 302.

36. In fact, the very title of his 1964 speech may have been influenced by the pages of *Muhammad Speaks*. In 1962, journalist Sylvester Leaks penned a front-page story on the civil rights struggle in Fayette County, Tennessee, to register Black residents to vote. The subtitle of Leaks's story read: "Fayette Fought for Freedom with Bullets and Ballots." Sylvester Leaks, "Fayette's Fantastic Fight," *Muhammad Speaks*, September 15, 1962, 1, 12–13.

37. "Elect Your Own Candidates," *Muhammad Speaks*, March 18, 1963.

38. Summary report, New York, April 30, 1958, 119–20, MX-FBI.

39. Summary report, 112.

40. Summary report, 124.

41. Summary report, New York, November 19, 1958, 7, 9, MX-FBI.

42. Summary report, 8–9.

43. Summary report, April 30, 1958, 109, MX-FBI.

44. "Christians Walk Out on Moslems," *Amsterdam News*, April 26, 1958.

45. According to police surveillance, Malcolm's task was to unify the temples on the West Coast. Using similar language to that of Malcolm himself, a report noted that he "obviously saw the fertile field in Los Angeles." See "Muhammad's Temple of Islam."

46. Summary report, New York, November 19, 1958, 45, 54, MX-FBI.

47. See Morrow, "Malcolm X and Mohammad Mehdi," 12–13.

48. "Malcolm X Speaks at Univ. S. Cal." *Amsterdam News*, April 5, 1958.

49. "Los Angeles Police Called Next Worst to Birmingham's," October 6, 1961, 2, General Office File, Police Brutality—California, Colorado, and Connecticut, Part 24: Special Subjects, 1956–1965, Series C: Life Memberships-Zangrando, PNAACP. See also "NAACP Civil Rights Rally Disappointing," *Los Angeles Sentinel*, October 5, 1961.

50. "NAACP Claims Brutality by Police in L.A.," *Los Angeles Times*, February 19, 1962.

51. LAPD estimated roughly 360 Muslims in Los Angeles. However, the *Washington Post* in 1962 cited police as reporting 3,500 members in Southern California. Clegg, *An Original Man*, 114; "Black Muslims' Fight Coast Police," *Washington Post*, April 29, 1962. See "Muhammad's Temple of Islam."

52. "Muhammad's Temple of Islam."

53. Summary report, New York, May 17, 1962, 11, 19–20, MX-FBI.

54. Summary report, New York, November 19, 1958, 1, MX-FBI 3.

55. Lincoln, *Black Muslims*, revised ed., 5.

56. Knight, "Justifiable Homicide," 185.

57. For testimony regarding the UCLA case, see *People v. Buice*: Troy Augustine (pp. 1307–65); Robert Washington (1,170–202); Arthur Coleman Jr. (1,990–2,072); Joseph Moreton Jr. (1,128–60); and Jack Gustafson (1,160–74). On Coleman's injuries, see testimony of Donald Weese (p. 8) and Coleman Jr. (99–100, 110).

58. Loren Miller, "Loren Miller Says . . . Tale of Two Men," *California Eagle*, May 10, 1962.

59. Loren Miller, "Farewell to Liberals: A Negro View," *Nation*, October 20, 1962.

60. Robert Carter to Loren Miller, November 8, 1962, box 10, folder 5, LMP.

61. Robert Carter to Loren Miller.

62. Kenneth Clark, "Liberalism and the Negro," *Commentary* 37 (March 1964): 39.

63. Press release, n.d., box 12, folder 1, MXC. See also "Makes Bail," *California Eagle*, May 10, 1962.

64. King, "Black Leadership in Los Angeles."

65. Telegram from Roy Wilkins, *Muhammad Speaks*, June 1962, 5.

66. "Los Angeles Tensions Up over Police Brutality," *Pittsburgh Courier*, May 19, 1962.

67. Grace Simons, "Chief Parker Called 'Drunk with Power,' Muslims Supported," *California Eagle*, May 10, 1962.

68. Hugh R. Manes, "A Report on Law Enforcement and the Negro Citizen in Los Angeles," 40, box 24, folder 15, LMP.

69. Gene Hunter, "Yorty Calls Racial Situation Tense, Asks Federal Help," *Los Angeles Times*, May 10, 1963.

70. Grace E. Simons, "I Killed Stokes, Says Officer," *California Eagle*, May 17, 1962.

71. Dr. J. Raymond Henderson, press release for mass meeting, May 12, 1962, box 12, folder 1, MXC.

72. This group was likely renamed the Citizens Committee on Police Brutality on June 19, 1962. Run by Christopher Taylor, the group was "formed out of the Citizens Protest Rally held at Second Baptist church, May 13, 1962, attended by over three thousand persons." The Stokes case and the NOI's calls for a Black United Front prompted the formation of the Citizens Committee, which eventually grew into the UCRC, a broader multi-issue coalition that was not committed to an all-Black model of organizing.

73. Keynote speech by Wendell Green, May 13, 1962, box 25, folder 1, LMP.

74. Telephone account from Althea Simmons, May 15, 1962, Geographical File, Los Angeles, 1962, Part 27: Selected Branch Files, 1956–1965, Series D: The West, PNAACP.

75. "Digest of News Account of Muslims-Police Riot in Los Angeles," May 18–25, 1962, General Office File, Police Brutality—California, Colorado, and Connecticut, Part 24: Special Subjects, 1956–1965, Series C: Life Memberships-Zangrando, PNAACP.

76. Ron Karenga to Dr. Lincoln, April 5, 1961, box 70, folder 5, CELC; Ron Karenga, "Protest Rally Demands Chief Parker's Removal," *Los Angeles Herald-Dispatch*, May 24, 1962, 1.

77. Althea Simmons to Gloster Current, May 23, 1962, General Office File, Police Brutality—California, Colorado, and Connecticut, Part 24: Special Subjects, 1956–1965, Series C: Life Memberships-Zangrando, PNAACP.

78. Arnold Trebach, notes from informal conference at Los Angeles County Conference on Community Relations, July 27, 1962, box 3, Records of the U.S. Commission on Civil Rights, Record Group 453, Police-Community Relations in Urban Areas, 1954–1966, NARA.

79. L. I. Brockenbury, "Negro Ministers Blast Muslims as Hate Group," *Pittsburgh Courier*, June 2, 1962.

80. "Digest of News Account of Muslims-Police Riot in Los Angeles."

81. "Ministers Disown Muslims: Also Hit Police Brutality," *Los Angeles Sentinel*, May 24, 1962.

82. "Pastors Accused of Splitting Ranks in Fight on Brutality," *California Eagle*, May 31, 1962.

83. Trebach, notes from informal conference, 14, 17.

84. "Pastors Accused of Splitting Ranks in Fight on Brutality."

85. "Muslim Rally Denied Use of Church," *Los Angeles Herald Examiner*, May 23, 1962.

86. King, "Black Leadership in Los Angeles."

87. Henderson, press release.

88. Malcolm X, "An Open Letter to America's Five Negro Congressmen," n.d., box 12, folder 1, MXC.

89. Brockenbury, "Negro Ministers Blast Muslims."

90. Ward, *In Love and Struggle*, 296.

91. "Alternative Paths to Negro Freedom," ad, *Los Angeles Sentinel*, February 14, 1963; "Discussion Unlimited Program Set," *Los Angeles Sentinel*, February 14, 1963.

92. The NOI often rented public halls under the auspices of business, as many disallowed their use by religious or political groups. This was the case with New York's Afro-Asian bazaars.

93. Warren debated Malcolm at Los Angeles State College the year before. Summary report, New York, May 17, 1962, 19–20, MX-FBI.

94. Gladwin Hill, "Muslims' Defense Opened on Coast," *New York Times*, May 12, 1963.

95. Gloster Current, March 26, 1963, General Office File, Black Muslims, 1961–1965, Part 24: Special Subjects, 1956–1965, Series A: Africa-Films, PNAACP. See also Warren Hill, "'We Are Black Folks First,'" 175.

96. "14 Muslims Go on Trial in Fatal Riot," *Los Angeles Times*, April 8, 1963.

97. "Begin Jury Selection in L.A. Muslim Trial," *Chicago Daily Defender*, April 10, 1963.

98. "Pick Jury for L.A. Black Muslim Trial," *Chicago Daily Defender*, April 24, 1963.

99. "Row Flares over Jurors in Muslim Riot Trial," *Los Angeles Times*, April 25, 1963.

100. "Extend Jury Selection in Muslim Trial," *Chicago Daily Defender*, April 15, 1963.

101. *People v. Buice*, 136–37.

102. See box 11, folders 4–5, MXC.

103. "Mass Unity and Protest Rally," May 19, 1963, box 12, folder 1, MXC.

104. "What Happened?," *Muhammad Speaks*, April 29, 1963.

105. See box 12, folder 3, MXC.

106. "Unity Urged for Muslims and NAACP," *Times-News*, February 16, 1963.

107. Telegram to John F. Kennedy, box 3, folder 4, MXC.

108. Malcolm X, "'And This Happened in Los Angeles.'"

109. "Foreman of Black Muslim Jury Says Strange Man Shadowed Him," *Los Angeles Times*, June 17, 1963.

110. A. S. Doc Young, "Negroes Here Speak Out on Race," *Los Angeles Sentinel*, June 13, 1963.

111. Self, *American Babylon*, 178. Malcolm X and the NOI did not simply draw parallels to Birmingham but also took steps to support and cover the protests. Soon after returning from Los Angeles, Malcolm spoke at a Harlem rally sponsored the Emergency Committee to Support Birmingham with Rev. A. D. King and Rev. George Lawrence of the SCLC. Jeremiah X, an NOI minister who split his time between Atlanta and Philadelphia, went to Birmingham to observe and write a piece for *Muhammad Speaks*. See Summary report, New York, November 15, 1963, 18–19, MX-FBI; C. Portis, "Celebrities and Celebrators Pour into City," *New York Herald-Tribune*, May 15, 1963.

112. Gladwin Hill, "Negro Foes of Black Muslims Picket at Trial," *New York Times*, April 30, 1963.

113. "Negro Picket Slugged at Black Muslim Rally," *Los Angeles Times*, May 5, 1963.

114. As Malcolm X had explained to Judge Henderson in Buffalo the year before, "Segregation means to regulate or control. . . . A *segregated* community is that forced

upon inferiors by superiors. A *separate* community is done voluntarily by two equals." Emphasis added. *SaMarion v. McGinnis*, 172.

115. "Tells of Cop Beating at L.A. Muslim Trial," *Chicago Defender*, May 4, 1963.

116. Lawrence Lamar, "Judge Bars Segregation of Muslims," *Amsterdam News*, May 11, 1963.

117. "Top New York Muslim Says L.A. Is on Trial," *Los Angeles Times*, May 4, 1963.

118. *People v. Buice*, 719–20.

119. "Muslim Trial Interrupted by Attorney," *Los Angeles Times*, May 7, 1963.

120. *People v. Buice*, 524–36.

121. *People v. Buice*, 1332–33.

122. *People v. Buice*, 1770.

123. *People v. Buice*, 2135.

124. *People v. Buice*, 1056–57.

125. *People v. Buice*, 1357.

126. *People v. Buice*, 1814–16.

127. *People v. Buice*, 1814–21. The testimonies given at trial regarding ripped clothing, racial epithets, and forcing the men to walk outside with their pants down were consistent with statements taken nearly a year earlier immediately after the shooting. See statements by defendants, n.d., box 4, Police-Community Relations in Urban Areas, Records of the Commission on Civil Rights (RG 453), NARA.

128. *People v. Buice*, 2138–39.

129. True to the NOI's strategy in Queens and other cases that brought physical evidence of police violence into the courtroom, Broady and Miller repeatedly asked the men to try their torn suits on, asking them to explain how they arrived in such a condition. *People v. Buice*, 1397, 1469.

130. "Attorney Suggests Need for 'White Muslims' Too," *Los Angeles Times*, May 24, 1963. Emphasis added.

131. "Judge Warns Audience at Muslim Riot Trial," *Los Angeles Times*, May 23, 1963.

132. "Muslim Trial to Jury," *Los Angeles Sentinel*, May 23, 1963.

133. "Muslim Riot Trial Ends," *Los Angeles Times*, May 25, 1963; "Convict 4 Black Muslims in Fatal Riot," *Chicago Tribune*, June 11, 1963.

134. "Call Night Jury Meet in Black Muslims Case," *Chicago Daily Defender*, June 5, 1963; "4 Convicted in Calif. Muslim Riot," *Boston Globe*, June 11, 1963.

135. Buice, Coleman, Jingles, and Rivers all received one to five years in prison; Craft, Jones, Sidle, Walker, Zeno, and Robert Rogers all received up to a year in jail and five years of probation; and William Rogers received four years of probation without a jail term. "Black Muslims Sent to Prison," *San Jose Mercury*, August 1, 1963. "Black Muslim Jury to Set Record Today," *Los Angeles Times*, June 14, 1963; Seymour Korman, "9 Convicted in L.A. Muslim Riot," *Chicago Tribune*, June 15, 1963.

136. "9 Muslims Guilty," *Los Angeles Times*, June 15, 1963.

137. "Battle Against Jim Crow Goes West to Los Angeles, *Chicago Daily Defender*, June 4, 1963; Bauman, *Race and the War on Poverty in Los Angeles*, 40.

138. Althea Simmons to Tarea Pittman, July 11, 1963, West Coast Regional Office, Correspondence, July–December 1963, Part 25: Branch Department Files, Series B: Regional Files and Special Reports, 1956–1965, PNAACP.

139. Structure, NAACP and the United Civil Rights Committee, Althea Simmons, January–June 1963, Part 25, Series B, PNAACP.

140. Report of Althea Simmons, West Coast Region, May 15–June 14, 1963, Part 25, Series B, PNAACP.

141. "Six Bills Proposed to Reform Police Methods," *Los Angeles Times*, March 14, 1963; Jack Langguth, "Los Angeles Racial Protests Bring Mixed Results," *New York Times*, August 17, 1963.

142. Paul Weeks, "Negroes Assail L.A.'s Inaction on Rights Plea," *Los Angeles Times*, June 22, 1963.

143. Langguth, "Los Angeles Racial Protests."

144. "The 'Review Board' Should Be Rejected," *Los Angeles Times*, March 27, 1963.

145. "Review Board Called Police Demoralizer," *Los Angeles Times*, June 12, 1963.

146. Robert Blanchard, "Two-Year Study Set on Police Review Boards," *Los Angeles Times*, May 29, 1963.

147. Langguth, "Los Angeles Racial Protests."

148. Weeks, "Negroes Assail L.A.'s Inaction."

149. See Langguth, "Los Angeles Racial Protests"; Weeks, "Negroes Assail L.A.'s Inaction."

150. Hugh Manes, "A Report on Law Enforcement and the Negro Citizen in Los Angeles," July 1963, box 40, folder 1, HMP; Lee Brown, "Black Muslims and Police Officers," ca. 1967, box 1, folder 42, LBP; "Police-Minority Group Relations in Los Angeles and the San Francisco Bay Area," Report of the California Advisory Committee to the United States Commission on Civil Rights, August 1963 (Washington, DC: United States Commission on Civil Rights, 1963).

151. Theoharis, "Hidden in Plain Sight."

Chapter Five

1. Gordon Parks, "The Violent End of the Man They Called Malcolm X," *Life*, March 5, 1965, 26–31.

2. For an account of Robert's role in infiltrating the OAAU and the Black Panthers, see Elaine Rivera, "The Man Who Spied on Malcolm X" and "Undercover Cop: Years of Peril Took Their Roll," *Newsday*, July 23–24, 1989.

3. Marable, *Malcolm X*, 455. See Jimmy Breslin, "Malcolm X Slain by Gunmen as 400 in Ballroom Watch: Police Rescue Two Suspects," *New York Herald Tribune*, February 21, 1965.

4. Ula Taylor is one of the few historians to explore the NOI between Malcolm X's death in 1965 and Elijah Muhammad's in 1975. She begins chapter 9, for example, with the question: "Why would the revolutionary poet Sonia Sanchez convert to the NOI after the assassination of Minister Malcolm X?" *Promise of Patriarchy*, 140–68. Jeffrey Ogbar is another, but writes that the while the "NOI was the chief benefactor of the Black Power movement. . . . [it] no longer captured the media spotlight or grew as rapidly" after Malcolm's departure. Ogbar, *Black Power*, second edition, 37–38.

5. Fujino, *Heartbeat of Struggle*.

6. For a deep description of Wood's infiltration into CORE and the BLF, see his testimony before the House Un-American Activities Committee in 1967, "Subversive Influences in Riots, Looting, and Burning," 1,030–47.

7. David Burnham, "Thesis Provides Clues on Undercover Police," *New York Times*, March 8, 1971.

8. "GOP Gave Lessons on Making Bombs," *Afro-American*, May 29, 1965.

9. "Rookie Given 2nd Promotion for Foiling Plot," *Los Angeles Times*, February 18, 1965.

10. Bouza wrote that "Raymond Wood, the 'Black militant,' was promoted to Detective 2nd grade and was transferred to a field assignment far removed from his former area of operations. Before he was transferred, he was required to attend the Police Academy where the presence of a Detective 2nd grade in a recruit's grey uniform caused some consternation until his undercover work was revealed. Detective Wood received the highest decoration the Police Department award—Honorable Mention—and today he is married and is a functioning field detective." Bouza, *Police Intelligence*, 77.

11. Bouza, *Police Intelligence*, 165.

12. Umoja, "Repression Breeds Resistance," 96, in Cleaver and Katsiaficas, *Liberation, Imagination, and the Black Panther Party*. Edith Evans Asbury, "Undercover Agent Recalls How Role Was Almost Discovered by Black Panthers," *New York Times*, December 2, 1970. For more on Panther 21 trial, see Kempton, *The Briar Patch*.

13. Goldman, *Death and Life of Malcolm X*.

14. Flamm, *In the Heat of Summer*, 53.

15. Hinton, "MLK Now," forum response, *Boston Review*, September 10, 2018.

16. *Riots, Civil, and Criminal Disorders: Hearings Before the Permanent Subcommittee on Investigations of the Committee on Government Operations*, 90th Cong., 1st sess., 6 (1967).

17. Spilerman, "Causes of Racial Disturbances."

18. *Attica: The Official Report*, 104–5, cited in Camp, *Incarcerating the Crisis*, 80.

19. Lindsey Lupo argues that "race riot" commissions operate to manage violence by "dismissing, neutralizing, and marginalizing the violence as anomalous." See Lupo, *Flak-Catchers*, 2.

20. Singh, *Black Is a Country*, 6.

21. Burton, "Organized Disorder."

22. Gilmore and Wilson Gilmore, "Restating the Obvious" and Story, *Prison Land*, 17.

23. Wilson Gilmore, *Golden Gulag*, 27.

24. Berger, *Captive Nation*, 141–42.

25. For more on the social constructions and political uses of crime in creating moral panics and a more repressive police state, see Hall et al., *Policing the Crisis*.

26. "Police Arrest 52 as Raid on Muslims Shatters the Calm," *Austin Statesman*, August 18, 1965. Newspaper articles differed dramatically. Another reported a "heavy exchange of gunfire" after National Guardsmen "tried to stop a group of men carrying firearms into the building." See John Dart, "Fired First, Police Say," *New Journal and Guide*, August 21, 1965.

27. Thompson, *Blood in the Water*, 22, 30, 32 and Burton, "Organized Disorder."

28. Clark, interview.

29. Quoted in Felker-Kantor, *Policing Los Angeles*, 64.

30. "Rockefeller Beams New York Blueprint at Nation," *Los Angeles Times*, January 9, 1964.

31. "New Police Laws Scored at Rally," *New York Times*, March 8, 1964.

32. Douglas Dales, "Rockefeller Signs Bills Increasing Powers of Police," *New York Times*, March 4, 1964.

33. Malcolm Nash, "3000 to Join in March on Albany," *Amsterdam News*, March 7, 1964; Fred Powledge, "3,000 in Rights Protest March on Albany in Snow," *New York Times*, March 11, 1964; "Rocky Confers with Leaders of State March," *Newsday* (Albany Bureau), March 10, 1964. The focus of the march was on an increase in the minimum wage, the legalization of rent strikes, collective bargaining for workers at voluntary hospitals, aid for integrated education, and the elimination of English-only literacy tests for voting.

34. OAAU working papers, June 6, 1964, and Notes from May 30 and "Second Research Meeting," box 14, folder 3, MXC.

35. For more on the OAAU's local organizing, see Felber, "Harlem is the Black World."

36. "Notes on an Organization and Possible Issues around Which to Struggle and Raise the Level of Consciousness of the People," undated, box 14, folder 3, MXC.

37. OAAU working papers, June 6, 1964.

38. Junius Griffin, "Whites Are Target of Harlem Gang," *New York Times*, May 3, 1964.

39. "The Harlem 'Blood Brothers,'" *New York Times*, May 8, 1964.

40. Junius Griffin, "40 Negro Detectives Investigate Anti-White Gang," *New York Times*, May 7, 1964.

41. Griffin, "Whites Are Target of Harlem Gang."

42. Jerry Weinberg, "The Infamous Statue of Liberty Bombing Plot Case," *The Realist* 65 (March 1966), 9.

43. Commanding Officer to Chief of Detectives, September 5, 1964, 2, BOSS, Municipal Archives, New York City. I am grateful to Jonathan Karp for sharing this document with me.

44. Other panelists included Quentin Hand of the Harlem Action Group, William Reed of Harlem CORE, and Clifton DeBerry, 1964 presidential candidate of the Socialist Workers Party. "Blood Brothers Meeting," box 11, folder 19, MWC.

45. "N.Y. Mayor Declares All-Out War on Roving Negro Terrorist Gangs," *Washington Post*, June 3, 1964; Griffin, "40 Negro Detectives Investigate Anti-White Gang."

46. Les Matthews and George Barner, "They Still Can't Prove That 'Blood Gang' Lie!," *Amsterdam News*, May 23, 1964.

47. Griffin, "Whites Are Target of Harlem Gang."

48. "Red and Racist Agitators Accused of Whipping up Violence in N.Y.," *Los Angeles Times*, July 22, 1964.

49. Bob Greene and Tom Johnson, "The Riots: A Few Fanned the Flames," *Newsday*, September 21, 1964.

50. Peter Kihss, "Police in Harlem Reduce Patrols," *New York Times*, July 27, 1964; John Sibley, "2 Harlem Demands Accepted by Mayor," *New York Times*, August 7, 1964.

51. "L. Joseph Overton," *New York Times*, August 10, 1964.

52. "Unity Pleas Made at Harlem Rally, *New York Times*, August 2, 1964.

53. Junius Griffin, "Coalition of 69 Negro Groups Gives Shaky Unity to Harlem," *New York Times*, August 1, 1964; "Harlem Leaders Joining Hands," *Amsterdam News*, August 8, 1964. For more on the role of the Harlem YMCA as a public and political space, see Weisenfeld, "Harlem YWCA and the Secular City." Anna Arnold Hedgeman had begun working for the YWCA in 1924 and had been the executive director in Harlem before 1938.

54. David Willis, "Police and Harlem Search for Peace," *Christian Science Monitor*, September 24, 1964.

55. Shifflett to Overton, August 3, 1964, box 14, folder 2, MXC.

56. Randolph was out of town, and despite being invited, Governor Rockefeller, Mayor Wagner, and Commissioner McGinnis did not reply. "Those Who Will Participate," undated, box 14, folder 2, MXC.

57. Shifflett to Overton, August 3, 1964, box 14, folder 2, MXC.

58. David Willis, "N.Y. Riot Causes Tackled," *Christian Science Monitor*, September 30, 1964.

59. Willis, "N.Y. Riot Causes Tackled."

60. As one flyer had emphasized, "All sincere so-called Negro leaders must step forward, take part in the mass rally. . . . Let us forget our religious and political differences, we must come together on the same platform in a great display of unity." Flyer advertising mass rally sponsored by the NOI, July 21, 1962, box 2, folder 5, JHP.

61. "Harlem Leaders Joining Hands."

62. Sibley, "2 Harlem Demands Accepted."

63. OAAU-FBI, Memo, Chicago, November 10, 1964, 21–22.

64. Ethel Minor would eventually join SNCC and author the influential critique of Jewish Zionism, "The Palestine Problem," in 1967. See "Third World Round Up: The Palestine Problem: Test Your Knowledge," *SNCC Newsletter*, June–July 1967, 4–5. As Robin Kelley notes, the article was the primary catalyst in moving "Black identification with Zionism as a striving for land and self-determination . . . to a radical critique of Zionism as a form of settler colonialism akin to American racism and South African apartheid." Kelley, "Yes, I Said, 'National Liberation,'" 149.

65. Marable, *Malcolm X*, 429.

66. Penn Warren, *Who Speaks for the Negro?*, 200.

67. Gerald Horne, *Fire This Time*, 3, 68.

68. Murakawa, *First Civil Right*, 50.

69. Wilson Gilmore, *Golden Gulag*, 39.

70. "To the Peoples of Afroamerica, Africa, and to all the Peoples of the World," *Soulbook* 1 (1964): 1.

71. "L.A. Teacher Rips City Officials; Says: 'Riot Could Easily Have Been Avoided,'" *Muhammad Speaks*, November 5, 1965.

72. Ted Lewis, "Capitol Stuff," *Daily News*, August 18, 1965; Tom Goff, "Police-Negro Stress Noted 3 Years Ago," *Los Angeles Times*, August 22, 1965; Laurence Stern, "Coast Rioting Foreshadowed by Rights Data on Hostility," *Washington Post*, August 18, 1965.

All in Records of the Commission on Civil Rights, Police-Community Relations in Urban Areas, 1954–1966, box 3 (RG 453), NARA.

73. *Paramilitary Organizations in California*, Attorney General Thomas Lynch to Senator Eugene McAteer, April 12, 1965.

74. Horne, *Fire This Time*, 124.

75. "Driver Who 'Ignited Spark' Speaker at Black Muslims," *Austin Statesman*, August 16, 1965.

76. Horne, *Fire This Time*, 125.

77. "Cops Say Black Muslims Worked to Fan Riot in L.A.," *Newsday*, August 16, 1965.

78. Horne, *Fire This Time*, 144.

79. Dart, "Fired First, Police Say."

80. "Police Arrest 52 as Raid on Muslims Shatters the Calm," *Austin Statesman*, August 18, 1965. Newspaper articles differed dramatically. Another reported a "heavy exchange of gunfire" after National Guardsmen "tried to stop a group of men carrying firearms into the building." See Dart, "Fired First, Police Say."

81. Branch, *Pillar of Fire*, 296.

82. Horne, *Fire This Time*, 127; "LA Lifts Curfew, Clash Follows," *Newsday*, August 18, 1965.

83. Special Report by Councilman Billy G. Mills, November 22, 1965, 7, 13, box 180, ACLU-SC.

84. Taylor Branch, handwritten notes from interview with Robert Reynolds, October 11, 1991, folder 1,097, TBP.

85. Horne, *Fire This Time*, 126.

86. Leroy Aarons, "'Master of Conspiracy' Tells of Police Intrigue," *Washington Post*, October 17, 1971. For more on Tackwood, see Saunders, *Combat by Trial*, 208–9.

87. Parker's full quote was: "Then, like monkeys in a zoo, others started throwing rocks." Felker-Kantor, *Policing Los Angeles*, 29.

88. Elijah Muhammad, "Police Brutality," box B-6, folder 17, ANC. Parker later claimed that his statement describing rioters as "monkeys in a zoo" was taken "out of context." See David Kraslow, "Parker Puts Blame for Riot on State Highway Patrolman," *Los Angeles Times*, August 30, 1965.

89. Chester Wright, "TALO Reiterates Its Position," *Los Angeles Times*, August 6, 1966; Donald Wheeldin, "The Situation in Watts Today," *Freedomways* 7, no. 1 (Winter 1967): 56.

90. For more on TALO, see Felker-Kantor, *Policing Los Angeles*, 69–71.

91. "Group Meets Chief Brown," *Los Angeles Sentinel*, October 6, 1966; Ray Rogers, "Negro Rights Alliance Racked by Quarrels," *Los Angeles Times*, July 19, 1966.

92. Single-leaf press release, September 9, 1965, box B-6, folder 17, ANC.

93. "Black Community United Against: Wild Police Assault on Muslim Mosque," *Muhammad Speaks*, December 31, 1965.

94. Hugh Manes, "A Report on Law Enforcement and the Negro Citizen in Los Angeles," July 1963, box 40, folder 1, HMP; Lee Brown, "Black Muslims and Police Officers," ca. 1967, box 1, folder 42, LBP; "Police-Minority Group Relations in Los Angeles and the San Francisco Bay Area," Report of the California Advisory Committee to the

United States Commission on Civil Rights, August 1963 (Washington, DC: United States Commission on Civil Rights, 1963).

95. "The McCone Commission Report—a Bitter Disappointment: An Analysis of the McCone Commission Report" (Washington, DC: United States Commission on Civil Rights, California Advisory Committee, January 1966), 2.

96. Loren Miller, "Relationship of Racial Segregation to Los Angeles Riots," October 7, 1965, box 33, folder 16, LMP.

97. Governor's Commission on the Los Angeles Riots (McCone Commission), *Violence in the City: An End or a Beginning?*, December 2, 1965, 28.

98. In fact, Moynihan was interviewed in the aftermath of Watts, and his report on the collapse of the Black family was cited as an explanation for the uprising. See *CBS Reports: Watts—Riot or Revolt?* Bayard Rustin also noted the similarity of the two reports. See Bayard Rustin, "The 'Watts Manifesto' and the McCone Report," *Commentary*, March 1, 1966.

99. McCone Commission Report, 27, 85–86.

100. In an interesting twist, the two attorneys who had represented Muslims in the *People v. Buice* case were now on either side of the McCone Commission report. Earl Broady was a member of the McCone Commission, and Loren Miller was a member of the California Advisory Council, which denounced it.

101. "The McCone Commission Report—a Bitter Disappointment," California Advisory Committee to the United States Commission on Civil Rights, January 1966, 5–6.

102. Horne, *Fire This Time*, 130.

103. "The McCone Commission Report," 2.

104. Gottschalk, *Prison and the Gallows*, 175.

105. For example, James Jacobs writes that the "success of the Muslims on the constitutional issue of free exercise of religious rights brought the federal courts into the prisons." Jacobs, "Prisoners' Rights Movement," 435.

106. Judge William Lawless opinion in J. D. Steinmetz, "Black Muslim Religious Practice in New York State Prisons," memo, January 8, 1968, 6, box 45, NCICF. The previous year, McGinnis had redrafted the policies governing Islam in prisons, allowing for a place of worship, the purchase of the Qur'an, and religious literature that was not deemed "inflammatory." But Lawless demanded that he redraft a clause that prohibited any new Muslims from joining for a year and a provision that continued to ban outside ministers with criminal convictions. Still, the right to a special diet was denied, *Muhammad Speaks* was censored, and limits were placed on the number of people who could attend a religious service.

107. Judge William Lawless opinion in Steinmetz, 9.

108. As Dan Berger and Toussaint Losier point out, prison organizing efforts were "more explicitly interconnected and more self-consciously radical than those in the early 1950s." *Rethinking the American Prison Movement*, 72–73.

109. J. H. O'Dell, "Introductory Comment," *Freedomways* 6, no. 3 (Summer 1966): 227.

110. Cited in Story, *Prison Land*, 15.

111. Berger, *Captive Nation*, 59. Brett Story adds that "Thinking about the city and the prison as dialectical spaces whose transformations are structurally bound by shared

imperatives and relations of power not only reveals the prison as an expression of property relation and its centrality to contemporary urban economies but also simultaneously invites us to consider the prison as an urban exostructure." *Prison Land*, 49–50.

112. "Report on California Prisons," *Muhammad Speaks*, October 8, 1971.

113. Woodward to Sampson, memo, May 20, 1964, box 24, items 850–59, NCICF.

114. Cleaver, *Soul on Ice*, 54.

115. Lieutenant W. C. Lovelock to Central Files, memo, January 25, 1965, box 24, items 970–79, NCICF.

116. Nadle, "Martin Sostre Up Against the Wall," 10.

117. King, *Separate and Unequal*, 165–66.

118. As Herbert X Blyden recalled, the consciousness of prisoners was "raised by the uprisings throughout America from '67, '68, '69, the split I think in the party, West Coast and the East Coast faction of the Panthers, Malcolm's teachings, the diverse militant groups that was set up, the Weathermen, the Young Lords, the Five Percenters and, of course, the Nation of Islam's contingent." Blyden, interview.

119. On correspondence, see May 1970 and "Clinton Prison Muslims"; on visitation, see Guard Room office to Warden's Office, Clinton Correctional Facility, July 19, 1971; on infractions, see Deputy Warden to Warden's Office, May 15, 1968, Clinton Prison, all in box 47, NCICF.

120. While the NOI may have benefited from Judge Lawless's opinion that they be considered a legitimate religious group, the ruling may have also ensnared other Islamic groups in an ever-widening web. For example, see mail surveillance between August and September 1971, box 47, NCICF.

121. See transition between "Muslim Report, July 1969," August 2, 1969, and "Muslim-Black Panther Report, October 1970," November 5, 1970, box 47, NCICF.

122. One "Muslim report" concluded that "there were no legal actions of any type submitted . . . which pertained to the Muslim or Panther movement." Harry Fritz and Michael Kany to Commissioner McGinnis, Muslim Report, August 1970, box 47, NCICF.

123. For more on Tombs, see Burton, "Organized Disorder"; Losier, "Against 'Law and Order' Lockup." For more on the Folsom manifesto, see Mirpuri, "Mass Incarceration."

124. New York State Special Commission on Attica, Minutes of Meeting, November 15, 1971, box 86, ACIF.

125. Juan Vasquez, "Guard Is Indicted with 8 Prisoners in Riots at Tombs," *New York Times*, January 26, 1971.

126. Black Solidarity Day was created the previous year by playwright Carlos Russell. On the first Monday in November before election day, all people of African descent would boycott all commercial activity.

127. Thompson, *Blood in the Water*, 22–30.

128. Berger and Losier, *Rethinking the American Prison Movement*, 90.

129. Thompson, *Blood in the Water*, 32.

130. Clark, interview.

131. "Books and Things: Specializing in Islamic Literature," box 84, ACIF.

132. Duties of Lieutenant Captain, box 1, AID.

133. Secretary General Instructions, seized September 14, 1971, box 1, AID.

134. Orientation class notes, box 1, AID.

135. Henry X, notes on "Courtesy and Discipline," box 84, ACIF.

136. Notes on meeting, August 22, 1971, box 1, AID.

137. WBAI Transcript of Speeches Made in D-Yard, New York State Special Commission on Attica, March 6, 1972, 5–6. Neither Farrakhan or Walker came. Joe Walker, a reporter for *Muhammad Speaks* who covered Attica extensively after the uprising, wrote that he was overseas at the time, and the main office in Chicago was never contacted. See Walker, "The Attica Rebellion: Day-to-Day Account," *Muhammad Speaks*, October 22, 1971.

138. It's unclear whether Norman Butler was actually at Attica during the rebellion. Clark recalled that he "got shipped out a little bit after." But in a later interview Butler said he had only corresponded with Johnson. See "Who Killed Malcolm X?," 8. I am grateful to Ori Burton for making me aware of this inconsistency.

139. Blyden, interview; Thompson, *Blood in the Water*, 66.

140. Smith, interview.

141. Clark, interview.

142. Clark, interview.

143. Thompson, *Blood in the Water*, 79–80.

144. Joe Walker, "The Attica Rebellion: Day-to-Day Account," *Muhammad Speaks*, October 22, 1971, 19.

145. Speech by Herbert Blyden, September 12, 1971, 3, box 83, ACIF.

146. Blyden, interview.

147. Quoted in WBAI Transcript of Speeches Made in D-Yard, March 6, 1972, 44–45, 50, 52, box 83, ACIF.

148. Clark, interview.

149. WBAI Transcript of Speeches, 45. Importantly, Smith made this comment before Muslim security from the metal shop kept him from being killed both by the prisoners who had decided to execute a hostage and by the forces of the state, which attacked at that moment.

150. Walker, "Attica Rebellion," 21.

151. Blyden, interview.

152. Thompson, *Blood in the Water*, 168.

153. Walker, "Attica Rebellion," 20–21.

154. Sostre, *The New Prisoner*, 253, JLC.

155. Thompson, *Blood in the Water*, 482; *Al-Jundi v. Mancusi*, 113 F. Supp. 2d 441 (W.D.N.Y. 2000).

156. Walker, "Attica Rebellion."

157. "Demands of Attica Prisoners Can Serve as Model for Others," *Muhammad Speaks*, October 22, 1971.

158. Sister Sandra 17X, "Muslim Wife Details Attica Horrors of Husband Inmate," *Muhammad Speaks*, October 29, 1971.

159. Larry 22X, "Attica Victims Cry Out for Justice," *Muhammad Speaks*, October 1, 1971.

160. While Clark remembered not being able to receive it, a monthly report from D block in 1970 reported that Melvin X "continues to write many notes dealing with all phases of Islam, especially from the paper (*Muhammad Speaks*)." "Monthly D-Block Report," December 1, 1970, box 1, AID.

161. Joe Walker, "Attica Inmate Sees Prisons Used as Labs," *Muhammad Speaks*, October 29, 1971.

162. Samuel 17X, "Prison News in Black," *Muhammad Speaks*, September 1, 1972, 29.

163. Samuel 17X, "Inmate Reviews Epic Struggle of Muslims for Prison Reform," *Muhammad Speaks*, September 15, 1972, 23. Most of the article is written by Lester 2X Gilbert from inside.

164. *Attica: The Official Report*, 104–5, cited in Camp, *Incarcerating the Crisis*, 80.

165. Sostre, *The New Prisoner*, 251.

166. See section on "Political Prisoners" in *Proceedings of the 102nd Annual Congress of Correction of the American Correctional Association*, 103–13.

167. Robert Bright, Administrator of the Department of Correction in Illinois, noted that "1972 finds one heck of a lot of minority persons languishing in our jails and penal institutions. Of the approximate 2 million in confinement and under community supervision, about 33 per cent are Black, and increasing numbers are Puerto Ricans and Chicanos—a disproportionate inclusion of the excluded." See Bright, "The Self-Proclaimed Political Prisoner," in *Proceedings of the 102nd Annual Congress*, 109–10. Dan Berger adds that "though the overall prison population fell during the 1960s, the rates of Black and Latino incarceration relative to white incarceration rose, as did the overall numbers of Black and Latino prisoners." *Captive Nation*, 55.

168. Sostre, *The New Prisoner*, 244.

169. Sostre, *The New Prisoner*, 245.

170. Sostre describes this distinction in Fischler, *Frame-Up*. It is unclear where Justice Motley's quote ends in the original article. See Schaich and Hope, "Prison Letters of Martin Sostre," 287. Amnesty International echoed the idea of Sostre as a political prisoner in 1973 by adding Sostre to its "prisoner of conscience" list: "We became convinced that Martin Sostre has been the victim of an international miscarriage of justice because of his political beliefs . . . not for his crimes," 297.

171. Berger, *Captive Nation*, 188.

172. Brother Al Morris, "Death of Jackson Shows 'America Itself a prison,'" *Muhammad Speaks*, October 8, 1971. For more on this theme, see Berger, *Captive Nation*, 49–90.

173. In one interview, Sostre said, "Many call it prisoners' rights, but I don't make any separation. This is a prison out here, too. As long as you are oppressed by the State and the State is in control this is a minimum security prison. Inside is a maximum security." Sostre, "Open Road Interview," 28.

174. Marx, "Eighteenth Brumaire."

175. Will Lissner, "Malcolm Fought for Top Power in Muslim Movement, and Lost," *New York Times*, February 22, 1965; Philip Benjamin, "Malcolm X Lived in Two Worlds, White and Black, Both Bitter," February 22, 1965.

176. Hinton, "MLK Now."

177. Berger, *Captive Nation*, 80.

Epilogue

1. Jon Swaine, Oliver Laughland, Jamiles Lartey, Kenan Davis, Rich Harris, Nadja Popovich, Kenton Powell, and Guardian US Interactive Team. "The Counted: People Killed by Police in the United States—Interactive." *Guardian*. Accessed June 21, 2019. https://www.theguardian.com/us-news/ng-interactive/2015/jun/01/the-counted -police-killings-us-database.

2. Megan Garber, "Funerals for Fallen Robots," *Atlantic*, September 20, 2013; and Kari Hawkins, "'Caveman' Teaches Robotics to Troops in Iraq," January 7, 2009. Accessed June 19, 2019. https://www.army.mil/article/15602/caveman_teaches_robotics _to_troops_in_iraq.

3. Jackie Wang, *Carceral Capitalism*, 51; and Jon Swaine, "Dallas Police Reveal Details of Bomb-Carrying Robot it Used as a 'Last Resort,'" *Guardian*, July 10, 2016.

4. Samuel Alioto, "Islamic Connection: Some Suspects in Dallas Shooting Sympathized with Nation of Islam," *Santa Monica Observer*, July 10, 2016.

5. Heidi Beirich and Ryan Lenz, "Dallas Sniper Connected by Black Separatist Hate Groups on Facebook," *Hatewatch* blog, July 8, 2016.

6. Travis Andrews, "Black Dallas Police Officer Sues Black Lives Matter on Behalf of 'Christians, Jews and Caucasians,' others," *Washington Post*, September 21, 2016.

7. Alice Speri, "Fear of a Black Homeland," *Intercept*, March 23, 2019.

8. Daryl Johnson, "Return of the Violent Black Nationalist," *Intelligence Report* magazine, August 8, 2017.

9. Heidi Beirich interview with Daryl Johnson, "Inside the DHS: Former Analyst Says Agency Bowed to Political Pressure," *Intelligence Report*, June 17, 2011. The FBI's memo also cited a 2015 SPLC article.

10. Anne Branigin, "FBI Launches COINTELPRO 2.0, Targeting 'Black Identity Extremists': Report," *The Root*, October 6, 2017; and "COINTELPRO 2? FBI Targets 'Black Identity Extremists' Despite Surge in White Supremacist Violence," *Democracy Now*, October 16, 2017.

11. Jana Winter and Sharon Weinberger, "The FBI's New U.S. Terrorist Threat: 'Black Identity Extremists,'" *Foreign Policy*, October 6, 2017.

12. Mike Wallace, interview by Blackside, Inc.

13. Megan Garber, "An Indelible Image from Trump's 'On Both Sides' Press Conference," *Atlantic*, August 16, 2017 and Michael D. Shear and Maggie Haberman, "Trump Defends Initial Remarks on Charlottesville; Again Blames 'Both Sides," *New York Times*, August 15, 2017.

14. Malcolm made this speech at an Organization of Afro-American Unity rally held at the Audubon Ballroom on January 24, 1965. Malcolm X, "Malcolm X on Afro-American History," in *Malcolm X on Afro-American History*, 11–72.

15. Trevor Aaronson, "Terrorism's Double Standard: Violent Far-Right Extremists are Rarely Prosecuted as Terrorists," *Intercept*, March 23, 2019.

16. Platt, *Beyond These Walls*, 131.

17. "Manning Marable Book Revisits Assassination of Malcolm X," *Washington Post*, April 3, 2011.

18. Shaila Dewan, "Justice Department Declines to Reopen Malcolm X Case," *New York Times* blog, City Room, July 23, 2011.

19. Senate Report 110-88, Emmett Till Unsolved Civil Rights Crime Act, June 22, 2007.

20. The majority of the 126 victims pursued over the course of the bill came from an initial inquiry to SPLC. "SPLC Provides List of Unresolved Civil Rights Era Deaths to FBI," February 21, 2007, https://www.splcenter.org/news/2007/02/21/splc-provides -list-unresolved-civil-rights-era-deaths-fbi; Also see "The Attorney General's Fifth Annual Report to Congress," January 2014.

21. "Racial Discrimination and Domestic Implementation of Human Rights: The Responsibility of the U.S. Government to Investigate Cases of Civil Rights Murders to Ensure Due Process and Equal Protection Under the Law," A joint submission to the United Nations Periodic Review by the Georgia Peace and Justice Coalition, Southern Christian Leadership Conference, and the Cold Case Justice Initiative at Syracuse University College of Law, April-May 2015.

22. David Wilson, *Inventing Black-on-Black Violence: Discourse, Space, and Representation* (Syracuse University Press, 2005). For more on myth of "Black-on-Black" violence, see Elizabeth Hinton, LeShae Henderson, and Cindy Reed, *An Unjust Burden.*

23. The 2016 strike began on September 9 and the 2018 one began on the anniversary of George Jackson's murder on August 21 and ended on September 9.

24. Schlanger, "Trends in Prisoner Litigation as the PLRA Enters Adulthood," 157.

25. Akbar and Theoharis, "Islam on Trial."

26. For example, see John-Paul Pagano, "The Women's March has a Farrakhan Problem," *Atlantic*, March 8, 2018. As Marc Lamont Hill explained, "There's this weird litmus test that gets applied to Farrakhan and Farrakhan only . . . This isn't about Minister Farrakahn's ideology; the question is why he's positioned as the brook of fire for everyone to pass." See Tanasia Kenney, "Marc Lamont Hill Has No Plans to Denounce Farrakhan," *Atlanta Black Star*, December 17, 2018. Also see Garrett Felber, "Black Zionism, Reparations, and the 'Palestine Problem,'" *Black Perspectives*, August 28, 2016. https://www.aaihs.org/black-zionism-reparations-and-the-palestine-problem/.

27. James Boggs and Grace Lee Boggs, *Revolution and Evolution in the Twentieth Century* (New York: Monthly Review Press, 1974), 22.

28. Malcolm Little, "Abolishment of Capital Punishment: The Death Penalty is Ineffective as a Deterrent," *The Colony* 20, no. 2 (January 15, 1950), 9.

29. "Prison Vengeance," *The Colony* 20, no. 18 (September 15, 1949), 13.

30. Matthew Schwartz, "Justices Let Alabama Execute Death Row Inmate Who Wanted Imam by His Side," *NPR*, February 8, 2019.

Bibliography

Manuscripts and Archives

California

American Civil Liberties Union of Southern California, Charles E. Young
Research Library, UCLA

Hugh R. Manes Papers, Charles E. Young Research Library, UCLA

Loren Miller Papers, The Huntington Library, San Marino

Margaret Meier Collection of Extreme Right Ephemeral Materials, Department of
Special Collections, Stanford University

Subject Files, Muslims, Division of Criminal Law, Attorney General's Office,
California State Archives

Georgia

C. Eric Lincoln Collection, Robert W. Woodruff Library, Archives Research
Center, Atlanta University Center

Illinois

Alfred Balk Papers, The Newberry Library, Chicago

Maryland

Malcolm X FBI File, National Archives and Records Administration at
College Park

Nation of Islam FBI File, National Archives and Records Administration at
College Park

Organization of Afro-American Unity FBI File, National Archives and Records
Administration at College Park

Records of the Bureau of Prisons, Record Group 129, National Archives and
Records Administration at College Park

Records of the U.S. Commission on Civil Rights, Record Group 453, National
Archives and Records Administration at College Park

Records of the Department of Justice, Record Group 60, National Archives and
Records Administration at College Park

Massachusetts

Malcolm X Prison File (#22843), Massachusetts State Archives

Marvin Worth Collection, Howard Gotlieb Archival Research Center, Boston
University

Papers of John F. Kennedy, John F. Kennedy Presidential Library and Museum,
Boston

Michigan

Joseph A. Labadie Collection, University of Michigan Special Collections
Library

Missouri
  National Archives and Records Administration–Kansas City
Nevada
  Louis E. Lomax Papers, Ethnicity and Race Manuscript Collection, University of
    Nevada–Reno
New York
  Amsterdam News Collection, Division of Rare and Manuscript Collections,
    Cornell University Library
  Appellate Division Law Library, Rochester
  Attica Commission Investigation Files, New York State Archives
  Attica Inmate Documents Seized, 1971, #22421, New York State Archives. These
    documents were once held at NYS archives but were later deemed government
    property and have been withdrawn from public access
  Columbia Center for Oral History, Rare Book and Manuscript Library, Columbia
    University
  James Haughton Papers, Schomburg Center for Research in Black Culture,
    New York Public Library
  Malcolm X BOSS File, in author's possession
  Malcolm X Collection, Schomburg Center for Research in Black Culture,
    New York Public Library
  Malcolm X Project Records, Rare Book and Manuscript Library, Columbia
    University
  Municipal Archives, New York City
  National Archives and Records Administration–Northeast Region, New York City
  Non-Criminal Investigation Case Files, New York State, Division of State Police,
    New York State Archives
North Carolina
  Taylor Branch Papers, The Southern Historical Collection at the Louis Round
    Wilson Special Collections Library, University of North Carolina–Chapel Hill
Pennsylvania
  Albert Bofman Papers, Swarthmore Peace Collection, Swarthmore College
  American Civil Liberties Union, National Committee on Conscientious Objectors,
    Swarthmore Peace Collection, Swarthmore College
  American Friends Service Committee, Swarthmore Peace Collection, Swarth-
    more College
  Center on Conscience and War, Swarthmore Peace Collection, Swarthmore
    College
  Juanita and Wallace Nelson Papers, Swarthmore Peace Collection, Swarthmore
    College
Texas
  Lee Brown Papers, Woodson Research Center, Rice University
Washington, D.C.
  A. Philip Randolph Papers, Library of Congress
  Bayard Rustin Papers, Library of Congress
  Papers of the NAACP, Library of Congress

Government Publications

Attica State Prison: Its History, Purpose, Makeup and Program. New York: New York State Department of Correction, 1949.

Federal Prisons, 1946: A Report of the Work of the Federal Bureau of Prisons. Leavenworth, KS: U.S. Penitentiary, 1947.

Langan, Patrick A., John V. Fundis, Lawrence A. Greenfield, and Victoria W. Schneider. *Historical Statistics on Prisoners in State and Federal Institutions, Yearend 1925-86.* Washington, DC: U.S. Department of Justice, 1988.

Lynch, Thomas C. *Paramilitary Organizations in California.* Sacramento: Office of the Attorney General, April 12, 1965. https://archive.org/stream/foia_Paramilitary_Orgs_in_California_1965_84p/Paramilitary_Orgs_in_California_1965_84p_djvu.txt.

New York State Commission of Correction Annual Report, 1960. Albany: State Commission of Correction, 1961.

New York State Commission of Correction Annual Report, 1961. Albany: State Commission of Correction, 1962.

New York State Commission of Correction Annual Report, 1963. Albany: State Commission of Correction, 1964.

Subversive Influences in Riots, Looting, and Burning: Hearings before the Committee on Un-American Activities House of Representatives, 90th Cong. 1030–47 (1967).

Multimedia

Bagwell, Orlando, dir. *Malcolm X: Make It Plain.* 1994; Alexandria, VA: PBS Video. DVD.

CBS Reports: Watts — Riot or Revolt? 1965. CBS.

Fischler, Steven, Joel Sucher, and Howard Blatt, dirs. *Frame-Up: The Imprisonment of Martin Sostre.* 1974; Brooklyn, NY: Pacific Street Films, 2008. DVD.

Shaykh Imran Hosein. "Dr Maulana Fazlur Rahman Ansari, His Life, Works and Thoughts." February 16, 2009. https://archive.org/details/DrMaulanaFazlurRahmanAnsariHisLifeWorksAndThoughts.

Published Interviews

Blyden, Herbert. Interview by Blackside, Inc. December 22, 1988. *Eyes on the Prize II: America at the Racial Crossroads, 1965 to 1985.* Washington University Libraries, Film and Media Archive, Henry Hampton Collection. http://digital.wustl.edu/e/eii/eiiweb/bly5427.0435.018herbertxblyden.html.

Clark, Richard X. Interview by History Makers. Accessed May 25, 2019. https://www.thehistorymakers.org/biography/richard-x-clark.

King, Celes, III. "Black Leadership in Los Angeles: Celes King III." Interview by Bruce M. Tyler and Robin D. G. Kelley. August 7, 1985. http://www.oac.cdlib.org/view?docId=hb9z09p6tg&brand=oac4&doc.view=entire_text.

Malcolm X. "'And This Happened in Los Angeles': Malcolm X Describes Police Brutality against Members of the Nation of Islam." Interview by Dick Elman.

WBAI radio, Pacifica Radio Archives, BB0541. http://historymatters.gmu.edu /d/7041.

Smith, Michael. Interview by Terry Rockefeller. Blackside, Inc. August 22, 1988. *Eyes on the Prize II: America at the Racial Crossroads, 1965 to 1985.* Washington University Libraries, Film and Media Archive, Henry Hampton Collection. http://digital.wustl.edu/e/eii/eiiweb/smi5427.0724.153michaelsmith.html.

Sostre, Martin. "The Open Road Interview with Martin Sostre." *Open Road,* Summer 1976, 12–13, 28–29.

Wallace, Mike. Interview by Blackside, Inc. October 12, 1988. *Eyes on the Prize II: America at the Racial Crossroads, 1965 to 1985.* Washington University Libraries, Film and Media Archive, Henry Hampton Collection. http://digital.wustl.edu/e /eii/eiiweb/wal5427.0729.168mikewallace.html.

Theses and Dissertations

Chase, Robert. "Civil Rights on the Cell Block: Race, Reform, and Violence in Texas Prisons and the Nation, 1945–1990." PhD diss., University of Maryland, 2009.

Gill, Gerald. "Afro-American Opposition to the United States' Wars of the Twentieth Century: Dissent, Discontent, and Disinterest." PhD diss., Howard University, 1985.

Lucander, David. "'It Is a New Kind of Militancy': March on Washington Movement, 1941–1946." PhD diss., University of Massachusetts, Amherst, 2010.

Morrison, Adam. "Religious Legitimacy and the Nation of Islam: *In re Ferguson* and Muslim Inmates' Religious Rights in the 1950s and 1960s." Master's thesis, University of California–Santa Barbara, 2014.

Pihos, Peter. "Policing, Race, and Politics in Chicago." PhD diss., University of Pennsylvania, 2015.

Stein, David. "Fearing Inflation, Inflating Fears: The End of Full Employment and the Rise of the Carceral State." PhD diss., University of Southern California, 2014.

Wood, John. "Wally and Juanita Nelson and the Struggle for Peace, Equality, and Social Justice: 1935–1975." PhD diss., Morgan State University, 2008.

Articles, Books, and Chapters

Akbar, Amna, and Jeanne Theoharis, "Islam on Trial," *Boston Review,* February 27, 2017.

Alhassen, Maytha. "Islam in America by Mahmoud Yousef Shawarbi." *Comparative American Studies* 13, no. 4 (December 2015): 254–64.

Allen, Ernest, Jr. "Religious Heterodoxy and Nationalist Tradition: The Continuing Evolution of the Nation of Islam." *Black Scholar* 26, nos. 3–4 (Fall 1996–Winter 1997): 2–34.

———. "When Japan Was 'Champion of the Darker Races': Satokata Takahashi and the Flowering of Black Messianic Nationalism." *Black Scholar* 24, no. 1 (1994): 23–46.

Armstrong, Andrea. "Slavery Revisited in Penal Plantation Labor." *Seattle University Law Review* 35, no. 3 (2012): 869–910.

Armstrong, Elisabeth. "Before Bandung: The Anti-Imperialist Women's Movement in Asia and the Women's International Democratic Federation." *Signs: Journal of Women in Culture and Society* 41, no. 2 (Winter 2016): 305–31.

Attica: The Official Report of the New York State Special Commission on Attica. New York: Praeger, 1972.

Ayer and Sons Directory of Newspapers and Periodicals. Philadelphia: Ayer Press, 1957.

Bauman, Robert. *Race and the War on Poverty in Los Angeles: From Watts to East L.A.* Norman: University of Oklahoma Press, 2008.

Beale, Frances. "Double Jeopardy: To Be Black and Female." In *Sisterhood is Powerful: An Anthology of Writings from the Women's Liberation Movement*, edited by Robin Morgan, 353–59. New York: Random House, 1970. Reprinted from *Third World Women's Alliance* pamphlet in 1969.

Bennett, Scott H. *Radical Pacifism: The War Resisters League and Gandhian Nonviolence in America, 1915–1963*. Syracuse, NY: Syracuse University Press, 2003.

Berg, Herbert. *Elijah Muhammad and Islam*. New York: New York University Press, 2009.

Berger, Dan. *Captive Nation: Black Prison Organizing in the Civil Rights Era*. Chapel Hill: University of North Carolina Press, 2014.

Berger, Dan, and Toussaint Losier. *Rethinking the American Prison Movement*. New York: Routledge, 2017.

Beynon, Erdmann Doane. "The Voodoo Cult among Negro Migrants in Detroit." *American Journal of Sociology* 43, no. 6 (May 1938): 894–907.

Biondi, Martha. *To Stand and Fight: The Struggle for Civil Rights in Postwar New York City*. Cambridge, MA: Harvard University Press, 2003.

"The Black Man and Islam." *Moslem World and the U.S.A.* 1, no. 5 (August/ September 1956).

"Black Muslims in Prison: Of Muslim Rites and Constitutional Rights." *Columbia Law Review* 62, no. 8 (December 1962): 1488–1504.

Blain, Keisha. "'Confraternity among All Dark Races': Mittie Maude Lena Gordon and the Practice of Black (Inter)nationalism in Chicago, 1932–1942." *Palimpsest: A Journal on Women, Gender, and the Black International* 5, no. 2 (2016): 151–81.

———. *Set the World on Fire: Black Nationalist Women and the Global Struggle for Freedom*. Philadelphia: University of Pennsylvania Press, 2018.

Blain, Keisha, Asia Leeds, and Ula Taylor. "Women, Gender Politics, and Pan-Africanism." Special issue, *Women, Gender, and Families of Color* 4, no. 2 (Fall 2016).

Boggs, James and Grace Lee Boggs, *Revolution and Evolution in the Twentieth Century*. New York: Monthly Review Press, 1974.

Bouza, Tony. *Police Intelligence: The Operations of an Investigative Unit*. New York: AMS Press, 1976.

Branch, Taylor. *Pillar of Fire: America in the King Years, 1963–1965*. New York: Simon and Schuster, 1998.

Breitman, George. *The Last Year of Malcolm X: The Evolution of a Revolutionary*. New York: Pathfinder Press, 1967.

Brown, Lee. "Black Muslims and the Police." *Journal of Criminal Law, Criminology, and Police Science* 56, no. 1 (March 1965): 119–26.

Brown, Michael. *Working the Street: Police Discretion and the Dilemmas of Reform.* New York: Russell Sage Foundation, 1981.

Browne, Simone. *Dark Matters: On the Surveillance of Blackness.* Durham: Duke University Press, 2015.

Burns, William Haywood. *The Voices of Negro Protest in America.* London: Oxford University Press, 1963.

Burton, Orisanmi. "Organized Disorder: The New York City Jail Rebellion of 1970." *Black Scholar* 48, no. 4 (November 2018): 28–42.

Caldwell, Wallace F. "Black Muslims behind Bars," *Research Studies* 34, no. 4 (December 1966): 185–204.

Camp, Jordan. *Incarcerating the Crisis: Freedom Struggles and the Rise of the Neoliberal State.* Oakland: University of California Press, 2016.

Canaday, Margot. *The Straight State: Sexuality and Citizenship in Twentieth-Century America.* Princeton, NJ: Princeton University Press, 2009.

Chase, Robert. "We Are Not Slaves: Rethinking the Rise of the Carceral States through the Lens of the Prisoners' Rights Movement." *Journal of American History* 102, no. 1 (June 2015): 73–86.

Childs, Dennis. *Slaves of the State: Black Incarceration from the Chain Gang to the Penitentiary.* Minneapolis: University of Minnesota Press, 2015.

Clark, Kenneth. "Liberalism and the Negro." *Commentary* 37 (March 1964): 25–42.

Cleaver, Eldridge. *Post-Prison Writings and Speeches.* New York: Random House, 1969.
———. *Soul on Ice.* New York: McGraw-Hill, 1967.

Clegg, Claude Andrew, III. *An Original Man: The Life and Times of Elijah Muhammad.* New York: St. Martin's Press, 1997.

Clemmer, Donald, and John M. Wilson. "The Muslim in Prison." In *Proceedings of the 90th Annual Congress of Correction of the American Correctional Association.* College Park, MD: American Correctional Association, 1960.

Cohen, Naomi W. *Not Free to Desist: The American Jewish Committee, 1906–1966.* Philadelphia: Jewish Publication Society of America, 1972.

Colley, Zoe. *Ain't Scared of Your Jail: Arrest, Imprisonment, and the Civil Rights Movement.* Gainesville: University of Florida Press, 2013.
———. "'All America Is a Prison': The Nation of Islam and the Politicization of African American Prisoners, 1955–1965." *Journal of American Studies* 48, no. 2 (May 2014): 393–415.

Crawford, Malachi. *Black Muslims and the Law: Civil Liberties from Elijah Muhammad to Muhammad Ali.* Lanham, MD: Lexington Books, 2015.
———. "Neo-Houstonian Studies: Edward W. Jacko, the NOI and the Struggle for Afro-Muslim Civil Liberties." In *Charles H. Houston: An Interdisciplinary Study of Civil Rights Leadership*, edited by James Conyers, 231–50. Lanham, MD: Lexington Books, 2012.

Cummins, Eric. *The Rise and Fall of California's Radical Prison Movement.* Stanford: Stanford University Press, 1994.

Curtis, Edward E., IV. *Black Muslim Religion in the Nation of Islam, 1960–1975.* Chapel Hill: University of North Carolina Press, 2006.
———. *Islam in Black America.* New York: State University of New York Press, 2002.

————. "Islamism and Its African American Muslims Critics: Black Muslims in the Era of the Arab Cold War." *American Quarterly* 59, no. 3 (2007): 683–709.

————, ed. "New York City." In *Encyclopedia of Muslim-American History*, 429–36. New York: Facts on File, 2010.

Cushmeer, Bernard. *This Is the One.* Phoenix: Truth Publications, 1970.

D'Emilio, John. *Lost Prophet: The Life and Times of Bayard Rustin.* New York: Free Press, 2003.

DeCaro, Louis A., Jr. *On the Side of My People: A Religious Life of Malcolm X.* New York: New York University Press, 1996.

Domanick, Joe. *To Protect and Serve: The LAPD's Century of War in the City of Dreams.* New York: Pocket Books, 1994.

Domino, John Michael. *Attica: A Survivors Story.* Maitland: Xulon Press, 2006.

Donner, Frank. *Protectors of Privilege: Red Squads and Police Repression in Urban America.* Berkeley: University of California Press, 1990.

Drzazga, John. "Muslim Terrorists," *Law and Order* 11, no. 5 (May 1963).

Essien-Udom, E. U. *Black Nationalism: A Search for an Identity in America.* Chicago: University of Chicago Press, 1962.

Evanzz, Karl. *The Messenger: The Rise and Fall of Elijah Muhammad.* New York: Pantheon Books, 1999.

Farmer, Ashley. *Remaking Black Power: How Black Women Transformed an Era.* Chapel Hill: University of North Carolina Press, 2017.

Felber, Garrett. "Harlem is the Black World" The Organization of Afro-American Unity at the Grassroots." *Journal of African American History* 100, no. 2 (Spring 2015): 199–225.

————. "'Integration or Separation?' Malcolm X's College Lectures, Free Speech, and the Challenge to Racial Liberalism on Campus." *Journal of Social History*, (April 2019, online only).

Felder, James. *Civil Rights in South Carolina: From Peaceful Protests to Groundbreaking Rulings.* Charleston, SC: History Press, 2012.

Felker-Kantor, Max. *Policing Los Angeles: Race, Resistance, and the Rise of the LAPD.* Chapel Hill: University of North Carolina Press, 2018.

Ferguson, James. *The Anti-Politics Machine: "Development," Depoliticization, and Bureaucratic Power in Lesotho.* Minneapolis: University of Minnesota Press, 1994.

Flamm, Michael W. *In the Heat of the Summer: The New York Riots of 1964 and the War on Crime.* Philadelphia: University of Pennsylvania Press, 2017.

Forman, James, Jr. *Locking Up Our Own: Crime and Punishment in Black America.* New York: Farrar, Straus, and Giroux, 2017.

Fortner, Michael. *Black Silent Majority: The Rochefeller Drug Laws and the Politics of Punishment.* Cambridge, Massachusetts: Harvard University Press, 2015.

Foucault, Michel. *Discipline and Punish: The Birth of the Prison.* 2nd vintage books ed. New York: Random House, 1995. Originally published in French in 1975 by Editions Gallimard.

Frankino, Steven. "The Manacles and the Messenger: A Short Study in Religious Freedom in the Prison Community." *Catholic University Law Review* 14, no. 1 (1965): 30–66.

Friedman, Lawrence. *Crime and Punishment in American History*. New York: Basic Books, 1993.

Fujino, Diane C. *Heartbeat of Struggle: The Revolutionary Life of Yuri Kochiyama*. Minneapolis: University of Minnesota Press, 2005.

Gaines, Kevin. *Uplifting the Race: Black Leadership, Politics, and Culture in the Twentieth Century*. Chapel Hill: University of North Carolina Press, 1996.

Gallicchio, Marc S. *The African American Encounter with Japan and China: Black Internationalism in Asia, 1895–1945*. Chapel Hill: University of North Carolina Press, 2000.

Garfinkel, Herbert. *When Negroes March: The March on Washington Movement in the Organizational Politics for FEPC*. New York: Atheneum, 1969.

Gellman, Erik S. *Death Blow to Jim Crow: The National Negro Congress and the Rise of Militant Civil Rights*. Chapel Hill: University of North Carolina Press, 2012.

Gibson, Dawn-Marie, and Jamillah Ashira Karim. *Women of the Nation: Between Black Protest and Sunni Islam*. New York: New York University Press, 2014.

Gilmore, Ruth Wilson. *Golden Gulag: Prisons, Surplus, Crisis, and Opposition in Globalizing California*. Berkeley: University of California Press, 2007.

Gilmore, Ruth Wilson, and Craig Gilmore. "Restating the Obvious." In *Indefensible Space: The Architecture of the National Security State*, edited by Michael Sorkin, 141–61. New York: Routledge, 2007.

Gilroy, Paul. "Black Fascism," *Transition* 81/82 (2000): 70–91.

Goldman, Peter. *The Death and Life of Malcolm X*. 2nd ed. Urbana: University of Illinois Press, 1979.

Gómez, Alan Eladio. "Resisting Living Death at Marion Federal Penitentiary, 1972." *Radical History Review* 96 (Fall 2006): 58–86.

Gooch, John Casey. "Illegal Search and Seizure, Due Process, and the Rights of the Accused: The Voices of Power in the Rhetoric of Los Angeles Police Chief William H. Parker." *Pólemos: Journal of Law, Literature, and Culture* 9, no. 1 (2015): 83–98.

Gordon, Sarah. *The Spirit of the Law: Religious Voices and the Constitution in Modern America*. Cambridge, MA: Harvard University Press, 2010.

Gottschalk, Marie. *The Prison and the Gallows: The Politics of Mass Incarceration in America*. Cambridge: Cambridge University Press, 2006.

Griffin, Farah Jasmine. "'Ironies of the Saint:' Malcolm X, Black Women, and the Price of Protection." In *Sisters in the Struggle: African American Women in the Civil Rights–Black Power Movement*, edited by Bettye Collier-Thomas and V. P. Franklin, 214–29. New York: New York University Press, 2001.

Gross, Kali Nicole. "African American Women, Mass Incarceration, and the Politics of Protection." *Journal of American History* 102, no. 1 (June 2015): 25–33.

Guglielmo, Thomas. "A Martial Freedom Movement: Black GIs' Political Struggles during World War II." *Journal of American History* 104, no. 4 (March 2018): 879–903.

Haas, Jeffrey. *The Assassination of Fred Hampton: How the FBI and the Chicago Police Murdered a Black Panther*. Chicago: Lawrence Hill Books, 2010.

Haley, Sarah. *No Mercy Here: Gender, Punishment, and the Making of Jim Crow Modernity*. Chapel Hill: University of North Carolina Press, 2016.

Hall, Stuart, Chas Critcher, Tony Jefferson, John Clarke, and Brian Roberts. *Policing the Crisis: Mugging, the State, and Law and Order.* London: Macmillan, 1978.

Hartman, Saidiya. *Wayward Lives, Beautiful Experiments: Intimate Histories of Social Upheaval.* New York: W.W. Norton and Co., 2019.

Hassan, Amina. *Loren Miller: Civil Rights Attorney and Journalist.* Norman: University of Oklahoma Press, 2015.

Heatherton, Christina. "University of Radicalism: Ricardo Flores Magón and Leavenworth Penitentiary." *American Quarterly* 66, no. 3 (September 2014): 557–81.

Hernández, Kelly Lytle. *City of Inmates: Conquest, Rebellion, and the Rise of Human Caging in Los Angeles, 1771–1965.* Chapel Hill: University of North Carolina Press, 2017.

Hill, Laura Warren. "'We Are Black Folks First': The Black Freedom Struggle in Rochester, NY, and the Making of Malcolm X." *The Sixties: A Journal of History, Politics and Culture* 3, no. 2 (December 2010): 163–85.

Hill, Robert A., ed. *The FBI's RACON: Racial Conditions in America during World War II.* Boston: Northeastern University Press, 1995.

Hinton, Elizabeth, LeShae Henderson, and Cindy Reed. *An Unjust Burden: The Disparate Treatment of Black Americans in the Criminal Justice System.* New York: Vera Institute of Justice, 2018.

Horlick, Reuben S. "The Black Muslim in Prison: A Personality Study." *Proceedings of the 93rd Annual Congress of Correction of the American Correctional Association.* New York: American Correctional Association, 1963.

Horne, Gerald. *Fire This Time: The Watts Uprising and the 1960s.* Charlottesville: University Press of Virginia, 1995.

"International Relations Club." *Brown and Gold, 1949.* Kalamazoo: Western Michigan University Yearbooks (1949): 98.

Irwin, John. *Prisons in Turmoil.* Boston: Little, Brown, 1980.

Jacobs, James. "The Prisoners' Rights Movement and Its Impacts, 1960–1980." *Crime and Justice* 2 (1980): 429–70.

———. *Stateville: The Penitentiary in Mass Society.* Chicago: University of Chicago Press, 1977.

Jeffries, Bayyinah Sharief. *A Nation Can Rise No Higher Than Its Women: African American Muslim Women in the Movement for Black Self Determination, 1950–1975.* Lanham, MD: Lexington Books, 2014.

Jamal, Hakim. *From the Dead Level.* New York: Random House, 1972.

Jonas, Gilbert. *Freedom's Sword: The NAACP and the Struggle against Racism in America, 1909–1969.* New York: Routledge, 2005.

Jones, William P. *The March on Washington: Jobs, Freedom, and the Forgotten History of Civil Rights.* New York: Norton, 2013.

Kearney, Reginald. *African American Views of the Japanese: Solidarity or Sedition?* Albany: State University of New York Press, 1998.

Kelley, Robin D. G. *Africa Speaks, America Answers: Modern Jazz in Revolutionary Times.* Cambridge: Harvard University Press, 2012.

———. *Freedom Dreams: The Black Radical Imagination*. New York: Beacon Press, 2002.

———. *Race Rebels: Culture, Politics, and the Black Working Class*. New York: Free Press, 1996.

———. "Yes, I Said, 'National Liberation.'" In *Letters to Palestine: Writers Respond to War and Occupation*, edited by Vijay Prashad, 139–53. London: Verso, 2015.

King, Desmond. *Separate and Unequal: Black Americans and the U.S. Federal Government*. Oxford: Clarendon Press, 1995.

Knight, Frederick. "Justifiable Homicide, Police Brutality, or Governmental Repression? The 1962 Los Angeles Police Shooting of Seven Members of the Nation of Islam." *Journal of Negro History* 79, no. 2 (Spring 1994).

Knight, Michael Muhammad. *The Five Percenters: Islam, Hip Hop, and the Gods of New York*. Oxford: Oneworld, 2007.

Kraus, Jeffrey. "William Parker." In *The Social History of Crime and Punishment*, edited by Wilbur Miller, 1321–23. Thousand Oaks: SAGE Foundation, 2012.

Kruse, Kevin, and Stephen Tuck, eds. *Fog of War: The Second World War and the Civil Rights Movement*. New York: Oxford University Press, 2012.

Kurashige, Scott. *Shifting Grounds of Race: Black and Japanese Americans in the Making of Multiethnic Los Angeles*. Princeton, NJ: Princeton University Press, 2008.

Larsen, Charles. "A Prisoner Looks at Writ-Writing." *California Law Review* 56, no. 2 (April 1968): 343–64.

Lightfoot, Claude. "Negro Nationalism and the Black Muslims." *Political Affairs* 41, no. 7 (July 1962): 3–20.

Lincoln, C. Eric. *The Black Muslims in America*. Boston: Beacon Press, 1961.

———. *The Black Muslims in America*, revised ed. Boston: Beacon Press, 1973.

———. *The Black Muslims in America*, 3rd ed. Grand Rapids: W.B. Eerdmans Press, 1994.

Lipsitz, George. "'Frantic to Join . . . the Japanese Army': Black Soldiers and Civilians Confront the Asia-Pacific War." In *Perilous Memories: The Asia-Pacific War(s)*, edited by Geoffrey M. White, Lisa Yoneyama, and T. Fujitani, 347–77. Durham, NC: Duke University Press, 2001.

Little, Malcolm. "Abolishment of Capital Punishment: The Death Penalty is Ineffective as a Deterrent." *The Colony* 20, no. 2 (January 15, 1950): 9.

Lomax, Louis. *The Negro Revolt*. New York: Harper, 1962.

Losier, Toussaint. "Against 'Law and Order' Lockup: The 1970 NYC Jail Rebellions." *Race and Class* 59, no. 1 (June 2017): 3–35.

———. "'. . . For Strictly Religious Reasons': *Cooper v. Pate* and the Origins of the Prisoners' Rights Movement." *Souls: A Critical Journal of Black Politics, Culture, and Society* 15, nos. 1–2 (2013): 19–38.

Lubin, Alex. *Geographies of Liberation: The Making of an Afro-Arab Political Imaginary*. Chapel Hill: University of North Carolina Press, 2014.

Lupo, Lindsey. *Flak-Catchers: One Hundred Years of Riot Commission Politics in America*. Plymouth, UK: Lexington Books, 2011.

Mack, Kenneth. *Representing the Race: The Creation of the Civil Rights Lawyer*. Cambridge, MA: Harvard University Press, 2012.

Malcolm X. *February 1965: The Final Speeches.* Edited by Steve Clark. New York: Pathfinder, 1992.

———. "Malcolm X on Afro-American History." In *Malcolm X on Afro-American History*, 3rd ed., edited by Steve Clarke, 11–72. New York: Pathfinder Press, 1990.

———. *Malcolm X: The Last Speeches.* Edited by Bruce Perry. New York: Pathfinder Press, 1989.

———. Malcolm X. "We Arose from the Dead!" *Moslem World and the U.S.A.* 1, no. 5 (August/September 1956).

Malcolm X and Alex Haley. *The Autobiography of Malcolm X.* New York: Ballantine Books, 1999.

Mamdani, Mahmood. *Good Muslim, Bad Muslim: America, the Cold War, and the Roots of Terror.* New York: Three Leaves Press, 2005.

Marable, Manning. *Malcolm X: A Life of Reinvention.* New York: Viking, 2011.

Marable, Manning, and Garrett Felber. *The Portable Malcolm X Reader.* New York: Penguin, 2013.

Marx, Karl. "The Eighteenth Brumaire of Louis Bonaparte." In *The Karl Marx Library*, vol. 1, edited and translated by Saul K. Padover, 245–46. McGraw Hill: New York, 1972.

McCubbin, Bob, ed. *Martin Sostre in Court.* Buffalo: Martin Sostre Defense Committee, 1969.

McGuire, Danielle. *At the Dark End of the Street: Black Women, Rape, and Resistance — a New History of the Civil Rights Movement from Rosa Parks to the Rise of Black Power.* New York: Alfred Knopf, 2010.

McLennan, Rebecca. *The Crisis of Imprisonment: Protest, Politics, and the Making of the American Penal State, 1776–1941.* New York: Cambridge University Press, 2008.

Meriwether, James. *Proudly We Can Be Africans: Black Americans and Africa, 1935–1961.* Chapel Hill: University of North Carolina Press, 2002.

Messerschmidt, James W. "'We Must Protect Our Southern Women': On Whiteness, Masculinities, and Lynching." In *Race, Gender, and Punishment: From Colonialism to the War on Terror*, edited by Mary Bosworth and Jeanne Flavin, 77–94. New Brunswick: Rutgers University Press, 2007.

Metzl, Jonathan. *The Protest Psychosis: How Schizophrenia Became a Black Disease.* Boston: Beacon Press, 2009.

Mirpuri, Anoop. "Mass Incarceration, Prisoner Rights, and the Legacy of the Radical Prison Movement." In *The Punitive Turn: New Approaches to Race and Incarceration*, edited by Deborah E. McDowell, Claudrena N. Harold, and Juan Battle, 131–55. Charlottesville: University of Virginia Press, 2013.

Morrow, John Andrew. "Malcolm X and Mohammad Mehdi: The Shi'a Connection?" *Journal of Shi'a Islamic Studies* 5, no. 1 (Winter 2012): 5–24.

"Mr. Elijah Muhammad and the MOSLEM WORLD AND THE U.S.A." *Moslem World and the U.S.A.* 1, no. 6 (October–December 1956).

Muhammad, Elijah. *Supreme Wisdom: Solution to the So-Called Negroes Problem.* Newport News, VA: National Newport News and Commentator, 1957.

Muhammad, Khalil Gibran. *The Condemnation of Blackness: Race, Crime, and the Making of Modern Urban America.* Csmbridge, MA: Harvard University Press, 2010.

Murakawa, Naomi. *The First Civil Right: How Liberals Built Prison America.* New York: Oxford University Press, 2014.

———. "The Origins of the Carceral Crisis: Racial Order as 'Law and Order' in Postwar American Politics." In *Race and American Political Development,* edited by Joseph Lowndes, Julie Novkov, and Dorian Warren, 234–55. New York: Routledge, 2008.

Naeem, Abdul Basit. Editorial. *Moslem World and the U.S.A.* 1, no. 1 (January 1955).

———. Introduction to *Supreme Wisdom: Solution to the So-Called Negroes Problem* by Elijah Muhammad, . Newport News, VA: National Newport News and Commentator, 1957.

———. "Moslem World and the U.S.A. Editor-Publisher's Brief Address at the Moslems' Convention." *Moslem World and the U.S.A.* 2, no. 3 (March–April 1957).

———. "Pakistan and U.S.A." *Muslim World* 41, no. 3 (July 1951).

———. "The Rise of Elijah Muhammad." *Moslem World and the U.S.A.* 1, no. 4 (June/July 1956).

———. "The South Chicago Moslems." *Moslem World and the U.S.A.* 1, no. 3 (April/ May 1956).

Ngai, Mae. *Impossible Subjects: Illegal Aliens and the Making of Modern America.* Princeton, NJ: Princeton University Press, 2004.

Ogbar, Jeffrey. *Black Power: Radical Politics and African American Identity,* 2nd ed. Baltimore: Johns Hopkins University Press, 2019.

Oshinsky, David M. *"Worse Than Slavery": Parchman Farm and the Ordeal of Jim Crow Justice.* New York: Free Press, 1996.

Parks, Gordon. "The Violent End of the Man They Called Malcolm X." *Life,* March 5, 1965, 26–31.

Pendergast, Sara. *Contemporary Black Biography: Profiles from the International Black Community.* Detroit: Gale Press, 2006.

Platt, Tony. *Beyond These Walls: Rethinking Crime and Punishment in the United States.* New York: St. Martin's Press, 2018.

Plummer, Brenda Gayle. *Rising Wind: Black Americans and U.S. Foreign Affairs, 1935–1960.* Chapel Hill: University of North Carolina Press, 1996.

"The Power to Change Behavior." Paper presented at a seminar conducted by the Bureau of Prisons, April 22, 1961. Republished in *Corrective Psychiatry and Journal of Social Therapy* 8, nos. 1–4 (1962): 101.

Prashad, Vijay. *The Darker Nations: A People's History of the Third World.* New York: New Press, 2007.

"Prison Vengeance." *The Colony* 20, no. 18 (September 15, 1949): 13.

Proceedings of the 90th Annual Congress of Correction of the American Correctional Association. College Park, MD: American Correctional Association, 1960.

Proceedings of the 93rd Annual Congress of Correction of the American Correctional Association. New York: American Correctional Association, 1963.

Proceedings of the 102nd Annual Congress of Correction of the American Correctional Association. College Park, MD: American Correctional Association, 1972.

Race Relations: A Monthly Summary of Events and Trends. Vol. 3, *1945–1946.* New York: Negro Universities Press, 1969.

Randolph, Sherie. *Florynce "Flo" Kennedy: The Life of a Black Feminist Radical*. Chapel Hill: University of North Carolina Press, 2015.

Satter, Beryl. "Cops, Gangs, and Revolutionaries in 1960s Chicago: What Black Police Can Tell Us about Power." *Journal of Urban History* 42, no. 6 (November 2016): 1110–34.

Saunders, Nancy Miller. *Combat by Trial: An Odyssey with 20th Century Winter Soldiers*. New York: iUniverse, 2008.

Scanlon, Jennifer. *Until There Is Justice: The Life of Anna Arnold Hedgeman*. New York: Oxford University Press, 2016.

Schaich, Warren, and Diane Hope. "The Prison Letters of Martin Sostre: Documents of Resistance." *Journal of Black Studies* 7, no. 3 (March 1977): 281–300.

Schein, Edgar. "Man against Man: Brainwashing." Paper presented at a seminar conducted by the Bureau of Prisons, April 22, 1961. Published in *Corrective Psychiatry and Journal of Social Therapy* 8, no. 2 (1962): 101.

Schlanger, Margo. "Trends in Prisoner Litigation as the PLRA Enters Adulthood." *UC Irvine Law Review* 5, no. 1 (April 2015): 153–78.

Schrader, Stuart. "More Than Cosmetic Changes: The Challenges of Experiments with Police Demilitarization in the 1960s and 1970s." *Journal of Urban History* (April 2017, online only).

Seigel, Micol. *Violence Work: State Violence and the Limits of Police*. Durham: Duke University Press, 2018.

Self, Robert. *American Babylon: Race and the Struggle for Postwar Oakland*. Princeton, NJ: Princeton University Press, 2003.

Shapiro, Herbert. *White Violence and Black Response: From Reconstruction to Montgomery*. Amherst: University of Massachusetts Press, 1988.

Sheehy, Donald F. "The Black Muslims and Religious Freedom in Prison." In *Proceedings of the 93rd Annual Congress of Correction of the American Correctional Association*. New York: American Correctional Association, 1963.

Sides, Josh. *L.A. City Limits: African American Los Angeles from the Great Depression to the Present*. Berkeley: University of California Press, 2003.

Singh, Nikhil Pal. *Black Is a Country: Race and the Unfinished Struggle for Democracy*. Cambridge, MA: Harvard University Press, 2005.

Smith, Cristopher E. "Black Muslims and the Development of Prisoners' Rights." *Journal of Black Studies* 24, no. 2 (December 1993): 131–46.

Sostre, Martin. *Letters and Quotations*. Northampton, MA: Mother Jones Press, 1975.
———. *The New Prisoner*. New York: Martin Sostre Book Store, 1973.

Spencer, Robyn. *The Revolution Has Come: Black Power, Gender, and the Black Panther Party in Oakland*. Durham, NC: Duke University Press, 2016.

Spilerman, Seymour. "The Causes of Racial Disturbances: A Comparison of Alternative Explanations." *American Sociological Review* 35, no. 4 (August 1970): 627–49.

Spivak, Gayatri Chakravorty. "Can the Subaltern Speak?" In *The Post-Colonial Studies Reader*, edited by Bill Ashcroft, Gareth Griffiths, and Helen Tiffin, 24–28. London: Routledge, 1995.

Stanford, Karin L., ed. *If We Must Die: African American Voices on War and Peace.* Lanham, MD: Rowman & Littlefield, 2008.

Story, Brett. *Prison Land: Mapping Carceral Power Across Neoliberal America.* Minneapolis: University of Minnesota Press, 2019.

Taylor, Ula. *The Promise of Patriarchy: Women and the Nation of Islam.* Chapel Hill: University of North Carolina Press, 2017.

Theoharis, Jeanne. "Hidden in Plain Sight: The Civil Rights Movement outside the South." In *The Myth of Southern Exceptionalism*, edited by Matthew Lassiter and Joseph Crespino. 49–73. New York: Oxford, 2010.

Thompson, Heather Ann. *Blood in the Water: The Attica Prison Uprising of 1971 and Its Legacy.* New York: Pantheon Books, 2016.

Thuma, Emily. *All Our Trials: Prisons, Policing, and the Feminist Fight to End Violence.* Urbana: University of Illinois Press, 2019.

Turley, David. *American Religion: Religion in the New Nation.* New York: Taylor and Francis, 1998.

Turner, Richard Brent. *Islam in the African-American Experience.* 2nd ed. Bloomington, IN: Indiana University Press, 2003.

Vogelman, Richard. "Prison Restrictions—Prisoner Rights." *Journal of Criminal Law, Criminology, and Police Science* 59, no. 3 (September 1968): 386–96.

Von Eschen, Penny M. *Race against Empire: Black Americans and Anticolonialism, 1937–1957.* Ithaca, NY: Cornell University Press, 2001.

Wang, Jackie. *Carceral Capitalism.* Cambridge, MA: MIT Semiotext[e], 2018.

Ward, Stephen M. *In Love and Struggle: The Revolutionary Lives of James and Grace Lee Boggs.* Chapel Hill: University of North Carolina Press, 2016.

———. "The Third World Women's Alliance: Black Feminist Radicalism and Black Power Politics." In *The Black Power Movement: Rethinking the Civil Rights Black Power Era*, edited by Peniel Joseph, 119–44. New York: Routledge, 2006.

Warren, Robert Penn. *Who Speaks for the Negro?* 2nd ed. New Haven, CT: Yale University Press, 2014.

Weinberg, Jerry. "The Infamous Statue of Liberty Bombing Plot Case." *The Realist* 65 (March 1966): 9–10, 32.

Weisenfeld, Judith. "The Harlem YWCA and the Secular City, 1904–1945." *Journal of Women's History* 6, no. 3 (Fall 1994): 62–78.

———. *New World A-Coming: Black Religion and Racial Identity during the Great Migration.* New York: New York University Press, 2016.

West, Cynthia S'thembile. "Revisiting Female Activism in the 1960s: The Newark Branch Nation of Islam." *Black Scholar* 26, nos. 3–4 (Fall 1996/Winter 1997): 41–48.

Wilford, Hugh. "American Friends of the Middle East: The CIA, U.S. Citizens, and the Secret Battle to Shape American Public Opinion in the Arab-Israeli Conflict, 1947–1967." *Journal of American Studies* 51, no. 1 (September 2015): 1–24.

Wilson, David. *Inventing Black-on-Black Violence: Discourse, Space, and Representation.* Syracuse, NY: Syracuse University Press, 2005.

"Who Killed Malcolm X? One of the Men Convicted Speaks Out!" *Black News* 4, no. 5 (February 1979): 6–9, 35.

Index